Children's Journeys Through the Information Age

McGraw-Hill Series in Developmental Psychology

CONSULTING EDITOR: ROSS A. THOMPSON

Children's Journeys Through the Information Age

Sandra L. Calvert

Georgetown University

McGraw-Hill College

Boston   Burr Ridge, IL   Dubuque, IA   Madison, WI   New York   San Francisco   St. Louis
Bangkok   Bogotá   Caracas   Lisbon   London   Madrid
Mexico City   Milan   New Delhi   Seoul   Singapore   Sydney   Taipei   Toronto

McGraw-Hill College

*A Division of The **McGraw-Hill** Companies*

CHILDREN'S JOURNEYS THROUGH THE INFORMATION AGE

This book is printed on acid-free paper.

1 2 3 4 5 6 7 8 9 0 DOC/DOC 9 3 2 1 0 9 8

ISBN 0–07–011664–4

Editorial director: *Jane E. Vaicunas*
Executive editor: *Mickey Cox*
Editorial coordinator: *Sarah C. Thomas*
Marketing manager: *James Rozsa*
Project manager: *Vicki Krug*
Production supervisor: *Deborah Donner*
Designer: *Laurie Jean Entringer*
Senior photo research coordinator: *Carrie K. Burger*
Compositor: *ElectraGraphics, Inc.*
Typeface: *10/12 Palatino*
Printer: *R. R. Donnelley & Sons Company/Crawfordsville, IN*

Cover image: Courtesy of WGBH Boston. Drawing done by William S. Pride. Arthur Character © Marc Brown. "Arthur" is a trademark of Marc Brown. © 1997 WGBH.

Library of Congress Cataloging-in-Publication Data

Calvert, Sandra L.
    Children's journeys through the information age / Sandra Calvert.
    — 1st ed.
        p.   cm. — (McGraw-Hill series in developmental psychology)
    Includes bibliographical references and index.
    ISBN 0–07–011664–4
    1. Television and children—United States.   2. Computers and children—United States.   3. Internet (Computer network) and children—United States.   4. Mass media and children—United States.
5. Sex role in mass media—United States.   6. Violence in mass media—United States.   I. Title.   II. Series.
HQ784.T4C24   1999
303.48´33´083—dc21   98–28385
                                                                                            CIP

www.mhhe.com

About the Author

SANDRA L. CALVERT is an Associate Professor of Psychology at Georgetown University. She graduated magna cum laude from West Virginia University, where she was elected to Phi Beta Kappa. She received her masters degree in Human Development and Family Studies from the Pennsylvania State University, and she was awarded her doctoral degree in Developmental and Child Psychology from the University of Kansas. Professor Calvert has published numerous articles about the impact of media, including television, computers, virtual reality, and Internet applications, on children's understanding of information. She also investigates the impact of media images on viewers' understanding of gender roles. Professor Calvert is a fellow of the American Psychological Association, a member of the Society for Research in Child Development, and a member of the International Communication Association. She guides the development of children's media by serving on advisory boards and by consulting for children's programs.

For my family and friends

Brief Contents

Contents

Foreword

Last week I ordered a software game for my younger son that builds math skills in the context of interplanetary exploration. He lacks confidence in math, so I thought he might benefit from the opportunity for some nonstressful practice of problem-solving skills in the midst of an enjoyable game. (I also ordered a computer game for myself to occupy my "spare" moments.) Later, I watched the NCAA basketball finals with both sons, who had been following the March Madness basketball tournament as avidly as I. We also watched an episode of *Star Trek* together, a regular weekly activity we share. I listened patiently as Brian announced that he "really, really" wanted to see a movie that was previewed in a commercial—a film that was clearly inappropriate for a 10-year-old. Yesterday I helped his older brother, Scott, search the Internet for information on a class project. My wife also videotaped a special program on Public Broadcasting about Thomas Jefferson to watch with the boys at a more convenient time.

It is as difficult for me to imagine family life without information technology as it would have been for my parents to imagine family life without electricity or refrigeration. Yet unlike electricity or refrigeration, the nature and scope of information technology—and its effects on us—are continuing to evolve. Cable television offers, for those who purchase it, unprecedented variety in entertainment and educational programs that will continue to broaden in the future. The World Wide Web provides access to expanding networks of knowledge and information—along with advertising, extremist rhetoric, and pornography. Computer software allows people to edit photographic and video images, compose music, create artwork, manage personal finances, communicate (through e-mail and chat rooms) with others worldwide, and engage in a growing range of personal and professional pursuits. And with the advent of virtual reality technologies, users can explore the full range of human experience upon request. Each of these technologies, and others under development, are changing our lives moment-by-moment; trying to understand their impact on children, as well as adults, is like trying to hit a moving target.

In *Children's Journeys through the Information Age*, Sandra Calvert tackles this challenge with thoughtfulness and insight. As a prolific contributor to research concerning the media's impact on children, Dr. Calvert describes the current and emerging information technologies that influence children's lives, summarizes what is known about their effects, and discusses their meaning for parents, teachers, and policymakers. She does so with the excitement of one who has watched sophisticated technologies become increasingly accessible to children in their homes and schools, and with the concern of a developmental scholar who is committed to children's well-being. Because the newer technologies have emerged so recently on the landscape of family life, research on the effects of CD-ROMS, virtual reality interfaces, and even computer games on children is ground-breaking work. In light of this, Dr. Calvert focuses much of her discussion on the impact of television, which has been studied for many years, and enlists this research in a thoughtful exploration of its implications not only for the effects of TV but also for the effects of other technologies on children. Because research findings inform us of the consequences of televised violence for children, for example, they also offer a valuable perspective on the potential consequences of video games with violent themes. Because studies of educational TV provide insight about how technology can assist children's learning, they have implications for our appreciation of computer games with educational goals. In this manner, Dr. Calvert provides an analysis of information technologies that is not only informative and up-to-date, but anticipates future issues concerning the impact of newer and rapidly developing technological innovations on children.

Dr. Calvert also identifies the major messages that television, computer games, CD-ROMS, and other information technologies convey to the children who use them. We learn about the gender roles and ethnic and racial stereotypes that are implicit in many programs (on TV, CD-ROM, and diskette). We discover the power of the media to educate and to heighten either aggressive or prosocial tendencies in young viewers. We learn about the media as well as the messages they convey. We find, for example, that television and other media convey implicit lessons in their use of symbols, in how action is represented (through visual perspective, special effects, and background music), and in the strategies that enlist the viewer's participation in its content. We also learn about the media industry, especially the commercial interests that shape the content and form of television, the Internet, and other technologies. Dr. Calvert insightfully discusses the children who use information technologies. We discover that children of different ages respond differently to the television they watch or the computer games they play because of their developing capacities to remember, interpret, critically appraise, and act on what they view. In learning about children as viewers, we also discover how the media can sensitize or desensitize children to violence, displace other activities (like reading), reinforce cultural stereotypes and schemas, offer positive (or negative) role models, manipulate through advertising ploys, and motivate new learning and understanding. Finally, we learn about the responsibilities of parents, government, and the media themselves for regulating children's exposure to the media and the content of what they view. The text thoughtfully considers current issues concerning V-Chip technology, First Amendment rights, and the Children's Television Act.

Throughout this fascinating journey down the highway of information technology, Dr. Calvert cautions her readers against simplistic conclusions about the media's influence on children. Contrary to those who either idolize or demonize the information technologies, her assessment is a more balanced recognition of its multifaceted potential for improving or blunting children's understanding, depending on how it is used. Yes, the media (primarily TV) contribute to sexist and racist stereotyping, and media content is overwhelmingly violent (even when it is intended for children), but the media also have the potential to challenge those stereotypes and foster children's awareness of nonviolent forms of dispute resolution and the human costs of violence. Yes, the media have considerable potential to educate and inform, but as we are now learning from the Internet, we must manage information for children to find it beneficial. In offering a more judicious assessment of children's journeys through the information age, Dr. Calvert enables readers to draw more thoughtful and informed conclusions about the uses of the media and the responsibilities of the parents, educators, and policymakers who care for children.

The McGraw-Hill Series in Developmental Psychology, of which this volume is a part, has been designed to enrich and expand our common knowledge of human development by providing a forum for theorists, researchers, and practitioners to present their insights to a broad audience. As a rapidly expanding scientific field, developmental psychology has important applications to parents, educators, students, clinicians, policymakers, and others concerned with promoting human welfare throughout the life course. Although the fruits of scholarly research into human development can be found on the pages of research journals, and students can become acquainted with this exciting field in introductory textbooks, this series of specialized, topical books is intended to provide insightful, in-depth examinations of selected issues in the field from which undergraduates, graduate students, and academic colleagues can each benefit. As forums for highlighting important new ideas, research insights, theoretical syntheses, and applications of knowledge to practical problems, I hope these volumes will find many uses: as books that supplement standard general textbooks in undergraduate or graduate courses, as one of several specialized texts for advanced coursework, as tutorials for scholars interested in learning about current knowledge on a topic of interest, and as sourcebooks for practitioners who wish to traverse the gap between knowledge and application. The authors who contribute to this series are committed to providing a state-of-the-art, accurate, and readable interpretation of current knowledge that will be interesting and accessible to a broad audience with many different goals and interests. We hope, too, that these volumes will inspire much-needed efforts to improve the lives of children, adolescents, and adults through research and practice.

We can be certain that the information highway children travel (along with adults) will change and grow in the years to come. Fortunately, *Children's Journeys through the Information Age* equips us all to be better travelers along the way.

Ross A. Thompson
Series Editor

Preface

Each and every evening, flickers of light illuminate millions of American homes. Television, a pervasive medium in the lives of our children, unites us by providing a common source of information, a common source of cultural stories. Now the flickers of video games join those of the television set, and virtual reality games are not far behind. Children's journeys through the information age begin early in development. They are journeys that will last a lifetime.

In the past, children observed the content depicted on their television sets. They listened to the songs broadcast on their radios. As a mass audience, they made choices only by selecting the specific reception channel they wanted to watch or listen to.

Newer information technologies now afford more choices to the audience. As members of the information age, children now have many more options for selecting television content because of videocassette recorders, cable television, and even the remote control device. Increasingly, media experiences require interaction. Computer, video game, CD-ROM, and virtual reality interfaces call upon children to act, not observe.

The content depicted in newer technologies often bears a close resemblance to its predecessor. For instance, the "action-and-violence" formula, in which actors injure or kill each other in fast-action chase scenes, appears in television programs, video games, and now virtual reality games. Similarly, simple formulas about men and women and about people of different ethnic backgrounds are used to convey cultural messages via television programs, advertisements, and even educational computer games. For example, girls play with Barbie while boys play with G.I. Joe in children's toy commercials, thereby promoting gender-stereotyped activities. Similarly, computer math programs are often paired with race cars, thereby stereotyping the computer with stereotypical male school subjects and leisure-time activities.

But while the content is much the same, the forms of presentation are changing. Visual and auditory experiences from television are expanding to include touch and smell in virtual reality games. These expansions represent a fundamental breakthrough in human experience as representations of events become increasingly enmeshed with computer-generated images. No longer do we always have a direct link between perceptual experiences and what is "really" there. Young minds may be deceived into believing that programmed representations of experience really exist, thereby blurring the distinction between what is pretend and what is real.

All information technologies share one common link: each is a symbolic medium accessed by a real person. Much of the past research has portrayed children as passive players in the information technology maze. As children learn to control media interactions, active choices and decision making can become more prevalent outcomes in these symbolic interactions.

Although the potential for children to use technologies to learn and to expand their educational horizons has always existed, children have historically used media for entertainment. This paradox between education and entertainment means that we will either become an illiterate nation addicted to visual information at the expense of reading, as many fear, or that we will rise to the occasion and learn to utilize these technologies for educational purposes to enhance learning, as many hope. This challenge is extremely pressing for us now because we will increasingly access information via technologies in the future.

The purpose of this book is to examine how children's journeys through the information age impact their development. Our study of changes in information technologies will focus on three trends: (1) the shift from observational to interactive technologies; (2) the shift to technologies that present increasingly realistic experiences; and (3) the potential use of media to educate children as it entertains them.

The child will take center-stage in this experience as he or she organizes choices about media interactions around personal cognitive skills and goals. In this text, we will pay special attention to the characteristics of children that impact their learning and behavior. For instance, we will examine exactly how children learn from information technologies, and how characteristics, such as age, gender, and ethnic backgrounds influence children's decisions to watch, play with, and master different technologies. We will also examine the link between learning and action. For instance, a child may learn how to hit another child from watching a violent television program, but may choose not to do so. Why not? We will also consider the changes in technology, such as virtual reality games, that will diminish the boundaries between thought and action.

Our study will address the financial incentives to present violent and sexual content, based on an advertising system designed to maximize profits. We will also discuss legislative and social policy initiatives designed to limit sex and violence in the media and to promote educational content in television and computer programs.

Ultimately, our final destination will be to make education interesting for those who are growing up in the information age, to maximize what we know about integrating education with entertainment. In doing so, we will consider ways to use production techniques like action to convey educational and prosocial messages.

As children journey through the changing landscape of the information age, behavioral and cognitive effects will be unprecedented. The children who master this journey, who learn to control our information technologies, will ultimately control our future. Thus, it is timely and important for our society to make that journey accessible and interesting to all of our children, and to ensure them a safe passage during their journey.

Sandra L. Calvert

The Medium as the Messenger

My four-year-old niece, Kristen, and I played a computer game together called *Get Ready for School, Charlie Brown.* Kristen used her mouse to move around the main menu. She decided to play a game where she could dress Charlie Brown.

Charlie Brown wore several outfits before she was satisfied. My favorite was a zebra suit, sandals, a ball cap, and sun glasses. She found his outfits amusing. After spending a considerable amount of time with different clothing combinations, Kristen moved on to another part of the package.

Prior to the twentieth century, information was communicated primarily through words on paper or by word of mouth. Then in rapid succession came the dawn of radio, television, and computers. The flow of information took on a new character as visual images were captured and then viewed by adults and children.

Kristen and many children like her are growing up in the information age, an age in which she is in control of the computer from a young age. Games like *Get Ready for School, Charlie Brown* are often a child's first experience with computers, and these games are teaching children certain skills during their play time (Greenfield, 1996). For example, Kristen is learning to navigate through computer interactions as she loads software packages, accesses menus, finds her way to her favorite activities, and moves on to other parts of the package.

In 1964, Marshall McLuhan argued that the medium is the message. By this statement, he meant that the technology used to present content is just as important as the content itself. The content of the news, for example, may be similar when one learns about the presidential election via newspapers, television programs, or the Internet. But how one experiences these messages varies by the medium. More specifically, a newspaper story and a radio program present content in a verbal format; television uses an audiovisual format; and computer software and the Internet use verbal and sometimes visual methods of displaying content. In the information age, children like Kristen are using interactive audiovisual media that give them control of the content they are experiencing. Television programming, as we shall see in Chapter 10, will also become interactive by the end of this century. Ultimately, using and interacting with these different symbol systems may influence how we think and what we interpret the messages of a medium to be.

When I say that the medium is the messenger, I mean that media have become our gateway to information. As a society, we increasingly rely on electronic media as a primary source of information from the beginnings to the ends of our lives. We watch television, we listen to our radios and stereos, and we will increasingly interact with our computers virtually every day. These media form a backdrop for children's development in American society.

Kristen takes these computer experiences for granted. Interacting with computers is part of her everyday reality. However, computer interactions were not part of my everyday childhood experiences, and they were probably not part of yours, either. We had television. And if we go back in time just 70 years, the information technologies that we now rely on for recreational activities did not even exist.

What are these information technologies? What is unique about them, who has them, and why do we spend so much time using them? What influence do these media have on the daily lives and development of children? What will the future bring children as we make more advances in computer technologies? These are the kinds of questions we will explore in this first chapter and throughout this book.

WHAT ARE THE INFORMATION TECHNOLOGIES?

Mass Media: Television and Radio

Information technologies are electronic devices used to transmit and receive symbolically coded messages. One of our first technologies was radio, which was rapidly followed by television. We listen to radio and we watch television, yet both share the common characteristics of broadcast media. That is, both transmit information from a central source to a mass audience, who, in turn, "tunes in" to particular signals or frequencies.

The spectrum of signals available to the audience expanded greatly during the twentieth century, resulting in a proliferation of broadcast stations and channels (Condry, 1989). Cable and satellite television improved and expanded reception from a handful of choices to hundreds of them (Huston & Wright, in press). In cable television, an actual cable is connected to the home and broadcast signals are channeled from a central location through these wires. Satellite television is common in rural areas where the cost of running a cable to a home is high. Satellites are launched into orbit, and broadcast signals are relayed from the earth to the satellite and then back to homes equipped with a satellite dish. With these advances in technologies, listeners and viewers have more options to select music, stories, and other types of programming.

Selections also expanded with the advent and dissemination of phonographs, tape decks, and videocassette recorders. Individual choices, based on personal tastes and preferences, can now be selected and played at will. Children can purchase audio tapes and compact discs of their favorite musical artists, and they can rent, purchase, or tape their favorite movies and television programs to play on videotape recorders.

Stereo and video equipment are now being merged into personal home theaters, so that users can connect stereo receivers and speakers with television monitors and videocassette players. These consolidations across technologies make excursions to the movie theater increasingly obsolete. We can experience personal choices of content and clarity of audio and visual images in the privacy of our homes.

Computer Technologies: Personal Computers, CD-ROM, Video Games, Virtual Reality, and the Internet

Access to information has also expanded via computer technologies. Large mainframe computers were initially found only in the workplace, with access limited to those who could "speak" the binary "0" and "1" language of these early systems. Eventually, user-friendly interfaces emerged on mainframes, and desktop computers became commonplace in work and home environments. Microchips allowed computers to become more powerful, yet smaller. Eventually, computers became small enough to sit on our laps, small enough for us to carry and use anywhere we go. Business travelers, for example, now use their laptop computers on airplanes as they move from one destination to the next.

Over time, computer interfaces simplified, relying more on visual icons and mouses for effective interaction than on verbal, keyboarding skills. These new interfaces were initially designed for adults, but they also made it possible for children, such as my niece Kristen, to use computers much more easily. Ease of use, in turn, brought computers increasingly into the world of younger and younger children.

Computer software, in the early form of video games, has been available for children to use in their homes for some time. Child-friendly computer interfaces, however, brought CD-ROM games into children's homes, allowing youngsters to explore stories that interest them.

Software package speed has increased enormously over the past few years so that crude, static motion has given way to more realistic movements like those in animated or videotaped television programs. *Ruff's Bone,* for instance, is an educational CD-ROM game that teaches children to read as they interact with an animated story. Children can also explore objects on the screen with a mouse, with amusing outcomes as the child clicks on specific objects. For instance, clicking on the bird bath makes a diver surface, complete with unusual sounds.

The **Internet** is a gateway to information throughout the world. It consists of connections between personal computers and various computer systems throughout the world via our phone lines. When you type a phone number in on the keyboard, you are connected to a server, such as America Online. After you put in an address, the server connects you to various other networks of computers throughout the world as you head to your destination. The route you travel varies depending on how busy certain networks are. Once you reach your destination, information at that destination is then sent back over the phone lines to your personal computer.

Using the Internet, people can now sit in their homes or offices and call up a myriad of services, ranging from exploring a university library, to sending e-mail to colleagues, to booking airline reservations, to paying bills via banking services, to making stock purchases. Initially, the Internet was only a verbal medium, but it now includes visual images as children and adults explore the **World Wide Web** of information. The World Wide Web is a visual and verbal field of information that is connected (in a "web") by phone lines and computers throughout the world; the information is linked so that a person can easily move on to related information (Corcoran, 1996).

Computer technologies are often linked together so that users can take advantage of a multimedia environment. Desktop computers typically come with a CD-ROM drive, modems to connect through a phone line to the Internet, a printer, and peripheral devices such as speakers to enhance sound and

HOW THE INTERNET WORKS

The Internet is a huge network of computers around the globe that communicate through common computer commands, allowing users to send messages to other users, post and receive messages through communal "bulletin boards," and draw out information—text, sound, or images—from distant databases.

1 A user in California sitting at a computer decides to send an Internet message to someone in Washington. That message can cross through several independent networks to reach its destination. The link between a home user and a network may be an ordinary telephone line.

2 Each network reads the coding on the messages and decides where to send it next. Links between networks are typically fiber-optic or satellite data circuits leased from private companies.

3 Networks choose the least crowded route to send the message, so one message from the user in California going to Washington may take a route completely different from a second message from the same person going to the same destination at a different time.

4 The message ideally reaches the destination computer in less than a second.

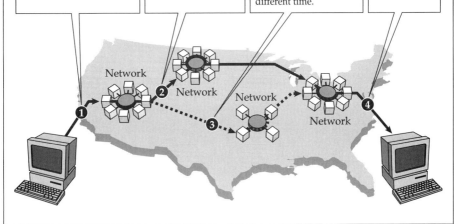

How the Internet works

scanners to capture print or visual images in a process that resembles xeroxing. Through the phone line, the user can bring in and interact with information from anywhere in the world.

The newest technology available is virtual reality. Virtual reality is a computer simulation that allows the user to become part of the computer experience. For example, in games like *Dactyl Nightmare,* you look out of the character's eyes and move through space, determining your virtual movements through your own physical movements. Virtual reality expands previous representational experiences by allowing us to enter into symbolic worlds never before possible (Calvert & Tan, 1996).

In summary, information technologies began as mass media like radio and television that broadcast over a few channels to the audience. Over time, three

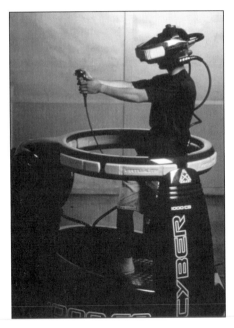

In the future, children will increasingly amuse themselves with virtual reality games in their homes as well as in video arcades.

significant developments occurred: (1) additional channels expanded access to information; (2) individual choices became more prevalent; and (3) information technologies, particularly when linked by personal computers, merged together to provide access to massive amounts of information. These technologies will be explored in relation to specific content areas throughout this book.

CHILDREN'S ACCESS TO INFORMATION TECHNOLOGIES

For media to be effective messengers of information, children must initially be exposed to the content. Before *exposure* can occur, children must first have *access* to a technology. Access is determined by parental decisions about purchasing a radio, television, video cassette recorder, or computer. Once they have access, children may be **actively exposed** to media messages based upon their personal choices and decisions, or they may be **passively exposed** by simply being present when someone else is using the medium.

Children often make decisions to use various media based on their search for entertainment and enjoyment (Zillmann & Bryant, 1994). They like to play computer games such as *Knights* or watch particular cartoons such as *Arthur*. When they make these choices, other activities are **displaced** and relegated to a less important role in their lives. For instance, if a child is watching a television program or playing a video game, he or she is not reading a book.

Ownership Patterns

Cost is the front line for initial access to information technologies (Condry, 1989). When first developed, all information technologies are expensive. Hence, the wealthy usually buy new technologies before the middle-class or the poor do. With the passage of time, cost drops and consumer demand increases. People want to own radios, television sets, videocassette recorders, and personal computers. Without consumer demand, for instance, the computer industry would not have developed personal computers for home use. People wanted their own computers, and the industry responded by making them. Similarly, multimedia computer systems, which involve visual, verbal, and musical presentations, are currently being developed in part because parents want their children to be *computer literate*, that is, to know how to use a computer. Consumer demand is also affected by advertising practices which arouse interest in particular products and new product lines. In Chapter 5, we will consider the role that advertising plays in children's media experiences.

In American culture, radio and television technologies are now present in virtually all households (Brown, Childers, Bauman, & Koch, 1990). Low cost and consumer demand led to the rapid dissemination of television sets into homes (Condry, 1989).

Children's access to new information technologies in their homes has skyrocketed over the past decade. Cable television is now present in approximately 60 to 70 percent of American homes (Wills, 1995). Sega and Nintendo video game systems are present in over 50 million American households (Elmer-DeWitt, 1993). Home computers were present in 22 percent of American households in 1987 (U.S. Department of Commerce, 1989), with ownership increasing to 33 percent by 1995 (Swerdlow, 1995). Households with children purchased home computers earlier than households that included only adults (Ancarrow, 1986).

Gender and Ethnic Issues

While almost all American children have access to television sets, the content is directed primarily at boys, not for girls or for children from ethnic minorities (Calvert, Stolkin, & Lee, 1997). Different access patterns are even more pronounced in the computer area. We will consider the role the media play in relation to gender and ethnic groups in Chapters 3 and 4, respectively.

Researchers documented four early trends in who owns a personal computer and who does not. The first trend is that boys are more likely to have a home computer than girls are, presumably because parents perceive computers as more relevant to the lives of their sons than of their daughters (Lepper, 1985). The second trend is that older children have greater access to personal computers than younger children do (Wartella et al., 1990). The third trend is that wealthier children are more likely to have computers than poorer children (Ancarrow, 1986; Kubey & Larson, 1990; Lepper, 1985). Ethnic trends in computer ownership reveal a fourth trend: more Asian Americans (39 percent) are likely to buy computers than are Caucasians (29 percent), Native Americans (21 percent), Hispanics (13 percent), or African Americans (11 percent) (Marriott with Brant, 1995). Modems, which link computers together via a phone line, were found in 11 million Caucasian homes, but only in 520,000 African-American homes (Farhi, 1996a); this is a proportionally small number even when differences in population size are considered. Different financial resources account for one reason that certain groups are more likely to have computers than other groups, but software that appeals to particular groups account for another.

Apparently, certain ethnic groups see computers as relevant to their lives, and others do not. Efforts are underway to expand young African Americans' interest. For example, Black Entertainment Television of the District of Columbia joined Microsoft Corporation in a joint venture to produce interactive computer software aimed at and about African Americans (Farhi, 1996a). This type of joint venture should provide the kind of content that will improve African-American participation in computer technologies.

Access issues also apply to other information technologies. Specifically, older children have more radios, stereos, computers, and television sets than younger children (Wartella et al., 1990), and wealthy families have the most television sets, videocassette recorders, computers, and radios (Kubey & Larson, 1990).

If children have access to these information technologies, particularly those that provide educational content, they may eventually be in a better position to obtain access to future jobs, status, and wealth (Montgomery, 1995). For instance, low-income preschoolers who watch educational television programs are better prepared for school when they arrive (Wright & Huston, 1995). Children who grow up using computers will know how to gain access to the information they need to succeed in school. With phone lines, computers will link children to libraries and other information sources, placing vast amounts of information at their fingertips. We will consider the educational implications of technologies in Chapter 8.

SELECTIVE EXPOSURE

Although we know that media affect children's lives, we often ignore the crucial question of how children are exposed in the first place. Why do children listen to music, watch television, or interact with computers? In American culture, a main reason is to be *entertained*.

Uses and Gratification Theory

Various theories attempt to explain the impact of media on children. Throughout this book, we will apply particular theories to areas where they explain many of the research findings. A key theory used to explain selective exposure to media is **uses and gratification theory.**

According to uses and gratification theory, children use certain media to fulfill emotional and social needs (Rubin, 1994). The *uses* of television refer to the choices children make to obtain information, entertainment, and the like. *Gratification* refers to the needs children fulfill when they use these various information technologies. Children, for example, watch television or play video games (the uses) for stimulation, companionship, or pleasure (the needs that are gratified). Spending time with television characters (uses) can provide company and amusement (gratification).

Viewers with certain needs often look to television as a potential source of gratification. Kippax and Murray (1977), for example, found that adults who reported needs for information watched more news and informational programming than those who watched television to escape from the pressures of life. Those who needed to escape, by contrast, spent as many as 40 hours per week watching any kind of television programming.

Because American culture often perceives information technologies as a recreational activity, the driving gratification in the creation of most programming is entertainment (Zillmann & Bryant, 1994). Even educational television programs like *Sesame Street* are marketed as fun, recreational activities, for children must view these programs in their leisure time. If children don't enjoy these experiences, they will simply do something else. Broadcasters' beliefs that children really don't like educational television programming is a major obstacle to the development of high-quality educational and prosocial programs for children (Jordan, 1997a). Social policy initiatives to improve children's television programming will be examined in Chapter 6.

Children may perceive computers somewhat differently than earlier technologies. Specifically, after the preschool years, computers are used more for intellectual pursuits than for recreation (Ancarrow, 1986). Thus, computers often fill the intellectual and informational needs of children. Nevertheless, one must keep in mind that children's first exposures to computers are often via video games, an activity that fulfills entertainment needs (Greenfield, 1996).

Active Versus Passive Exposure

Active choices are an inherent assumption of the uses and gratification model, for according to the model, children and adults choose the media and content that they experience (Perse, 1990). Children, however, do not always choose the programs that they watch. For instance, children are often present when parents watch adult television programs, giving the children **passive exposure** to the content (Huston et al., 1990). Some information may be gained simply by being present while someone else is selecting the content, but it's not the same level of involvement that occurs when a child selects a favorite television or computer program, engaging in **active exposure** (Comstock, 1991). When children express preferences by selecting programs with particular content, they gain maximum enjoyment and involvement. For instance, children are more selective and excited when watching videotapes and video games than when watching television, in part because the former maximize their personal choices (Dorr & Kunkel, 1990). For this reason, active exposure may well impact children's lives more than passive exposure does.

The demands inherent in using various technologies also influence passive and active exposure. Children expend less effort to watch a television program or listen to a radio show than they do interacting with a computer or a video game. Television and radio often serve as backdrops for daily experience. For example, adolescents play their radios or even watch television programs as they do their homework (Beentjes & Koolstra, 1995). Even young children can easily divide attention between television viewing and playing with their toys (Anderson & Lorch, 1983).

Dividing attention among competing activities is more difficult when one's actions make the program work. Although children can divide attention between computing and television viewing, computer interaction requires ongoing attention to the activity. For example, when I exposed children to several educational computer games with a television program playing in the background, the children were far more attentive to the computer programs than to the television program (Calvert, 1994a). Their attention moved to the television programming primarily when we were booting a different computer program, making the television program mostly a back-up activity.

It is also far easier to discern when children are actively involved with interactive computer technologies than when they are actively involved with broadcast media like television and radio. Children punch the keys and react to the screen when they interact with computers. They make things happen. But how do you know when a child is actively involved with television content? Before one can answer this important question, we must first tackle the more basic issue of what it means to view television.

What Is Television Viewing?

This deceptively simple question is central to our understanding of television effects, but researchers define viewing in different ways. Being able to measure television viewing precisely is important, for we must know how much children are exposed to the medium to understand how it impacts their lives. For advertisers, knowing who is in the audience determines how much they will pay to broadcast commercials (Condry, 1989). The commercial issues associated with television and the Internet will be explored in more depth in Chapter 5.

Some researchers measure viewing by whether or not *the television set is on*. Nielsen (1981) ratings, the industry standard for determining audience size, were once based on this definition. The programs that were broadcast and the commercials shown reflect their findings. However, children are sometimes out of the room when the television is on and programs are being aired. Even if they are in the room, children may be involved in another activity. Children are not viewing television in these examples, but some statisticians used to assume they were. Those who use this definition may overestimate viewing.

Viewing can also mean that *a child is in the viewing room while the television set is on*. However, a child may be in the room but not be watching the

In this photograph, all family members are in the viewing room and looking at the television set.

program at all. Using this definition, the children that I described earlier in my computer study would always be defined as viewing, which was clearly not the case. In home situations, parents may be watching the news while the child is on the floor, playing with toys. Again, under this definition, television viewing is probably overestimated.

Nielsen now uses a **people meter** to measure viewing. The television set is wired to capture the viewing frequency, or station, a particular household is viewing, and this information is stored on a small computerized device (Raymondo, 1997). When adults and children come into a viewing room and watch a television program, they are instructed to punch their personal code into a small remote control to let Nielsen know they are viewing the program. This remote control device is known as the people meter. Sometimes, however, people forget to punch in when they come into the room, and sometimes they forget to punch out when they leave. To correct for some of these problems, viewers must punch in every 70 minutes to reestablish their viewing, or else red lights flash at them. Red lights also flash every time the channel is changed until viewers punch in their codes again (Raymondo, 1997). This measure is relatively precise, but it may be difficult for children to handle accurately by themselves. The patterns of children's television viewing Nielsen has collected recently are presented in Figure 1.1.

Viewing can also mean that *a child is in the viewing room and looking at the television set.* "Eyes on the screen" is the definition I used in my computer study and

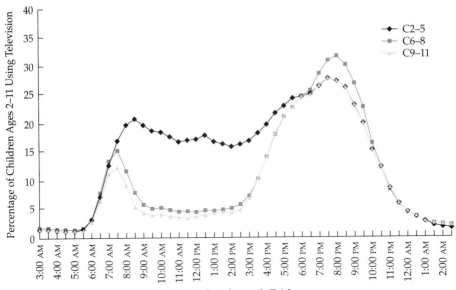

FIGURE 1.1 Children's TV Usage, Monday through Friday

in my other television studies as well (Calvert, in press). However, we ignore auditory attention when we use visual attention only to measure viewing. Unfortunately, we do not have a clear measure of auditory attention because it is difficult to know when a person is listening. With this definition, actual viewing may be underestimated because a child may be listening without looking.

A seminal study by Anderson and colleagues (1985) examined the issue of what home viewing is and how to measure it. To do so, they enlisted 334 families; 106 of these families had video cameras placed in their homes to record their actual television viewing. Whenever a television set was turned on, the video camera also came on and recorded the viewing of family members and friends who were in the room. Families also filled out viewing **diaries** in which they logged the programs that they were watching. In these diaries, parents wrote the names of the people who were in the viewing room every 15 minutes when the television set was on. This approach, as you may recall, was our second definition of television viewing. Parents also recorded the specific programs that were playing. In another measure, parents filled out a checklist of activities, including television viewing, that a child typically did on a given day.

To determine the best measure of home viewing, Anderson and colleagues (1985) then matched the actual videotapes of viewing behavior with parents' reports of viewing behavior (that is, the diaries and the activity checklists). The *diary was the most accurate index of children's presence in the viewing room*, as recorded by the camera on videotapes. A sample page from the diary is presented in Figure 1.2. The videotapes revealed that preschoolers were in the presence of an operating television set for about 13 to 14 hours per week, or

Time	TV Set		Channel Number	Name of Program	1	2	3	4	5	6	7	8	9	10		
1/4 hours	On	Off		(for movies, please list name of movie)												
				EXAMPLE:												
6:00–6:14																
6:15–6:29																
6:30–6:44																
6:45–6:59																
7:00–7:14	X		4	Today	X	X								X		
7:15–7:29					—									—		
7:30–7:44																
7:45–7:59					O											
8:00–8:14					—											
8:15–8:29					?											
8:30–8:44								X								
8:45–8:59								—								
9:00–9:14																
9:15–9:29																
9:30–9:44	X		3	Fred Flintstone		X										
9:45–9:59						—										
10:00–10:14				Movie "And Then There												
10:15–10:29				Were None"												
10:30–10:44																
10:45–10:59																

6:00 AM

11:00 AM

NOW, TURN THE PAGE TO BEGIN YOUR VIEWING DIARY . . . .

FIGURE 1.2 Sample Page from Home Viewing Diary

about 2 hours per day. Diaries indicated that children viewed 16.7 hours per week; activity checklists indicated 22 hours of viewing per week. Thus, the more specific the measure, the more accurate it was. Having an accurate measure is an issue of **reliability.** In this instance, it means that the diary is the most reliable way to tell us who is in the room when the television set is on. The videotapes are also an excellent measure to use, but it is not feasible to videotape all children as they view television in every study. Since this study was published, the diary has become the preferred measure for social scientists to assess children's presence in the viewing room as television programs are aired.

The more difficult issue of *what it means to view* was also targeted in this study. What it means to view is a **validity** issue. Validity examines whether we are measuring what we claim to measure. In this instance, we are claiming to measure television viewing. The diary indexed whether or not a child was in the room when a particular television program was on. Were children actually watching that program? Specifically, were they looking at the television set? To answer this question, the researchers scored each child's visual attention to the television screen from the videotapes. Then they related each child's visual attention to the television screen to that child's presence in the viewing room when the television set was turned on.

The researchers found *little relation between being present in a room with an operating television set and actually viewing the programs.* Some children spent little time looking at the television set even though they were in the room when the television set was playing. One preschool boy, for instance, spent 39.8 hours in one week in the presence of an operating television set. However, he only spent 3.4 hours actually watching the programs. While in the room, he played with toys, climbed on his dad, slept, and participated in other activities with television as the backdrop for those activities. If one uses the diary to measure his viewing, he is one of the highest viewers in the study. If one uses eyes on the screen to measure viewing, he is one of the lowest viewers. The implication of this study is that the definition of viewing is central in understanding children's exposure to television content.

Passive versus active exposure is an important consideration when examining what viewing means. Boys like the one Anderson and his colleagues (1985) encountered are being passively exposed to television content. In this case, someone else is actively choosing and watching the television programs. The boy just happened to be there because family activities were occurring in that room.

Passive exposure is most likely to occur during our second definition of viewing: when the child is in the room and a television set is on. In contrast, active exposure may occur most often with our third definition, when a child actually looks at the television screen. One can argue that we are most interested in a program when we look at it. However, children may choose to watch a program, an active decision, and pay little visual attention to the show. Alternately, they may be in the audience and become very interested in a program that someone else initially selected.

TABLE 1.1 Total Hours of Television Viewed Per Week

Younger Cohort			Older Cohort		
Age	M	SD	Age	M	SD
3	19.2	9.87	5	19.2	10.85
3½	19.9	10.75	5½	19.0	11.28
4	19.6	10.02	6	17.7	10.50
4½	19.1	10.09	6½	15.9	10.32
5	20.8	10.93	7	15.5	9.48

Note: M is the mean, or average, number of hours children view television each week. *SD* is the standard deviation, indicating the variability in the number of hours children view television each week.
Source: Huston, A. C., Wright, J. C., Rice, M. L., Kerkman, D., & St. Peters, M. (1990). Early television viewing. *Developmental Psychology, 26,* 409–420. Copyright © 1990 by the American Psychological Association. Reprinted with permission.

As it turns out, passive exposure to television content is prevalent during the early years of life. For example, Huston et al. (1990) explored family viewing patterns using the diary method. Contrary to the researchers' expectations, family viewing characteristics had more effect on a child's overall exposure to television programs than the child's individual characteristics, such as his or her age. That is, young children were often passively exposed to a television program because someone else in the family was watching it, not because the children themselves selected it. Adult programs often played on the television set while children were in the viewing room. Children's level of exposure to television programming appears in Table 1.1. Note that until age 6, children are in the presence of an operating television set about 19 to 20 hours per week, or about 3 hours per day. Exposure drops slightly after age 6 to about 18 hours and then to 15 to 16 hours of television exposure per week. This drop probably reflects the increased time children begin to spend in school.

Even though children don't select all the programs they see, passive exposure is still important in children's development. Programs adults watch form a context for children's daily life experiences; for example, tastes in programs may be cultivated when fathers and sons watch Monday night football together. The cultivation of viewing patterns at early ages may impact later viewing preferences and viewing styles when children make more active choices about their viewing. Consequently, parental decisions about what to view on television provide a *social context* for the development of their children (Huston et al., 1990). Along with other social contexts of development, including family relationships, neighborhoods, and schools, viewing habits formed in childhood can have an important impact on who that child will become.

Content indifference is yet another reason for passive exposure. When a television set is turned to a particular program, viewers often leave the channel on that station after the program that they are watching is over (Comstock, 1991). This is known as content indifference; the viewer does not really care about what he or she is viewing as long as some program is on. Hence, active intentional exposure can become passive exposure as one crosses program boundaries. Advertisers rely on content indifference to keep viewers watching commercials that interrupt the programming. With the advent of remote control devices, affording easier channel changes, this pattern may now be changing.

Impact of New Technologies on Viewing

Changing options in technological interfaces make definitions of television viewing even more difficult for researchers. The invention of the remote control has resulted in a viewing style called **"grazing"** (Huston et al., 1992) or "channel surfing." Grazing occurs when a person flips through an array of channels. Sometimes the person uses this strategy to select a program; at other times the person changes the channel whenever commercials appear; and sometimes the person "watches" more than one program at a time, flipping back and forth between two or more shows (Dorr & Kunkel, 1990). Viewers who are not in control of rapid channel changes may become frustrated and have difficulty following the thread of any story as discrepant visual images rapidly move by.

In a study of cable subscribers, Perse (1990) asked men and women about how they used the remote control device. About 2 percent of her sample said that they never changed channels. About 24 percent said that they changed channels between programs. About 44 percent reported changing channels when commercials appeared. About 30 percent reported changing channels during the actual programs. Not surprisingly, those who changed channels frequently reported the least attentional involvement in the programs. Conversely, those who rarely changed channels reported the most attentional involvement in the programs they watched. These findings suggest that surfing patterns can be an indicator of active versus passive involvement in television programming.

Grazing may make the measurement of television viewing more difficult to gage, for viewing diaries are very difficult to fill out for those who watch numerous channels in a minute or two. Moreover, the people meter Nielsen now uses does not pick up rapid channel changes. Those who are grazing and then select one channel for viewing may well be indicating an active preference for certain content. Alternately, one may select a program only because it's the "best" show on at that time. Or perhaps the viewer's thumb simply wears out.

DISPLACEMENT EFFECTS: WHAT ACTIVITIES DO INFORMATION TECHNOLOGIES REPLACE?

Information technologies have altered the way children and adolescents spend their free time. **Displacement** occurs when the introduction of a new technology replaces previous activities. When a child watches 2 to 3 hours of television each day (Condry, 1989; Huston et al., 1990), that time must come from other activities.

Presumably, spending time in an activity cultivates skills in that domain (Condry, 1989). The activities that receive less time are unlikely to develop as well because of displacement effects. That is why researchers have been particularly interested in the specific activities children give up when they use different technologies. Leisure reading has been a focal point, given our nation's commitment to literacy skills.

We will consider displacement in two ways. First, we will examine how the introduction of television displaced other activities. Then we will discuss how the introduction of new technologies has displaced television viewing.

The Introduction of Television

Because television penetrated American households so quickly, we know little about how daily life changed in the United States after the introduction of television. In one seminal U.S. study (Schramm, Lyle, & Parker, 1961), children who only had access to radio (lived in a community the researchers called *Radiotown*) listened to the radio, read more comic books, and went to the movie theater more often than children who had access to television (lived in *Teletown*). Why should one go out for entertainment when one can be entertained at home? These findings suggest that television displaced activities that were similar in meeting the entertainment needs of children and adults, findings in keeping with the uses and gratification theory we discussed earlier.

Researchers did examine the introduction of television into other cultures. Murray and Kippax (1978), for example, examined the social behavior of children living in three rural Australian communities. One community had no television. The second had had one public television station for a year at the time of the study. The third community had had one commercial and one public television station for five years. Eight to twelve years old children were the focus of the investigation. As Table 1.2 shows, access to television altered children's use of alternative media. Specifically, children without a television listened to the radio and records and read more comic books than children who had a television. Interestingly, children who had access to television read more books than those who did not have television, countering the claim that television impedes leisure reading. Children who had television did read fewer comic books than those who did not have television, suggesting that comic books and television viewing meet similar entertainment needs. There were no significant differences in newspaper reading across the three communities. When participation in all activities was considered, the researchers found that time devoted to some activities initially decreased, but then rebounded after the novelty of television wore off.

A cross-cultural study conducted in Canada (Williams, 1986) also found that television displaces activities that fill similar needs for its users. The study compared three communities: (1) *Notel*, which had no television reception; (2) *Unitel*, which received one television station; and (3) *Multitel*, which

TABLE 1.2 Children's Media Use

Media	High-TV Town	Low-TV Town	No-TV Town
Radio	2.00	1.82	2.27
Records	2.06	1.77	2.81
Books	1.85	1.61	1.08
Comics	2.76	3.91	5.84
Newspapers	2.30	2.42	2.32

Note: Mean figures refer to the number of hours allocated to radio listening and record playing on the average school day and the number of books, comics, and newspapers read each week.
Source: Murray, J. P., & Kippax, S. (1978). Children's social behavior in three towns with differing television experience. *Journal of Communication, 28,* 19–29. Reprinted by permission of Oxford University Press.

received several television stations. The researchers studied these three communities before and after television reception came to the Notel community. Canadian children who had television sets spent less time attending community events than those without television reception. Television also affected reading skills (Corteen & Williams, 1986); the second and third graders who lived in Notel scored better in reading than those who lived in Unitel, and Unitel children, in turn, scored better in reading than Multitel children. The reading advantage the Notel children exhibited, however, disappeared two years after television was introduced into their community. These results suggest that television viewing can have a negative impact on reading proficiency.

The initial fascination with television as a foreground activity eventually gives way to the acceptance of television as a background activity—that is, the novelty of television subsides somewhat over time (Huston et al., 1992). This shift from foreground to background does not diminish the importance of television in daily lives. Rather, it suggests that television is now accepted as an integral activity in children's and families' daily routines.

The Introduction of New Technologies

As new information technologies are developed, existing technologies must share time and compete with emerging ones. This alters selective exposure to various media. As we have seen, children and adults often use technologies for entertainment. If a new technology entertains better than a previous one, the old technology may well be displaced.

Consider how people once used radio and how we use it today. In earlier generations, families sat around the radio and listened to stories. When television appeared, visual depictions provided a more compelling story than a radio depiction with only a sound track. Over time, television stories replaced radio stories because television was a better story-telling device.

Radio, however, did not disappear. Instead, it retained viability by specializing and by filling a particular niche for listeners. Songs are a clear example of this specialization. Songs can provide an activity listeners can do as they work

Before the dawn of television, families once sat around the radio and listened to stories for entertainment.
Courtesy of Zenith Electronics Corporation.

on homework assignments (Beentjes & Koolstra, 1995). Even when they need vision for a task such as writing, children can still listen to the radio in the background. Radio, then, takes on a specialized role that fits user needs and that takes advantage of its auditory symbol system.

Even so, the more technologies compete with each other for scarce time resources, the less time any one technology will have. The home viewing studies conducted in the 1980s (Anderson et al., 1985; Anderson, et al., 1986; Huston et al., 1990) are obsolete in some respects because of the plethora of new technologies and stations now available in the home.

Several studies have examined the impact of the new technologies on children's use of media. Wartella et al. (1990), for example, examined the extent to which broadcast television, cable television, and videocassette recorders increased the availability of programming for children. Little diversity was found in network television, with cartoons being the main fare provided for children. Cable provided more diverse offerings than the networks, but only 5 percent of their programming was instructional and educational. Videocassette rentals yielded similar findings; most of the videocassettes involved programs presented on network television or cable. PBS provided the only major source of educational programming for children. The implication is that more programming did become available for children, but often it was more of the same type of programming broadcasters were already supplying.

When asked about their children's media use, parents reported that children with cable watched about 3 more hours of television per week. Many children watched Nickelodeon, a cable station that offers educational and prosocial programming for children. PBS programs were also very popular with young children; 59 percent of their favorite PBS programs were educational or prosocial. Parents used videocassette recorders to tape programs for later use or to build a video library for their children. Parents also rented three to four programs each month for their children to view (Wartella et al., 1990).

Brown et al. (1990) found that newer technologies did not displace television or radio use. In Brown's study, young adolescent boys and girls answered a **questionnaire,** a paper-and-pencil measure that asked them about their media usage patterns. African Americans and boys spent more time watching television than Caucasians and girls did. African Americans and girls listened to the radio more often than Caucasians and boys did. As they aged, children listened to the radio more and watched television less. Interestingly, having cable television or a videocassette recorder did not increase the amount of exposure to television offerings. Instead, the newer media allowed children more choices during the same viewing times. These findings suggest that new information technologies may promote active choices and viewing styles.

In another study of media behaviors, 9- to 15-year-olds carried electronic paging devices that periodically signaled them to report their activities (Kubey & Larson, 1990). Music videos, video games, and videocassette use was targeted. The youngsters reported using these media 18 percent of the times sampled. As Table 1.3 indicates, television viewing was by far the most frequently reported activity, accounting for 74 percent of their media time (13 percent of total time). Reading books came next, followed by listening to music. These preteens and teens used new video media infrequently. Video games, for example, accounted for only 3 percent of children's and adolescents' media time.

Gender differences also occurred in media usage patterns. Compared to boys, girls spent more time listening to music and less time watching television. For the new media, boys played more video games than girls, accounting for almost 80 percent of all video game play. Both boys and girls watched music videos, but boys liked hard rock videos whereas girls preferred a station featuring more ballads and Motown hits. Middle-class boys were the predominant users of videocassette recorders. Taken together, the results suggest that boys respond to the new media more positively than girls, perhaps because video games and video programming are often targeted at a male audience.

When personal computers began to enter American households, they, too, had little initial impact on children's use of time (Ancarrow, 1986). As Table 1.4 shows, computers lagged behind other information technologies in household purchases. People viewed books and magazines as more educational than computers, but informal learning did take place with computers, particularly for boys. After age 5, children increasingly used computers for intellectual

TABLE 1.3 Frequency of Media Use

	Number of Reports	*Percentage of All Media Time*	*Percentage of Total Time*
Traditional Media			
Television	2,355	74.3	13.1
Music	267	8.4	1.5
Reading	288	9.1	1.6
New Video Media			
Music video	56	1.8	.3
VCR	55	1.7	.3
Video games	105	3.3	.6
Other Media	46	1.4	.2
Total Media	3,172	100.00	17.6

Note: Based on 18,022 random samples. Other media include attending a movie at a theater (N=19), playing a video arcade game (N=13), using a computer for something other than playing a game (N=10), and listening to the news or advertisements on the radio (N=4).

Source: Kubey, R., & Larson, R. (1990) *Communication Research, 17,* 107–130. Copyright © 1990 by Sage Publications, Inc. Reprinted by permission of Sage Publications, Inc.

rather than recreational needs. The public appears to take computers more seriously as an educational medium when compared to other information technologies. Even so, the majority of children used computers less than 5 hours per week. Specifically, 78 percent of teens, 82 percent of 6- to 11-year-olds, and 98 percent of preschoolers used computers less than 5 hours per week.

United States Census data (1996) projects that similar media use patterns will continue through the end of the twentieth century. These data were collected through 1994, and patterns of use were projected from 1995–99. As

TABLE 1.4 Percentage of Persons with Various Information Technologies Available in 1986 (by Age Group)

Technology in Household	*Age Group*			
	Adults (18 yrs and older)	Teens (12–17)	Youths (6–11)	Preschoolers (2–5)
Television set	99%	99%	99%	99%
Cable television	48	51	53	53
Videocassette recorder	29	35	34	33
Personal/Home computer	13	26	22	17
Record player/Stereo	87	93	91	89
Audiocassette/Tape player	82	94	91	86
Number of Sample Cases	1,752	564	1,141	2,316

Source: Ancarrow, J. S. (1986). *Use of computers in home study* (U.S. Department of Education Statistics). Washington, D.C.: United States Government Printing Office.

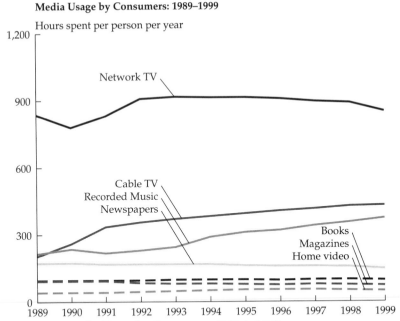

FIGURE 1.3 Media Usage by Consumers: 1989 to 1999
*Source: United States Bureau of the Census (1996). Statistical Abstract
of the United States (116th ed.), p. 558. Washington, D.C.: United States
Government Printing Office.*

Figure 1.3 shows, the general population spends considerably more time using
network television than cable television, recorded music, newspapers, books,
magazines, or home videos. As children are part of this audience, they will
continue to view substantial amounts of broadcast television.

In summary, new technologies appear to make little difference in children's media activities, for broadcast television remains the medium of choice
for both children and adolescents. Adolescence brings a preference for musical
offerings, particularly for girls. Nevertheless, over the years, children have
spent more time watching television than doing any other activity except
sleeping (Liebert & Sprafkin, 1988), and that trend is continuing.

Usage patterns, however, vary for different children who live in different
media environments. Many children who have video games, for example, play
as much as an hour and a half per day (Elmer-DeWitt, 1993). This figure rivals
the 2 to 3 hours of daily television exposure other investigators report (Huston
et al., 1990).

Impact of Television on Reading Skills

Many believe that books and the literacy skills cultivated by reading are the
major loser as technologies consume more and more of children's leisure time.

This conclusion has sparked debate since the first researchers examined the effects of television.

When Schramm, Lyle, & Parker (1961) studied the displacement effects television had on American children's activities in the early 1960s, they concluded that television had displaced comic book reading, but not serious book reading. Children preferred the light nature of televised stories over comic books. Hence, the entertainment television viewing provided fulfilled children's entertainment needs and displaced the entertainment comic book reading afforded. The cross-cultural research of Murray and Kippax (1978) supported this thesis; they found that comic books, but not books, faced displacement after the introduction of television in Australian communities.

More recently, others have challenged these early findings, particularly as more television stations and more competing technologies have emerged. For example, as you may recall, one set of researchers found that reading scores were initially higher for Canadian children who had no television reception in their town than for those who did have television reception. Children were followed over time, and new age groups, called **cohorts,** were added to the study. The investigators examined reading scores two years after the television came to the no-television town. The new group of young children, who had had television available for two years, had lower reading scores than the earlier cohort of children from that town, who had not had television available (Corteen & Williams, 1986). These findings implicate television viewing as an impediment in reading proficiency.

Similarly, recent research on Dutch children suggests that television viewing now has a more negative impact on reading books than comic books (Koolstra & van der Voort, 1996). The study followed children in the second and fourth grades for two years. Television viewing reduced children's reading of leisure books during both years. The authors suggest that television viewing creates negative attitudes about reading books and reduces children's reading concentration skills.

Neuman (1991), by contrast, argues that television viewing has had little impact on serious book reading at any time because children have always devoted little time to reading. Children in the 1940s and the early 1950s rarely read more than 15 minutes per day in their leisure time, and those figures are no different today. Therefore, television viewing is not responsible for the small amount of time children spend reading.

In a displacement study, however, Neuman (1988) did find that children who watched more than four hours of television per day were poorer readers. These findings suggest that excessive viewing does impede reading skills. However, children who live in homes where the television is always on may differ in other ways as well, such as in income levels; these other factors may be the reason their reading scores decline, rather than television viewing per se. The kind of program may also play a role in determining the complex relation between television viewing and reading. For example, children who view *Sesame Street* do better in school than those who watch programs designed only for entertainment (Wright & Huston, 1995).

In summary, some recent findings suggest that the need for entertainment may be growing for current generations and interfering with verbal literacy skills. Viewing more than four hours of television per day is related to poorer reading skills. However, few American children ever spent much of their leisure time reading, even before television was widely available in homes. Moreover, many middle-class American children read books rather than watch television programs before they go to bed (Welch, 1995). And if children view specific educational programs, viewing can actually have a positive effect on reading skills, as when children watch *Sesame Street* (Wright & Huston, 1995).

The implication is that we must be sensitive to the particular children we are describing, for not all children are alike, and they watch different television programs for different reasons. Moreover, the same child has different needs in different situations. For instance, reading stories is often a bedtime ritual for parents and their young children. Watching television together may also be a family activity, promoting group cohesion and entertainment for the entire unit.

THE SYMBOL SYSTEMS OF RADIOS, BOOKS, TELEVISIONS, AND COMPUTERS

One of the most unique aspects of information technologies is that they are representational media (Calvert, in press). More specifically, each medium relies on particular ways of transmitting messages by using visual, verbal, and musical forms of thought that parallel the way children and adults think. Visual images arouse children, teach them how to act, and present content in a believable form (Calvert, in press). We will consider the way a medium relates to children's thought in depth in Chapter 7.

One reason some researchers believe television may erode reading skills is because it focuses on visual rather than verbal symbol systems. Radio and books rely on words, whereas television relies on both pictures and words to present the content. An overreliance on television for entertainment may prevent children from developing an interest in reading books during their leisure time, thereby lowering reading skills for lack of practice (Condry, 1989).

Radio, television, books, and computer technologies all present a symbolic world to children. An effective form of communication presents information in ways that parallel the visual and verbal ways children think about information (Calvert, in press). Visual forms are called **iconic modes** of representation, and verbal forms are called **symbolic modes** (Bruner, Olver, & Greenfield, 1968). Visual modes characterize the representational thought of young children, whereas verbal modes characterize the thought of children in middle childhood (Bruner et al., 1968). Put another way, children tend to think first in pictures, later in words. Thus, television presentations may be easier for young children to understand than radio or book presentations.

Because radio presents information only in an auditory mode, the listener must decode the information and then create visual images from content that was previously stored in memory. As radio messages are broadcast, a listener has to pay close attention to the audio track for learning to occur. If attention lapses, there is no way to go back and rehear the content again to improve comprehension. For this reason, radio presentations are rather difficult for children to understand, particularly at young ages. Even so, children create their own visual images after listening to radio more often than after seeing a televised presentation of the same content (Meringoff, 1983). This issue will be explored in Chapter 9.

Just as radio relies on auditory verbal symbols, books rely on a written verbal symbol system to convey a story. Books for young children accentuate verbal messages with visual pictures. Unlike radio, books allow children to go back and reread passages as many times as they desire, thereby allowing them to master the content. However, children must be able to read, or someone must read to them, if they are to understand the story.

Television is a storybook of visual images that both move and talk (Lemish & Rice, 1986). Verbal dialogue combines with visual images to provide dual modes for children to think about content (Calvert et al., 1982): they simultaneously see an event and hear words that describe that event. Moreover, children acquire verbal information and vocabulary from their exposure to television programming (Rice et al., 1990; Rice & Woodsmall, 1988). Yet, like radio, television communicates in images that come and go quickly with little opportunity to review the content.

With the development of the videocassette recorder (VCR), children gained the opportunity to rehearse televised information by seeing and hearing it as many times as they desired. Children like to watch their favorite videotapes over and over, just as they enjoy hearing their favorite storybooks over and over (Rice & Sell, 1990). Children take advantage by rewatching favorite programs, perhaps improving their comprehension of their favorite stories. For example, children begin to predict story events of interest to them, and they tell others to watch. Children can view their favorite videotapes without adult assistance long before they can read their favorite books by themselves, making television a readily accessible medium for young children.

Technologies have now evolved from those in which an audience listens or watches to those in which children take an active role in deciding what will happen next. In CD-ROM games such as *Ruff's Bone,* children can select a version that tells the uninterrupted story, or they can explore the story screen by screen. The child can click the mouse on an object to see what happens—for example, clicking on the mop spurs a lively dance between the mop and broom. Computer interfaces are requiring children to think about and encode information in order to act on it. They must make choices, perhaps cultivating decision-making skills. They can go back and find their favorite story points, or they can explore new areas.

The probability that a child will get some message increases when the child must do something for the interaction to continue. Moreover, the message can be personalized for each child. *Ruff's Bone,* for example, can be presented in English or Spanish, while *Just Grandma and Me* can be presented in English, Spanish, or Japanese. These talking storybooks are entertaining and easy for children to control. The CD-ROM story is also packaged with a story-book, making this experience one that can foster literacy skills.

Virtual reality experiences even allow the child to enter the computer game. As a three-dimensional experience, virtual reality allows the person to enter a character's body and to control his or her movements (Calvert & Tan, 1996). As the character, the child looks out of his or her own eyes and touches nearby objects. These symbolic experiences allow the player to see, smell, hear, and touch objects just as they have been able to see and hear events in older technologies like television and video games. When the player can use all of his or her senses, the realism of symbolic experiences will become even more compelling. Aggressive thoughts, for example, increase when young adults participate in virtual reality experiences, a topic that we will pursue in the next chapter.

SUMMARY

Over the course of the twentieth century, the medium became the messenger. As a society, we increasingly get our information from various media. It's clear we enjoy these media because we choose to spend much of our free time using them. Our dependence on them is also clear from their penetration into every sphere of our lives, from homes to schools to workplaces.

Television became and continues to be the dominant technology in American society. Television initially displaced similar leisure activities, such as comic book reading, and newer technologies have failed to erode its popularity.

If written words on pages are becoming less interesting to children who have developed in a world of visual media, educational attainment may ultimately suffer. But this issue should not be one of visual versus verbal images. Indeed, both pictures and words are legitimate modes of thought. Instead, the issue is how we use pictures and words in our representations of experience. For young children, visual and verbal messages may assist information processing more effectively than strictly verbal messages. It is noteworthy that many computers now include visual iconic menus for younger and older users alike, for words will never capture the vast capacity human beings have for thinking in vivid visual images.

The current climate in America is one in which learning via words in books competes with enjoyment via television and video games. Many educators see computers as the answer to diminishing scholastic skills. But so, too, did others view radio and television in an earlier age. As children move fast-forward down the information highway, it is time to pause and reflect on where that journey is taking them.

CHAPTER 2

Media Violence

Censorship or V-Chip?

Summary

The Simpsons are watching television together. The three children sit directly in front of the television set and watch Itchy and Scratchy hit and hurt each other. In one scene, Itchy hits Scratchy on the head with a mallet. The two older children laugh. The baby watches and sucks her pacifier.

Later, Mr. Simpson makes his wife a spice rack in the basement. He looks up and screams as his baby daughter hits him on the head with a mallet. Mr. Simpson falls to the floor.

Back in the living room, Mrs. Simpson asks, "Where would a baby get such an idea?" The children are viewing another episode of the *Itchy and Scratchy Show.* This time Itchy stabs Scratchy with a knife. The baby then tries to stab Mr. Simpson with a knife. "Could it be," Mrs. Simpson asks, "that my baby is learning violence from watching a cartoon?!"

Although *The Simpsons* are only a fictional, animated television family, Mrs. Simpson asks a very important question that has serious implications for our society. Specifically, does viewing violent television content cause children to act aggressively? About one thousand empirical studies and two sets of Congressional hearings have examined this issue (Murray, 1998), yet the networks continue to rely on an action-and-violence formula to attract television viewers (Gerbner & Signorielli, 1990). The **First Amendment** guarantees their right to do so.

While social concerns about violence in American society continue (Kunkel et al., 1995b), the action-and-violence formula itself has spread to a new frontier: our new information technologies. Unlike television, where a viewer can simply watch violence without ever acting on that content, video games and other interactive technologies require a child to act aggressively for the game to continue. Through interaction, aggression is incorporated directly into a child's behaviors (Calvert & Tan, 1996).

In this chapter, we will examine the action-and-violence formula and the amount of aggressive content found in various media. We will consider the theories germane to the television-and-aggression issue, the evidence to support or refute each position, and the extent to which exposure to media violence impacts children's aggression in real life. Finally, we will examine social policy initiatives directed toward controlling media violence.

THE ACTION-AND-VIOLENCE FORMULA

Children's storybooks and fairytales often focus on clear themes of good and evil. Children's television programs rely on similar formulas that clearly depict themes of good versus evil. Action and violence are an integral facet of this formula.

The **action-and-violence formula,** in which a hero defeats a villain, pairs aggressive content with character movements. This simple either/or social formula, ready-made for an audience with limited cognitive skills, teaches children that "Good always triumphs over evil." The hero is an important role model who teaches children values, such as what is right versus wrong, or the importance of helping and protecting those who are in need of aid. However, when the "good guys" act almost as violently as the "bad guys," even when it's for a good cause, young children may also be learning that aggression is an acceptable way to solve problems.

Although American television productions rely on action and violence to present stories, action is different from violence. **Action** involves *movement*, whereas **violence** involves *aggressive content* or *behavior* (Huston-Stein et al., 1981a). One can show movement with little violent content. For example, rapid movement is present when someone skis through a challenging course. The rapid movement, in and of itself, can be exciting and interesting to children.

Our failure to separate the two dimensions of action and violence means that we think that nonviolent content is boring because it has no action. Prosocial content does not preclude movement. Prosocial stories can involve adventure, movement, and excitement without being aggressive.

Because of commercial goals, the networks rely on this simple, action-and-violence formula to deliver a large child audience to advertisers. Large audiences mean large financial gains via advertising revenues. In reality, violence is not the most popular type of programming in the United States, as calculated by Nielsen ratings (Gerbner, Morgan, & Signorielli, 1994). Rather, violent programs are more profitable in the larger international market because "action" is readily comprehensible in other cultures (Gerbner et al., 1994). Although the social costs of this formula can be high, it has become the formula of choice in many media presentations. The action-and-violence formula now appears in television programs, and in video, computer, and virtual reality games.

Violent Television Content

In the television area, Gerbner and his colleagues (Gerbner et al., 1980; Gerbner et al., 1986; Gerbner et al., 1979; Gerbner & Signorielli, 1990) have documented the amount of violence in commercial television programming over the past 30 years using **The Violence Index,** a measure of the frequency and rate of violent representations in network television drama. The researchers define **violence** as acts that threaten to hurt or kill other individuals (Gerbner & Signorielli, 1990). As Figure 2.1 indicates, the specific television programs have changed over time, but the amount of violent content has remained remarkably stable over the years (Gerbner, Morgan, & Signorielli, 1994). On average, 70 percent of prime-time television programs contained violent content from 1973–1995. Prime-time television programs contained approximately 5 acts of violence per hour. Almost half of prime-time characters were involved in violence, with 10 percent involved in actual killing (Gerbner & Signorielli, 1990). See Table 2.1.

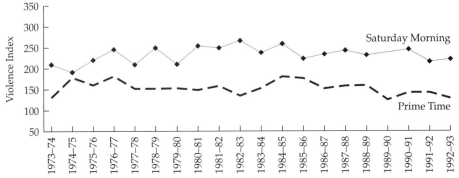

Note: To compute the Violence Index, Gerbner and his colleagues add
(1) The percent of television programs containing violence;
(2) The rate of violent incidents per program doubled;
(3) The rate of violent incidents per hour doubled;
(4) The percent of characters participating in violent activities; and
(5) The percent of characters involved in killing.

FIGURE 2.1 Violence Index of Network Prime Time and Saturday Morning Dramatic
Programs (1973–1993)
Source: Adapted with permission of the Cultural Indicators project, George Gerbner,
Director.

Children's cartoons contain more violence than prime-time television
programs (Gerbner & Signorielli, 1990). On average, 93 percent of children's
television programs contained violence over a 22-year period—20 percent
more violence than prime-time television programs showed. Seventy percent of characters in 90 percent of children's weekend television programs
acted violently from 1986–1989, a figure in keeping with the averages over
the previous 22 years. Table 2.1 depicts the amount of violence in television programs documented by Gerbner and his colleagues over a 22-year
period.

After 1989 to 1990, violence in prime-time programs began to drop when
legislative action was threatened (Gerbner et al., 1994). Reductions in Saturday
morning television violence also occurred, but they were less pervasive than
the reductions made in prime-time programs. Increases in educational and
prosocial television programming, which began in the Fall of 1997, may now
reveal a decline in Saturday morning violence.

Gerbner et al. (1994) also find that television often portrays different social
groups as perpetrators or victims of crimes. About half of major characters are
involved in violence in any given week. Young adult males, Hispanic males,
and settled adult males are the most frequent perpetrators of violence. These
same groups, except for settled males, are also most likely to be the victims of
violence, primarily because males are the most prevalent characters on television. However, when one considers the relative risk of being victimized by a
crime, women, children, the poor, the disabled, young people, and Asian

TABLE 2.1 Prevalence and Rate of Violent Acts in Prime-Time and Children's Television Programs

Season	Prime-Time Programs			Children's Programs		
	Number of Programs	Prevalence	Rate	Number of Programs	Prevalence	Rate
1973–74	62	59.7%	4.9	37	94.5%	13.2
1974–75	58	77.6%	5.5	38	92.1%	12.1
1975–76	66	69.7%	5.9	45	91.1%	16.3
1976–77	61	80.3%	6.0	49	100.0%	22.4
1977–78	68	66.2%	5.9	53	90.6%	15.6
1978–79	63	74.6%	4.5	48	97.9%	25.0
1979–80	64	70.3%	5.7	62	91.9%	17.2
1980–81	64	73.4%	5.7	66	97.0%	26.9
1981–82	65	80.0%	5.9	69	91.3%	30.9
1982–83	77	63.6%	4.6	44	97.7%	30.3
1983–84	63	73.0%	4.8	54	92.6%	25.5
1984–85	65	78.5%	6.9	55	98.2%	27.3
1985–86	67	79.1%	6.8	53	92.5%	21.3
1986–87	67	71.6%	5.2	38	92.1%	25.1
1987–88	75	70.0%	5.1	36	100.0%	25.5
1988–89	77	74.0%	6.2	31	87.1%	25.5
1989–90	69	56.5%	4.7	NA	NA	NA
1990–91	54	74.1%	4.0	40	82.5%	32.0
1991–92	61	62.3%	5.1	43	76.7%	26.2
1992–93	60	65.0%	2.9	31	90.3%	17.9
Fall 1993	121	66.1%	5.5	35	92.1%	26.6
Spring 1994	119	72.3%	5.7	44	97.8%	22.2
Spring 1995	80	66.3%	5.6	NA	NA	NA
Fall 1995	94	52.1%	3.4	35	88.6%	20
Total	1,720	70.0%	5.27	1,006	92.5%	23

Note: Prevalence = percentage of programs containing violence; rate = number of violent acts per hour. NA = data not available at the time of writing. Percentage of programs with violence on ABC, CBS, NBC, and FOX. (FOX appears in the data from 1993 on.)
Source: Adapted with permission of the Cultural Indicators Project, George Gerbner, Director.

Americans are much more likely to be victimized by adult males (Gerbner et al., 1994).

Critics of Gerbner's violence index argue that it examines violence out of context (Kunkel et al., 1995a). To address this issue, these authors launched a national study of violent television content at several sites in the United States. The first step was for Kunkel et al. (1995a) to define violence:

> *Violence* is defined as any overt depiction of a credible threat of physical force or the actual use of force intended to physically harm an animate being or group of beings. Violence also includes certain depictions of physically harmful consequences against an animate being or group that occur

as a result of unseen violent means. Thus, there are three primary types of violence depictions: credible threats, behavioral acts, and harmful consequences (p. 286; copyright © 1995 by the Broadcast Education Association).

In this three-year longitudinal study of televised violence, the first two years found steady rates of violence over both samples. In the first year, 58 percent of the programs contained some violence; in the second year, 61 percent contained violence. Violence was often glamorized, with "good guys" initiating 40 percent of violent actions. Thirty-seven percent of the programs featured "bad guys" who were never punished for their aggression (Donnerstein et al., 1997).

Contextual factors that place children at risk for imitating violence were also prevalent in these programs. These factors include: (1) attractive perpetrators; (2) violence that is justified; (3) violence that goes unpunished; (4) violence that has no pain or consequence to the victim; and (5) violence that seems realistic to the viewer (Donnerstein et al., 1997). In a typical week, young children could have potentially seen about 800 violent portrayals that were particularly dangerous to them; most of these acts were portrayed in cartoons (Donnerstein et al., 1997).

In this same study, 75 percent of the perpetrators of violence were male, but only 9 percent of the perpetrators were female (Kunkel et al., 1995b). Seventy-six percent of the perpetrators were Caucasian, 5 percent were African American, 3 percent were Native American, 3 percent were Asian, 2 percent were Hispanic, and 1 percent were Middle Eastern. In short, most perpetrators of television violence were white males.

The targets of violence were also white males. Seventy-five percent of the targets of violence were males, and only 9 percent were females. Seventy-five percent of the targets were white, 6 percent were African American, and other ethnic groups account for 3 percent of the targets (Kunkel et al., 1995b). Violent content, then, has remained a staple in television programming, whether it is measured within particular contexts or not. Most violent television interactions take place between white males.

Gerbner (1996) considers violence to be more than a one-dimensional act. He views violence as a social relationship, a demonstration of power, a lesson in domination, submission, and victimization. Violence is about who has control and who does not. White men dominate television casts and have access to power, while women do not. Violent depictions are social lessons that reinforce the power structure of American society.

Violent Content in the New Technologies: Video Games and Virtual Reality Games

Now that the action-and-violence formula has become the staple of video game programs, children are participants in the violence. No one has yet conducted comprehensive content analyses of the overall amount of violence in video games, but informal examination of the content in arcade games suggests the pervasive use of violence (Elmer-Dewitt, 1993). Kinder (1996), for example, documents the male focus of most video games, with arbitrary distinctions drawn between lawful and unlawful violence. Plots are minimized, and children, as players, are authorized to shoot anything that moves, an enactment of the action-and-violence formula.

Video game software is derived, in part, from television and movie counterparts (Gailey, 1996). The genres include crime and violence, military adventures, sports, and fantasy software. In most urban jungle warfare games, however, the television distinction between good and evil is apparently lost. Rival street gangs compete for dominance, and no pretense is made that a moral resolution will justify the violence. The goal is dominance over one's opponents, achieved by being more violent than the opponents are.

One can see from these examples that the action-and-violence formula has become less storylike and more blatantly aggressive as it has been adapted to video, computer, and virtual reality games. In the new technologies, the formula has been stripped to the essential aggressive actions. Like television and film, however, the content seems to portray acts of violence more graphically over time. In video games like *Mortal Kombat,* for example, the object of the game is a bloody battle to the death. Players can choose to be one of seven characters, including one violent female. One character rips out his opponent's heart in colorful detail, and the heart continues to beat in the character's hand. Scorpion, another character, kills people by igniting them and then watching them burn to death, while Subzero rips his opponent's head off, leaving a dangling spine and spurting blood. To use the character's unique weapons and killing behavior, the player must activate a "Bloodcode." By contrast, early games were more likely to involve shooting space invaders, an attack on an abstract spaceship rather than one involving graphic human violence.

Virtual reality games, the heir apparent of the action-and-violence formula, can blur the line between reality and fantasy for the players. In virtual reality experiences, a player wears glasses and gloves that allow him or her to experience a three-dimensional, computer-simulated world such as one in a video game. Virtual reality experiences rely on a person's perceptual systems to create the illusion that he or she is really part of that game. The player, "immersed" in this virtual world, sees this symbolic reality, moves through virtual space, and performs various actions, such as shooting a gun at another person (Calvert & Tan, 1996).

Just as the technologies before them relied on the action-and-violence formula, virtual reality games utilize action and violence as a way to involve adolescents in the game. In *Dactyl Nightmare,* for example, two cartoonlike characters shoot each other in a three-dimensional world that includes an attacking pterodactyl. Actions take place at the speed players choose, based upon pressure they exert on a joystick. Whenever a character is shot, he or she explodes and is then reassembled in another place in the game. The pterodactyl can also

Interacting with violent virtual reality games increases the player's arousal and number of aggressive thoughts.

pick up the player and drop him or her; this action also causes the temporary destruction of the character. Other violent virtual reality games like *Dactyl Nightmare* are readily available at video arcades (Corliss, 1993). Because the player is embodied in one of these characters, parts of the game are realistically experienced even if the game is imaginary.

Based on the proliferation of the older and newer games, we might presume that children and adolescents enjoy violence. Do they? In a content analysis of 11 different video games, Anderson and Ford (1986) found no relation between violence and undergraduates' ratings of enjoying the game. In fact, enjoyment did not relate to either violence or action. Instead, enjoyment related to how difficult and frustrating the games were. Adolescents enjoyed games that were not overly frustrating. Thus, these findings do not support the assumption that adolescents find only violent games "fun." The implication is that other challenging formulas, perhaps those that emphasize strategy, can entertain children and draw an audience.

Video parlors are including some action-oriented games not organized around violence. This type of game appears on a large video screen in front of the player, and the screen makes the player feel like he or she is part of the game. Many sports games make use of rapid action and have excellent graphics, and yet are low in violence. These include *Alpine Racer,* a ski game in which players speed down a mountainside; *Virtua Striker,* a soccer game;

and *Virtua Indy Car,* a race car game that accommodates up to eight players at a time.

TECHNOLOGICAL INTERFACES: FROM OBSERVATION TO INTERACTION

Although all information technologies use the action-and-violence formula, the impact this violent message has on children may increase in the future for two reasons: (1) a consistently violent message is presented across video experiences, thereby reiterating and increasing children's exposure to violent content; and (2) children are active participants in, not just observers of, violent messages in the new technologies. Violence is pervasive in both television and video game interfaces. But do these technologies have the same impact on children? Are media messages more powerful, for example, when "I" am shooting or being shot than when a distant television character is shot? These are important questions that researchers are beginning to address.

The Observational Television Experience

Even if children are passively exposed to television programs as part of the audience, they must still actively process the content in order to comprehend it (Huston & Wright, 1983). Active versus passive exposure involves who controls what is being viewed. Comprehension requires children to look at, listen to, and actively process content. But children do not have to perform aggressive acts they see to comprehend these acts, even though they certainly do copy these acts at times.

Young children may be particularly vulnerable when it comes to imitating aggression because they are just learning how to control their impulses. Young children tend to be actors, not reflectors. They are less likely, for example, to "count to 10" before hitting another child. (Indeed, many young viewers of violence don't even know how to count yet!) Young children are also less likely to discuss their conflicts in rational ways, for their verbal skills are lacking. It's difficult for them to understand how another child feels. They may believe an act is morally wrong only if one gets caught and punished (Kohlberg, 1984). Because of these cognitive limitations, young children may copy the behaviors of aggressive televised models.

As children mature, they develop additional strategies to cope with conflicts. They become more reflective and less impulsive. They are more likely to think before they act. As children grow older, they are also socialized into moral ways of interacting with others. Their tendency to imitate social models is increasingly mediated by their ability to think about the appropriateness of those behaviors. They are able to inhibit certain behaviors, even if those behaviors could lead to a desired result.

Biology and culture both play a role in children's aggression (Huesmann & Miller, 1994). Certain children are more aggressive than others, for both genetic and social reasons. Boys, for example, are generally more physically aggressive than girls (Maccoby, 1980). And differences in aggression exist within gender groups, not just between them. In other words, certain boys and girls are more likely than others to act aggressively.

Aggression is a stable characteristic of children (Huesmann et al., 1984). More specifically, children who are aggressive when they are young tend to be aggressive when they grow older (Huesmann & Miller, 1994). Moreover, aggressive children react most strongly to depictions of television violence (Freedman, 1984). Even so, parents, teachers, and even other children may amplify or reduce aggressive tendencies by rewarding or discouraging aggressive responses. For instance, if I reward an aggressive child who imitates aggression, she will likely do it again. But if I punish a child by sending her to her room, she will be less likely to imitate the aggression again. Nature and nurture work together to produce all behaviors.

The Interactive Experience

While violent television amplifies the aggressive tendencies of children, violent video games require action. After children observe aggressive television models, they still must act on that content to exhibit aggression (Bandura, 1965). Some children do so, but some just watch (Kunkel et al., 1995b). This is not the case with the new technologies.

The child is the aggressor in the new technologies, the player of the video or the virtual reality game. These games certainly amplify personal involvement, perhaps because the child identifies more with the character that wins or loses. The child who plays the game directly experiences success or failure when his or her own behaviors lead to those outcomes.

Virtual reality games provide especially potent personal experiences. As the player, the child is embodied inside the character. He "sees" out of the character just as you see through your own eyes. Being "inside" a character he can control with his own movements presents an unprecedented interactive experience. As the player shoots or is shot in these symbolic worlds, he personally experiences consequences in a way unlike other representational interfaces. Some speculate that this active participation will lead more directly to real-life violence than previous observational participation (Calvert & Tan, 1996; Kinder, 1996).

In the next section, we turn to the theories that attempt to explain the impact of violent content on children's behaviors and beliefs. We will pay special attention to the similarities and differences between televised and interactive experiences with violent content.

HOW DOES VIOLENCE AFFECT CHILDREN?

How does environmental exposure to the continual flow of media violence affect children's beliefs and actions, particularly children who tend to be aggressive? To examine this issue, we will view violence through the lenses of several developmental and communication theories that make predictions about

TABLE 2.2 Theoretical Predictions about the Impact of Violent Media on Children

Theory	Predictions
Arousal Theory	Children initially get pumped up after viewing aggression, with the energy directed in ways that are cued by children's environments. With repeated exposure, children habituate to aggression and no longer respond physiologically; they become desensitized to the violence. The level of media violence must be ever increased to recover earlier arousal levels.
Social Cognitive Theory	Children imitate aggressive behavior, and exposure to aggressive characters who are rewarded for violent acts disinhibits children's internal behavioral guides to control aggression.
Script Theory	Children create expectations and scripts about aggressive behavior early in development that come to guide their behavior over time.
Cultivation Theory	Children develop beliefs about aggression that reflect the mainstream media culture and that resonate with real-life experiences.
Psychoanalytic Theory	Children view media aggression experience catharsis, draining off destructive and aggressive impulses in harmless fantasy.

how exposure to violent content impacts children. These theories include **arousal theory, social cognitive theory, script theory, cultivation theory,** and **psychoanalytic theory.** Specific predictions about how violence impacts children according to each of these various theories is presented in Table 2.2.

Arousal theory, social cognitive theory, and script theory predict increases in aggressive behavior after children are exposed to televised and video game depictions of violence. Cultivation theory predicts an increase in either aggression or fearfulness after exposure to aggressive content. Only psychoanalytic theory predicts a decrease in aggressive behavior after exposure to violent television and video game content. The empirical literature provides far more support for the theories that predict a deleterious effect after exposure to televised and video game aggression. Specifically, children become desensitized to aggression (arousal theory), imitate aggression or have their internal controls that prevent aggression undermined (social cognitive theory), or come to expect a violent world (script theory and cultivation theory). Exposure to imaginary violence does not reduce aggressive actions (psychoanalytic theory).

Arousal Theory

Arousal involves physiological responses to real and imagined events. For instance, when children are exposed to violent depictions, their hearts race, their palms sweat, and their pupils dilate. The body prepares itself for an immediate response to a situation that signals danger. These responses involve the autonomic arousal system (Zillmann, 1982).

Although both types of arousal always occur simultaneously, the literature makes a useful distinction between **autonomic** and **cortical** arousal (Zillmann, 1982). Cortical arousal is measured by an electroencephalogram, an instrument that measures the action of brain waves (Zillmann, 1982). Cortical arousal involves attention, perception, alertness, and vigilance. Autonomic arousal, measured by heart rate, blood pressure, and skin conductance, relates to affect and emotion (Zillmann, 1982). To date, the literature on television, video games, and virtual reality games has focused on autonomic arousal.

In real life, physiological arousal has survival value because a child is prepared to fight or flee (Cannon, 1927). Symbolic media play upon this built-in biological response to create excitement and interest almong children who watch television or play video games.

Visual depictions elicit more physiological responses than nonvisual ones. For example, the action-and-violence formula is far more pervasive and effective in television, films, video games, and virtual reality games than it is in radio content or in print. When one sees a grisly murder on television, the visceral response is stronger than when one hears about the same murder on the radio. Could it also be that visceral responses to interactive visual experiences are stronger than our responses to observational experiences portrayed on television?

Because arousal calls for a burst in physiological responses, it would be maladaptive to respond every time to a perceived threat if there is no real danger. If we did, we would die from a heart attack before age 10! Hence, after repeated exposure to violent television and video game content, children and adults **habituate** to it (Zillmann, 1982). No longer does one's heart race as it once did when one views aggression. Habituation is our way of keeping arousal levels in check.

When media portrayals overuse the action-and-violence formula, adaptive arousal responses can become dulled by overexposure. Children become **desensitized** to violent content and no longer have the same emotional and physical responses they once did. Put another way, children become less responsive to violent media portrayals (Liebert & Sprafkin, 1988), and this attitude can carry over to real life. They begin to see violence as normal. They are less likely to respond to those in need of help. Violence does not seem so "bad" because it permeates their experiences every day.

The creators of television programs must also deal with this desensitization problem. To keep the audience aroused and interested, the producers must increase the graphic nature of the violent content or find another way to arouse viewers. That's why the television programs now are more violent than the ones you watched as a child. Viewers will then respond to this new level of graphic violence and become aroused again. And so the cycle continues in an escalating fashion.

Television producers also add sexual material to the action-and-violence formula to keep arousal levels high (Zillmann, 1982). Sexual and violent content paired in the form of pornography has become a serious social concern in films, video rentals, and computer content, both in the United States and abroad.

Another way to increase arousal levels is to involve the viewer in the aggressive material. Personal involvement is increased when children participate in video game and virtual reality game violence (Calvert & Tan, 1996). *Being the character* creates a powerful situation that can elicit player involvement and activity.

Both the form (for example, action) and the content (for example, violence) of a presentation can have independent or combined influences on children's arousal (Huston-Stein et al., 1981a). Movement, as a feature, excites and stimulates children. When movement is paired with violent content, arousal escalates even further.

Arousal, though, has no preordained direction for release (Zillmann, 1982). A child becomes pumped up, but the environment triggers the direction in which a viewer expresses that arousal. For instance, one child may play baseball to release energy. Another may hit a friend or sibling to release that energy. Still another could use that energy to help others or to study. The environment cues how the energy will be released.

According to arousal theory, then, children who view or interact with violent content should become aroused physiologically, as measured by heart rate, blood pressure, and galvanic skin response. After extensive viewing of violent content, habituation and desensitization should occur. Children would then have to see or interact with increased levels of violent content for arousal to occur. The video and virtual reality game studies suggest that initial exposure to media depictions of violence increases arousal levels; after heavy exposure, as television research now shows, desensitization to violence occurs (Zillmann, 1982).

Desensitization to Televised Violence

One strategy for examining arousal effects is to compare children who vary in the amount of violent content they have seen. High viewers of violent content should be less responsive to violent content than low viewers, demonstrating a desensitization effect. Boys are often selected as subjects in research studies since they tend to be more physically aggressive than girls, and they tend to view more violent television programs.

In one study in the television area, Cline, Croft, and Courrier (1973) showed two groups of boys, aged 5 to 12 and 7 to 14, television programs that varied in the amount of violence they depicted. The researchers measured physiological arousal by blood volume responses, a measure of heart rate, for both groups of boys. In addition, they measured galvanic skin response for the 7- to 14-year-olds. As expected, boys who were high viewers of television programs, and hence of violent content, were less aroused by the violent television programs than the boys who were low viewers. The results suggest that boys who are heavy television viewers can become habituated and desensitized to violent material.

Exposure to violence in television drama also reduces children's responsiveness to real portrayals of aggression. In a study by Thomas et al. (1977), 8- to 10-year-old children and young adults were shown excerpts from a violent police drama or excerpts from a nonviolent control film about an exciting, but nonviolent, volleyball game. The children then saw a film about preschoolers who were arguing and fighting; college students viewed riots of the 1968 Democratic National Convention. All subjects except for college-aged women were less aroused by real portrayals of violence, as measured by ongoing changes in skin resistance, when they had seen the violent police drama rather than the control film about volleyball.

Studies such as these suggest that viewers of violent television content become desensitized to it. Viewers are less aroused in experimental studies immediately after viewing violent programs, and heavy exposure to violent television content is associated with less responsiveness when children and adults are exposed to real violence through television. The implication is that our children may become desensitized to violence, in part because they view too much television violence.

Arousal Effects from the New Technologies

Playing video games can affect the *moods* of players, which is an autonomic arousal effect. In a study by Anderson and Ford (1986), college students played either: (1) a mildly aggressive video game called *Centipede;* (2) a violent video game called *Zaxxon;* or (3) no video game. Students who played either game reported feeling more hostile afterwards than those who played no game. Those who played the most violent video game also felt more anxiety than those who played the less violent game or no game at all.

One study, however, found that exposure to violent video games did not predict aggressive behavior. Winkel, Novak, and Hopson (1987) examined the impact of video game exposure on male and female eighth graders. The video games varied in the amount of aggression they contained, as defined by the number of human figures included and the duration of time involved in destroying those figures. Adolescents played either: (1) a very aggressive video game; (2) an aggressive video game; (3) a nonaggressive video game; or (4) no video game. The researchers monitored the students' heart rates, an autonomic arousal measure, during the video-game period. If aggressive video game content leads to more arousal, then one would expect an increase in heart rate as the adolescent is increasingly "pumped up." Girls' heart rates increased during the video game exposure, as arousal theory would predict, but boys' heart rates did not. Moreover, the level of aggressive content in the video games had no effect on the subjects' subsequent aggressive behaviors, defined here as taking money away from other students who made errors on a test.

The action-and-violence formula, as a way of thrilling the audience, has moved on to the virtual reality frontier. In playing *Dactyl Nightmare*, adolescents hold devices and shoot their opponents in symbolic realities. Calvert and Tan (1996) had college students either: (1) play this violent game; (2) observe another person playing this game; or (3) participate in a control group that simulated game movements, except for pulling the trigger to shoot another person. The researchers took the subjects' pulse rate, a measure of autonomic arousal, prior to the treatments and immediately after treatments were finished. Adolescents who played the violent virtual reality game showed significantly increased arousal levels, as measured by pulse rate, than those who viewed the game or who simulated the nonviolent aspects of the game movements. These results provide support for arousal theory.

In summary, video game play is associated with increased hostility (Anderson & Ford, 1986), but aggressive effects are not a given (Winkel, Novak, & Hopson, 1987). Playing a violent virtual reality game leads to stronger arousal effects than observing another person play the game (Calvert & Tan, 1996). The latter finding suggests that being "inside" the character is an unprecedented and powerful experience for game players.

Social Cognitive Theory: Violent Characters as Social Models

Although the action-and-violence formula becomes less arousing as children are overexposed to it, the learning effects of violent content continue to accumulate. Specifically, media exposure teaches children aggression as a problem-solving strategy.

In the simple formulas of children's cartoons, attractive, aggressive characters serve as models for children to imitate. Their visual message teaches young children that aggression is an effective and acceptable way to deal with conflict, and the characters' actions show them exactly how to do so.

According to **social cognitive theory,** children may imitate aggressive behaviors they have observed in others. Violence can also undermine the internal controls that prevent children from acting aggressively, a process called **disinhibition.** Disinhibition occurs when children repeatedly see aggressive television models rewarded or see them go unpunished for the aggression. Disinhibition also occurs when a child wins a violent video game.

Even when a character is punished for aggression, young children often do not link the punishment to the character's aggressive behavior. For instance, Collins (1973) showed children an adult television program that sometimes separated the violent actions from the punishment with commercial interruptions. Second-grade boys who viewed the program with commercial interruptions were more likely to choose aggressive solutions to conflict situations than their peers who saw an uninterrupted version of the same program. Older boys, by contrast, were not influenced by the commercial interruptions. The results suggest that young viewers may become more aggressive after viewing televised violence because they do not understand that the characters are punished for their aggression. Thus, the children's own aggressive tendencies are disinhibited. From these findings, one can predict that children in the early years of grade school overestimate aggression as an effective problem-solving strategy.

Imitation of Televised Models

Some argue that imaginary characters have little impact on children's actions because these characters are not real. Do children, like the baby on *The Simpsons*, really imitate aggressive cartoon characters by hitting their dads on the head with mallets? Research on this issue suggests they do. Children imitate both real and animated characters.

One seminal study demonstrated that preschool children acted more aggressively after they had viewed Superman and Batman cartoons (Friedrich & Stein, 1973; Stein & Friedrich, 1972). For three times a week over a four-week period, one group of children viewed these violent cartoons, while the other two groups viewed either nature films or the prosocial television program, *Mister Rogers' Neighborhood*. The researchers observed children's social behaviors in their preschool classrooms: (1) for three weeks before viewing began (the baseline period); (2) for the four weeks during viewing (the treatment period); and (3) for two weeks after the treatments were completed (the follow-up period). Compared to baseline levels of aggression, children who watched the Superman and Batman cartoons acted more aggressively than those who watched nature films or prosocial television programs. The idea that children will copy cartoon characters is a very important finding because cartoons depict far more violent incidents per hour than prime-time television programs do (Gerbner & Signorielli, 1990). As Table 2.1 indicated, the average rate of violence is 23 violent acts per hour in children's programs and 5.27 violent acts per hour in prime-time programming.

Not all children become more aggressive after viewing violent content. In the Stein and Friedrich (1972) study, the children who were initially highly aggressive became the most aggressive after watching the violent cartoons. This was not the case for the children who were initially low in aggression. Hence, we must consider how violence affects individual children. Even so, note that the children who became more aggressive in this study were normal children, not children who were initially extremely aggressive (Friedrich-Cofer & Huston, 1986).

From other studies, we also know that children *learn* aggression even if they do not *act* upon this learning immediately. Bandura (1965) exposed children to violent films that showed various consequences to the perpetrator of the violence. The consequences ranged from rewards to punishment to no consequence at all. Bandura then observed the children as they played with toys such as the Bobo doll that had been used in the films. Children who saw the model rewarded for aggression were more likely to imitate his actions spontaneously than children who saw the model punished for aggression. Boys were also more likely than girls to imitate the aggressive actions and to punch the Bobo doll.

Bandura (1965) then took this study one step further, offering children incentives to show the experimenter what they had learned. When **motivational incentives** were offered, most children, including the girls, were quite capable of punching the Bobo doll as the television model had done. The implication is that children *learn* aggression whenever they are exposed to violent content, but they *perform* it only when they believe they will receive rewards. Because children can store and remember violent content, they can act on it at any time they choose. These findings suggest that the children described in the Stein and Friedrich (1972) study may have learned aggression even if they did not act aggressively in their preschool classrooms.

Imitation of Video Game Characters

Storing information for later use is not a necessary skill in the newer technologies, for children act on that information as they play the game. Aggressive actions are encoded directly into the child's behavioral repertoire (Calvert & Tan, 1996). For example, the person learns how it feels to shoot the gun as the game is played. The literature suggests that playing video games has similar effects to observing violent television content. Children imitate the aggressive actions from a video game interaction just as they imitate violent television content.

One study (Silvern & Williamson, 1987) compared violent video game play to violent television viewing. Preschool boys and girls were exposed to a violent *Space Invaders* video game and a violent *Road Runner* cartoon. Playing the game and watching the television program both led to increased aggressive behaviors, thereby supporting social cognitive theory. Boys demonstrated more aggression in their subsequent play than girls did.

The impact of playing games that vary in the amount of violence they contain has also been examined. Schutte et al. (1988) compared the impact of interacting with a violent karate game to a nonviolent swinging jungle vine video game on 5- to 7-year-old children's subsequent play. Children tended to imitate the game they had just played. That is, children who interacted with the karate video game later played more aggressively, while those who interacted with the jungle vine game played with a jungle vine. In this study, both girls and boys acted aggressively after playing the violent video game.

Playing violent video games can also reduce children's **prosocial behaviors,** that is, their socially positive behaviors. Chambers and Ascione (1987) exposed third and fourth graders versus seventh and eighth graders to: (1) a prosocial Smurfs video game; (2) an aggressive boxing video game; or (3) no video game. Children either played the game alone or with one other child. After exposure, children could donate money to poor children and could help the experimenter by sharpening pencils. Children who played the aggressive game alone or with another child donated less money than children who played the prosocial game alone. However, exposure to the prosocial Smurfs game did not increase helping, as social cognitive theory would predict.

The virtual reality study reported earlier (Calvert & Tan, 1996), in which college students played, observed, or had no experience with *Dactyl Nightmare*, also examined the possibility of observational learning effects. The game players did report more aggressive thoughts. However, although the investigators also expected the observers of the aggressive game to report more aggressive thoughts, they did not. Instead, the observers and the control group (those who simulated nonaggressive game movements) reported low levels of aggressive thoughts. This study, then, showed that participating in the game had stronger effects on aggression than observing it did.

Summary of Effects

Taken together, the studies suggest that viewing violent television content and interacting with violent video games can increase children's aggression and reduce their prosocial responding. When age or gender differences occur, they are stronger for younger children and boys than for older children and girls. However, interaction with violent content in video games sometimes eliminates the gender differences traditionally found in the literature on television and aggression. These findings suggest that the interactive effects of newer technologies may have a stronger impact on players than the observational effects of earlier technologies such as television and films.

Cultivating Aggressive Beliefs and Scripts

Acting aggressively or becoming desensitized to aggressive content are two ways children may respond to depictions of violence, but what do children believe about aggression? How do they expect other children to act when a conflict occurs, and how do they think they should act? Two theories, script theory and cultivation theory, shed insight in answering these kinds of questions. According to script theory, children's prior knowledge affects their understanding, and one source of knowledge is television. Similarly, cultivation theory also views television as a source for children's knowledge of and beliefs about aggression. Cultivation theory focuses on fearful as well as aggressive responses when children view violent television content.

Script Theory

Schemas are cognitive beliefs that children construct, based upon the events that happen to them. **Cognitive scripts** are a type of schema in which children create and then follow a "script" of the behaviors they will perform. These schemas and scripts are constructed from real events, but they are also constructed from symbolic media experiences.

Huesmann and Miller (1994) use cognitive scripts as a mechanism for explaining the durability of aggressive behaviors. **Observational learning** is involved when children initially acquire aggressive scripts by observing aggression. **Enactive learning** comes into play as children perform these actions and encode them into their repertoire of behaviors (Huesmann & Miller, 1994). These scripts become stronger and more resistant to change as they are rehearsed and enacted over time.

Script theory predicts that early experiences with aggression will exert considerable influence over later aggressive behavior (Huesmann & Miller, 1994). Early television viewing causes a child to create aggressive scripts that he then rehearses, replays, and enacts throughout development, eventually leading to later adult aggression. The research by Huesmann and his colleagues, which we will discuss in detail later, supports this long-term prediction (Huesmann & Miller, 1994; Lefkowitz et al., 1972).

Aggressive schemas can increase real-life aggressive behaviors (Dodge, 1985). Aggressive boys, for example, expect everyone to respond as aggressively as they do. This expectation is particularly noticeable in ambiguous situations that could actually be accidental. While many of us, for example, would give another person the benefit of the doubt in an ambiguous situation, such as pushing in line, aggressive boys believe the other person acted aggressively on purpose. By expecting aggression, aggressive boys may create a situation in which an accident escalates into real aggression. Moreover, as their expectations are confirmed, future aggressive actions become even more likely.

Other children also construct schemas about these more aggressive boys (Dodge, 1985). More specifically, less aggressive boys begin to view aggressive boys as acting aggressively, even when the aggressive boy has done so accidentally. For instance, when an "aggressive" boy accidentally pushes another child in line, others may believe he committed this act deliberately. In general, children are less likely to give a child they perceive as aggressive the benefit of the doubt. These expectancies can entrench "aggressive" children in aggressive modes of responding and interacting.

Exposure to television violence affects children's expectations or schemas about other children's aggression. Thomas and Drabman (1977) showed third- and fifth-grade children either a 15-minute aggressive television program or a nonaggressive nature program. Children were then given hypothetical situations and asked to predict how their peers would resolve conflicts. Children who viewed the aggressive television program believed their peers would react aggressively to a conflict situation more so than those who had viewed the nature program.

The Cultivation Hypothesis

Cultivation theory also focuses on the role television plays in the development of children's expectancies about others. The more television children view, the more it should influence their views about violence. It is in this area of expectancy that televised violence may have its most insidious effects. Television presents a world of power, a world that defines who controls, and of who is the victim (Gerbner & Signorielli, 1990).

Take, for example, the impact of violent television content on girls. Some girls (and boys, for that matter) will not become aggressive. Instead, they may feel fear in a world of male violence. By observing symbolic role portrayals, children and adults learn their respective places in the power structure in American society. Women learn they need protection, and men learn to protect them. Repeated exposure to violent, stereotyped television portrayals cultivates violent expectations and schemas. Gerbner calls this expectation of violence a **cultivation effect** (Gerbner & Signorielli, 1990).

Cultivation effects include **mainstreaming** and **resonance** (Signorielli, Gross, & Morgan, 1982). In mainstreaming, heavy viewers of television create a shared vision of reality. Heavy viewers tend to see the world as mean and gloomy, to overestimate the likelihood that they will be involved in violence, to think their neighborhoods are unsafe, to fear crime, and to believe that crime is increasing, regardless of the facts (Gerbner et al., 1994). For example, about one half of heavy viewers but fewer than one third of light viewers think it is unsafe to walk on their own street at night (Gerbner et al., 1994). This fear, in turn, creates a situation that strengthens the schema because the person stays home and watches even more violent television and becomes even less likely to go out at night. If such viewers do not go out at night because of their fear, the cycle of fear will probably never be broken. Heavy viewers are also more likely to take steps to protect themselves from violence, such as buying new locks, guns, and watchdogs (Gerbner et al., 1994).

A resonance effect occurs when the media portrayal resonates with and reinforces one's own life experiences (Signorielli, Gross, & Morgan, 1982). For example, suppose a woman was attacked when she went out alone one night. Media portrayals of attacks would have a very strong impact on her because they reflect her real experiences. People selectively remember personal life experiences that are consistent with media-generated schemas. In these ways, viewers construct schemas that mirror both real events and symbolic media experiences.

Effects of New Technologies on Aggressive Scripts and Beliefs

At present, neither script theory nor Gerbner's cultivation hypothesis has been examined in light of the new technologies. However, the pervasive violence in video and virtual reality games suggests that violent beliefs and scripts will become stronger as children encounter these sources of violent content. To the extent that the new media reinforce the power roles other media depict, they will amplify and solidify the same formulas about the social roles of different groups of people.

Psychoanalytic Theory

Perhaps the only optimistic view of exposure to violent content, though not of human nature itself, is presented in psychoanalytic theory. According to psychoanalytic theory, people are inherently aggressive (Hall, 1954). Therefore, they must devise ways to release their aggressive impulses in socially acceptable ways. In the symbolic world of media, viewers supposedly channel and release innate aggressive impulses via imaginary violent experiences. Through symbolic acts of aggression, **catharsis,** a process that harmlessly releases aggressive drives, occurs.

Catharsis via Television Viewing

Empirical support for psychoanalytic theory and aggression is weak in television research. At first glance, one study conducted by Feshbach and Singer (1971) seems to provide some support for catharsis. In this study, 400 adolescent boys were examined in natural settings such as private schools serving middle-class students or institutional schools serving lower-class students with social and personality problems. Within the schools, boys were assigned to either an aggressive or a nonaggressive television diet for six weeks. Each day, the boys were rated on aggressive behavior. Boys who viewed the less aggressive television programs became more aggressive than those who viewed the more aggressive television programs. These findings seemed to support psychoanalytic theory.

Closer examination of these results revealed that this lowered aggression only occurred for boys in the institutional homes. These boys reported that they did not like the nonaggressive television programs, which may have led to increased frustration, and hence more aggression, because they could not watch the aggressive programs they preferred. Moreover, boys in one institution protested their nonviolent viewing diet so vehemently that they were allowed to watch one of their favorite violent television programs.

By contrast, the boys who attended the private schools became less aggressive after viewing the nonaggressive television diet and more aggressive after watching the aggressive television diet. For these boys, the results fit social cognitive theory predictions, not psychoanalytic theory. The results suggest that one must consider the characteristics of the viewer if one is to understand the impact of aggressive television content on their behavior; one such characteristic is their prior tendency to act aggressively. This study also suggests that passive exposure to nonaggressive television content will not always reverse the effects of the more established active viewing choices adolescent viewers make.

In another study, Siegel (1956) showed preschoolers an aggressive *Woody Woodpecker* cartoon and a nonaggressive film, *The Little Red Hen.* The children viewed the films one week apart, and researchers observed the children's play after viewing each film. If catharsis takes place, preschoolers should have acted less aggressively after viewing the violent *Woody Woodpecker* cartoon. The results were exactly the opposite of this prediction. Instead of acting less aggressively after watching *Woody Woodpecker,* children acted more aggressively. The psychoanalytic theory prediction of drive reduction via catharsis was not supported here.

Catharsis via New Technologies

Catharsis has also been examined as children play video and virtual reality games (Calvert & Tan, 1996; Graybill, Kirsch, & Esselman, 1985; Graybill et al., 1987; Silvern & Williamson, 1987). For instance, children who played an aggressive rather than a nonaggressive video game reported fewer aggressive thoughts afterwards, suggesting a discharge of aggression in a socially acceptable way (Graybill et al., 1985). However, Graybill et al. (1987) noted that the nonaggressive video game in the 1985 study was more difficult, and hence potentially more frustrating, than the aggressive video game. The frustration, they argued, rather than the particular context of the game, could have increased aggressive activity. When the level of difficulty was controlled, there were no differences in aggressive behavior for children who played a violent or a nonviolent game (Graybill et al., 1987). Hence, upon closer examination, the catharsis hypothesis was not supported.

Other studies in the video game and virtual reality game literature report little evidence of catharsis. Silvern and Williamson (1987) found no reduction in aggressive play for players of video games. Similarly, Calvert and Tan

(1996) found no reduction in aggressive thinking for those who played or observed a violent virtual reality game.

Summary of Catharsis Effects

In summary, studies have rarely supported the notion of catharsis, which predicts a decrease in aggression after exposure to aggressive content via television, film, or video or virtual reality game interactions. In the one study where aggression was higher for viewers of nonviolent television content, boys had lost control of their typical viewing choices and had to give up their preferred violent television programs. The boys who preferred the violent programs also had prior social and personality problems. Boys in the same study who had no prior behavior problems decreased in aggression after viewing nonviolent television programs. Moreover, players of video games and virtual reality games show little, if any, reduction in aggressive behavior or thoughts after participating in aggressive interactions. Taken together, the studies raise serious doubts about the fit between psychoanalytic theory and children's viewing of violent television programs or their interactions with violent video or virtual reality games.

Is There a Causal Link between Media Violence and Real-Life Aggression?

Does exposure to media violence *cause* children to act aggressively? Social scientists who study media violence generally agree that it does (Huesmann & Miller, 1994), but there are those who take the other side of the argument.

In a review of the television-and-violence literature, Freedman (1984) argued that there was insufficient evidence to support the premise that television violence *causes* children to act aggressively. His arguments were predominantly methodological. He did believe that the laboratory studies of television aggression, such as Bandura's classic Bobo doll studies on imitation and learning, support a causal link between viewing violence and engaging in aggressive behavior. However, Freedman argued that this type of study has little relevance to children's real lives. Support for causality, he argued, must come from studies of aggression in natural surroundings, such as Feshbach and Singer's study of adolescent boys in detention facilities or private schools. He found the evidence weak in the latter kind of studies.

A reply by Friedrich-Cofer and Huston (1986) addressed these methodological issues. For example, in their original study of preschoolers who viewed Superman and Batman cartoons versus *Mister Rogers' Neighborhood*, children did become more aggressive after viewing the violent television programs. This study was a **field experiment** that studied children in the natural environment of their preschool. Moreover, Friedrich-Cofer and Huston argued that researchers do not show children the extremely violent television programs they may see elsewhere for moral and ethical reasons.

We also know from the work of Gerbner and his colleagues that some people see themselves as victims rather than as perpetrators of aggression. These people would not act aggressively after exposure to violence; instead, they would be more likely to feel afraid. Therefore, not every child or person would be expected to act aggressively after they see a violent television program or play a violent video game. Even so, the children and adults that do act aggressively influence us all.

Generalizations of Television Effects to Real-Life Experiences

One way to study the causal relationship between television violence and aggression is to follow children over time in a longitudinal study. In one such study (Eron, 1963), 8-year-old children rated each other on how violently they acted. The children's mothers also reported on the television programs the children watched. Boys who watched violent television programs were rated as aggressive by their peers, but girls were not. (As we will see in a moment, Eron reexamined these children a decade later to see how violent television viewing would affect them over time.)

A later study of both U.S. and Finnish children yielded similar results with one important exception. As Table 2.3 shows, this study found positive correlations between viewing television violence and peer-nominated aggression for both boys and girls (Huesmann, Lagerspetz, & Eron, 1984). In fact, the correlations for girls were slightly higher than those found for boys. These findings suggest that viewing television violence is related to aggression for both genders and for different cultures. Even so, cultures that reward violence as a socially acceptable response to conflict may find stronger links between media violence and long-term aggressive behaviors than cultures that are less tolerant of aggressive acts.

TABLE 2.3 Correlations between TV Violence Viewing and Peer-Nominated Aggression

		Males				*Females*			
Cohort	Grade	U.S.	N	Finn	N	U.S.	N	Finn	N
First Grade	1	.16*	188	.03	55	.22**	201	.14	64
	2	.20*	144	.27*	54	.25*	158	.02	48
	3	.15	114	.09	50	.28***	124	.33**	44
Third Grade	3	.24**	167	.04	49	.13	168	.05	51
	4	.18*	131	.38**	44	.26***	138	−.16	46
	5	.20*	99	.28*	43	.29***	107	.04	41

N=number of children studied.

*$p<.05$ **$p<.01$ ***$p<.001$. "p" values indicate the probability that a significant statistical relationship has actually occurred by chance. Specifically, $p<.05$ means that there are five chances in one hundred that this relation occurred by chance; $p<.01$ means that there is one chance in one hundred that this relation occurred by chance; $p<.001$ means that there is one chance in one thousand that this relation occurred by chance. In this table, a significant positive correlation means that those who watch more violent television programs are also more likely to be named by their peers as a highly aggressive child.

Source: Huesmann, L.R., Lagerspetz, K., & Eron, L. (1984). Intervening variables in the TV violence-aggression relation: Evidence from two countries. *Developmental Psychology, 20,* 746–775. Copyright © by the American Psychological Association. Reprinted with permission.

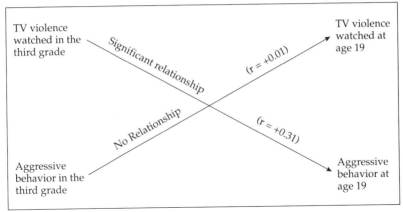

FIGURE 2.2 Correlations between Television Violence and Aggression over a 10-Year Period
Source: Lefkowitz, M. M., Eron, L. D., Walder, L. R., & Huesmann, L. R. (1972). Television violence and child aggression: A follow-up study. In G. A. Comstock & E. A. Rubenstein (Eds.), *Television and social behavior. Vol. III: Television and adolescent aggressiveness.* Washington, D.C.: U.S. Government Printing Office.

Although a relationship between viewing violence and childhood aggression seemed to exist, the more important questions involved the causal direction of the relation. To address this issue, the children from the original Eron (1963) study were examined again 10 years later. As Figure 2.2 indicates, boys who watched the most violent television content when they were 8 years old were the most aggressive at age 19 (Lefkowitz et al., 1972). (These effects were found for boys, but not for girls.) On the other hand, being violent at age 8 did not predict violent television viewing 10 years later. These findings suggest that viewing television violence may cause boys' aggressive behavior, not the reverse.

A 22-year follow-up of these same subjects revealed that by age 30, those who were heavy viewers of violent television content at age 8 were more likely to have been convicted of violent crimes (Huesmann & Miller, 1994). By this time, however, the sample had only 162 male subjects, so the results should be interpreted with caution (Huesmann & Miller, 1994). Although one could not conclude that viewing violent television is the sole cause of children's aggressive behavior, one could well propose that viewing violent television is one cause of aggressive behavior (Liebert & Sprafkin, 1988).

Imitation via observational learning is a potent force for teaching antisocial acts to criminals. Criminals can get their ideas for violent activity from watching or reading about violent terrorist acts. For example, a 1995 Arizona train derailment was linked to a magazine article that had published information about a similar act of sabotage committed 50 years earlier. These "copy cat" crimes are imitative acts. We all go through metal detectors at airports now because some criminals learned how to hijack and bomb planes from news reports and then copied these crimes. This means that the news media are not just reporting crimes, they are inadvertently contributing to them by providing detailed descriptions about how to commit them. Criminals also get extensive news coverage for committing antisocial acts, thereby receiving rewards for antisocial behavior. Social cognitive theory provides clear evidence that these kinds of rewards for violence increase aggressive behavior.

Television violence has also impacted everyday life via desensitization. According to arousal theory, desensitization carries over into real life. For example, children in the first through the fourth grades were less responsive to real-life conflicts after exposure to a violent film (Drabman & Thomas, 1974; Drabman & Thomas, 1976). Specifically, Drabman and Thomas (1974) examined the behavior of third- and fourth-grade children who had either viewed or not viewed an aggressive cowboy film. After the treatment, children watched a videotape, presumably a live-action view of younger children in an adjacent room, who became increasingly aggressive with each other as time passed. Children who had watched the aggressive film waited longer before getting an adult to intervene in the younger children's aggressive play than those who had not seen any film. Put another way, those who had viewed violent films tolerated "real-life" aggressive action by the younger children longer than those who had not viewed violent films. Similar effects occurred in a follow-up study in which the control group viewed a baseball game rather than no film whatsoever (Drabman & Thomas, 1976). In the study by Thomas et al. (1977) discussed earlier, children and college students were less responsive to real-life aggressive depictions after viewing violent television dramas. Children and adults become desensitized to violence in these situations and therefore do not respond as readily to real-life violence (Kunkel et al., 1995b).

Friedrich-Cofer and Huston (1986) concluded that the link between television violence and childhood aggression is probably **bidirectional.** A bidirectional relationship means that children who tend to be more aggressive watch more violent television, and watching violent television makes them even more aggressive. In this way, a cycle of violent behavior is established and reinforced in an escalating fashion. We can see this bidirectional relation in the longitudinal work of Eron (1963); children who were aggressive to their school classmates at age 8 were also high viewers of violent television, and high viewers of violent television were also aggressive (a bidirectional relation). However, by age 19, causality was clearer. Viewing television violence predicted aggressive behavior (Lefkowitz et al., 1972), but not the reverse.

Finally, one must look at all the studies together and see if there is a *convergence* of findings—that is, whether the findings all point to the same conclusion. There are about one thousand studies in the television-violence-and-children's-aggression literature (Murray, 1998); I provided only a sampling of some important studies here. Each study has weaknesses and flaws. However, when you take the literature as a whole, the studies supplement each other and lead to the same general conclusion: viewing television violence is one cause of children's aggressive behavior.

Meta-analyses, in which large numbers of television studies are examined in relation to a particular issue, support this conclusion. In such a meta-analysis, Hearold (1986) found that most studies support the conclusion that television violence causes children to be aggressive. Although television is not the only cause, it is a cause we should be concerned about, particularly since the new technologies present similar messages and yield similar empirical findings.

Generalizations of New Technology Effects to Real-Life Experiences

Long-term effects from the newer technologies have not yet been documented. From the history in television research, we can expect similar deleterious effects for those who frequently play violent video and virtual reality games. In addition, the constant bombardment of violence and action from all entertainment media should result in a greater resonance of violence throughout the culture, particularly as children act directly on violent content in the newer interactive media.

CENSORSHIP OR V-CHIP?

The responsibility for preventing children from seeing violent television programs has been passed back and forth between the networks and parents. Networks argue that parents are responsible for what their children view. Parents argue that they have limited resources to determine what programs are acceptable unless they view television and play video games with their children. Unfortunately, many parents do not take the time to watch cartoons or play video games with their children, an approach fostered by busy schedules and beliefs that television viewing and video game playing are, after all, only harmless entertainment.

The First Amendment states that the government shall not censor freedom of speech. The television and computer industries are protected by the First Amendment, but various laws also impact the kind of content these industries transmit.

In 1996, for example, the Telecommunications Act was passed and signed into law. One facet of this law is a technological innovation called the V-Chip, which has promise for assisting parents who want to monitor their children's exposure to violent and sexual television content (Chandrasekaran, 1997). The V-Chip is a computer chip that will be installed in all new television sets with screens larger than 13 inches in diameter. The chip will be used in conjunction with the content ratings of television programs that the networks provide. Although the American Civil Liberties Union argued that the First Amendment, which protects freedom of speech, may be violated when the government requires networks to rate depictions of media violence, the networks did voluntarily create a rating system for television programs.

Initially, the networks based their system on the rating system used for movies, but then they modified it. This television rating system, which debuted in January 1997, entails the following ratings: *TV-Y* for all children;

TV-Y7 for children who are at least age 7; *TV-G* for a general audience; *TV-PG* for parental guidance; *TV-PG14* for content that should be shown to adolescents who are at least 14 years old; and *M* for mature audiences only. After less than a year, pressure from parent groups and researchers led the broadcasters to expand their system to include content ratings (Cantor, 1997): *V* for violence; *S* for sexual material; *D* for suggestive dialogue; *L* for language; and *FV* for fantasy violence. These ratings appear at the beginning of each television program. Parents will eventually be able to program the V-Chip to eliminate television programming they do not want their children to see.

The networks are concerned about the impact of this rating system on viewership. If parents use the V-Chip to delete aggressive and sexual content from children's viewing schedules, an erosion in the viewing audience can occur. Advertisers might then refuse to buy time in certain programs. This type of pressure could eventually lead to changes in television programming for young audiences.

The V-Chip, however, is not a panacea or a solution to violent television. Children who most need it, for instance those coming from violent homes, may not have it at all (Simon, 1995). Children may also be able to unravel the V-Chip computer code and watch violent programs, for children are often more computer literate than their parents are. In spite of these problems, the V-Chip is one tool that parents could potentially use to limit the amount of televised violence their children see. Parents could also turn the television set off.

Controlling the amount of violence and sexual content on the Internet poses unique problems. The First Amendment forbids censorship, and it is difficult to prevent minors from gaining access while allowing adults access to any type of content that is legal. The **Communications Decency Act** made it a crime to transmit indecent material to minors over the Internet (Chandrasekaran, 1997). The U.S. Supreme Court overturned this law on June 26, 1997, but a revised bill is now pending in Congress to address this issue (Chandrasekaran, 1997). Companies are attempting to prevent Internet regulation by implementing voluntary controls, such as software that blocks Internet sites with adult content (Chandrasekaran, 1997).

Ultimately, the action-and-violence formula will only move from the foreground to the background if parents take entertainment media as seriously as the business world does. If parents do not allow their children to watch violent television or to play violent video games, and if parents do not watch violent television programs themselves, advertisers and television industry executives will follow the marketplace and change what they produce. After all, advertisers only want to make money. The actual program material used to deliver the audience to the advertiser is immaterial to them.

SUMMARY

An overall examination of the literature suggests the following conclusion: Viewing violent televised or filmed content or playing violent video or virtual reality games can lead to increased aggression for both children and adolescents. Effects are most pronounced for those who are initially more prone to violence, for the youngest viewers, and for boys. By requiring children to act on content, newer technologies appear to be eliminating some of the gender differences traditionally found in studies of observational aggression.

Pervasive depictions of violence in all information technologies result in multiple opportunities for children to experience, rehearse, and incorporate aggression as a personal behavior. As children move from observing to interacting with violent content, aggressive behavior may become an even more serious social issue than it already is.

Let us be conservative and say that only a small proportion of our children and our population are severely affected by viewing or interacting with aggressive media content. If only 1 percent of our nearly 270 million Americans become aggressive after watching violent content, that is 2.7 million people. This minority can and does impact the character of our nation.

Our nation ranks first in homicides per capita in developed nations, and our entertainment media have been implicated as one source of our violence (Kunkel et al., 1995b). Imaginary families like the Simpsons highlight the violent realities American families experience. In the future, children may become even more aggressive after exposure to multiple sources of media violence.

CHAPTER 3

Pink and Blue Media Images

Four-year-old Rachel and two-year-old Sara repeatedly view the same episode of *The Big Comfy Couch* on their videocassette recorder. This prosocial program features Loonette, a girl, and her doll, Molly, who play with each other on their big comfy couch.

In this episode, Molly puts a Band-Aid on her face. I later observe that the two girls put Band-Aids on their faces, too. At one point in the program, there is a 10-second tidy where the characters on the show race around in fast motion and put their toys away. Rachel comes tearing through the family room to do the same activities in her home. A prime place that the characters put their objects is under the big comfy couch and its cushions. Guess where Rachel keeps many of her toys and clothes?

Learning and abiding by the pink and blue messages about being a male or female are central organizers of children's experiences, for gender is a key ingredient for constructing our worlds and our identities. Although children do not understand gender in the same way adults do, they do understand early in development that they are boys or girls (Huston, 1983).

Information technologies amplify cultural messages about the activities boys and girls should do, their relative status in society, and even the occupational and social roles they can expect to assume (Huston, 1983). Not surprisingly, children look to media as a way to learn about who they are and what they should do. As you can see from the opening vignette, very young children use same-sex models to guide their own behaviors.

In this chapter, we will examine the impact of television programs, video games, and computer content on children's: (1) **gender schemas** (their expectations about males and females); (2) **gender identity** and **gender constancy** (their own sense of self in relation to gender); and (3) **gender roles** (the kinds of behaviors and occupations they expect to do, based on their gender). These three areas represent **information processing theory, cognitive developmental theory,** and **social cognitive theory,** respectively. Although the specific focus varies across the theories, the main message is consistent: The information highway is the color "blue," and both girls and boys know and respond to gender-stereotyped messages about our information technologies. We will begin with the content depicted on the information highway, then turn to theories and research about gender in relation to information technologies, and end with implications for the different paths we as a society are promoting for girls and for boys.

PINK AND BLUE MESSAGES ON THE INFORMATION HIGHWAY

Television, video games, and computers often depict a pink and blue world. This world is mostly designed for boys rather than girls, as can be seen in: (1) the numbers of male and female characters portrayed in media roles; (2) the personality traits of male and female characters; and (3) the occupational roles of males and females. Television program content and advertisements, as well as computer software content, transmit somewhat homogenous messages—though they sometimes attempt to present counterstereotypical content as well.

Television Content: Content Analyses

To understand portrayals of gender in the media, researchers initially tape television programs broadcast during a given year. Then they score the programs for **gender-stereotyped content:** content that portrays traditional values about men and women. For the past 30 years, **content analyses** of large numbers of television programs have documented pervasive gender-stereotyped content (Calvert & Huston, 1987; Calvert, Stolkin, & Lee, 1997; Gerbner, 1972; Gerbner et al., 1979; Mackey & Hess, 1982; Williams et al., 1986). Although these messages partly reflect the true power structure in American culture, they also exaggerate stereotyped modes of behavior (Huston, 1983).

Toy Advertisements

Long before children even understand that their gender will always be the same, they are learning about gender, particularly through their toy play. Children's toys and play activities are very gender-stereotyped (Huston, 1983). Boys play with action figures and girls play with dolls. Researchers long overlooked this fact, but advertisers did not.

Children's toy advertisements reflect cultural stereotypes of appropriate play for boys and girls. Barbie dolls are pitched to the girls in the audience, and action figures like G.I. Joe are pitched to the boys. Action toys are advertised during cartoons filled with action and violence so that the right audience will be delivered to the advertisers—but Barbie is also advertised in that time slot. The networks believe that girls will watch programs made for boys, but that boys will not watch programs made for girls (Jordan, 1997a). That assumption may not be true. Young girls like Rachel and Sara are interested in programs that feature female characters, just as boys are interested in programs that feature male characters. Not surprisingly, boys view more Saturday morning cartoons than girls do (Huston et al., 1990), a time frame that targets boys, not girls.

Toy advertisements also reflect cultural changes in gender roles. Although the female role has less status than the male role, the female role is also more flexible. Hence, girls perform traditionally masculine activities on television more often than boys perform traditionally feminine activities. Barbie, for example, can now go camping or be a doctor. However, Barbie was also programmed to say, "Math is hard," a stereotyped belief about girls' analytical skills.

Even the *form* of television commercials reflects traditional views of masculinity and femininity. Masculine "hardness" is reflected in rapid pace, fast action, and the use of loud sound effects. By contrast, the "softness" of femininity is connoted through dreamy dissolves and background music (Welch et al., 1979).

Number of Men and Women in Television Programming

Determining the number of men and women portrayed in television programming, compared to the real-life presence of these groups, is one way we can tell who "counts." One way to convey that message is making some people visible and others invisible via major and background roles. Another way is simply to count the number of men and women portrayed on television.

Although census data reveal approximately equal numbers of men and women in the U.S. population (U.S. Bureau of the Census, 1986; 1994), there are three men for every woman in the world of television (Calvert & Huston, 1987; Calvert, Stolkin, & Lee, 1997; Gerbner et al., 1979; Mackey & Hess, 1982; McArthur & Eisen, 1976; Sternglanz & Serbin, 1974; Williams et al., 1986). Such a pattern makes men far more visible to children than women are and reflects men's relative power and stature in contemporary culture.

In the 1970s, both children's and adults' television programs and commercials reflected this gender bias. Cartoons often had no female characters dur-

ing the 1970s (McArthur & Eisen, 1976; Streicher, 1974), with equal representation of men and women on network television found only in daytime soap operas (Turow, 1974). Portrayals of the sexes were not much better on public than
on commercial television. On public television, men outnumbered women 2 to
1 in children's programs, and only 15 percent of the major characters in adult
programs were female (Cantor, 1977).

Commercials on children's and adults' programs present an even more ex-
treme pattern of male presence than the programs do. Eighty percent of the
characters in a sample of Saturday morning advertisements were male
(McArthur & Eisen, 1976). Although women outnumbered men on daytime
commercials, men remained the voice of authority: 90 percent of *commercial
voice overs,* in which an off screen person attempts to persuade viewers to buy
particular products, featured male voices (Courtney & Whipple, 1974). Commercial voice overs remained the province of men throughout the 1980s and
1990s. DeBell (1993), for example, found that 92 percent of commercial
voiceovers used male voices during 1987, and 97 percent used male voices in
1993.

The prevalence of women on television changed slightly during the 1980s.
During the 1984 season, women filled 47 percent of the roles. By 1985 and
1986, however, the trend had reversed, with a reduction of female roles; moreover, a number of programs appeared with exclusively all-male casts (Huston
et al., 1992).

A recent content analysis of children's Saturday morning television programs continued to reflect a male-dominated world (Calvert, Stolkin, & Lee
1997). As Table 3.1 shows, children's television programs during the 1995–96
season portrayed three male characters for every female character. Male characters also spoke three times as much as female characters did. In fact, male
characters spoke more than female characters appeared on the screen! Female
heroes were notably absent. Since Saturday morning has traditionally been the
time for children's television programs, the relative importance of men and
women is communicated to children early in their development.

Occupational Roles of Television Characters

Portrayals of women and men often reflect stereotypes about the roles expected of them. In the programming of the 1960s and 1970s, for example, men
on television virtually always had careers, while women were frequently portrayed as wives and mothers (Downs, 1981; McArthur & Eisen, 1976). These
portrayals reflected that time period, for many women did work in their
homes to raise and care for their families.

When women on television in the 1970s had occupations, they held either
unidentifiable jobs or they held gender-stereotyped, often low-status jobs,
such as nurses, secretaries, maids, or entertainers. Men, too, held gender-
stereotyped jobs such as police officers, doctors, musicians, and diplomats
(Seggar & Wheeler, 1973). Traditional division of labor by gender was still the
norm in prime-time television portrayals sampled in 1979. Men assumed more

TABLE 3.1 Number of Males and Females in Children's Saturday Morning Television Programs by Network

	Male Characters	Female Characters	Male/Female Ratio
ABC	164	53	3/1
NBC	270	202	1/1
CBS	256	66	4/1
FOX	642	171	4/1
Totals	1,332	492	3/1

Source: Calvert, S.L., Stolkin, A., & Lee, J. (1997, April). Gender and ethnic portrayals on Saturday morning television programs. Poster presented at the biennial meeting of the Society for Research in Child Development, Washington, D.C.

task-oriented roles, while women assumed more social and emotional roles (Mackey & Hess, 1982).

Content analyses conducted in Canada and in the United States during the 1980s found that portrayals of women's occupational roles were changing, but men's were not (Calvert & Huston, 1987). In a content analysis of 1985 Canadian prime-time programming, Williams et al. (1986) reported that major female characters were just as likely to be cast in nontraditional as traditional occupational roles. However, minor female and male characters remained in gender-stereotyped occupations. Women were also more likely than men to be cast as sex objects.

Content analyses of American television programs during the 1980s revealed that two-thirds of female characters were working outside their homes on television, a number that accurately reflected the real number of women who were working outside their homes during that time frame (National Commission on Working Women, 1986). However, the fictional world of women's work differed from the reality of 1984; specifically, many women lived an extremely affluent life style on television, whereas only 0.2 percent of U.S. women actually earned more than $75,000 per year (Huston et al., 1992).

Commercial portrayals of women have changed less than program portrayals. When DeBell (1993) analyzed commercials from 1985, 1987, and 1993, she found remarkable stability in the stereotyped occupational portrayals of men and women. Men were cast in traditionally masculine occupations, such as medical doctor, construction worker, and police officer, while women were cast in traditionally feminine occupations, such as elementary school teacher, nurse, and waitress. Men were more frequently shown in occupational roles and assumed more diverse occupational roles than women did. DeBell concluded that little change had occurred in the gender-related occupations portrayed in commercials since tracking began in the early 1970s (for example, Courtney & Whipple, 1974).

Another message television transmits about women and work is that women must often choose between a family or a job (Calvert & Huston, 1987).

Men typically appear in traditional occupations; they provide financial support for their families, but they have few responsibilities for running the household or caring for children when at home. This portrayal may accurately reflect contemporary problems associated with two-career families, for women often both run the household and hold down a job.

Personality Characteristics of Television Characters

Male and female television characters are often portrayed with traditional masculine and feminine personality characteristics. "Masculine" personality characteristics, such as dominance, aggression, and autonomy, are typically portrayed in men's roles. Negative "feminine" attributes such as passivity and deference are used to portray female television characters (Huston, 1983; Williams et al., 1986) rather than positive "feminine" characteristics such as helping (Sternglanz & Serbin, 1974).

Video Game and Computer Content

Content analyses of video game and computer content are far less common than in the television area. Even so, what we do know suggests that video game and computer software content typically reflects male interest patterns, just as television content does.

Programming Directed at Boys

Early computer arcade and home games focused on adventure and sports programs directed primarily at boys (Miura, 1984). Much of the content in early games involved violence.

Industry figures reveal that video game companies in recent years have targeted 99 percent of their products for boys (Oldenburg, 1994). Recent efforts may target both boys and girls as a consumer group, but software specifically designed for girls remains limited. For example, when the researchers examined 82 popular video games, they found 61 directed at traditional patterns of male interest such as violence and sports; 18 directed at both genders; and only 3 directed specifically at girls (Oldenburg, 1994), one of which was extremely masculine.

The support for male interest patterns continues in the newest virtual reality technologies. Recent products such as *Virtual Boy* target boys (Oldenburg, 1994).

Even educational software relies on gender-stereotyped content. Computers are often introduced to children in math and science classes; the games emphasize male themes; computer-related occupations are stereotyped as a male profession; and many software products emphasize visual spatial features of programming that are more attractive to boys than to girls (Hess & Miura, 1985). Even if children take separate computer classes, the software still carries names and activities that specify male interest patterns such as *Speedway Math*, a math game involving race cars. Because newer software such as the Carmen Sandiego Math Detective program features a female character, girls may increasingly perceive math as for them, too.

In *Orly's Draw-a-Story* CD software, boys and girls are taught to write creative stories, a traditionally feminine area of expertise.

By pairing female images with traditionally masculine areas of expertise, such as being a Math detective, Carmen is teaching girls that math is for them, too.

Personality Characteristics of Video Game Characters

The themes of video games further reflect a male bias. In an examination of video games, Gailey (1996) described content reflecting male fantasies. Blond-haired princesses are often the reward for male success. The few active female characters participate in the "male world" of aggression; they are tough, dangerous, and sexy. Old crones occasionally offer advice, but male wizards display more power.

Presentational Features

Video game and computer presentational features may also be gender-stereotyped. Formal features such as action (the amount of movement), pace (the rate of scene and character change), and sound effects (unusual audio noises) used to present television content (Huston et al., 1981) also exist in video games (Silvern & Williamson, 1987) and in educational software as well (Calvert, 1991). These features are associated with male content, such as action-adventure cartoons and action-adventure programs.

In television content, **perceptually salient** features are more densely concentrated in entertainment than in educational programming (Huston et al., 1981). That is, one finds packages of rapid pacing, rapid action, and sound effects clustered together in entertainment programming. One might also expect higher concentrations of perceptually salient features in video games than in educational software packages because of the entertainment focus of video games, but no one has systematically examined this relation.

Summary on Content

Much of the content and many of the forms used in television, video games, and computer programs reflect gender stereotypes. For the most part, television presents messages about men and women that reinforce traditional gender-role expectations. While portrayals of women's occupational roles have changed, few changes have occurred for men. Moreover, gender stereotyping is most prevalent in children's programming. For instance, there are virtually no female heroes in children's television programming.

More computer and video games are targeted at boys than at girls. Masculine presentational features (such as rapid action, loud music, and sound effects) as well as violence are common in both television and video games. In addition, virtual reality games now coming to the home market replay these formulas. Let's turn next to theories of gender and how gender-stereotyped images from information technologies impact children's development.

GENDER AS AN ORGANIZER OF HUMAN EXPERIENCE

Regardless of the theory one selects, gender is a major organizer of children's experiences. Cognitive approaches such as **information processing theory** and **cognitive developmental theory** emphasize the cognitive constructs children create about being boys or girls (Huston, 1983). Learning theories such as **social cognitive theory** and **behaviorism** argue that gender roles and gender behaviors are learned, just as all behavior is learned, through rewards and punishments (Huston, 1983). Table 3.2 summarizes the theoretical predictions regarding gender and media.

Gender Schema Theory

Just as children construct aggressive schemas (Dodge, 1985), so too do they construct schemas about gender (Bem, 1981; Martin & Halverson, 1981). According to schema theories, thought is a primary organizer of behavior, and a child uses the content he or she encounters to construct thoughts and beliefs about gender.

Schemas, as we have learned, are cognitive constructs reflecting learned expectations that guide perception, memory, and inference (Fiske & Taylor, 1984). **Gender schemas** are cognitive constructs that guide an individual's information processing activities about men and women (Martin & Halverson, 1981). **Gender stereotypes** are a very simple type of gender schema (Calvert & Huston, 1987).

Gender Schemas for Self-Definition

Gender schemas may well become one of the most important constructs a child develops, for the child links this information to a growing understanding

TABLE 3.2 Theoretical Predictions about the Impact of Media on Children's Gender Roles and Behaviors

Theory	Predictions
Schema Theory	Children create expectations about gender early in development, and these expectations come to guide their behavior over time.
Cognitive Developmental Theory	As they develop, children gradually come to understand the immutable nature of gender as a personal characteristic.
Social Cognitive Theory	Children imitate behavior portrayed by same-sex role models that they view on television or interact with in video and computer games.
Behaviorism	Children perform behaviors that are reinforced, and they avoid behaviors that are punished. These behaviors often vary according to a child's gender.

of him or herself. In Martin and Halverson's (1981) theory of gender, concepts associated with being a boy or girl are a primary organizer of self-definition. Children look for information about how boys and girls should act, and they create and refine these conceptual categories based upon incoming information. More importantly, children use some of this information to define who they are. Increasingly, children look for information that confirms their gender schemas, and they ignore or distort information that violates their gender schemas. With development, gender schemas become increasingly differentiated, and potentially more flexible, organizers of experience (Calvert & Huston, 1987). Even so, 6- to 10-year-old children make more gender-stereotyped judgments than 4- to 6-year-old children (Martin, Wood, & Little, 1990).

All children learn the cultural expectations for both boys and girls, but information about one's own gender develops earlier (Martin, Wood, & Little, 1990) and in more depth (Huston, 1983) than information about the opposite gender. For example, boys know that dolls are a girls' toy, but girls have more knowledge about the kinds of accessories that exist for Barbie dolls. Because that type of information is relevant to a girl's world, girls look for the information, and boys ignore it. These increasingly elaborated and differentiated schemas can become linked to interest patterns.

Androgyny

Although all children and adults acquire gender schemas, Bem (1981) argues that gender schemas are not a central organizer of self-concept for all individuals. For some, gender moves from the foreground to the background as a definer of personality. Bem describes these people as *androgynous*.

In Bem's (1981) gender schema theory, masculinity and femininity are cultural expectations about personality characteristics that have historically been deemed as appropriate for men and women, respectively. **Masculinity** reflects stereotypical male personality characteristics such as dominance, aggression, independence, and ambition. **Femininity** reflects stereotypical female personality characteristics such as compassion, loyalty, and sensitivity. We once thought people had to be either masculine or feminine, but that is not the case. Individuals can also be **androgynous,** blending traditionally "masculine" and "feminine" personality characteristics. For Bem, those people who demonstrate androgynous personality styles are more adaptable and function better than those who organize their personalities around traditional stereotypes of masculinity and femininity. Individuality is a focus of this approach, for androgyny can be described as relative freedom from gender-based judgments (Bem, 1981). Personality scales of masculinity and femininity have been developed for children (Spence & Helmrich, 1978) as well as for adults (Bem, 1981; Spence & Helmrich, 1978).

Summary on Gender Schemas

For some theorists, gender schemas are major identity concepts (Martin & Halverson, 1981), whereas for other theorists, gender schemas can fade to background concepts (Bem, 1981). Nevertheless, the construction of gender schemas carries importance for a child's acceptance in any society. As an organizer of self-concept and of group membership, gender becomes a guide for what children should and should not do (Liss & Calvert, 1994; Maccoby, 1988). Given the ubiquitous presence of gender-stereotyped information in the real world and in the symbolic world of information technologies, it would be useful for us to now look at the ways gender-stereotyped content impacts the cognitive activities of perception, attention, memory, and inference.

Television Effects on Gender Schemas: Activation versus Differentiation

Schema theories often use a computer as an analogue for how information flows through our minds (Thomas, 1996). We are human computers, for we built computers to parallel the way we think. The computer has input; a child has perception. The computer has a working memory and a long-term storage system; so, too, does a child. The computer has programs that operate on information; a child has mental operations that act on information. A computer has output; a child has action. These are the ways we take in, operate on, and ultimately act on information (Thomas, 1996). Much of the content children encounter, as documented by content analyses, is filled with gender-stereotypes. What do children do with this gender-stereotyped content?

Perception and Attention to Gender-Related Content

Children initially pick up incoming information through their perceptual systems. More specifically, children pick up information through their sensory systems, by seeing, hearing, touching, smelling, and tasting.

The world of television is a world of sight and sound. One way to document that children are picking up information is to examine their visual attention to televised material. In this method, researchers examine children's visual attention to gender-stereotyped content, such as men and women performing stereotypical occupations, or their attention to gender-stereotyped formal features, such as action, sound effects, and loud foreground music (masculine forms) versus dreamy dissolves and background music (feminine forms).

Attention to television programs is typically measured by visual orientation to a television screen (Anderson et al., 1981; Calvert et al., 1982; Wright et al., 1984). When a child looks at a television screen, we consider that child attentive. By contrast, when that child looks away from the television screen, we consider that child inattentive.

Boys' viewing patterns in their homes suggest that gender schemas influence their attention to television programs (Calvert & Huston, 1987). Boys are in the viewing audience more than girls during cartoons and action-adventure programs (Huston et al., 1990), and this type of content targets boys. These naturalistic patterns of exposure to gender-stereotyped television content document the role gender schemas play in determining children's viewing selections. Children look for content that is "for them," and gender is one indicator of self-relevant content.

Children's attention to television programs in laboratory situations also links gender schemas to children's attentional patterns. When children view television programs in laboratory studies, boys are often more attentive to the television programs than girls are (Alvarez et al., 1988). Children sometimes selectively attend to characters of their own gender or to behavior that is stereotyped for members of their gender (Huston, 1983). These patterns are particularly pronounced when children are viewing gender-stereotyped content (Sprafkin & Liebert, 1978), such as fighting scenes. The patterns suggest that children are more likely to look when the content is directed at their gender than when it is directed to children of the opposite gender.

Gender-stereotyped formal features used in children's programs also lead to different patterns of attention among boys and girls (Calvert & Huston, 1987). Boys attend to animated programs that feature high concentrations of action and sound effects more than girls do; by contrast, boys and girls attend equally to live programs with real people, which contain fewer gender-stereotyped forms (Wright et al., 1984). Young boys also attend to sound effects, a male gender-stereotyped formal feature, more than girls do (Calvert & Gersh, 1987).

Comprehension and Memory of Gender-Related Content

Children's understanding of a television program depends on their ability to: (1) select important content for processing; (2) order that content into a story scheme; and (3) draw inferences about hidden information, such as a character's motivations and emotions (Collins et al., 1978). What children select for processing and ultimately understand depends on what they already know, on what they have already stored in their memories.

As we have seen, children are likely to attend to gender-stereotyped television content. To remember content, children must take the material they have attended to and link it with information already stored in memory. Children's memories contain a vast amount of gender-stereotyped material. Therefore, it is easy for them to link new incoming information with a preexisting knowledge base formed from previous experiences. These experiences can be real or symbolic (that is, representational experiences) that the children encounter when they watch television or interact with computers.

In gender schema theory, stereotypes influence memory in the following way. Whenever a child encounters gender-stereotyped content, preexisting information is pulled into **working memory,** a form of memory that constitutes what one is conscious of at this moment. This process is called **activation.** Each time gender-stereotyped content is activated, the gender schema is strengthened because a child is thinking about it. Gerbner and his colleagues (1979) describe this process as a cultivation effect, for the world of television is transmitting messages that reinforce a pink and blue world to its young viewers.

Both children and adults use gender stereotypes to help them understand stories they see on television, and these gender stereotypes influence children's subsequent memories of that content. Some children and adults have gender-stereotyped schemas, believing that girls and boys should adhere to traditional beliefs about what men and women should do. By contrast, some children and adults have androgynous schemas, believing that girls and boys can and should do any activity they choose. Children who have gender-stereotyped schemas remember television information that conforms to gender stereotypes better than information that violates those stereotypes. From Gerbner's perspective, such information resonates with their real-world experiences.

A study by List, Collins, and Westby (1983) illustrates this point. Nine-year-old children viewed a traditional and a nontraditional television program. In the traditional program, the woman was a wife and mother. In the nontraditional program, the woman was a female surgeon and an army officer. Gender-stereotyped children remembered more information about the traditional than the nontraditional woman. By contrast, more androgynous children remembered information about both woman equally well.

It's not just children who are influenced by gender schemas; adults are also affected. Young adults who have developed strong gender schemas are likely to remember content that fits traditional gender roles and to forget role violations. Renn & Calvert (1993), for example, had college students rate their own gender-stereotyped personality characteristics on the Bem Sex Role Inventory, a measure of masculinity and femininity. The students then viewed a television episode of *Northern Exposure,* a program on in the early 1990s, that focused on stereotyped and nonstereotyped information about gender. In the story, a character named Maggie protects herself and her friend Joel after she makes an emergency plane landing in the Alaskan wilderness (nonstereotyped information). In a parallel plot, a women named Shelly feels jealous and insecure when her estranged husband wants a divorce so that he can marry another woman (stereotyped information). Three weeks after they viewed this program, subjects were asked to recall information about it. Everyone remembered the gender-stereotyped content. However, only the nontraditional individuals remembered the counterstereotypical information well. Perhaps children and adults who are highly gender-stereotyped remember gender-stereotyped information better than nonstereotyped information because it confirms their self-concepts.

Gender-stereotyped individuals not only forget nontraditional gender role portrayals, they also distort memory to reflect their gender stereotypes. For example, Cordua, McGraw, and Drabman (1979) showed children a television program about a male nurse and a female doctor. When asked about the program, children remembered a male doctor and a female nurse. Real-life experiences can alter expectancies and memories, however. The children who had met a real male nurse at their school or who had mothers employed outside the home remembered the profession of the televised male nurse better than children who had never had such experiences (Cordua, McGraw, & Drabman, 1979).

Children understand even the subtle gender-stereotyped forms of television programs. In one research group, experiments paired neutral content with either: (1) rapid action and sound effects (masculine gender-stereotyped formal features); or (2) dreamy camera dissolves and background music (feminine gender-stereotyped features). Children understood that the rapid action and sound effects were for boys and that the background music and dreamy dissolves were for girls. Children who were heavy viewers of Saturday morning cartoons, where these features are concentrated, understood the masculine and feminine forms best (Huston et al., 1984; Leary, Huston, & Wright, 1983).

The Construction of Social Reality: Cumulative Exposure

Because television content is highly gender-stereotyped, frequent viewers of television should construct a view of reality that reflects gender stereotypes more so than infrequent viewers, reflecting a cultivation effect. These stereotypes are often implicit, rather than explicit, throughout much of the programming. From viewing these programs, children create gender-stereotyped beliefs over time. Beuf (1974), for example, asked 3-year-old children what they wanted to be when they grew up. Heavy television viewers chose gender-stereotyped occupations more frequently than light viewers did. More importantly, these beliefs became more pronounced over time. Specifically, elementary-aged children who remained heavy viewers increasingly chose gender-stereotyped occupations, while those who remained light viewers chose less gender-stereotyped careers (Frueh & McGhee, 1975; McGhee & Frueh, 1980). Heavy viewers of television also hold more sexist attitudes (Gross & Jeffries-Fox, 1978) and see others' personalities in gender-stereotyped ways (Caplan & Watkins, 1981).

These studies are **correlational,** which means researchers studied effects but did not manipulate variables. Thus, it's not clear whether television caused children to become more gender-stereotyped and sexist; it could be that gender-stereotyped and sexist children watch more television simply because it confirms their beliefs and attitudes. This is the same issue we encountered in the television and violence area—the direction of the relation is often difficult to state with certainty. Naturalistic studies, however, suggest that when gender-stereotyped television content comes to a new geographical area, children become more gender-stereotyped (Kimball, 1986).

Altering Gender Schemas: Counterstereotyped Television Programs

Television activates gender schemas by repeatedly calling upon children to use these schemas as they interpret televised stories (Calvert & Huston, 1987). While children can distort information to fit their expectancies, there are instances when television exposure alters gender schemas.

One way to help children perceive men and women as individuals, rather than as a stereotype reflecting group membership, is to expose them to **counterstereotypical** television programming (Calvert & Huston, 1987). Counterstereotypical programs show content that is nontraditional, for example, female astronauts and male nurses. Although this type of programming should alter children's gender schemas, we also know that children and adults often ignore, distort, or forget information that violates their gender schemas (Huston, 1983). How, then, can gender schemas be changed?

People can remember schema-inconsistent information accurately if additional time is available for them to process content that violates their expectancies and if their memories are tested immediately after exposure (Calvert & Huston, 1987). Obviously, additional processing time is problematic in television portrayals that come and go quickly. Videocassette recorders, however, can remedy that issue. Parents can show their children nonstereotyped television programming repeatedly, thereby reinforcing nontraditional messages.

Children are also more likely to modify their schemas when conflicting information first appears. Otherwise, the inconsistency may go unnoticed. When the discrepancy is clearly apparent, schema-inconsistent information often elicits high levels of attention and careful processing (Crocker, Fiske, & Taylor, 1984; Martin & Halverson, 1981). To call attention to nontraditional information about gender, a sound effect, placed strategically before the discrepant event, can be used to elicit attention and promote processing of that content.

While it is not easy to alter children's gender schemas, some experimental studies in which children view counterstereotypical television programs have shown effects. For example, Davidson, Yasuna, and Tower (1979) showed young girls one of three programs: (1) *Kid Power,* in which gender stereotypes were reversed; (2) *Scooby Doo, Where Are You?* a neutral control cartoon; and (3) *Jeannie,* a gender-stereotyped cartoon. The girls who viewed *Kid Power* had lower sex-stereotyping scores than the girls who viewed the other two programs.

An entire series called *Freestyle* was developed to alter gender stereotypes. The series targeted gender stereotypes by presenting men and women in nontraditional roles and careers (Johnston & Ettema, 1982; Williams, LaRose, & Frost, 1981). For example, women in the series were sometimes auto mechanics, and men sometimes cooked meals. Although children's beliefs about what men and women *could do* were altered by exposure to this program, their attitudes about what men and women *should do* were not altered. Behaviors were highly resistant to change, particularly for boys (Johnston & Ettema, 1982).

These findings point to an important issue. Children's gender schemas rarely change dramatically. Instead, the child allows exceptions to the rules; for example, a man can cook if he is a great chef. The implication is that exposure to counterstereotypical television programs will lead to more flexible gender schemas, but it will not eliminate gender stereotyping (Calvert & Huston, 1987).

Indeed, children continue to use male and female conceptual categories after viewing nontraditional television programs. O'Bryant and Corder-Bolz (1978) showed children commercials of women performing jobs traditionally held either by men or by women. Girls who viewed the nontraditional commercials were more likely to prefer nontraditional jobs than girls who viewed women performing traditional jobs. Although boys considered the nontraditional jobs more appropriate for women after viewing the nontraditional commercials, they did not choose those jobs for themselves. These data suggest that the manipulation did not affect the tendency to categorize occupations as "for men" or "for women," but rather that the children altered the content (occupations) within those categories.

Counterstereotypical portrayals can even induce more prejudice. Pingree (1978), for example, showed children in elementary and junior high schools commercials portraying women in traditional and nontraditional occupations. Girls had less stereotyped attitudes toward women after viewing the nontraditional than the traditional portrayals. However, eighth-grade boys who viewed the nontraditional portrayals responded with heightened stereotypes about women when compared to the boys who saw the traditional portrayals.

Taken together, the studies suggest that counterstereotyped portrayals can alter the content of children's gender schemas, but the gender schema itself can be highly resistant to change. Girls are more likely to change than boys are, probably because they receive more rewards than boys who assume nontraditional gender roles. Durkin (1985) argues that counterstereotyped programming is most effective when the programming builds on what children already know rather than directly contradicting children's social knowledge.

Summary on Television Effects and Gender Schemas

Television is a daily influence in children's lives that affects their expectations of men and women. Pervasive gender stereotypes about the importance, roles, and personality characteristics of men and women typically activates and reinforces traditional gender schemas. The gender schemas children bring to the television viewing situation affect their program selections, their attention to television programs, and their memories of the content they view. The impact is strongest for children who are already gender-stereotyped, for boys, and for heavy viewers of television, a major source of gender-stereotyped content.

Exposing children to nontraditional gender portrayals can alter children's beliefs about men and women, particularly for girls, but changes do not always occur. Expectancies change slowly, in part, because both television and real-life experiences continue to emphasize the importance of gender stereotypes to children.

Computers and Children's Gender Schemas

As children develop, their experiences with video games and computers accumulate. Because much of the content reflects gender stereotypes, children may well construct beliefs that computers are more relevant to boys than to girls.

This process occurs in the following manner: Every time a child experiences a computer interaction that reinforces gender stereotypes, these belief structures are activated and reinforced. Repeated interaction increases the strength of this category so that children are more likely to believe computers are for boys. That means that each time a child interacts with a computer or a video game that presents stereotyped male content (for example, science and math, or violence) or male forms (that is, action, sound effects), the game activates the gender schemas of both boys and girls, and thereby strengthens those schemas. If young children learn to define a technology as gender-inappropriate, they are less likely to be interested in it and motivated to use it.

In the television area, presentations that violate traditional gender stereotypes affect perceptions and memory more than behaviors and attitudes (Calvert & Huston, 1987). But surprisingly little literature is available on perception and memory in the computer area. Instead, behaviors and attitudes have been a focal point in the computer literature.

Perceptions of Computer Program Titles

Miura and Hess (1984) found that adolescents and adults perceived more computer program titles as relevant only to boys than as relevant only to girls. Junior high school students and adults classified the titles of 75 computer software programs. Although they perceived the majority of the titles to be relevant to both genders, they judged 37 percent of the titles as exclusively for males, but only 5 percent of the titles as exclusively for females. Boys and girls were similar in their ratings. These findings suggest that boys are more likely to perceive computer software titles as central to their interest patterns. Such an interpretation can cultivate and reinforce the schema that computers are for boys more than for girls and decrease girls' interactions with computer programs.

Comprehension and Memory of Computer Content

In the television area, researchers typically examine memories and inferences about gender-stereotyped content after subjects view television stories. The stories often present social stereotypes about men and women, and children often exhibit memory distortions after hearing or seeing stories, particularly when they draw inferences. Inferences about motivations and character feelings are central to story comprehension (Collins, 1983). When inferential reasoning requires a child to go beyond the information explicitly presented, the child must rely on what is already stored in memory.

Stories have been less focal in the development of computer software, so no one has yet undertaken studies of this kind. The recent increase in CD-ROM story production, however, has increased the opportunities for story exposure. With this technological development, one could expect studies about gender-stereotyped content to occur.

Interacting with Computer Content

If children are creating gender schemas about computers, then gender differences in the use of computers should become more pronounced as children age. That is indeed the case.

During the early years, relatively few differences in children's computer use emerge. As children age, however, boys increasingly interact with computers more than girls do. The ratio of boys to girls increases when the software requires more effort, is more difficult, or is more expensive (Hess & Miura, 1985; Lepper, 1985). These findings suggest that young children do not have schemas that define the computer on the basis of gender. Instead, children appear to develop gender-stereotyped schemas about computers.

During the preschool years, computer usage patterns do not differ for boys and girls. Essa (1987), for example, found no gender differences in preschoolers' use of computers. Similarly, no gender differences were found when a computer was placed in a preschool classroom with a small number of children; however, boys did use aggression to control access to the computer more than girls did when numerous children were present in a preschool classroom (Lipinski et al., 1986). The implication is that if computers are a scarce resource, less aggressive children, typically girls, will not have equal access to newer technologies.

Young children actually view the computer as feminine if they are girls and masculine if they are boys (Williams & Ogletree, 1992). And researchers found no gender differences in children's competence at completing three matching activities on the computer. As Table 3.3 shows, girls and boys performed similarly on the tasks, although 4-year-olds of both sexes were more competent than 3-year-olds. The authors believe that early experiences with computers are necessary for positive attitudes to develop (Williams & Ogletree, 1992). These results suggest that young children find computers interesting and define their own use as gender-appropriate.

Both boys and girls as old as age 7 continue to believe they are good at using computers. Yelland (1995) examined Australian children's beliefs and attitudes about computers. While girls believed both genders were equally good at using a computer, boys believed boys were better than girls. Boys were also more likely to own a computer than girls were, replicating earlier patterns reported in the United States (Lepper, 1985).

By the middle of grade school, gender differences emerge in children's participation with computers. Programming activities appear to be a key reason girls rapidly depart from computer use. Hess and Miura (1985) studied

TABLE 3.3 Means by Sex and Age on Number of Completions of Computer Game

	Dinosaurs Mean	Numbers Mean	Shapes Mean	Composite Mean
3-year-olds				
Males	2.357	4.167	3.993	11.000
	(n=14)	(n=15)	(n=15)	(n=13)
Females	2.455	4.231	2.577	9.874
	(n=11)	(n=13)	(n=13)	(n=9)
4-year-olds				
Males	3.450	7.690	6.525	17.667
	(n=20)	(n=21)	(n=20)	(n=18)
Females	3.533	9.500	8.056	20.231
	(n=15)	(n=18)	(n=18)	(n=13)

Note: Children had to participate in all three games to include their score in the composite mean. The mean is the average score; the "n" is the number of children who completed a particular game.
Source: Williams, S., & Ogletree, S. (1992). Preschool children's computer interest and competence: Effects of sex and gender role. *Early Childhood Research Quarterly, 7,* 135–143. Copyright © 1992 by Ablex Publishing Corporation. Adapted with permission.

age differences in the proportion of boys and girls who voluntarily enrolled in summer computer camps. Computer camps typically offer programming courses in languages such as BASIC, PASCAL, or assembly languages. This type of programming experience provides students with the background to later become computer programmers. Twenty-three camp directors provided information on 5,533 students. Students were sorted into groups by grades, designated as primary (kindergarten through fourth), middle school (fifth through eighth), and high school (ninth through twelfth). The overall ratio of boys to girls who enrolled in these computer camps was approximately three to one. More importantly, sex differences in enrollment patterns increased with age and with class difficulty. The proportion of girls in computer classes declined steadily from primary (30 percent) to middle school (26 percent) to high school grades (24 percent). When examined by difficulty level, these patterns became even more striking. Approximately 28 percent of girls enrolled in beginning or intermediate classes, 14 percent enrolled in advanced programming classes, and only 5 percent enrolled in assembly language classes. Boys also enrolled in more expensive computer camps than girls did, a pattern that suggests parents may be more willing to invest financial resources when their children develop what they perceive as culturally appropriate, gender-stereotyped skills.

By grade school, children never identified girls as computer experts, but interestingly, they did call upon girls to help other children who were stuck (Hawkins et al., 1982). This suggests that a gender-appropriate activity, such as helping, mediates children's involvement as a computer expert. Nevertheless, girls' programming experiences with LOGO, a beginning programming language, and their interest in spending their free time at computer classes and camps to acquire programming skills drops over time.

Some of the skills necessary in computer programming include **debugging skills,** which allow children to analyze and correct errors to make their programs run. Girls fared less successfully than boys when learning debugging techniques. For example, 8-year-old boys who were taught LOGO programming skills improved in debugging techniques when compared to a control group, but girls did not. By contrast, **procedural skills,** which allow the programmer to break the program into subroutines in order to create a program, are not related to training in LOGO, and no gender differences appeared here in boys' and girls' performance (Poulin-Dubois, McGilly, & Shultz, 1989). The authors suggest that school-aged boys' greater interest in computing activities may have led them to commit increased interaction and effort, and to learn more from the computer task.

Miura (1987) reported both gender and socioeconomic (SES) differences in computer use during middle school. Although the SES differences mediated the gender differences, a clear pattern emerged: boys increasingly use computers as they get older, while girls use computers less, particularly when the computer interaction teaches or requires programming expertise. Because programming activities center on traditional male activities involving mathematical expertise, programming is probably less interesting to girls than to boys.

Children's Attitudes about Computers

Children's gender schemas are also reflected in their attitudes about computers. Griffiths and Alfrey (1989) found gender differences in attitudes towards computers during primary school. Specifically, children linked men to computers, and boys used computers more frequently than girls did. Similarly, Sklorz-Weiner (1989) found that adolescent girls regarded computers with a critical attitude. Boys' interest in computers was related to their interest in technologies and natural sciences, but no such relation existed for girls.

Altering Children's Gender Schemas about Computers

Evidence indicates, then, that the schema that computers are a boys' technology is learned. In gender schema theory, at least two paths are available for preventing gender stereotyping of computer usage. The first path is to get girls to construct conceptual categories that define computers as gender-appropriate, a process that already occurs at young ages. In the second path, girls who have classified computers as a boys' technology can be taught that the computer is relevant to them as an individual, even if it is not typically a girls' technology. This allows a girl to see herself as an exception to the rule. Using computers in areas that interest girls is one way to alter girls' gender schemas about computers.

Interacting with Nonsextyped Computer Content

When computers are paired with areas girls enjoy, girls are as involved with computers as boys are. For example, word processing packages focus on verbal skills, an area of expertise traditionally acceptable for girls. Therefore, few gender differences would be expected in children's selection of word processing activities, and this is in fact the case. Kurland and Pea (1984) found equal involvement for two classes of 10-year-old boys and girls in word processing activities. Similarly, Linn (1985) found equal enrollment patterns for 10- to 16-year-old boys and girls in word processing classes, although boys did select more programming classes. Thus, computer interest patterns are more similar for boys and girls when girls perceive the activities as gender-appropriate.

Personal Relevance

Personal relevance also mediates children's interest in computer activities, even for programs traditionally defined as relevant to males. One set of researchers examined Science and math curricula for fourth through sixth graders. Although boys interacted with and liked the tools used to gather data more than girls did, gender differences were eliminated when the software experiments focused on measurements of the children's own body temperatures rather than measurements of water temperature. In fact, 80 percent of both boys and girls liked experiments that were personally relevant—that is, that focused on their own body temperatures (Char et al., 1983).

During grade school, boys and girls sometimes perform similarly on computers even on a stereotypically masculine spatial task. Men often perform **spatial tasks,** which require visual processing skills, better than women do (Greenfield, 1996). Hay and Lockwood (1989) examined 6- and 10-year-old boys' and girls' strategies on a computer video game that involved hunting prey in order to survive. Success at this task required visual-spatial skills, or the ability to visualize spatial layouts of objects and places, traditionally a masculine area of expertise. While 10-years-olds performed better than 6-years-olds did, boys and girls were equally successful in their hunting strategies. Girls were somewhat more careful in their strategies than boys were. In particular, girls avoided mistakes and maximized the capture of highly valued prey. Even so, the most striking finding was the absence of gender differences in a personally relevant task, even though the content of the task and the skills required to solve it favored boys.

Personal relevance even equalizes boys' and girls' programming skills. Kafai (1996) had children construct their own video games about learning fractions. She found that boys created programs that reflected the current video game prototype: violent content in a fast-action format. Girls, by contrast, were more likely to create nonviolent programs. The goals in girls' games involved diverse tasks such as landing a helicopter, skiing down a mountain slope without falling, and avoiding a spider. The reward for completing these tasks often involved some type of treasure or reward.

Motivational Appeal of Computer Forms

Another area of research involves children's interest in forms traditionally associated with boys or girls. When interacting with an educational computer game about fractions, boys preferred visual action fantasies like shooting arrows that popped balloons, whereas girls preferred musical rewards of songs (Malone, 1981). These findings suggest that boys and girls enjoy different computer forms; the implication is that games with certain forms will attract girl's interest more effectively.

The Impact of Computer Interactions on Attitudes

Participation with computers can alter girls' attitudes about computers. During middle school, for example, girls actually held more positive attitudes toward computers than boys did. As computer experience increased, interest also increased and anxiety decreased (Loyd, Loyd, & Gressard, 1987). Similarly, Campbell (1988) found no gender differences in computer anxiety for adolescents. Instead, *familiarity* with computers was the key to feeling comfortable. These findings suggest that direct interaction with computers can translate into positive attitudes about the technology.

One longitudinal study that tracked students from middle school until high school found persistent gender differences in students' attitudes about computers. Krendl, Broihier, and Fleetwood (1989) tracked 2,500 fourth through tenth graders. At the end of each year, students were asked questions about computers. Girls consistently reported less confidence and interest in computers than boys did. However, all children felt less confidence and interest in computers as time passed. In addition, enjoyment declined as children became more familiar with computers. The authors did not separate math interests from computer attitudes, nor were they able to get accurate assessments of how much time children spent actually using the computer. Thus, they were not able to get a good indicator of how familiar these children became with computers over time. Nevertheless, the results suggest that access to computers at school alone is insufficient to improve girls' attitudes about computers.

In a study of college students, Arch and Cummins (1989) shed light on why girls do not succeed when computers are simply made available to them. In this study, college students either had access to computers in a formal class that required participation, which was the *highly structured situation,* or they had access to computers whenever they liked, but participation was not mandatory, the *nonstructured situation.* Although males initially had better attitudes about computers than females did, the females in the structured class situation improved in their perceived efficacy (their belief that they could control the computer), equaling the males within one term. By contrast, females in the unstructured situation, where they were not required to interact with the computer, were more likely to avoid the computer and to sustain negative attitudes about the technology. Interestingly, only females with prior experiences with computers made substantive efforts to develop their computer skills in the unstructured situation. By contrast, males in the unstructured situation voluntarily developed computer expertise, regardless of prior exposure. The results suggest that mandatory computer classes should be required for both genders, but particularly for females, from the beginnings of formal schooling.

In a study of male and female college students, Colley, Gale, and Harris

(1994) found that males had less computer anxiety, more confidence, and liked computers more than females. However, when prior experiences and gender-stereotyped personality characteristics were included in their analyses, gender differences disappeared. Therefore, it seems that experiences and beliefs about one's gender play key roles in females' attitudes about computers, as we saw in the previous study of college students (Arch & Cummins, 1989). Females' attitudes are also more positive when their mothers use computers, and males' attitudes are more positive when their fathers use computers. Having an older brother who uses a computer has a positive influence on both genders (Colley, Gale, & Harris, 1994).

In summary, girls who use computers generally develop positive attitudes and feel less anxiety about using them. Apparently there is no substitute for use, since actual experiences seldom support fearful expectations. Content that is interesting to girls maximizes their participation with computers.

Summary on Gender Schemas and Computers

Taken together, the findings suggest that gender schemas about computers are not present for preschoolers, but these schemas develop after school entry and become more pronounced as children age. The implication is that children are learning gender stereotypes as they get older and are increasingly incorporating these schemas into their activity choices. Boys often perceive computers as relevant to their lives and make active efforts to learn the skills needed to control computers. Girls, too, tend to view computers as a boys' technology, but this is not an inevitable belief. Personal relevance mediates children's interest in computer activities, even in nontraditional interest areas. When girls interact with computers, they take control of the technology, create games of interest to them, and develop positive attitudes about computers.

COGNITIVE DEVELOPMENTAL THEORY: FROM GENDER IDENTITY TO GENDER CONSTANCY

We have been discussing gender as a concept that children understand just as adults do. Adults understand that their sex is an unchangeable personal characteristic. But do children have this same kind of knowledge? Cognitive developmental approaches, such as those Piaget advanced, describe age changes in the way that children understand information. Kohlberg (1966) adapted Piaget's approach to describe age changes in the ways that children understand gender.

Kohlberg (1966) argued that **gender constancy,** the knowledge that you are a male or female and will remain so throughout life, is acquired in successive stages throughout the first seven years of life. By about age 3, children have acquired the concept of **gender identity**, the knowledge that one is either a boy or a girl. By about age 7, children acquire gender constancy. **Gender constancy** consists of **gender stability,** the knowledge that gender does not change over time (for example, boys do not grow up to be mothers), and

gender consistency, the knowledge that physical transformations, such as changing the clothing one wears, will not alter one's gender.

For Kohlberg, the acquisition of these cognitive structures serves as a major organizer of experience. Early concepts are very stereotyped. For example, I've heard young girls state emphatically that only men wear belts or carry briefcases. These beliefs are rather inflexible, even when these girls face a woman wearing a belt or see their mother's briefcase beside them in the car. Once gender constancy is achieved, however, gender concepts become more flexible, for children understand the true and immutable nature of gender. Children also look for models as guides for their gender-role behaviors, but cognitive developmental theory views thought as the primary organizer of behavior. As in gender schema theory, thought precedes action.

Gender Constancy and Television Content

For Kohlberg (1966), the impact of television portrayals on children should be filtered through the child's knowledge about his or her gender, particularly after gender constancy is achieved. Gender constancy is important because children understand that their gender will never change and will thus be a reliable category to guide behavior throughout the life span. In the research on television, most findings are associated with the final outcome of gender constancy, the knowledge that gender is an immutable personal characteristic. Effects are stronger for boys than for girls.

The development of gender constancy influences boys' attention to television characters. For example, Slaby and Frey (1975) measured children's visual attention as they viewed a depiction of a man and a woman performing similar activities at the same time. Boys who had achieved gender constancy were more attentive to the male character than boys who had not yet achieved gender constancy. However, there were no effects for girls.

Citron, Serbin, and Conner (1979) reported similar results. In this study, a male and a female character performed exactly the same activities on a videotape. The two tapes were shown simultaneously on adjacent monitors. Boys who had achieved gender constancy were more attentive to the male than to the female character. Once again, no effect was found for girls.

Both of these studies were laboratory studies that gave children no control of their viewing selections. A naturalistic study by Luecke-Aleksa and her colleagues (1995), however, replicated the same findings. In this study, the researchers examined 24 children's viewing behaviors by using video equipment and diaries in the subjects' homes. The children also completed various measures, including a gender constancy test, in which the researchers tested their understanding of their gender. Compared to the preconstant boys, boys who had achieved gender constancy: (1) viewed more programs featuring male television characters; (2) viewed more sports and action-adventure programs; and (3) attended more to male characters. As in the earlier laboratory studies, there were no effects for girls. Patterns of attention to television characters for gender preconstant and constant boys and girls appear in Table 3.4.

TABLE 3.4 Mean Percentage Attention to Television Characters by Level of Gender Constancy

Sex/Level of Constancy	Human Adult		Human Child		Nonhuman Adult	
	Male	Female	Male	Female	Male	Female
Boys						
High	55.6%	47.4%	73.7%	67.9%	82.7%	79.1%
Low	55.2%	61.0%	60.4%	63.6%	71.1%	74.7%
Girls						
High	47.9%	56.7%	65.3%	69.9%	67.4%	69.7%
Low	56.2%	61.6%	72.1%	73.9%	75.8%	79.8%

Source: Luecke-Aleksa, D., Anderson, D. R., Collins, P. A., & Schmitt, K. (1995). Gender constancy and television viewing. *Developmental Psychology, 31,* 773–780. Copyright © 1995 by the American Psychological Association. Adapted with permission.

Gender constancy also affects children's behavior. Again, the effects are most pronounced for boys. Ruble, Balaban, and Cooper (1981) showed children toy commercials in which either boys or girls used a gender-neutral toy, but a child character expressed toy preferences. Children who had achieved gender constancy avoided the toy used by the opposite-sex model. In another study (Frey & Ruble, 1992), children saw a television segment in which child characters expressed their toy preferences. Gender-constant boys played with a less desirable toy if a male character had endorsed it. However, there was no effect for girls.

In summary, gender constancy is associated with different viewing selections, different patterns of attention to models, and different patterns of behavior. These effects occur only for boys. Perhaps cultural pressures for boys to adhere to traditional gender roles make televised portrayals of these roles more salient for them. For girls, the higher status traditionally associated with the male role may allow more flexibility in their own behaviors. For example, boys are more likely to be punished for violating traditional gender roles than girls are, providing more incentive for boys to pay attention to how they should act and then to act accordingly.

Gender Constancy and Computer Content

Children have not been classified as gender constant or gender preconstant in computer studies. However, if one uses age 7 as a rough index for attaining gender constancy, then one can make inferences about the impact of gender constancy on computer participation. Preschool children, who should be gender-preconstant, do not vary in their use of computers when both genders have equal access to the technology (Essa, 1987; Lipinski et al., 1986). However, computer usage patterns reveal increased use by boys and decreased use by girls during the elementary school years (Hawkins, 1985), the age at which gender constancy emerges. Moreover, gender differences in usage patterns become increasingly pronounced as children age (Hess & Miura, 1985).

There are exceptions to this pattern, however, that reflect girls' beliefs that certain types of computer content are relevant to them (Char et al., 1983; Kafai, 1996). These exceptions can be compatible with the concept of gender constancy if girls perceive computer use as gender-appropriate. In this case, girls would construct categories that allow computing activities to be defined as "girls' activities." Put another way, computer use need not be incompatible with a feminine identity.

Summary on Gender Constancy

While television shows a greater impact on gender roles for boys than for girls, computers show a pronounced effect on both girls and boys. In the computer area, boys become more involved as they age, while girls become less involved. The implication is that gender constancy may have a stronger overall impact on children in computer usage than in their response to television. It would be useful to empirically examine this thesis with studies of gender-constant and preconstant children; this area has important social policy ramifications if girls begin to avoid computers after they develop gender constancy in a society that targets computers at male interest patterns.

SOCIAL COGNITIVE THEORY

The search for models who can guide appropriate gender behaviors is best described by **social cognitive theory,** an approach that has historical links to behaviorism. **Behaviorism** holds that children's behavior responds to reinforcements and punishments delivered for performing "gender-appropriate" and "gender-inappropriate" behaviors, respectively. Social cognitive theory expands the idea to include cognitive processes, such as attention and memory, that organize thoughts before action takes place. Specifically, a child attends to, retains, produces, and is motivated (via self or other reinforcers) to acquire and perform gender-stereotyped behaviors (Bandura, 1986).

Social cognitive theory considers the impact of television role models as children acquire and perform gender-stereotyped behaviors. Children seek, find, and imitate symbolic models that portray behaviors in keeping with appropriate gender roles. Hence, television can alter gender roles, according to this theory, by portraying men and women in diverse ways. For instance, portraying women as doctors and men as school teachers would help alter what children define as acceptable occupations for both genders. Similarly, viewing female heroes could empower young girls.

As children observe powerful and nurturant role models, they incorporate that information into their own schemas about how men and women should behave. Through attention and memory, cognitive processes organize experiences. Knowledge is translated into action when the appropriate situation arises. If children believe models for either gender-stereotyped or gender-nonstereotyped behavior have been reinforced, they are likely to imitate that behavior in the future. By contrast, if children believe that models violating gender-stereotyped behavior have been punished, they will be unlikely to alter their own behavior. Reinforcement and punishment, as is true in behaviorism, are key mechanisms that affect imitation.

Self-efficacy, the belief that one can control the events in one's life, may regulate a child's attention, retention, production, and motivation (Bandura, 1986). When a child believes he or she can control events, the child is likely to imitate reinforced behaviors. However, if a child believes events are beyond his or her control, imitation is less likely to occur. According to this theory, then, belief structures about personal control affect the performance of gender-stereotyped, and particularly gender-nonstereotyped, behaviors.

Gender Roles and Television Content

Children look to the media for heroes—role models they can emulate. Gender is one defining characteristic of who is an appropriate model. Power and nurturance are the dynamic duo that invite imitation. Interestingly, these reflect the traditional masculine and feminine principles, respectively. It is notable, therefore, that television heroes are almost exclusively male, particularly in children's television programming.

Although children's television is a Saturday morning enterprise, children actually are exposed to more adult than children's programming, simply because more adult programs are on the air waves at other times (Huston et al., 1990). Consequently, children often see gender roles and sexual roles portrayed on prime-time television programs. In action-oriented programs, men often rescue women (Calvert & Huston, 1987). A notable exception is *Xena Warrior Princess,* an adult program that features a female hero from ancient Greece. Such programs could alter the roles that females see as appropriate and possible for them. We have already discussed the role gender plays in children's attention to, and memory of, information. The gender-stereotyped content that children view is also reflected in their play, their understanding of occupational roles, and their understanding of sexual relationships.

Impact on Imaginative Play

Young children will at times incorporate the behaviors of models into their **imaginative play.** Superheroes who are crime fighters, like Superman and Batman, have long been a major interest in boys' play. Female superheroes, however, are rarely portrayed for girls to imitate in their play.

Although some women are now portrayed as aggressive characters on television, aggression has historically been a male behavior (Mischel, 1966). That may explain, in part, why so few females are portrayed as heroes. Specifically, heroes often use aggression as one way to resolve conflicts. Yet heroes also provide children with guides to important personal qualities, such as standing up for what is right, sacrificing one's own self interest for the good of others, and persevering in the face of adversity. If children can incorporate these constructive behaviors into their imaginative play, exposure to heroes of their own, as well as the opposite gender, can be beneficial.

Occupational Role Models

Because children prefer same-sex role models (Huston, 1983), same-sex television characters may serve as potential **occupational role models** for children. For example, when 9- to 12-year-old children were asked about television characters they wanted to be like, boys chose male characters and girls chose female characters. But boys all chose male characters, whereas girls chose females two-thirds of the time (Miller & Reeves, 1976).

From content analyses, we know that women have traditionally held low-status, stereotyped occupational roles or ambiguous roles in television portrayals. More recently, female characters have assumed higher-status occupational roles, but men continue to play the most powerful roles. Children who are heavy viewers of television can store information about occupational roles as guides for their future behavior. Beuf (1974) found that 3-year-old children who were heavy television viewers chose gender-stereotyped occupations for their future careers more frequently than light viewers did, and these choices were durable over time.

Recent occupational shifts in the television portrayals of women can lead girls to select nontraditional careers, but it depends on what they view. Fifth- and sixth-grade girls had higher aspirations and more positive attitudes toward nontraditional careers portrayed frequently in the media, such as being a lawyer. By contrast, girls who saw frequent portrayals of traditional gender-stereotyped occupations had more conventional career aspirations (Wroblewski & Huston, 1987). The implication is that television programs may encourage girls to pursue nontraditional occupations, and these aspirations can lead to success. However, high aspirations may be unrealistic because women, as a group, are not as affluent as the media now portrays them to be (Huston et al., 1992). Because the occupations of men have changed little over time, boys should continue to select gender-stereotyped occupations.

Guides to Sexual Behavior

Children also look to television for information to guide **sexual behavior.** Girls tend to look for romance, whereas boys tend to look for sexual encounters with many partners. These different interest patterns are also reflected in television program choices. Girls, for example, watch romantic television programs like soap operas by the end of grade school.

The explicit content of soaps operas provides information about how to engage in sexual behavior, particularly for those with little real-world knowledge about sex. For example, high school and college students who are less sexually experienced use the media to gain knowledge about sexual information more than sexually experienced viewers do (Courtright & Baran, 1980). Research on pornography and college-aged men also reveals more callousness toward women as exposure increases (Comstock, 1991).

Adolescent boys also rent pornographic videotapes more than girls do. The sexual content on cable is more graphic than that depicted on network television, creating issues of censorship or close monitoring of children's viewing behaviors. The V-Chip, which will allow parents to censor television content, should assist them in screening out explicit sexual material.

Summary on Gender Roles

In summary, the literature indicates that children: (1) imitate television characters in their play; (2) use television actors as guides to develop expectations for future occupational roles; and (3) use the media as a source of information about sexual roles.

Social Cognitive Theory and Computer Interactions

The main computer literature on social cognitive theory involves self-efficacy, the belief that children can control the events around them. In general, boys are more likely than girls to develop the belief that they can control computers (Hawkins, 1985).

Self-Efficacy and Computer Interaction

Since computers have become a gender-stereotyped instrument in American society, one might expect men to perceive greater self-efficacy in relation to computer experiences than women do. They do. Teachers report that 8- to 9-year-old boys want control of the computer more than girls do (Hawkins et al., 1982). Men reported higher self-efficacy for completing a computer course than women did (Miura & Miura, 1984), and gender differences favor boys in their perceived self-efficacy in computer programming, their computer course work, and their personal computer usage patterns from the sixth through eighth grades (Miura, 1984). Female college students who were required to take a structured computer class increased in their perceived efficacy with computers, but females in an unstructured situation did not (Arch & Cummins, 1989).

Patterns of perceived self-efficacy have important social implications, for schemas about personal competence influence decisions to participate in a task, the effort expended to accomplish the task, and task persistence (Bandura, 1989). Sex differences in perceived self-efficacy in computer usage suggest that boys will develop more motivation, interest, and persistence in computer interactions than girls will. This pattern, as we discussed earlier, is reflected in the literature.

Sexuality and Computer Interaction

Computers allow interactive sexual activities. Males are more likely than females to access pornographic computer software, including virtual reality sexual encounters (Prime Time Live, 1991). Software can block Internet sites with explicit sexual material, but these packages are not infallible. When blocking software fails or is unavailable, repeated exposure to sexual content can result in disinhibition. Adolescents may become less likely to delay real sexual experiences when explicit sexual computer interactions are undermining their inhibitions. Realistic virtual reality encounters may magnify these issues.

SUMMARY

The information highway has become a male superhighway. Male interests are linked to both old and new technologies more than female interests are. Television is incorporating changes in its portrayals of occupational roles for women, but women are rarely portrayed or perceived as computer experts.

Various theories all point to the relevance we attach to gender and the way it affects our choices and behaviors. Cognitive theories emphasize the acquisition of gender constancy or gender schemas as organizers of human thought and experience. In cognitive theories, concepts about gender guide actions. In social cognitive theory, rewards and punishments shape behavior, with cognitive processes mediating actions. All theories acknowledge the importance of gender in human functioning, but some approaches suggest that gender is a more malleable category than others do. Stereotyped functioning begins in the early years of life, even though this is also the same time frame when children least understand the true nature of gender.

Media have the potential to alter children's gender-related beliefs and behaviors. To alter children's beliefs, television and computer programs can include themes that are interesting to both girls and boys, and parents and teachers can encourage all children to interact with computers. Decisions about how the media portray gender roles will shape our children's futures.

Black and White Media Images

In a *Sesame Street* vignette, a Caucasian girl spends the night with her African-American friend, Ieshia. The two girls play on skateboards, brush their teeth together, go to bed, and have breakfast the next morning with Ieshia's family.

Awareness of ethnic differences appears during the preschool years for both African-American and Caucasian children (Cross, 1991). Yet as a group, children sometimes have limited access to children of different racial and ethnic backgrounds. American neighborhoods and day care settings are often racially segregated, restricting opportunities for children to form firsthand opinions of others.

While real-life exposure may be limited, television exposure to different groups is widely available to children. In the privacy of their homes, children are exposed to about 2 to 3 hours of television a day (Huston et al., 1990). African-American children watch about 1 to 2 hours of television more each day than their Caucasian counterparts do (Greenberg & Brand, 1994). Many of the images children view are racially stereotyped (Graves, 1993; Palmer, Smith, & Strawser, 1993).

Yet television content can promote racial integration rather than racial stereotypes. As we saw in the opening vignette, television can provide children with information that is not stereotypical in nature, potentially leading to a better understanding of one another and better race relations. The Ieshia vignette, which portrays typical social interactions between friends, is part of a curriculum designed to improve children's racial understanding (Lovelace et al., 1994). As children watch these images, they learn about themselves and others. Television is providing an important source of information about cultural similarities and differences as well as potential role models.

What are the racial images children see in the privacy of their homes? Do they view vignettes like Ieshia's friend spending the night, and if so, how do these images affect children's attention, learning, and attitudes about race and ethnicity? What kinds of television role models do children have available, and do children use ethnicity to select role models? What do the new technologies teach us about race? These are the kinds of questions we will address in this chapter.

CONTENT ANALYSES OF MINORITY PORTRAYALS

If we consider the number of minority people in the media, their roles, and their behaviors, the world of television quickly becomes a black and white medium. Specifically, Caucasian and African Americans are presented in far greater numbers than Hispanics, Asians, or Native Americans (Geiogamah & Pavel, 1993; Hamamoto, 1993; Subervi-Velez & Colsant, 1993). Moreover, portrayals of all ethnic groups have often been stereotyped (Berry, 1988). We will examine representation in two ways: (1) mere presence on the screen, which evokes what is sometimes referred to as *recognition;* and (2) the roles characters play, which may or may not evoke *respect* (Clark, 1972).

The Number of Ethnic Minority Television Characters

The number of ethnic minorities in television roles typically falls short of their real-life numbers. Table 4.1 presents the proportions of various ethnic groups at different times in the U.S. population. We'll compare these data with content analyses of the media.

In the 1950s, only 2 percent of all television characters were African Americans (Smythe, 1954); in reality, African Americans represented 10 percent of the population (U.S. Bureau of the Census, 1983). The census did not even count other ethnic minorities, suggesting their perceived unimportance in American society.

The Civil Rights Movement of the 1960s, led by African Americans who protested discriminatory practices, eventually led to changes in the number of African Americans presented on television (Murray, 1993). African Americans began to appear on television in proportion to their real presence in the United States population. Between 1969 and 1974, for example, the proportion of non-white characters nearly doubled from 6.6 percent to 12.5 percent (U.S. Commission on Civil Rights, 1977). According to the 1970 census, the U.S. population at this time was approximately 88 percent Caucasian and 11 percent African American. Although minority groups as a whole were presented in numbers close to their real prevalence, there were three times as many minority men as women on television.

From 1970 to 1976, Gerbner and his colleagues examined television characters who were members of various ethnic minorities. Ethnic minority members comprised 16 percent of their sample; they were 10 percent African American, 3 percent Hispanic, 2.5 percent Asian, and less than 0.5 percent Native American (Gerbner et al., 1979). Ethnic minority members were shown in numbers that paralleled their numbers in the U.S. population, except for Hispanics, who were underrepresented.

Throughout the 1980s, however, about 8 percent of television roles featured African Americans, once again falling short of their real-life proportion

TABLE 4.1 Percent of U.S. Population by Racial or Ethnic Origin

Race	1950	1960	1970	1980	1990
Caucasian*	89%	88.5%	87.7%	83%	80.3%
Caucasian, not Hispanic					75.6%
African American	10%	10.5%	11%	12%	12.1%
Native American, Eskimo, or Aleutian					.8%
Asian or Pacific Islander					2.9%
Hispanic**					9%

*Caucasian includes white Hispanics.
**Hispanic origin of any race.
Source: United States Bureau of the Census. (1992, 1983). *1980 U.S. Census of Population; 1990 U.S. Census of Population.* Washington, D.C.: Government Printing Office.

TABLE 4.2 Percent of Ethnic Groups Appearing in Children's Television Programs by Network Affiliate

	Total Presence		Major Characters		1990 U.S. Census Data	
	Caucasian	Ethnic Minority	Caucasian	Ethnic Minority	Caucasian	Ethnic Minority
ABC	68%	32%	100%	0%	75.6%	24.8%
NBC	70%	30%	73%	27%		
CBS	59%	41%	62%	38%		
FOX	80%	20%	89%	11%		

Source: Calvert, S. L., Stolkin, A., & Lee, J. (1997, April). Gender and ethnic portrayals in children's Saturday morning television programs. Poster presented at the biennial meeting of the Society for Research in Child Development, Washington, D.C.

in the population (Berry, 1980; Williams & Condry, 1989). Asian, Hispanic, and Native American characters also lost ground during this decade. Specifically, these groups already had fewer roles than their real-life numbers would call for, and their representation decreased even more during the 1980s (Berry, 1980; Williams & Condry, 1989). Hispanics were the most underrepresented group. Within minority groups, African-American men outnumbered women by a 3 to 1 ratio (Baptista-Fernandez & Greenberg, 1984), but Hispanic men outnumbered women by a 5 to 1 ratio, making minority women virtually invisible (Greenberg & Baptista-Fernandez, 1984).

Representations of African Americans rose again in the 1990s. African Americans made up 11 percent of prime-time characters and 9 percent of daytime characters, but only 3 percent of the characters in children's television programming; other minority groups remained absent (Gerbner, 1993).

A content analysis conducted on Saturday morning children's television programs during the fall of 1995 revealed that minority portrayals were increasing, approximating the overall proportions of minority groups within the U.S. population (Calvert, Stolkin, & Lee, 1997). As Table 4.2 shows, Caucasian and ethnic minority portrayals were presented in similar proportions to their real-life numbers in the U.S. population. Moreover, the overall amount of time that ethnic minorities were present on the screen roughly paralleled these proportions. Within ethnic groups, African-American males were overrepresented, while other ethnic groups were underrepresented when compared to their real-life prevalence. Caucasian males were also more prevalent than they are in real life.

Educational television programming from the early 1990s presented considerable racial diversity. Neopolitan and Huston (1994a) found that 38 percent of the characters on PBS and 27 percent of the characters on commercial educational programs were minorities. Similarly, Williams and Cox (1995) found at least one major character from a minority group in 70 percent of informational programming and in 33 percent of noninformational programming in a sample of U.S. and Canadian television programs.

Taken together, the studies suggest that Caucasian and African-American males are prevalent in television depictions, but other minority groups are still rarely seen. These numbers suggest the invisibility and relative unimportance of other ethnic groups.

Television Roles of Ethnic Minority Characters

Minority presence in television programming is an important part of visibility, but the *kinds of roles* people of a certain race play are equally important. Role portrayals influence children's perceptions of the races and their access to appropriate models. Minority characters who play major television roles in a series provide consistent and potentially salient role models for children. Roles have recently improved, but stereotypes are still prevalent.

In the beginnings of television, stereotypes of African-American people abounded. For example, *Amos and Andy* portrayed African-American men as lovable buffoons (Liebert & Sprafkin, 1988).

Changes in the roles of African Americans came with the civil rights movement. Favorable roles for African Americans sprung up in situation comedies, where diverse portrayals of family life were presented. Interestingly, African Americans exerted more influence and control over Caucasians in situation comedies than Caucasians exerted over African Americans (Lemon, 1977). However, Hispanic characters remained seriously underrepresented. Of 3,549 characters analyzed in programming from 1975 through 1978, only 53 were Hispanics with speaking roles; put another way, Hispanic characters had less than 1.5 percent of the total number of speaking roles, even though they made up about 6 percent of the U.S. population (Greenberg & Baptista-Fernandez, 1984).

In a content analysis of African-American television families, Greenberg and Neuendorf (1980) found that almost all African-American families were presented in nuclear, but not extended, families. Television featured more African-American mothers than fathers and more African-American brothers than sisters. Most interaction within the African-American family occurred between males, and the son was the most active member of the family. There was also considerable conflict within African-American families, particularly between spouses and among siblings.

The Cosby Show represented a major breakthrough in African-American portrayals on American television. The Huxtables, a middle-class family, presented a humorous scenario of family life that appealed to Caucasians and minorities alike. African Americans in this program appeared in a variety of family situations and occupational roles. *The Cosby Show* presented a different scenario of African-American family life than the American people had viewed in the past (Calvert & Huston, 1987).

The roles of African Americans in situation comedies have been more favorable than their roles in prime-time dramatic television. In prime-time programs, ethnic minorities, women, and the elderly are frequently victims (Gerbner & Signorielli, 1990; Graves, 1996). Prime-time television roles for

African-American women are often low-status and menial (Greenberg & Brand, 1994).

Presentations of ethnic minority children and adults fared best on PBS. Perhaps the best known children's program targeted at an ethnically diverse audience is *Sesame Street*. *Sesame Street,* with a multicultural cast of African-American, Caucasian, and Hispanic children and adults, presents cognitive activities targeted at a preschool audience. A key scene for the live action sequences is Sesame Street, an integrated street in an inner-city neighborhood. The program's appeal extends beyond racial boundaries to children of diverse ethnic backgrounds, and the program is now aired in many countries including the United States, Israel, Palestine, and Saudi Arabia (Cole, 1997). *Sesame Street* coproductions, in which countries adapt the series to their own cultures, are also prevalent. A recent coproduction with Israel and Palestine teaches Israeli and Palestinian children about each other to reduce negative stereotypes and to foster mutual respect and peace (Children's Television Workshop, 1997).

Other PBS programs such as *Barney* and *Wishbone* also include children from different ethnic backgrounds who interact with each other at school and at play. In *Reading Rainbow,* an African-American male serves as the host as he introduces children to the world of books.

While children's commercial programs featuring African-American casts have been rare, some well-produced programs have been developed in this area. In the 1970s, CBS broadcast *Fat Albert and the Cosby Kids,* a prosocial series featuring an animated cast of African-American boys. The boys dealt with a variety of childhood issues such as how it feels when one's parents divorce, or how to cope with changing gender roles when a girl plays sports well and a boy loves to cook. Recently, FOX created *C-Bear and Jamal,* an animated program about a boy and the hip teddy bear who guides him through the challenges of childhood.

Overall, children's programs on the network stations in the 1990s provide few positive Hispanic, Asian, or Native American role models. In a content analysis of Saturday morning television programs broadcast in 1992, Greenberg and Brand (1993) found only one Hispanic character, and no Asian Americans or Native Americans. Most minority characters were African-American males. Only 3 of 20 programs featured regularly occurring characters from racial minorities.

NBC provided the most racial diversity. NBC ran a public service campaign in which African-American musicians told children to stay in school, and it broadcast two programs featuring African-American characters in central roles. However, African-American females appeared only in minor roles on one program.

Interestingly, the commercials often provided more racial diversity than the programming. Nevertheless, children typically played in segregated groups in commercials, no African-American female adults were ever present, and children from Asian, Hispanic, or Native American backgrounds rarely appeared (Greenberg & Brand, 1993).

Saturday morning entertainment programming from the 1995 season shows similar problems when major and minor roles are considered. **Major roles,** which require characters to speak and to be present on screen at least 20 percent of the total program time, favored Caucasians. ABC and FOX underrepresented members of ethnic minorities in major roles, but CBS actually overrepresented minority group members. NBC presented ethnic minorities in major roles consistent with their real-life presence in the U.S. population, until the gender of characters was considered. Except for CBS, minority females were invisible (Calvert, Stolkin, & Lee, 1997). In a comparison of U.S. and Canadian programs broadcast during the early 1990s, minority characters played powerful roles in 59 percent of the informational programming, but in only 11 percent of the noninformational programming (Williams & Cox, 1995).

Summary of Content

In summary, content analyses conducted over the past twenty-five years reveal some changes in the numbers and kinds of television roles members of ethnic minorities play. Educational programming, on PBS or on the network affiliates, presents the most racial diversity. Gains are most noticeable for African-American males; other minority groups remain virtually invisible, as do all women of color. The implication is that social activism, such as the civil rights movement, leads to increased representation in the media. Those who do not demand change do not gain visible media roles (Greenberg, 1988).

A THEORETICAL LENS FOR PREDICTING ETHNIC PORTRAYAL EFFECTS

Schema theory, social cognitive theory, and cultivation theory all predict that television conveys messages about minority groups to children in two ways: (1) by the number of minority members shown; and (2) by the kinds of roles minority members play (Huston & Wright, in press). The **drench hypothesis,** by contrast, focuses on the salient roles a few important minority characters play rather than on the overall number of minority characters portrayed. Specific theoretical predictions about media racial depictions are presented in Table 4.3.

According to **schema theory,** children develop beliefs about what other people are likely to do. Stereotypes, such as racial stereotypes, are one type of schema children construct, a schema based on skin color.

While we all have real-life experiences to draw upon to understand gender roles, information about minorities may be less available in everyday experience. Concentrations of minority groups in certain settings, such as large urban cities, may result in different levels of exposure to various cultural groups. Those not exposed to ethnic minorities in everyday life may be more dependent on television for information about these groups than those who play and live with members of ethnic minorities every day.

TABLE 4.3 **Theoretical Predictions about the Impact of Minority Media Portrayals**

Theory	Predictions
Schema Theory	Children will perceive, attend to, and remember information about race that fits with their prior beliefs.
Social Cognitive Theory	Children use television characters, particularly those of their own race, as role models.
Cultivation Theory	The racial images on television cultivate beliefs that Caucasian children are more prevalent and more important than minority children are.
Drench Hypothesis	A few very good images of racial minorities that are repeated over time can compensate for the more pervasive stereotyped media images.

Because television often uses stereotypes to depict different groups in society, television programming may cultivate and reinforce racial schemas. These racial schemas, in turn, are likely to influence children's selective attention to, and their memory of, televised information.

Racial schemas may also influence children's interactions with the new technologies. For instance, if children perceive computer interaction as a valued activity for their race, they are more likely to use computers than if computers are perceived as an activity for others (Marriott with Brant, 1995).

According to **social cognitive theory,** children search for models who can serve as guides for their own behavior. Models of the same race may more often guide children's behavior because children may perceive these models as being similar to them. Children use attention, retention, production, and motivation to acquire and perform behaviors (Bandura, 1986). Self-efficacy, the belief that you can control events, organizes the child's use of these subprocesses (Bandura, 1997). That is, as children's belief in their personal control increases, they are more likely to attend to, remember, and act on information, even when reinforcers are not immediately available to motivate them (Bandura, 1986). Observing attractive minority members as they perform professional activities, including computer-related activities, should theoretically increase the observer's performance of those behaviors.

According to **cultivation theory** (Gerbner et al., 1994), children who are continuously exposed to media images about race construct beliefs that are congruent with the dominant media images. This occurs via *mainstreaming effects,* when viewers construct a view of the world based on the dominant media images that they see. It also occurs via *resonance effects,* when media images reinforce real-life impressions. Therefore, children who repeatedly view racial stereotypes on television should construct similar world views, particularly if other sources of knowledge reinforce this stereotyped view.

The **drench hypothesis** predicts that the quality of a few media images may be more important than the overall quantity of images (Greenberg, 1988). According to the drench hypothesis, programs like *The Cosby Show* can override many of the stereotyped media images that children see. The drench hypothesis argues that the image of a Claire Huxtable, a Heathcliff Huxtable, or an Oprah Winfrey can impact the viewer more than a quantity of other images, in effect "drenching" the viewer with a positive image. The **drip hypothesis,** by contrast, predicts that all images slowly "drip" into the viewer's consciousness, making an impact on his or her impressions of other groups.

EFFECTS OF RACIAL TELEVISION PORTRAYALS ON CHILDREN

Although there have been numerous content analyses and theoretical predictions about the impact of racial depictions in television programming, there have been relatively few studies about the impact of programming on children (Greenberg & Brand, 1994). What we do know is often from older studies that typically examine only Caucasians and African Americans, not other ethnic groups. Therefore, we know relatively little about the current impact of racially stereotyped and nonstereotyped programs on children. With this limitation in mind, we will review what we do know through four lenses: schema theory, social cognitive theory, the drench hypothesis, and cultivation theory.

Schema Theory: Constructing Beliefs about the Races

Television creates two worlds for children: a white world and a nonwhite world (Palmer, Smith, & Strawser, 1993). That occurs, in part, because many television programs present children in segregated settings (Graves, 1993). Most programs feature predominantly black casts or predominantly white casts. Other minority children appear rarely.

All children are seeking information, including information about other people. Younger ethnic minority children, however, are relatively isolated from other sources that can meet those needs (Comstock & Cobbey, 1979). This occurs partly because racial segregation tends to occur when children are members of an ethnic minority; it also occurs because many minority children are poor (Montgomery, 1995). Poor children often do not have many books or computers in their homes, but they do have television. Thus, young children from ethnic minorities may rely on television for information more heavily than Caucasian children do (Comstock & Cobbey, 1979). As children from ethnic backgrounds grow older, social information about Caucasians surrounds them and saturates their daily experiences, leading to a relatively sophisticated understanding of majority values (Spencer & Markstrom-Adams, 1990). Caucasian children, who have less overall exposure to information about ethnic minority children, may continue to rely on racial portrayals on television as a primary source of information about different ethnic groups throughout their childhood (Greenberg & Brand, 1994).

Using schema theory, we can explore the impact of television portrayals on children of varying ethnic backgrounds. Although the learning processes are exactly the same for children of all ethnic backgrounds (Dorr, 1982), the schemas children have constructed should influence what they watch as well as what they take away from the television viewing experience.

Selective Attention

Although most children obviously watch a great deal of television, African Americans generally watch more television than Caucasians do (Comstock, 1991; Graves, 1996). Initially, researchers thought that people with lower incomes watched more television than those with higher incomes. While that is true for Caucasians, it is not true for African Americans; African Americans watch more television than their Caucasian counterparts at all income levels (Comstock, 1991). Because television viewing is more central to the daily lives of African-American than of Caucasian families, television plays an important role in the socialization of African-American children (Comstock, 1991).

The African-American preference for television emerges early and has been documented over time. African-American children and adolescents view more television than their Caucasian counterparts (Dominick & Greenberg, 1970; Greenberg & Dominick, 1970; Greenberg & Brand, 1994). As Table 4.4 indicates, Hispanic children in grades 4, 8, and 11 fall between their same-aged African-American and Caucasian peers in the number of hours of television viewing (Anderson, Mead, & Sullivan, 1986).

TABLE 4.4 Ethnicity and Daily Television Viewing for Children in Grades 4, 8, and 11

	Viewing		
Race/Ethnicity	0–2 hours	3–5 hours	6 hours or more
Grade 4			
White	35%	40%	25%
Black	21%	28%	51%
Hispanic	31%	36%	33%
Grade 8			
White	40%	50%	10%
Black	21%	48%	31%
Hispanic	34%	51%	16%
Grade 11			
White	61%	35%	4%
Black	36%	50%	13%
Hispanic	55%	38%	7%

Source: Adapted from Anderson, B., Mead, N., & Sullivan, S. (1986). *Television: What do national assessment results tell us?* Princeton, N.J.: Educational Testing Service.

Lyle and Hoffman (1972) found that Caucasian, Hispanic, and African-American children chose different programs as favorites. While differences in the first grade were negligible, they emerged for children in the sixth and tenth grades. Ethnic minority children prefer programs with performers from the same ethnic background (Greenberg & Atkin, 1982). African-American children particularly like programs about African-American families (Graves, 1996), and Hispanic youth prefer programs they find culturally relevant (Greenberg & Brand, 1994). African-American children identify with African-American characters and rate them highly on handsomeness, friendliness, and strength (Greenberg, 1972). Caucasian children also select African-American television characters as role models, but not as much as African-American children do (Greenberg, 1972); they also view programs featuring African Americans, but again, not as much as African Americans do (Graves, 1996). Little is known about the program preferences of Asian-American, Hispanic American, or Native American children (Graves, 1996).

Learning and Memory of Content

Schematic models of information processing predict that children will bring previously learned information to bear on the media messages they view. Thus, memory should reflect prior knowledge and expectations.

The predictions of schema theory with regards to race and memory are fourfold. First, children from minority groups will remember information about characters of their own ethnic group particularly well. Secondly, children who have little real-world knowledge about a minority group will rely on television images for racial information. Thirdly, children will attempt to preserve racial schemas by distorting incoming content to fit prior beliefs. Fourthly, when racial stereotypes are not activated, children of different races will rely more on other realms of experience besides race when processing information.

Nonstereotyped portrayals of ethnic minority children impact children's memory of that content. Children viewing *Sesame Street* attend to constructive messages, recognize positive feelings, and remember information about characters who are from their own ethnic backgrounds (Lovelace, Freund, & Graves, in press). This supports the first prediction schema theory makes.

Caucasian, more than African-American, children are likely to learn about the other race from watching television. Greenberg (1972) found that approximately 40 percent of Caucasian fourth and fifth graders said they knew about how African Americans look, talk, and dress from watching television. Reliance on television for knowledge about African Americans was much more pronounced in rural than in suburban or urban settings. In a later study (Atkin, Greenberg, & McDermott, 1983), in which Caucasian fourth-, sixth-, and eighth-grade children interacted frequently with African Americans, television played a smaller role in the children's knowledge about African Americans. Only 24 percent of these children relied on television for their knowledge about African Americans. These effects suggest, as the second prediction of schema theory states, that real-life interactions influence beliefs about other

Children learn the most about different races from real-life experiences, which sometimes involves watching TV programs together.

racial groups more than television portrayals unless children have little real-life experiences with these groups.

As new technologies are integrated into American schools, children are learning about other cultures on their computers as well as from television. For example, six fourth and fifth graders who used a computer package called Multicultural Links talked about cultural similarities and differences involving dress, lifestyles, homes, and customs (Moore-Hart, 1995). This **qualitative analysis,** which describes children's responses without statistical comparisons, should be followed with more in-depth examinations of what children learn about other cultures through computer-generated environments.

Schema theory also predicts that children will distort information to fit their prior beliefs. We know little about how children distort media messages, but we do have some information that adults distort racial information. When an African American and a Hispanic rated television commercials, they overestimated the number of significant television commercial roles members of their own ethnic minorities played (Wilkes & Valencia, 1989). Perhaps seeing one's ethnic minority in any role makes that portrayal more salient and memorable to group members, thereby leading one to distort the actual media prevalence of that minority.

While no formal studies were conducted on the O. J. Simpson trial, polls demonstrated clear racial divisions about his innocence or guilt in the murder of Nicole Brown Simpson. Millions of people viewed the trial, which was televised for more than a year. After hearing the same evidence, 83 percent of

African Americans, but only 37 percent of Caucasians, believed that the jury was correct in finding Simpson not guilty of murder (ABC Nightline, 1995). The audience's racial schemas, based on viewing the trial and upon other occurrences in their own lives, may well have influenced the way in which they interpreted the evidence.

Children of different races also have much in common with one another. When a presentation does not invoke racial schemas or stereotypes, children process the message primarily by age and other kinds of experiences. All children, for example, learn moral messages from television programs that feature African-American cartoon characters. In an evaluation of *Fat Albert and the Cosby Kids,* CBS (1974) found that 90 percent of a sample of children learned one or more messages from viewing the series. In other experimental studies of *Fat Albert,* both Caucasian and minority children learned the program messages, and comprehension increased with age (Calvert et al., 1982; Calvert, Huston, & Wright, 1987). These studies focused on children's comprehension of story plots, such as their gender roles or their parents' divorce, that are common experiences of children during middle childhood. Although none of these studies examined whether learning the messages altered children's beliefs about other races, the findings do support the fourth hypothesis about racial schemas.

Similarly, economic similarity can sometimes provide more common ground for processing television content than racial similarity. For example, Newcomb and Collins (1979) found that children remembered televised information about people who were similar to them in social class more than they remembered information about those of the same race. Social class, one organizer of experiences, may be one reason Caucasians related to the middle-class portrayals of *The Cosby Show.*

Attitudes about Race

The racial schemas viewers bring to the viewing situation affect their perceptions of program themes. For example, Vidmar and Rokeach (1974) examined portrayals of bigotry on prejudiced or nonprejudiced American adolescents and Canadian adults who viewed *All in the Family,* a situation comedy pitting Archie, a conservative, prejudiced patriot against Mike, his liberal son-in-law. The investigators measured prejudice by asking questions such as whether black and white students should attend the same schools. The researchers examined two hypotheses: (1) the **selective perception hypothesis,** which predicted that viewers who are high or low in prejudice would perceive this program in different ways; and (2) the **selective exposure hypothesis,** which predicted that highly prejudiced individuals would view this series more often than less prejudiced individuals, because Archie's views were similar to their own. The authors found support for both hypotheses. Specifically, highly prejudiced viewers were more likely to admire Archie Bunker than less prejudiced viewers, thereby supporting the selective perception hypothesis. American adolescents, but not Canadian adults, who frequently watched *All in the Family* were also more likely to be high in prejudice, to admire Archie Bunker, and to find nothing wrong with his racial and ethnic slurs than were those who watched the program infrequently, thereby partially supporting the selective exposure hypothesis.

Roots, a television miniseries about slavery, also impacted viewers differently, depending on who the viewer was. Hur and Robinson (1978) conducted a telephone interview with 529 African Americans (18 percent of the sample) and Caucasians (82 percent of the sample) soon after the last episode of the series was broadcast. Interviewers asked questions about the respondents' views of the series as well as questions about their racial attitudes, such as their views on open housing. Seventy-five percent of the sample viewed at least one of the eight episodes; African Americans viewed more of the episodes than Caucasians did. Caucasians who viewed the program were more liberal than those who did not watch the series. These findings support the selective exposure hypothesis. Compared to Caucasians, African Americans believed more of the program messages and discussed the program more after viewing. One-third of white viewers were unconvinced that African Americans endured more hardship than white immigrants, a finding that supports the selective perception hypothesis. Overall, then, what viewers believed before the series was broadcast influenced whether they watched the programs and what they believed after viewing them.

Taken together, these research studies demonstrate the importance of examining what a child or an adolescent brings to a viewing situation when determining the effects that television program may have on him or her. Selective attention is determined in part by the preexisting schemas and attitudes viewers bring as an audience. Learning is influenced by prior racial beliefs, which in turn are influenced by real-life exposure more than by media exposure.

Modifying Racial Schemas

Television programs can alter the racial schemas children have of ethnic minorities. The focus has been upon African-American perceptions, but perceptions of children from other cultures can also change.

Sesame Street promotes ethnic diversity by portraying an integrated city neighborhood. After being encouraged to view the program for two years, both Caucasian and African-American preschoolers had more favorable beliefs and perceptions about children from ethnic backgrounds other than their own (Bogatz & Ball, 1971). However, one year of exposure was insufficient for improving racial attitudes.

Short-term media exposure to other ethnic groups can improve racial attitudes when the content is specifically targeted at that topic. For example, Gorn, Goldberg, and Kanugo (1976) found that preschool-aged children who viewed only two racially integrated vignettes from *Sesame Street* became more interested in playing with peers from different ethnic backgrounds. Vignettes that portrayed multiracial themes worked well when nonwhite groups were presented in mixed racial settings or in segregated ethnic settings that presented information about the culture (for example, scenes in which Asians or

Native Americans demonstrated traditional dances). Hence, any positive exposure to other ethnic groups was sufficient for improving children's interracial attitudes.

The goals of *Vegetable Soup,* a magazine television series, were to reduce racial prejudice, racial barriers, and stereotyped thinking by presenting ethnic minority characters in nonstereotyped roles. Six- to 10-year-old Caucasian and African-American children who repeatedly viewed this series were friendlier toward various ethnic minority members; for African-American children, self-acceptance of their own heritage also increased (Mays et al., 1975).

In an effort to counteract racial unrest in the United States in 1989, *Sesame Street* embarked on the explicit goal of promoting racial harmony. Over a period of four years, the curriculum emphasized friendships among people who were African American, Native American, Latino, and white American. In one assessment of viewing effects, preschoolers were asked to "Make a Neighborhood" with drawings of characters from different racial backgrounds. African-American, Chinese-American, Crow-Native American, and Puerto Rican children all created integrated neighborhoods. Caucasian children integrated their neighborhoods with all races except African Americans, who they kept segregated. *Sesame Street* vignettes were then created in which African-American and white children visit each other's homes. (Visiting Ieshia, from our opening scenario, was one such vignette.) Although children of both races wanted to be friends, they thought that the televised African-American and Caucasian mothers would feel sad or angry if their child visited a friend of the other race. Vignettes featuring parental support of interracial friendships may be a necessary ingredient for improving racial relationships (Lovelace et al., 1994).

Using schema theory, the results of these studies suggest that positive portrayals of peoples from different ethnic backgrounds lead to more favorable perceptions of those groups. These effects occur for children from age 3 through 10, indicating a plasticity that implies that nonstereotyped portrayals can alter schemas. Because children indicate more willingness to interact with members of other ethnic backgrounds after exposure to television programs about them, television can pave the way to a better understanding between children of different ethnic backgrounds. To maximize differentiated schemas, the media can depict role models for children from diverse ethnic backgrounds. To maximize interaction, television messages can focus on how children are similar; they can also depict parents who support interracial friendships.

Social Cognitive Theory: Role Models for Children

Social cognitive theory posits the importance of positive role models who can guide children's behaviors (Bandura, 1986). According to this theory, children will identify with characters of their own race and use those characters as models. Identification with same-race role models is one reason so much attention has been focused on the kinds of roles minority characters play on television.

African Americans prefer programs that feature members of their own ethnic group, and they identify with those characters (Graves, 1980). In some instances, self-esteem is associated with viewing minority members who serve as positive role models. African-American children have higher self-esteem when they perceive African-American television characters favorably (McDermott & Greenberg, 1984), and African-American girls who are heavy television viewers have positive self-concepts (Stroman, 1986). When first- and second-grade African-American children were shown either a prosocial episode of *Fat Albert and the Cosby Kids* or a control episode of *Charlie Brown*, their self-perceptions improved, but only when the recipient of the prosocial actions was the same sex as the viewer (Freeman & Huston, 1995). More research is needed in this area, including studies of children who are Latino, Asian, and Native American.

Caucasian and African-American children will also select characters of other races as role models. In an early study by Greenberg (1972), for example, fourth- and fifth-grade children were asked to name the television characters they would most like to emulate. Forty-three percent of Caucasian and 75 percent of African-American children identified with an African-American television character. Identification with African-American characters increased when African-American children viewed more television. Twenty-five percent of African-American children also identified with Caucasian television characters. Although television provides role models for children, why children identified with certain television characters remains unknown.

The Drench Hypothesis: Assessing the Value of a Few Nonstereotyped Media Images

The idea of salient role models is also applicable in understanding the drench hypothesis. According to the drench hypothesis, the roles minority characters play are more important than the sheer number of minority characters shown (Greenberg, 1988). Even if minority children view characters of their own race infrequently, a few portrayals can have a profound effect on racial schemas, particularly if children are exposed to a series over an extended period of time.

Little research has been conducted to support the drench hypothesis, but there is some indication that racial portrayals are salient to members of the same race. As we discussed earlier, African-American children prefer to watch portrayals of African-American characters (Comstock, 1991), and African-American and Hispanic scorers overestimate the number of positive roles people from their ethnic group play (Wilkes & Valencia, 1989).

The Cosby Show, a program which supposedly led to drench effects, is now seen only in reruns. However, positive portrayals of African Americans and Native Americans followed in other programs such as *Dr. Quinn, Medicine Woman*, a series about a Caucasian female physician and her family in the late 1800s. In this series, an African-American family plays a central role. Prejudice issues are sometimes featured in the plot lines. For example, questions arise about whether Anthony, an African-American child, will be allowed to attend the school for white children, or whether his parents can buy a house in the predominantly white town. A Native American character, Cloud Dancing, introduces viewers to the customs of his people, including religious beliefs. Through his eyes, we see how the U.S. government treated Native Americans. Caucasian children who view this series are likely to create more differentiated schemas about other ethnic groups than those who do not. If one accepts the drench hypothesis, this program could make an important difference in the beliefs and attitudes children develop about other ethnic groups, just as *The Cosby Show* seemingly did. For underrepresented minority groups such as Hispanics, Greenberg (1988) argues that one television program that presents characters who are strong, positive role models for children could be an important first step in making inroads in their group representation. Nonetheless, we still need empirical verification of the drench theory.

Cultivation Theory: Cultivating Racial Beliefs

The cultivation theory has more of a "drip," rather than a drench approach, to assessing the impact of television on children's racial perceptions. Specifically, the constant flow of stereotyped images shapes children's views of minority groups. According to Gross and Morgan (1980), television provides information the child does not have (mainstreaming) or reinforces information the child has already assimilated (resonance).

So what happens to minority children who view racial depictions on television? One prediction of cultivation theory is that if children rarely see members of their own race, they may come to believe they are unimportant, creating feelings of low self-esteem. However, there is little data to support that prediction. Even though African-American women appear infrequently on television and often take on stereotyped roles when they do appear, African-American girls who are heavy viewers of television programs have high self-esteem (Stroman, 1986). Another prediction from cultivation theory is that children who see their race portrayed in stereotyped roles may come to believe that those are the roles society expects their group to take. No one has examined this area. Cultivation theory also predicts that television will shape the beliefs of Caucasian children, particularly those who have little personal contact with minority children. Early research by Greenberg (1972) found that Caucasian children who lived in rural America relied on television for general information about ethnic minorities, but suburban children believed the depictions of African Americans were accurate more than those who lived in rural or urban settings. Clearly, we need more research about the effects of racial portrayals, for little has been conducted and what has been done is somewhat dated.

Summary of the Theoretical Findings

In summary, while the evidence about the impact of racial portrayals on children is scant, it generally supports theories that depict children as active processors of media content. Selective exposure plays an important role as viewers choose the kinds of programs they see, and selective perception influences how viewers remember the characters they watch. Viewers sometimes distort their memories of a program to fit their prior beliefs and expectations. Children also seem to search for certain information, including attractive role models. In short, total exposure is less important than the kind of beliefs viewers have about other races they see on television.

This evidence supports schema theory, social cognitive theory, the drench hypothesis, and the resonance aspect of cultivation theory. However, the data do not support the mainstreaming aspect of cultivation theory, which focuses on exposure, particularly when viewers have real-life exposure to members of other races. The implication is that children bring a great deal of information to the television viewing experience that influences what they view, remember, and believe about other races.

THE INFLUENCE OF NEW TECHNOLOGIES

As we saw in Chapter 1, many minority children, who tend to be poor, have limited access to personal computers. Being part of a poor family also means living in a poor school district. The lack of resources in poorer schools also results in less exposure to the new technologies.

We know that Asian Americans are most likely to purchase computers for home use, followed by Caucasians, Hispanics, and African Americans, respectively. Although Asians appear to value access to the information highway, we know little about why they do. The popular press reports that many African Americans do not purchase computers because of their negative perceptions of the technology (Marriott with Brant, 1995), but this premise has no empirical confirmation.

The joint venture between Microsoft and Black Entertainment Television to produce interactive information for and about African Americans could make the Internet more interesting to African Americans (Farhi, 1996a). There are also other African-American role models for children on the Internet. For instance, numerous sites feature accomplished African-American athletes such as Arthur Ashe and Jackie Robinson. Blackwings, a project linked to The National Air and Space Museum, teaches the user about African-American pilots, including Bessie Coleman, the first African American to receive a pilot's license. These sites can provide historical information to educate children about prominent members of African-American culture.

One educational computer package that includes children from minority groups is the Multicultural Links program. In this package, children use a word processor to read and write about other cultures in a multimedia format of words, pictures, sounds, and music. In an exploratory study, Moore-Hart (1995) reported that fourth and fifth graders who used this computer program in conjunction with the Multicultural Literacy Program improved more in their reading, writing, and attitudes about writing than those who participated in a traditional reading program or who used the Multicultural Literacy Program without the computer link. However, no conventional tests of statistical significance were reported, making the magnitude of these children's gains unclear. The results suggest that computer programs with a multicultural focus may improve the academic performance of minority children, but more definitive research is needed.

Kramer (1987) reported that African-American adolescent women have limited access to computers in their homes. Even when computers were available at inner-city schools, high school math and science teachers reported that less than 10 percent of the school population used them. Lack of computer use was also prevalent among the teachers; 54 percent of the teachers reported that they did not use the computers. If we are to provide children with access to the information highway, we must also teach the teachers to use computers.

The lack of research about minority computer use in American culture suggests that few are seriously concerned about equal access to the new technologies. This lack of concern is a mistake, for jobs and future roads to success will be open to those who travel the information highway (Montgomery, 1995). In 1986, less than 5 percent of computer programming degrees were awarded to African-American or Hispanic women, and less than 5 percent of computer-related jobs were held by women who were African-American or Hispanic (Kramer & Lehman, 1990).

Minority girls benefit when taught to program a computer. Black and white 11- and 12-year-old children from Zimbabwe were pretested on four WISC-R subtests which measured their mathematical intelligence. For the next year, children were assigned either to a LOGO condition, where they were taught computer programming skills, or to a control condition. Then posttests were given on the WISC-R. Children in the LOGO group improved their performance on the WISC-R Arithmetic scale more than the control group did. In addition, black girls who learned LOGO increased on the WISC-R Block Design task more than the other groups did. The results suggest that minority girls experience cognitive benefits when they are taught to be computer programmers (Mundy-Castle et al., 1989). Educational experiences like these are needed to improve the position of minority children for future occupational success.

SUMMARY

Although children from ethnic minorities view television extensively (Greenberg & Brand, 1994), few quality commercial programs are targeted to that audience. Over the past two decades, innovations such as cable television and public television failed to alter two important facts: (1) Americans primarily view commercial television programs; and (2) American children primarily view television programs designed for adult audiences (Comstock & Cobbey, 1979; Huston et al., 1992). Thus, we must also examine adult programs on the commercial networks to assess television's effects on children's attitudes about ethnic minorities.

Television programs can affect children's racial perceptions, attitudes, and behaviors. Caucasian children who have little firsthand exposure to minority groups learn a great deal about these groups from television presentations, but most children bring prior beliefs about others based on real-life experiences to the screen. Nonstereotyped television portrayals can alter and modify children's attitudes towards members of different races. A few nonstereotyped characters can teach children about people from different ethnic groups, particularly if they appear in a series on a regular basis.

Providing minority children with access to quality television programs and to the new information technologies can pave the way for future careers and greater racial equality. Minority children can gain information about their own cultures, about other cultures, and about their futures in American society. Asian Americans are ensuring their access by purchasing computers, but other minority groups are not. While price is one obstacle in computer acquisitions, a bigger obstacle is the perception that computers are irrelevant to the lives of minority children. Content of interest to minority children could improve their desire to travel on the information highway.

Green Media Images: The Color of Money

I once talked to a girl who was about 10 years old about advertisements on children's television. She told me that when she was younger, she believed that Tony the Tiger would really come out of the cereal box and into her kitchen. Needless to say, she had viewed that scene many times in Kelloggs' Frosted Flakes commercials.

Each day, children are exposed to about one hundred advertisements as they watch television in their homes (Van Evra, 1995). Many young children, such as the girl who spoke to me, do not understand commercials as older children or adults do (Comstock, 1991). In particular, they rarely understand that someone is trying to sell them a product (Van Evra, 1995). At about age 9 to 10, children begin to understand the motives and intentions of advertisers, but by this age, most have viewed approximately 40,000 commercials each year (Comstock, 1991).

What do children understand about commercials? When do they want their parents to buy the products they see? How do children come to understand that commercials are designed to sell them products?

Although commercial television has been one of the most effective sellers of goods in America, the Internet may soon provide some stiff competition. As children are spending more time online, they are also spending less time watching television, and hence, they are being exposed somewhat less to television advertisements (Williams, Montgomery, & Pasnik, 1997). Because of online marketing, however, children's overall exposure to advertisements has not declined.

Some of the concerns raised in television advertising have also been raised in Internet advertising, such as having a familiar host sell products. Additional concerns arise when familiar characters interact with children on the Internet by sending them mail, thereby forming personal relationships with them (Montgomery & Pasnik, 1996).

In this chapter, we will explore the green images of commercial television and the impact those images have on the youngest viewers. We will then examine the newest commercial medium: the Internet.

CONTENT ANALYSES OF CHILDREN'S ADVERTISEMENTS

American children represent a market with buying power. In 1995, children and adolescents influenced 160 billion dollars of their parents' spending; in addition, children spent 14 billion dollars themselves, and adolescents spent an additional 67 billion dollars (Montgomery & Pasnik, 1996). Commercial advertisers want to attract this audience, and television is an ideal medium for reaching them because children are in the viewing audience about 2 to 3 hours each day (Comstock, 1991; Condry, 1989; Huston et al., 1990).

In content analyses of children's commercial television programs, researchers have documented the amount of time, the number of advertisements, the kind of products, and the kinds of commercial practices that advertisers use to sell products to children. Content analyses conducted during the 1970s and the 1980s demonstrated that the amount of time devoted to commercial advertisements remained relatively constant (Barcus, 1980; Condry, 1989). However, because commercials became shorter, children are now exposed to far more advertisements than they were two decades ago. The kinds of products advertised to children have also remained constant over three decades.

In early research, Barcus (1980) tracked children's television programs in the Boston area from two samples taken during 1971 and one taken during 1975. About 20 to 25 percent of Saturday morning broadcast time was devoted to commercials in 1971. Children, on average, viewed about 26 commercials each hour. When child advocacy groups, such as Action for Children's Television, brought pressure to bear on industry, and when the Federal Communications Commission initiated investigations, the National Association of Broadcasters, who sets up broadcaster guidelines within industry, decided to implement steps to reduce the amount of advertising on children's television (Barcus, 1980). These changes were reflected in a subsequent content analysis. In the 1975 sample, a decrease in commercial time occurred so that 15 percent of each broadcast hour was devoted to commercials, meaning about 20 advertisements were aired per hour. Nevertheless, children still saw almost the same number of commercials as in 1971 because the length of many commercials had decreased to about 30 seconds (Barcus, 1980). Most of the advertisements were for cereal, candy, toys, and fast food restaurants, a pattern that is still constant two decades later (Comstock, 1991; Kunkel & Gantz, 1992).

In a later longitudinal sample of television programming, Condry (1989) examined commercial advertising patterns at two-year intervals during 1983, 1985, and 1987. Although the time devoted to commercials remained relatively constant, the number of advertisements rose. Once again, commercials were shortened so that many were only 15 seconds long, resulting in what the researchers described as "clutter" (Condry, 1989). If one looked at the number of commercials over time, the frequency of commercials increased from 13.8 per hour in 1963 to 19.3 in 1987 (Condry, 1989).

Children's television, however, showed fewer commercials than most other programming times. Across all three periods, commercials were broadcast on Saturday mornings for an average of 8.3 minutes each hour, or about 13 percent of each broadcast hour (Condry, 1989). This amount was lower than all other times except Sunday morning.

So what did advertisers want children to buy? It depended partly on the season. Not surprisingly, toy commercials dominated the schedule during the Christmas holidays. Cereals, candy, soft drinks, snacks, and fast food restaurants were the other major products advertised to children (Condry, Bence, & Scheibe, 1988).

With increased access to cable and independent television stations, new channels are now advertising to children. Kunkel and Gantz (1992) examined a composite week of programming that focused on the child audience. They sampled programs from three sources: (1) the major network affiliates of ABC,

TABLE 5.1 Type of Product Advertised by Channel

		Percentage of Ads				
Channel	Toys	Cereals & Breakfast	Snacks & Drinks	Fast Food	Healthy Food	Other
Broadcast Networks (ABC, CBS, NBC) (N = 1,706)	17.3	31.2	32.4	8.7	4.6	5.8
Independents (N = 6,110)	42.1	22.7	15.6	5.6	1.7	12.4
Cable Networks (Nick, USA) (N = 2,509)	24.7	15.9	15.8	3.8	4.3	35.5
Total (N = 10,325)	33.8	22.4	18.4	5.7	2.8	16.9

Note: All figures represented statistically significant differences across broadcast networks, independents, and cable networks; chi square test for each product type, $p < .01$.
Source: Kunkel, D., & Gantz, W. (1992). Children's television advertising in the multichannel environment. *Journal of Communication, 42*, 134–152. Adapted with permission of Oxford University Press.

CBS, and NBC; (2) independent broadcast stations; and (3) cable channels. The results indicated that the major network affiliates spent more of each hour broadcasting commercials than the cable networks did, with the independent stations falling in between. Specifically, the major networks broadcast 10:05 minutes of commercials each hour, whereas the independent stations broadcast 9:37 minutes per hour, with cable channels at 6:48 minutes per hour. For the major network affiliates, the amount of advertising in children's programs had increased by about 2 minutes per hour since the Condry, Bence, and Scheibe (1988) study conducted in the mid to late 1980s.

As Table 5.1 shows, Kunkel and Gantz (1992) found that toys, cereal products, and sugared snacks and drinks remain the major products sold to children, accounting for three-fourths of the commercial advertisements on children's programs. When the researchers compared channels, they found that toy advertisements were most prevalent on independent stations. Cereals and breakfast foods, sugared drinks and snacks, and fast foods were most prevalent on the network affiliates. Cable stations offered the most diversity in advertisements. Cable stations advertised some products that the other broadcasters did not even carry and that have not been marketed to children in the past, such as telephone services for children to call.

In summary, over the past three decades, the amount of time spent broadcasting commercials generally has accounted for about 15 to 20 percent of each broadcast hour. The kinds of products that children see—toys, cereals, candy, and fast foods—have also remained constant over time. Even so, the total number of commercials that children view has increased because advertisements have become briefer in length.

COMMERCIAL SELLING TECHNIQUES

To sell products, advertisers use certain techniques to increase the products' appeal to children (Van Evra, 1995). Barcus (1980) found that children's advertisers often used attention-getting production techniques such as unusual sounds, camera "magic," and other interesting visual effects to attract children to commercials. For example, advertisers often mix real characters with animated ones, particularly when selling cereal (Kunkel & Gantz, 1992).

These attention-getting techniques, or **perceptually salient** features, embody characteristics like contrast, incongruity, movement, and surprise that are likely to elicit children's attention and interest (Huston & Wright, 1983). Applied to television production techniques, Huston and Wright (1983) classified certain visual and audio features as perceptually salient. The salient visual techniques included: (1) the amount of **action** on the screen; (2) how rapidly the scenes change, or the **pacing;** and (3) **visual special effects** that present impossible events, such as an animated rabbit talking to children. Perceptually salient auditory features included: (1) *sound effects* involving unusual, prominent noises; and (2) loud, prominent *foreground music.*

Commercials often use perceptually salient production techniques to present content to boys. For example, commercials directed at boys present content quickly, accompanied by loud noises, fast action, and loud music (Welch et al., 1979).

Premiums, small toys offered with the purchase of the product, are another common and effective selling technique (Comstock, 1991). For instance, many cereals include small toys as a prize for buying the product (Ward, 1980). Kunkel and Gantz (1992) found that premiums were featured in about 10 percent of all advertisements directed at children, and particularly in commercials by fast food restaurants, who use premiums in about 36 percent of their advertisements. Barcus (1980) also found that cereal advertisements were primary utilizers of premiums, with about 28 percent using premiums in 1971, 47 percent in 1975, and 25 percent in 1977. The problem with premiums is that children often choose a product for the wrong reason, thus raising issues of fairness in advertising (Rossiter, 1980a).

Celebrity endorsements are another technique used to sell products (Comstock, 1991). Advertisers pay celebrities to put their images on a product and to use the product; thus, Michael Jordan eats Wheaties on the cereal aisle or plays basketball in Nike athletic shoes. Children who identify with these stars may desire the product and buy it for themselves (Condry, 1989).

What is the impact of this multimillion-dollar effort to sell products to children? Do children attend to advertisements, do they understand and remember them, and most importantly, from the advertiser's perspective, do they buy those products? Common sense tells us that businesses wouldn't spend millions of dollars on advertisements if it wasn't an effective selling technique. But children don't ask for or buy all the products they see on television. From a psychological perspective, we need to understand how children perceive, understand, and are influenced by commercial messages. Two theoretical models are particularly useful for doing so: (1) Piaget's theory of cognitive development; and (2) information processing theory.

THEORETICAL MODELS IN RELATION TO ADVERTISING

Early research about children's advertising often looked to Piaget's theory of cognitive development. Because of consistent age differences in the way children understand commercials (Costley & Brucks, 1986; Wartella, 1980), researchers used Piaget's cognitive developmental theory to explain why young children did not understand commercial material (Macklin, 1987). Information processing theory more often guided the later research. This theory focuses on the cognitive activities children must engage in to process and understand commercials.

In Piaget's theory, children pass through four stages of cognitive development: (1) sensorimotor thought (from about ages 0 to 2); (2) preoperational thought (from about ages 2 to 7); (3) concrete operational thought (from about ages 7 to 12); and (4) formal operational thought (after about age 12). During sensorimotor thought, children represent information with their bodies. Thinking is limited because children are bound to the present time. Preoperational thought sees children beginning to use symbols and representational thinking. Thus, it is here that television's influence begins because television is a representational medium. Preoperational children often think intuitively, without extensive logical knowledge of the world. That's why many young children believe in magical beings like Santa Claus, the Easter Bunny, and the Tooth Fairy, or believe that animated characters like Tony the Tiger may jump out of a cereal box. Researchers have raised concerns that children in this stage cannot distinguish fantasy from reality, including the content in commercial advertisements (Wartella & Ettema, 1974). The implication is that young children cannot understand commercial intent because of their cognitive limitations based on age. During concrete operational thought, children begin to think logically, more as adults do, but concrete experiences continue to set boundaries on their thinking. At this stage, children are able to discriminate the difference between commercials and programs and between imaginary and real experiences. Finally, formal operational thought is characterized by abstract thinking and the ability to live in the realm of possibility, not just the actual (Flavell, 1963).

Information processing theory, a refinement of Piagetian theory (Thomas, 1996), examines the specific activities children must do to understand commercial material. There are many different information processing approaches. The model we will follow here considers the following cognitive activities: **perception, attention, comprehension, memory,** and **behavior.** Perceptual qualities of television initially influence children's attention. Once children attend, they will understand and remember certain parts of the messages. Ultimately, these activities will influence children's behavior: that is, their buying activities.

To organize the literature, we will follow an information processing approach. Because of the shift that occurs at around age 7 between preoperational and concrete operational thought, we will also pay close attention to that time frame. In particular, we will examine whether children can understand commercials and commercial intent before and after that age.

IMPACT OF ADVERTISING ON CHILDREN

The intent of any advertisement is to get the audience to buy a particular product. Before buying a product, however, children must first *attend* to the advertised message and then *recognize* the product when they next shop or go out to eat. To obtain some products, children must be able to convey their desires and convince their parents to buy those products. In short, there is a tier of activities children must first do before they can obtain an advertised product.

Attention to Advertisements

Because young children do not understand implicit media messages well (Huston & Wright, in press), researchers have been concerned about whether children "know" that a change is occurring when the program they are watching transits to and from commercials. One way researchers have examined this issue is by studying children's attentional shifts to and from the television program. When a major change in content occurs, children typically look away from the television screen momentarily if they have been looking at it; if they have not been looking, a change in content will often elicit a look back to the screen. This type of measure tells researchers that children have noticed a discrepancy or change in content.

Research on children's **attention** to advertisements suggests that older children notice changes more often than younger children do. In an early study by Ward, Levinson, and Wackman (1972), mothers were trained to observe their children's attention to advertisements during Saturday morning viewing. Younger children, ranging in age from 5 to 8, did not increase or decrease their attention when commercials began. By contrast, children who were older than 8 stopped looking at the television set when the commercials began. These findings suggest that older children not only notice, but tend to screen out, commercial messages, but younger children are less likely to make these discriminations (Wartella, 1980). It also provides support for a Piagetian interpretation of the findings: when concrete operational thought begins, children are better able to detect commercial material.

Children may attend to commercials because of the attention-getting features of commercials, not because they understand that they are now viewing commercials. To get children to attend to their messages, commercial advertisers use television production techniques such as catchy sound effects, lively music, and commercial jingles that are likely to attract and to hold children's attention (Stewart & Ward, 1994; Stutts & Hunnicutt, 1987; Van Evra, 1990).

These techniques, as you may recall, are perceptually salient (Huston & Wright, 1983).

Greer, Potts, Wright, and Huston (1982) found that preschool children, particularly boys, were more attentive to commercials that contained high, rather than low, levels of these perceptually salient features (action, sound effects, loud music). Wartella and Ettema (1974) found that 3- to 8-year-old children were more attentive to commercials high in auditory complexity than those high in visual complexity, another way of describing perceptually salient features. Taken together, these findings suggest that rapid change in the auditory track is the most effective technique for attracting the attention of young viewers to commercial material.

Product Recognition

Once an advertiser gets children to attend to a commercial message, the next step is to make sure that children *recognize* the product so that they will buy it. Yet commercials are often short in duration, lasting only 15 or 30 seconds. How do advertisers get young children, who are notably deficient in memory skills, to remember to ask for their product?

One way to get children to remember any information better is to repeat it (Calvert & Billingsley, 1998). Advertisers also use *repetition* to get children to remember commercials (Condry, 1989; Stewart & Ward, 1994). When children are repeatedly exposed to the same commercials over and over, they are more likely to remember, and less likely to forget, that product (Gorn & Goldberg, 1980; Rossiter, 1980b). Within a commercial, considerable repetition of content may also occur, such as repeating the name of the product.

Another method advertisers use to enhance memory is to include catchy auditory features in commercials, such as jingles or catchy songs. Musical jingles are often used to reach child audiences (Barcus, 1980). Repeated exposure to a song can make verbal information memorable to children and adults (Calvert & Tart, 1993). Songs get "stuck" in listeners' heads, leading them to automatically rehearse the lyrics, thereby increasing the memorability of the content (Calvert & Tart, 1993).

A third way advertisers enhance memory is through attractive visual techniques (Condry, 1989). For example, Stoneman and Brody (1983) showed preschool, kindergarten, and second-grade children food commercials that presented the products in three ways: visually, audiovisually, or aurally only. Children recognized the products that were presented visually or audiovisually better than products that were presented aurally. Moreover, exposure translated into better recognition and interest for general classes of products (cereal, in this instance).

Comprehension of Commercial Intent

Detecting a change in content or recognizing a product name does not necessarily mean that children understand the commercial intent of the message: to persuade viewers to buy products. This is a comprehension issue (Comstock, 1991).

Comprehension of commercial intent is clearly linked to age. As children get older, they increasingly understand that the underlying motive in commercial advertising is to persuade them to buy products (Comstock, 1991; Van Evra, 1990; Young 1990). In one study, Robertson and Rossiter (1974) examined first- , third- , and fifth-grade boys' understanding of commercial intent. The boys answered questions such as "What is a television commercial? Why are commercials shown on television? What do commercials try to get you to do?" Their responses revealed their comprehension of **assistive** and **persuasive intent.** When they viewed commercials as having assistive intent, children understood commercials as informative messages about products. When they viewed commercials as having persuasive intent, children understood that the commercial was trying to get them to buy products. As they got older, children increasingly answered these questions in ways that reflected their comprehension of persuasive intent. Approximately 50 percent of first graders gave answers reflecting their comprehension of assistive and persuasive intent. By the third grade, 68 percent of the answers revealed comprehension of assistive intent, but 87 percent indicated comprehension of persuasive intent. By the fifth grade, children overwhelmingly understood advertisements as persuasive messages. Specifically, 55 percent of fifth graders gave responses indicating comprehension of assistive intent, but 99 percent gave responses indicating comprehension of persuasive intent. These results suggest that children begin to understand persuasive intent at about 7 to 8 years of age, with most children mastering this concept by about 10 or 11 years. Comstock (1991) argued that unless children understand the persuasive intent of commercials, their ability to discriminate the commercial from the program is irrelevant.

According to Macklin (1987), researchers have relied too much on verbal methodologies when examining children's comprehension of commercials. She assessed preschoolers' understanding of commercials using a nonverbal methodology. For example, she showed children a commercial and asked questions about what the elves (the product endorsers) wanted them to do. To answer, they pointed at a picture using an "answer wand." The correct response was a picture of a shopping trip in which they go to the store and buy a product. As Table 5.2 shows, none of the 3-year-olds, 7.5 percent of the 4-year-olds, and 20 percent of the 5-year-olds answered the nonverbal item correctly. Therefore, although a few children could answer this question, most could not. In a second study, Macklin (1987) had children view a commercial and then act out the commercial intent (that is, buying a product) in a play situation. None of the 3- or 4-year-olds were able to do so, but 40 percent of the 5-year-olds could. The results suggest that by age 5, some children are beginning to understand that advertisers want them to go to a store and buy their product. Even so, the results do not indicate that these children understand the underlying persuasive function of advertising (Macklin, 1987).

With comprehension of persuasive intent comes cynicism and distrust about the advertised goods (Rossiter, 1980b). Distrust begins to emerge by the second grade and is evident for most sixth graders (Rossiter, 1980b).

Cynicism about advertised products comes about, in part, because advertisers use production techniques that mislead a child about what a toy can do. Multiple

TABLE 5.2 Children's Understanding of the Informational Function as Demonstrated by Game: Study I

Understanding of Informational Function (Raw Number and Percent)	Age			
	3 Years	4 Years	5 Years	Total
Correct sketch selected	0	3	8	11
	0%	7.5%	20%	9%
Incorrect sketch selected	40	37	32	109
or no response	100%	92.5%	80%	91%
Total number of responses	40	40	40	120

Source: Macklin, N. C. (1987). Preschoolers' understanding of the informational function of television advertising. *Journal of Consumer Research, 14,* 229–239. Copyright © 1987 by the American Marketing Association. Adapted with permission.

tapings allow a toy race car to take the hairpin turn and make three major loops just right. Similarly, a wide-angle lens can make a toy look larger than it really is. Children's real-life experiences rarely duplicate the promises of the advertisements. Over time, children learn that the promise of the commercial does not match the reality of the product. Even so, children who view many advertisements are more likely to believe the advertisements than light viewers are (Atkin, 1980).

Adolescents continue to develop knowledge about advertiser tactics, even after they understand persuasive intent. Boush, Friedstad, and Rose (1994) examined the skeptical attitudes of sixth and eighth graders over the course of an academic year. Students completed a questionnaire on two occasions: when the school year began and when it ended. In addition to assessing their skepticism about advertisements, the questionnaire also asked students about their knowledge of advertiser tactics, such as the use of celebrity endorsements, animation, and humorous content. Knowledge about advertiser tactics increased over the course of the year. The more students knew about advertiser tactics, the more skeptical they became. The findings suggest that teaching adolescents about advertiser tactics may create discerning consumers.

Knowing that advertisements are designed to sell products presumably leads older children to develop **defensive safeguards** (Kunkel & Roberts, 1991). Defensive safeguards are mechanisms children develop to protect themselves from commercial manipulation once they understand the persuasive intent of advertising. However, this knowledge may be insufficient to alter children's interest in advertised products (Young, 1990). For example, children who knew that commercials were designed to sell them products initially chose fewer advertised products than those who did not realize advertisers' intent; however, repeated exposure to advertising during the Christmas season eliminated those "defenses" (Rossiter & Robertson, 1974). Similarly, 14-year-old boys wanted a toy race car that a celebrity endorsed just as much as 8-year-old boys did, with both sets of boys overestimating how big and fast the toy race car was (Ross et al., 1981).

Cynicism, then, does not necessarily mean that children will not succumb to advertisements (Comstock, 1991; Condry, 1989; Van Evra, 1990). There is no evidence, for example, that children apply cynical attitudes about advertisements in general to specific products (Rossiter, 1980b). It's much like the American public's view of politicians. Although we are cynical about Congress, we like our own particular representatives, and we continue to reelect them.

Behavioral Effects: Product Requests and Purchasing Patterns

As we have seen, commercials influence children's attention and their recognition of product names, but do they get children to buy the product? It's far easier to produce changes in knowledge than to prompt behavioral change.

Prior attitudes and consumer characteristics influence children's interest in products (Stewart & Ward, 1994). Children's age and the amount of exposure that they have had to commercial advertisements influence their purchasing decisions (Robertson & Rossiter, 1977). The more children are exposed to commercial messages, the more likely they are to request advertised toys and foods (Atkin, 1980; Atkin, 1982; Goldberg, Gorn, & Gibson, 1978). For example, heavy viewers of Saturday morning advertisements asked to go to fast food restaurants and requested more cereals and toys than light viewers did (Atkin, 1980).

Since many television programs advertise children's food products, particularly cereal, researchers sometimes study children and their parents at the supermarket. In a study by Galst and White (1976), 3- through 11-year-old children viewed advertisements in a laboratory setting. The researchers also collected data on the children's viewing of commercial television at home, and then observed them with their parents at the supermarket. Children who were most attentive to the commercials in the laboratory and who viewed the most commercial television at home made the most requests for products at the supermarket.

Similarly, Stoneman and Brody (1982) examined children and their parents at the supermarket after they had viewed television programs that: (1) had no advertisements; or (2) had advertisements interspersed in the programming. Children who viewed the programs with the commercials asked for more of the advertised products than children who did not see the commercials.

Premiums also influence children's cereal selections. For example, Atkin (1980) asked mothers about what children said when they asked for particular cereals. Forty-five percent of the mothers spontaneously reported that children asked for the premium, and an additional 36% percent mentioned the premium when asked directly about it. The more Saturday morning television children viewed, the more likely they were to ask for premiums.

Requests sometimes lead to conflict when parents do not buy the desired product. For example, Atkin (1980) found that the more children viewed advertisements, the more conflict they had with their parents about purchasing

Television commercials influence children's interest in advertised products.

advertised products. Twenty-one percent of children who were heavy television viewers reported a lot of arguing when their parents denied their requests for cereals and toys, but only 9 percent of the light television viewers reported a lot of arguing. Arguments over cereals occurred most often when a premium was involved.

DECEPTIVE PRACTICES IN CHILDREN'S ADVERTISEMENTS

Fairness issues and deceptive practices have been important issues in children's television advertising (Condry, 1989). Deception comes down to a simple point: if children do not understand the persuasive intent of commercial advertisements, is it fair to influence their buying patterns? The Federal Trade Communication (FTC) is charged with ensuring fair advertising practices, and, as we shall see in the next chapter, it has examined the issue of children's television advertising in considerable depth.

One way advertisers deceive children is by using terms like *fruit* to describe artificial flavors. Ross and colleagues (1981) examined 5- to 12-year-old children's understanding of whether fruit was really included in cereals and beverages labeled as: (1) real fruit; (2) nonfruit; or (3) artificial fruit flavor. Although children could understand the presence or absence of fruit in the real fruit and the nonfruit conditions, they were confused about whether fruit was present in the artificial fruit-flavor products. This confusion was still prevalent for older children, suggesting that the commercial practice of describing products as "fruit flavored" is misleading to children.

One potential way to improve children's understanding of commercial material is to use disclaimers that tell viewers about the limitations of the product, such as "batteries not included" (Young, 1990). About half of commercial advertisements directed at children have at least one disclaimer

(Kunkel & Gantz, 1992). Commercial advertisers, however, do little to make these disclaimers clear and comprehensible to children. For example, many disclaimers are presented only on the audio track or in small print at the bottom of the screen (Van Evra, 1990). Perceptually salient techniques (for example, sound effects) that are likely to recruit attention and improve comprehension of the message are rarely used in disclaimers (Van Evra, 1990). For example, kindergarteners and first graders do not understand the disclaimer "part of a balanced breakfast," which is typically presented only on the audio track (Palmer & McDowell, 1981). Indeed, children may believe that they need the cereal for a balanced breakfast (Barcus, 1980), and they remember relatively little about the other products that are portrayed with the cereal.

Incomprehensible dialogue is another problem with disclaimers. Not many youngsters understand "assembly required," but they do readily understand the words "you have to put it together" (Liebert et al., 1977). Similarly, Stutts and Hunnicutt (1987) found that the majority of a sample of preschoolers did not understand disclaimers, even when researchers used nonverbal methods to assess their comprehension. Based on their findings, the authors recommended that simpler disclaimer wording be investigated, such as: "You'll have to buy the batteries" rather than "Batteries not included," or "You have to buy each toy by itself" rather than "Each sold separately."

Because many young children have difficulty in understanding the difference between the commercial content and the program material (Blatt, Spencer, & Ward, 1972; Palmer & McDowell, 1979), **commercial separators** are used to mark off the commercial from the program content. Commercial separators are brief, often animated segments presented just after the program goes to commercials, and then again just before the program returns. Palmer and McDowell (1979), for example, showed kindergarteners and first graders one of four conditions: a control program with commercials and no separators, or one of three network separators breaking apart the commercials and the program content. Periodically, the investigators stopped the tape and asked the children if they were viewing the program or a commercial. Children in the control condition correctly discriminated the commercials from the program content just as often as children in the experimental conditions. Specifically, their comprehension was not much better than chance. These findings suggest that commercial separators are not particularly effective in aiding children's understanding of the differences between commercials and programs.

CONSUMER EDUCATION PROGRAMS

Since the commercial nature of television continues to be its reason for being, educators and researchers have attempted to design programs that will teach children about the intent of advertisements. They expect these programs to help children construct defenses to protect themselves from commercial messages (Pecora, 1995). Though the programs have been somewhat successful, very young children do not understand persuasive intent.

Using information processing theory, Costley and Brucks (1986) attempted to eliminate age differences in children's understanding of advertisements by teaching them about products. They compared boys who were 8 to 9 and 11 to 12 years old, that is, those who would be in the early versus late part of Piaget's concrete operational stage. The younger boys were assigned to one of two conditions: a low-knowledge condition or a high-knowledge condition, induced by teaching children about products. The older boys were all in the high-knowledge condition because they all understood quite a bit about products. The boys saw a print commercial about a new bike that included deceptive information in it. Boys in the treatment condition received additional information to enable them to understand contradictions in the advertisements. The researchers then asked the boys about the bike and coded their responses according to the amount they elaborated on the messages by providing either counterarguments or support arguments for the product. Boys who received more knowledge did not show improved cognitive evaluative skills regarding the advertisements. In fact, inaccurate supportive arguments for the product, rather than counterarguments based on the contradictions shown in the product advertisement, increased. Moreover, product knowledge did not eliminate age differences in children's evaluative skills. These findings suggest that age differences in comprehension cannot be eliminated just by increasing product knowledge, a finding consistent with Piagetian theory.

Older children often do show benefits from carefully constructed consumer education programs. For example, Roberts and colleagues (1980) examined two instructional films designed to teach children about the persuasive techniques used in advertising. One was called *The Six Billion $$$ Sell* and the other *Seeing Through Commercials*. These two fifteen-minute films taught children about the tactics advertisers use in commercials, including celebrity endorsements, exaggerations about the effectiveness of the product, and special camera effects that make a product look better than it is.

Two studies were conducted. In the first study, fourth, sixth, and eighth graders viewed either *The Six Billion $$$ Sell* or a control film. After viewing, children were tested on their *general skepticism* about advertisements. One week later, children watched five commercials and were then tested on their *general sophistication* about the issues covered in *The Six Billion $$$ Sell* and on whether they applied the *specific techniques* discussed in the film to the commercials they watched. As Table 5.3 reveals, the authors found that the children who viewed *The Six Billion $$$ Sell* were more skeptical about advertisements, were more sophisticated about advertisements, and applied the techniques from the film to advertisements more than the control group did. Effects were strongest for the fourth graders and for children who were the heaviest television viewers.

The second study also examined the effects of viewing the second film, *Seeing Through Commercials*. Second, third, and fifth graders viewed either *The Six Billion $$$ Sell, Seeing Through Commercials,* or a control film and were then tested for their skepticism toward commercials. The next day, children viewed commercials and were tested with additional skepticism measures. Overall,

TABLE 5.3 Mean Scores for General Skepticism, General Sophistication, and Techniques Scales by Grade and Treatment

	*Fourth Graders**		*Sixth Graders*		*Eighth Graders*	
	Mean	Number	Mean	Number	Mean	Number
General Skepticism						
The Six Billion $$$ Sell	7.4	28	7.3	29	6.7	23
Control film	6.2	30	6.6	23	7.1	20
General Sophistication						
The Six Billion $$$ Sell	15.9	28	15.1	29	15.5	23
Control film	12.6	30	15.3	23	15.8	20
Techniques						
The Six Billion $$$ Sell	15.6	28	15.9	29	16.7	23
Control film	12.4	30	14.4	23	16.4	20

Note: Higher scores indicate more skepticism. Obtained ranges: General skepticism, 3–9; general sophistication, 7–21; techniques, 5–21.
*Among fourth graders, all the means for children viewing *The Six Billion $$$ Sell* were significantly higher than for children viewing the control film (p < .01 for general skepticism and p < .001 for general sophistication and techniques).
Source: Roberts, D. F., Christenson, P. C., Gibson, W. A., Mooser, L., & Goldberg, M. E. (1980). Developing discriminating consumers. *Journal of Communication, 30,* 229–231. Reprinted with permission of Oxford University Press.

the children who viewed the treatment conditions were more skeptical of advertisements than those who viewed the control film, with *The Six Billion $$$ Sell* having a slightly stronger impact. These studies demonstrate that older children can learn to be more critical of commercial messages.

Public service announcements (PSAs), brief segments inserted into commercial programs, are yet another way to educate children about commercials. Christenson (1982) created a three-minute public service announcement designed to educate young consumers. This public service announcement was inserted into programming and commercial content directed at children. Children in primary school who viewed the public service announcement distrusted the advertisements more and became more aware of their persuasive intent than children who did not see the public service announcement.

Public service announcements can also be effective in altering the kinds of snacks young children select for themselves. Goldberg et al. (1978) exposed 5- and 6-year-old children to programming punctuated by either sugared snack and breakfast food commercials or pro-nutrition public service announcements. Some children viewed these commercials or public service announcements twice, the repetition condition, whereas the other groups saw the material only once. A control group saw no television program or products at all. After viewing, children were asked to choose three of six products they wanted to eat. These products varied in nutritional value. This procedure was repeated for three sets of product choices, for a total exposure to eighteen products. Children who viewed the pro-nutrition public service announcements

TABLE 5.4 Mean Number of Sugared Foods Selected by Exposure to _Fat Albert_ and Other Stimuli

Exposure Condition	Number of Children	Mean Number of Sugared Foods Selected
Fat Albert	15	2.87
Fat Albert plus PSAs	10	5.60
Fat Albert plus commercials	16	6.06
Control	20	10.20

Source: Goldberg, M. E., Gorn, G. J., & Gibson, W. (1978). TV messages for snack and breakfast foods: Do they influence children's preferences? _Journal of Consumer Research, 5,_ 73–81. Copyright © 1978 by the American Marketing Association. Adapted with permission.

selected more nutritious foods than children who viewed the commercials. The repetition condition increased children's selection of nutritional foods, but not of the advertised foods. The results suggest that young children's food selections can change when the children view messages about nutritious foods.

In a second study, Goldberg et al. (1978) examined an episode of a children's cartoon, _Fat Albert and the Cosby Kids,_ that focused on junk food. Specifically, the message was for children to moderate their intake of sugared foods and to eat more vegetables and fruits. Children viewed this program in one of three viewing conditions: (1) the pro-nutrition program alone; (2) the pro-nutrition program plus pro-nutrition public service announcements; or (3) the pro-nutrition program with typical commercial inserts. Goldberg compared these treatment conditions with the control condition from the first study. As Table 5.4 indicates, children who viewed the _Fat Albert_ junk food episode selected fewer sugared snacks than those subjected to the control condition (no viewing at all). This finding was true regardless of which of the three viewing conditions they saw. Overall, the program was also more effective than the public service announcements used in the first study, as assessed by the number of sugared versus nutritional snacks that children selected.

Taken together, these studies suggest that consumer education is one way to moderate the impact commercials have on child audiences. Specific programs that teach children about commercials, public service announcements, and well-made television programs can all moderate the impact of commercial advertisements. Behavioral changes occur in children as young as age 5. However, a sophisticated understanding of commercial intent is best taught when children are about age 10, the time when general cognitive changes allow them to understand the intentions and motives of others. Even at this age, when there is a very attractive product presented with contradictory information, children do not always pick up the correct message. These findings provide some support for both information processing theory and the Piagetian theory of cognitive development.

COMMERCIAL ADVERTISING PRACTICES ON THE INTERNET

What is happening now that many children are spending their time on the Internet and having personal interactions with characters like Batman? What issues arise when advertisers sell to children in cyberspace? Montgomery and Pasnik (1996), at The Center for Media Education, pointed to two fundamental issues in online advertising to children: (1) violating children's right to privacy; and (2) unfair and deceptive advertising practices. Currently, no legal guidelines prevent advertisers from using either of these practices.

Violating Children's Right to Privacy

Advertisers want information about potential buyers. While television is limited to mass marketing techniques, such as directing advertisements at 2- to 11-year-olds, online advertisers can collect information about individual children and specifically target each child based on his or her personal interests. One way to do so is to build a personal relationship with each child when he or she is online. The goal of this type of marketing is to sell products to children by developing a trust relationship between the young consumer and the advertiser.

As Montgomery and Pasnik (1996) point out, one tactic advertisers use to get children into their sites is to offer them prizes and awards for entering their contests. In order to win, children must register and provide personal information, presumably to collect their prizes. This information can include name, age, gender, and e-mail address—information that enables the advertiser to contact that specific child easily.

Using sophisticated computer programs, advertisers can also track exactly what a child or an adult does during his or her online time. Netscape Navigator, for example, leaves "cookies" behind at every site visited (Montgomery & Pasnik, 1996). Advertisers can develop profiles of individual users for individualized marketing tactics. For example, if a child spends her time interacting with animated characters, marketers can send that child e-mail about visiting the latest animated characters at various commercial sites.

Unfair and Deceptive Advertising Practices

The unfair and deceptive advertising practices used on the Internet extend some of the practices now regulated in television advertising. Specifically, (1) the distinction between commercials and programming is blurred; (2) no limits are set on how much time children can spend at advertiser's sites; and (3) hosts are used to sell products (Montgomery and Pasnik, 1996).

Seamless programming occurs when there is no sharp defining line between parts of a program, or in this case, between the program and the advertisements (Montgomery and Pasnik, 1996). In a television program, advertisers must make distinctions between the commercials and the content, but in online programming, the advertisements are often integrated with the content. For instance, children can read an online story and see visual icons within the story. If a child clicks onto that icon, he or she may enter a commercial site where products can be purchased.

Fantasy worlds are created about products for children to explore. Crest, for instance, has a fantasy world about toothpaste, and Crayola has a fantasy world about crayons. The purpose of these sites is to sell products and to create brand loyalty among young consumers.

Unlike television commercials, these commercial Internet sites are unregulated when it comes to the amount of time children spend at them. The more time children spend at a site, the more successful the advertiser is. Because children often use computers by themselves, parents are not likely to regulate their interactions with commercial content (Montgomery & Pasnik, 1996).

Hosts also take active roles in getting children to visit, to stay, and to buy commercial products from Internet sites. For example, Batman sends children a personal greeting after they enter that site (Montgomery & Pasnik, 1996). Because many young children are still confused about what is real and what is pretend, this new interactive opportunity with their favorite television characters gives advertisers more leverage in getting children to buy their products.

For older children and adolescents, tobacco and alcohol sites on the Web can foster illegal activity. Williams et al. (1997) from the Center for Media Education conducted a content analysis of alcohol and tobacco sites on the Web. Although it is illegal for minors to consume alcohol, the researchers found fourteen liquor companies and ten large breweries with sites likely to attract underage youth. These sites used techniques such as adolescent humor, hip language, and interactive games. For example, Cuervo's animated "J. C. Roadhog" and the Budweiser frogs are icons that attract children and adolescents. Children remember the content associated with these characters. For instance, more 9- to 11-year-old children were able to say the frogs' "Bud-weis-er" slogan than Kellogg's Tony the Tiger's "Eat Kellogg's Frosted Flakes. They're Grrreat!" slogan (Williams et al., 1997).

Some sites had "cyberbars" where a friendly bartender "chatted" with and gave advice to the user. At these chat sites, advertisers use **relational marketing,** in which the advertiser interacts with and gets to know the consumer in order to build individual product loyalty and to discover information about each potential customer (Williams et al., 1997). Advertisers also give away products, such as screensaving devices, or sell merchandise such as tee-shirts and caps to visitors.

Williams et al. (1997) found more than fifty sites devoted to smoking. Most sites did not overtly advertise to customers, presumably because of the regulatory atmosphere that now surrounds the tobacco industry. The tobacco industry has not advertised on television since the end of the Super Bowl in 1971, when it became illegal to advertise cigarettes on television or on the radio. Regulatory restrictions that could be extended from the radio and television industry to the Internet may keep the tobacco industry from moving aggressively into the sale of tobacco products on the Internet. Nonetheless, there are numerous pro-smoking sites on the Internet as well as opportunities to order tobacco products online. Cigar sites, which often promote cigar smoking as the hip thing to do, are also a well-established feature on the Web.

Recently, internal documents emerged that showed company executives of R. J. Reynolds targeted underage adolescents for tobacco consumption (Mintz & Torry, 1998). Although the targeting is not explicitly stated, the documents appear to indicate that animated characters like Joe Camel were created to increase RJR's share of young smokers (Mintz & Torry, 1998).

Solutions to Internet Commercial Issues

Montgomery and Pasnik (1996) propose two solutions to protect children from the commercialization of the Internet. The first is regulatory. The second involves using software that blocks children's exposure to advertisements.

The Federal Communications Commission and the Federal Trade Commission regulate advertisements during television broadcasts (Condry, 1989). Broadcasters cannot use hosts to sell their products, they must provide clear breaks between the program material and the commercials, and they can only advertise for a certain amount of time during each broadcast hour. Similar regulations could be instated for children on the Internet.

Software that blocks advertisements is another possibility for limiting children's exposure to commercial sites. **Banners,** which are a bit like billboards, appear on the Internet for children to click on to, thereby moving them to another site. For example, if children see and then click on the Chester Cheetah banner, featuring the animated character who advertises Fritos corn chips, they will move directly into the commercial site. A program called "Web Filter" blocks children's access to these ad banners on the web. Nevertheless, this type of program cannot deal with messages that are integrated into story content, for these commercials are not presented with a banner (Montgomery & Pasnik, 1996).

Software can also keep track of where children spend their time on the Internet. Parents can later view their browsing habits and restrict their access to specific sites that advertise to children. Some software also allows parents to use key terms, such as *alcohol* and *tobacco,* to block children's access and exposure to these types of products (Montgomery and Pasnik, 1996).

Educating children about advertising practices on the Internet is another way to help children understand advertisers' commercial intent. Specific sites on the Internet can teach children about commercial selling techniques.

SUMMARY

Advertising is the financial backbone of the commercial television industry in the United States. We use advertisements to create and to sell products to an audience, and television and the Internet efficiently deliver that audience to the advertiser. Mass technologies like television target specific groups, including children, but the Internet can target individual children and create a personal relationship to sell products to them. The new technologies have more potential to sell, and are less regulated, than the older mass technologies.

Advertisers spend millions of dollars each year to influence young consumers' buying habits, and the evidence indicates that these commercial practices are effective. Children attend to advertisements, recognize the products, and try to get their parents to buy some of the products. Parents often buy what children request, but conflict sometimes occurs when they do not. Premiums are a particularly effective technique for selling products to children.

Information processing theory provides a useful approach for examining the specific cognitive activities that must take place for commercial advertising practices to be effective. Specifically, a chain of activities leads from perception to attention, comprehension and memory, and, ultimately, behavior. Certain comprehension activities, such as understanding commercial intent, are not well understood until children are well into grade school. This suggests that Piaget's cognitive developmental theory may also be useful in understanding the effects of advertising on children.

Selling products is part of a capitalist society. Even so, questions of unfairness and deception arise when young children, who do not comprehend the commercials' intent to sell, are targeted by advertisements. Rules and guidelines federal agencies have developed, which we will explore in more depth in the next chapter, offer one way of regulating advertisements so that they are as fair as possible to young children. Guidelines are not yet in place on the Internet, making the information highway a difficult place for young children to navigate.

CHAPTER 6

Media, Public Policy, and Government Regulation

Mrs. Simpson's friends come to her door to protest a nude statue that is coming to their town. It is Michelangelo's David. Mrs. Simpson does not think that David should be censored. She believes David is a work of art, and she wants to see him.

After serious thought, Mrs. Simpson concludes that the freedom that allows her to see Michelangelo's David is the same freedom that allows the broadcasters to show violent television programs like *The Itchy and Scratchy Show*. She visits the art museum to see David with her husband and abandons her campaign against violent television programs.

For decades, critics have raised issues such as: should television stations be allowed to broadcast violent television programs, even when they are cartoons like *The Itchy and Scratchy Show?* Should the commercial stations broadcast more educational and prosocial programming, like the public broadcasting system which features *Sesame Street* and *Mister Rogers' Neighborhood?* Is it unfair and deceptive to advertise products to young children who are incapable of understanding the intent of commercials (that is, to get viewers to buy products)? If the networks refuse to accept their fiduciary responsibility to young viewers, should the government regulate television content? If "Big Brother" watches you, can it lead to beneficial rather than to harmful effects, or is governmental intrusion to be avoided at all costs?

Business interests involve profits, not social agendas. However, because television stations use the public air waves to broadcast their programs, commercial stations have a responsibility to serve the interests of all viewers, including children. Put another way, broadcasters do not own the air waves; they are granted a license to use them for a specific period of time, and they must then renew their license. However, no television station has ever lost a license because of the kind of programming it broadcasts (Condry, 1989).

Because commercial television programs only exist so that viewers will buy the products they advertise, it is exceedingly difficult to alter industry practices without some form of government intervention. The Simpson episode illustrates the complexity involved in censoring content that certain groups find objectionable: what is unacceptable to one person may be acceptable to another. The tension between the First Amendment, guaranteeing freedom of speech, and the responsibility and right to protect children has driven the children-and-television agenda. It has also emerged as a concern in the computer industry, particularly in regard to the Internet.

OVERVIEW

Although the American people generally view television programming as harmless entertainment, the commercial networks see themselves as businesses that deliver an audience to advertisers. This revenue-based approach to programming shapes decisions that deliver the largest audience with the most money to purchase products to the advertisers (Huston, Watkins, & Kunkel, 1989). Television programs are the "bait" (Melody, 1973).

By contrast, the public television financial base comes from governmental support, individual contributions, and grants from corporations. The lack of advertising on PBS allows that system to broadcast different types of programming to a smaller audience. Quality children's television programs flourish in this kind of atmosphere (Huston et al., 1989).

Because of the First Amendment, guaranteeing freedom of speech, commercial networks have considerable freedom to broadcast any type of programming (Liebert & Sprafkin, 1988). However, the air waves that the broadcasters use actually belong to the people. Broadcasters are therefore obligated to address the needs of the entire audience. This mandate includes children, who have less money to support the commercial industry, and hence, who are a less desirable audience to advertisers (Jordan, 1997a).

The responsibility of broadcasters differs from the responsibility of newspapers or of magazines because the public owns the air waves, and thus a government agency, the Federal Communications Commission, regulates these air waves (Liebert & Sprafkin, 1988). By contrast, newspapers and magazines are privately owned, and no limits are placed on the number of publications that can be disseminated. There are, however, a limited number of air waves, which make them a valuable public resource (Condry, 1989).

After years of controversy about children's programs, Congress passed the **Children's Television Act of 1990.** This law requires television stations to broadcast educational and informational programming for young viewers, and it regulates the amount of time advertisers can show commercials on children's television. The **Federal Communications Commission (FCC),** which oversees television station license renewals, is enforcing this law. Because the networks broadcasted a minimal amount of children's programming to meet their obligation to the child audience, the FCC (1996) implemented a **three-hour rule** in 1996, mandating that each television station broadcast a minimum of three hours of educational and informational programming each week. This rule became effective in the fall of 1997 (Jordan & Sullivan, 1997).

In addition, a legislative movement to regulate television content led to a voluntary agreement with the networks to rate programs for content that may be objectionable to parents (Farhi, 1997a). These ratings will allow parents to block access to violent television content by using a V-Chip. Parents will also be able to censor other types of programming.

New technologies, including cable television, video games, computer software, virtual reality games, and the Internet, are not subject to the same kind of regulation because they do not use a scarce public resource: the public air waves. Even though the same content issues, such as children's exposure to violent and sexual images, are concerns in the new technologies, the marketplace will dictate the types of programs developed and distributed. That's because the government does not regulate computers or newspaper content as it does the broadcast air waves.

In 1997, the Supreme Court overturned legislation prohibiting the transmission of pornographic material to minors on the Internet (Chandrasekaran, 1997). Some authorities have proposed developing software that blocks access to pornographic material, similar to the V-Chip in television sets, as an alternative to regulating the content of video games and materials on the Internet (Chandrasekaran, 1997). To understand the legal aspects of this issue, we will begin by examining the structure of broadcast television and the government agencies that regulate the television industry.

STRUCTURAL ASPECTS OF THE TELEVISION INDUSTRY

When television first appeared in the 1930s, the broadcasters (that is, television stations) were placed under the authority of the Federal Communication Commission (FCC), just as broadcast radio was (Condry, 1989). The FCC's decisions and policies depend largely on the U.S. President, who nominates FCC members for seven-year terms, and on Congress, who confirms these appointments. The original networks, the American Broadcasting Company (ABC), the Columbia Broadcasting System (CBS), and the National Broadcasting Company (NBC), were granted licenses to broadcast programming to viewers. These networks are corporations that own and operate some stations and that attempt to gain the affiliation of other stations (Condry, 1989). As Table 6.1 shows, the FCC now grants licenses to three major types of local broadcasters: (1) owned-and-operated stations; (2) network-affiliated stations; and (3) independent stations (Jordan & Sullivan, 1997). In 1992, the networks owned and operated approximately 20 percent of the stations; another 60 percent were affiliated with a major network; and the remaining 20 percent were independent (Jordan & Sullivan, 1997). This means that the major networks influence most of the programming on television.

Licenses now last five years, so that the FCC must renew a station's license at the end of each five-year period (Condry, 1989). Historically, license renewal was virtually automatic for any station that applied to the FCC. Nevertheless, because the networks transmit their programs on public air waves free of charge, they are required to broadcast content that serves "the public interest, convenience, and necessity" (Communications Act of 1934, p. 51). In addition, the **Federal Trade Commission (FTC),** another government agency, enforces fairness rules and prevents advertisers from using deceptive practices (Condry, 1989).

TABLE 6.1 Types of Local Broadcasters

Type	Description
Owned and Operated	Stations owned by specific networks
Network-Affiliated	Stations that sign contracts with the major networks; 70 percent of network affiliate programming typically comes from the networks by satellite
Independents	Stations that buy their programming on the open market from syndicators, not from or through the networks

Television stations are protected by the First Amendment, which guarantees freedom of speech (Huston & Wright, in press). The American people did not want the government to control what the television industry broadcasts, for censorship could violate democratic principles. For instance, most Americans do not want the news they view subject to regulations and censorship, for politicians could interfere with stories that might harm their chances for reelection or hurt their own political agendas. The freedom of the press and of television ensured that media would be independent of government and an ally of the people. This dual responsibility, to regulate the content of television but also to protect the broadcasters' right of free speech, left the FCC in an awkward position to enforce policies and rules (Liebert & Sprafkin, 1988).

In the beginnings of television, legislative solutions were not a consideration. Although violent programs have been a concern since television began (Huston & Wright, in press), quality programming for children appeared abundantly in those early days. Melody (1973) reported that 27 hours of children's programs were available per week in 1951; most programs were broadcast on weekdays. Many programs were educational in nature, and many featured live actors (Huston et al., 1989).

The Financial Base of Television Programs

As the networks realized they could make enormous commercial profits, children's programs became less attractive to broadcasters (Condry, 1989). The profit motive operating within commercial television drove the creation of programs that attracted the largest audience at the lowest cost. The preferred audience was single, affluent, and 18 to 49 years old, for these individuals had the most control over financial resources (Liebert & Sprafkin, 1988). Sports programming on Sundays became common, and the advertisers flashed cars, beer, and other products across the screen. This commercial approach to financing television programs remains the norm today, and it is one of the reasons for the problems in children's television (Huston et al., 1992).

Segments of the audience with less disposable income were relegated to time blocks when more desirable members were absent. Romantic soap operas were broadcast to women at home in the afternoon, supported by a host of home cleaning products. Children's television programs became a standard feature of Saturday morning when adults were often sleeping. Commercials for toys and sugar-coated cereals were sprinkled throughout the children's schedule.

Television program development is a costly venture. Networks do not want to risk any audience loss, particularly by developing expensive new programs that might not attract large numbers of viewers (Liebert & Sprafkin, 1988). The broadcasters developed story "formulas" that seemed likely to deliver large audiences to advertisers (Liebert & Sprafkin, 1988). These formulas included action-and-violence stories for child-oriented cartoon adventures and for adult-oriented action adventures. These formulas reliably drew and kept their audiences, and the broadcasters retained them as one keeps a tried-and-true old friend. The networks could depend on them for bringing in the audiences they needed to attract advertisers.

Broadcasters determine the effectiveness of a program in attracting an audience by measuring viewership (Condry, 1989). Nielsen has long measured audience viewership of specific programs and sold this information to broadcasters. Advertisers pay more money to place their commercials in blocks of time that attract more viewers. Two basic statistical measures come into play: **ratings** and **shares.** Ratings measure the percentage of the total population watching a particular television program. If a program has a rating of 30, then 30 percent of those who have a television are viewing that program. Shares measure the percentage of the available audience watching television at a given point in time (Liebert & Sprafkin, 1988). For instance, fewer viewers watch television on Saturday morning than during prime-time programs broadcast in the evenings. A broadcaster will draw a certain share of the available audience during that time.

Whether a television program succeeds or is dropped from the schedule depends on its ratings and shares. Put another way, the size of the audience is a key determinant in selecting the programs television stations will broadcast. For a program to be viable, an audience share of one-third was once required, based on drawing an equal share of the audience split between the three major competitors: ABC, NBC, and CBS (Liebert & Sprafkin, 1988). Given the addition of FOX, cable stations, other independent stations, and PBS stations, the share of the viewing audience has been shrinking for specific stations. Profits drop when a program attracts insufficient viewers because advertisers do not want to pay to sponsor such a program. Educational television is thus not a priority for broadcasters, in part because the audiences are smaller, and hence, yield lower profit margins.

GOVERNMENT REGULATION OF TELEVISION CONTENT AND ADVERTISEMENTS

Because of governmental pressure, networks have altered some programming decisions (Condry, 1989). Political shifts in the priorities of Congress and the President and in the composition of the FCC and FTC lead to eras of regulation and of deregulation, depending on who is in power.

Hearings typically foreshadow potential changes in federal policy toward television stations. Foremost among the concerns of Congress has been the issue of television violence, with the first hearings taking place in 1955 (Huston & Wright, in press). In spite of periodic Congressional hearings about the impact of televised violence on children's aggressive behaviors, little changed. As a result of the hearings, the networks elected to examine the issue and to regulate themselves. **Self regulation,** in which broadcasters set policies for themselves, was in keeping with the legal issues associated with the First Amendment right. However, as we saw in Chapter 2, television stations did not substantially decrease the amount of violent television they broadcast.

Consequently, the Senate Subcommittee on Communications asked the Surgeon General to appoint a Scientific Advisory Committee on Television and Social Behavior in 1969 (Huston & Wright, in press). Representatives of academia and industry participated, and social scientists submitted proposals to examine the television violence issue. The body of research this group produced convinced most academics that television violence increased children's aggressive behavior (Huston et al., 1989).

The industry selected voluntary compliance as the implementation policy, with the networks arguing that they reduced violence during the 1970s. However, independent assessments of television content conducted by Gerbner and colleagues (1978) found little change in the level of violence on television.

In 1974, the FCC advanced a policy requiring stations to provide programming for children. Five years later, a 1979 FCC Children's Television Task Force found that virtually no changes had appeared in children's programming (Huston et al., 1992).

The regulatory atmosphere of the 1970s did impact advertising practices. Many child advocates believed—and still believe—that commercials should be abolished from children's television programs (for example, Huston et al., 1989). Because of age-based limitations in cognitive skills, children are inherently vulnerable to persuasive messages in advertising (Federal Trade Commission, 1981). Put simply, it is unfair to advertise to young children because they do not understand that someone is trying to sell them a product. In fact, many 5-year-olds believe commercials are helpful because they show you what products are "really" like (Dorr, 1986). Many young children are also vulnerable to advertisements because they believe that their favorite characters are truthful (Huston et al., 1989).

Because they are at a disadvantage in understanding the goals of advertisers (Meringoff & Lesser, 1980), FCC guidelines established in 1974 protect children from some unfair practices. The **separation principle,** which supports using techniques to divide the program from the commercial content, was established because young children confuse the advertisements with the program (Ward, 1972; 1980). The separation principle consists of three guidelines: (1) the program host cannot advertise products within or during blocks of time adjacent to the program; (2) products cannot be integrated within the program for advertising purposes; and (3) separation devices must divide the program from the commercials (Huston et al., 1989).

Host selling is restricted because it takes advantage of the special status children give their favorite characters. When I was a young child, the teacher in a program called *Romper Room* used to walk to a different section of the classroom to sell products. Interestingly, the founders of Action for Children's Television originally targeted host selling on *Romper Room* as an example of unfair advertising practices (Adler, 1980). Because of the separation principle, it is no longer permissible for television characters or hosts to sell products during their program or in commercial blocks that surround their program. Similarly, a program like the *Teenage Mutant Ninja Turtles* cartoon could not be broadcast simply to sell products such as Teenage Mutuant Ninja action figures. In such **program-length commercials,** or product-related programming, the "program" is really a commercial.

Program separators help children distinguish the commercial from the program content. Separators are typically animated vignettes that break apart the program from the commercial material. For example, ABC shows marching toy soldiers who chant a message to separate the program from the commercials.

Commercials can also deceive children by including many products that the buyer must purchase separately. For instance, accessories shown with products like Barbie, such as her spa, are additional purchases. Advertisers must now use a **tombstone shot** at the end of the commercial where only the unadorned product is shown.

Concerns about deceptive practices in children's advertising led the FTC to hold hearings in 1978 about the use of advertisements in children's television programs (Federal Trade Commission, 1978). Based on the evidence, the FTC proposed banning or severely limiting the amount of advertising on television programs for children under 8 years of age. Because young children are unable to understand the persuasive intent of commercials, the FTC reasoned, advertising practices were unfair. Nor was there any other straightforward solution to the problem, for young children did not have the cognitive ability needed to evaluate children's advertising (Federal Trade Commission, 1981).

Congress effectively terminated the proceedings in 1980 by eliminating the power of the FTC to rule on unfair advertising practices (Huston et al., 1989). The FTC ended their proceedings in 1981, concluding there was no workable solution to the problem of television advertisements for young children (Liebert & Sprafkin, 1988). Without the financial base of advertisers, limited revenue was available to produce children's programs.

The political climate for regulating children's television changed after Ronald Reagan, a previous radio broadcaster and television and movie actor, was elected President in 1980. President Reagan selected Mark Fowler as the Chairman of the FCC, and Fowler **deregulated** children's television during the 1980s. Children were no longer considered a special audience who deserved protection. The marketplace would regulate itself (Fowler & Brenner, 1982).

With this philosophy in place, educational children's programs virtually disappeared on commercial television during the 1980s. On average, each commercial network broadcast informative children's programs for less than one hour per week in 1983 (Kerkman et al., 1990). Individual networks were no longer obligated to broadcast programs for the child audience. Cable, computer options, and other pay services were to join them in meeting any obligation to children (FCC, 1984). Obviously, poor children were least likely to have access to any of these pay services (Huston et al., 1989). PBS was the major station that created quality programs for children during the 1980s (Kerkman et al., 1990).

Another commercial practice the FCC accepted during the deregulation era was the program-length commercial (FCC, 1984). This policy reversed the earlier FCC (1974) guidelines which prevented broadcasters from integrating products into children's television programs. Toy companies produced low-cost animated children's programs about their products, and they distributed them to television stations for little money so that the stations would air programs about their products (Kunkel, 1988). In the past, toys were a byproduct of children's programs. Now the purchase of toys dictated the development of children's programs.

Because many children's programs such as *Teenage Mutant Ninja Turtles* were developed to sell toys, this practice essentially meant that children were viewing advertisements any time they watched television because the "programs" were really commercials. In fact, children are often confused about whether they are viewing a program or a commercial. For example, 23 percent of 4- to 11-year-old girls thought that a *Beetlejuice* cartoon was a commercial (Wilson & Weiss, 1992).

When children weren't watching television programs about products, they were viewing commercial advertisements about products. With deregulation, commercial advertisements tripled on children's television from the late 1970s to the late 1980s (Condry, Bence, & Scheibe, 1988). Deregulation policies were having a major impact on children's television programming.

In the 1990s, the political climate changed again. Congress, President Clinton, Vice President Gore, and FCC Chair Reed Hundt brought legislation and political pressure to bear on the networks to improve children's television programming (Farhi, 1995a; 1996b; Kaplan, 1997). In an invited address at the Family and Violence Conference, former Senator Paul Simon of Illinois (1993) recommended that broadcasters voluntarily reduce the amount of violence on television or face Congressional regulation. Based on a three-year content analysis at four different sites, an independent research group reported that children's television programming continues to contain high levels of violence (Donnerstein et al., 1997).

IMPACT OF THE CHILDREN'S TELEVISION ACT ON CHILDREN'S PROGRAMS

The Children's Television Act of 1990 set the stage for government to play a more active role in mandating the quality of children's television programs. This legislation came into being partly because of grass roots efforts led by Peggy Charren, the founder of **Action for Children's Television (ACT)**. ACT, a nonprofit organization advocating quality programs for children, was central in keeping issues about children's television before Congress, the FCC, and the FTC for three decades.

The Children's Television Act had two basic components: (1) it required the networks to create educational and informational programming for children; and (2) it reduced the amount of commercial time allowed in children's programs to 10.5 minutes per hour on weekends and 12 minutes per hour on weekdays. As a condition for license renewal, stations had to demonstrate compliance with the Act.

Educational and Informational Programming

The FCC began to enforce the Children's Television Act by creating guidelines for the television stations to follow. In two rulings, the FCC (1) interpreted the law as including all children age 16 or younger, though it did not require age-specific programs; (2) defined educational and informative content, though it allowed broadcasters to decide whether their programs met that definition; (3) refrained from setting firm policies on the number of programs or on the time frames in which stations could offer programs; (4) decided that **short-form programs** less than five minutes in length would count; and (5) refrained from providing uniform guidelines about how individual stations should document compliance with the law (Kunkel & Canepa, 1994).

Compliance with the law became a matter of debate when stations applying for license renewal submitted their lists of educational programs. Some stations claimed that programs such as *GI Joe* and *Ducktales* were educational, thus meeting the requirements of the act (Center for Media Education & Institute for Public Representation, Georgetown University, 1992). Plot summaries were written so that almost any entertainment program could meet the law. For example, the license renewal application for WDIV-TV in Detroit, Michigan, described an episode of *GI Joe* as follows: "The Joes fight against an evil that has the capabilities of mass destruction of society. Issues of social consciousness and responsibility are show themes" (Center for Media Education & Institute for Public Representation, Georgetown University, 1992, p. 6).

One reason stations could make these claims was ambiguity about the definition of an educational television program. The FCC defined **educational programming** as content that serves to "further the positive development of the child in any respect, including the child's cognitive/intellectual or emotional/social needs" (FCC, 1991, p. 21). This definition made it possible for entertainment programs to qualify as "educational" when stations applied for license renewal. The earlier description of *GI Joe* as prosocial is an example.

Other content analyses verified problems with the FCC's flexible requirements. When all programs the stations submitted were taken at face value as educational, each network broadcast an average of only 3 and one-half hours of children's educational programming each week (Kunkel & Canepa, 1994). Educational programs typically aired only in the very early morning hours (Kunkel & Canepa, 1994), often beginning at 5:00 A.M. (Jordan, 1996). Twenty-one of the 48 stations simply listed children's programs, making no claim that a program was even educational (Kunkel & Canepa, 1994). The overall amount of educational programming was not much greater than it had been in the 1970s.

Short-form programs, educational formats less than five minutes in length, were another area of ambiguity. Initially, there was nothing to prevent broadcasters from using this format alone to meet the programming requirement for children. Short-form programs are attractive because they can reduce the cost of producing educational programs for a child audience, and they can be dropped into blocks of time within more profitable entertainment programming.

The FCC held hearings to provide additional clarification to broadcasters about programs that did and did not meet the requirements of the Children's Television Act. In June 1994, network executives and social scientists provided testimony about progress and obstacles that remained in implementing the Act at the En Banc hearings. Broadcasters were producing some high-quality programs, such as *Where in the World Is Carmen San Diego?* Overall, broadcasters believed that they were making more progress in meeting the guidelines of the Children's Television Act than social scientists and children's advocates did (for example, Charren, 1994; Kunkel, 1994; Trias, 1994). Clearer rules about the requirements of the Children's Television Act followed.

The Three-Hour Rule

In 1996, the FCC moved to strengthen the enforcement of the Children's Television Act. One important change was the three-hour rule, which requires each station to broadcast a minimum of three hours of educational and informational programming each week, effective September 1997. The rationale for the three-hour rule was to remove market disincentives for creating educational television programs (Hundt, 1995). Educational programs are expensive to produce, and educational programs attract a smaller audience because programs must target a narrow age range (Jordan, 1997a). By requiring all stations to broadcast a minimum of three hours of educational programming each week, the FCC attempted to ensure no station was put at an economic disadvantage.

Core educational programming became another focal point of changes for license renewal requirements. To receive an expedited review for license renewal, stations must broadcast core educational programs that meet several criteria. First, the programs must be specifically designed to serve the educational and informational needs of children aged 16 and under; second, the programs must air between 7:00 A.M. and 10:00 P.M.; third, the programs must be scheduled on a weekly basis; and fourth, the programs must be at least thirty minutes in length (FCC, 1996). These requirements address some of the concerns about how the stations were implementing the Children's Television Act. Programs must now be shown during times when children are likely to be in the viewing audience, and programs cannot simply be recast as prosocial without a strong rationale for labeling them as such. Short-form programs and public service announcements can supplement core programming, but they are insufficient in themselves to meet the guidelines of the law (Jordan & Woodard, 1997).

According to Jordan and Sullivan (1997), television stations create their schedules with three types of television fare: network programs, syndicated programs, and locally produced programs (see Table 6.2). Networks produce or barter for their programs. Independent producers often create syndicated programs and offer them directly to local broadcasters; some syndicated programs are also reruns of series the networks previously presented. Stations produce locally produced programs in-house for their viewing audiences.

TABLE 6.2 Sources of Television Programs

Type	Description
Network Programs	Produced or obtained in syndication by the actual TV network
Syndicated Programs	Developed by independent TV producers and sold directly to local broadcasters; also reruns of older series originally shown on network television
Locally Produced Programs	Produced by a local TV station for that station's use

After the three-hour rule came into being, most stations elected to use the core educational programs broadcast by the major networks to meet their obligation rather than produce their own programs (Jordan, 1997a). This decision means the creative efforts of local television stations, which often exemplify community values, may disappear from the schedule. The 1997 fall programs for the four major commercial stations, a result in part of the three-hour rule, appear in Table 6.3.

Stations must also identify educational programs so that parents and children can find them (FCC, 1996). **E & I logos** (that is, educational and informational logos) had to be placed in programming as of January 2, 1997. Each station uses a different visual logo to indicate educational and informational programs to viewers. For example, ABC uses a lightbulb that whirs across the screen and says "Illuminating Television." Jordan and Woodard (1997) found that the majority of stations did identify their programs as educational and informational, though the identifiers often lasted less than five seconds.

Because the FCC does not conduct content analyses to measure station compliance in providing educational and informational programs for children, independent research groups provide assessments of program content and station compliance. Jordan and Woodard (1997) conducted one such analysis by examining a 1996 sample of commercial, cable, and PBS television programming. In addition, they extended the content analysis to a later sample of programs from the spring of 1997 that broadcasters identified as educational and informational. The researchers used the FCC definition of educational and informational programming: any content that will "further the positive development of the child in any respect, including the child's cognitive/intellectual or emotional/social needs" (FCC, 1991, p. 21). Thus, both traditionally academic and prosocial television programs were scored as educational. Quality television programs were those that scored high on the presence of a lesson. When the researchers analyzed the entire sample of programs, they found that PBS broadcast the majority of the quality children's television programs (see Table 6.4) The researchers then analyzed the sample of children's programs the commercial stations labeled as educational and informational in terms of their educational strength. They defined and evaluated **educational strength** as:

TABLE 6.3. Network Educational and Informational Children's Television Programming for Fall 1997

ABC

Disney's 101 Dalmatians: The Series
Brand Spanking New Doug
Disney's Pepper Ann
Disney's Recess
Disney's Jungle Cubs
New Adventures of Winnie the Pooh
Science Court

CBS

Beakman's World
Wheel of Fortune 2000
The Sports Illustrated for Kids Show
The Weird Al Show
Fudge
Ghostwriter

NBC

City Guys
Hang Time (two half-hour slots)
Saved by the Bell: The New Class (two half-hour slots)
NBA Inside Stuff

FOX

Bobby's World (every weekday half-hour each day)
Life with Louie

(1) lesson clarity, (2) lesson salience, (3) lesson involvement, and (4) lesson applicability. The top ten educational and informational programs from commercial television appear in Table 6.5.

Jordan and Woodard (1997) scored approximately 43 percent of the programs identified by broadcasters as educational and informational as *highly educational,* 35 percent as *moderately educational,* and 22 percent as *minimally educational.* Overall, then, the majority of programs met the guidelines for educational and informational programs, but 22 percent did not. Thus, a gap exists between what some broadcasters and independent evaluators rate as an educational and informational television program.

Advertising Regulations

The second facet of the Children's Television Act was to reduce the amount of commercial material portrayed in children's programs. This area of the Children's Television Act has received less empirical attention than the requirements for educational and informational television programming. However, numerous violations have occurred, with stations broadcasting more than

TABLE 6.4. Favorite Educational and Informational Programs of Parents and Children

APPC's* High-Quality Programs	Station	Parents' List[1]	Children's List[2]	Encouraged List[3]
Amazing Animals	Disney			
Animal Adventures	Disney			
Arthur	PBS	X		
Big Bag	Cartoon Network			
Bill Nye the Science Guy	PBS, Fox	X	X	X
Bloopie's Buddies	PBS			X
Blue's Clues	Nick	X		X
Book of Virtues	PBS			
Charlie Brown and Snoopy	Disney			X
Feed Your Mind	TBS			
Gladiators 2000	WB			
Grounding Marsh	Disney			
Gullah Gullah Island	Nick	X		
Iris, Happy Professor	TLC			
Just For Me	PBS			
Kidsongs	PBS	X		
Kratt's Creatures	PBS	X		X
Lambchop's Playalong	PBS	X	X	
Madison's Adventures	48-Ind			
Mister Rogers	PBS	X		
Mr. Wizard's World	Nick			
News for Kids	CBS			
Newton's Apple	PBS			
Nick News	Nick			
Numbers Alive	PBS			
PE TV for Kids	NBC			
Puzzle Place	PBS	X		
Reading Rainbow	PBS	X		
Ready or Not	Disney			
Richard Scarry	Nick, Showtime	X		
Rory & Me	TLC			
Sesame Street	PBS	X		X
Shining Time Station	PBS	X		
Story Time	PBS	X		
Teen Summit	BET			
Under the Umbrella Tree	Disney			
Voyage of the Mimi	PBS			
Welcome to Pooh Corner	Disney			
Where in Time Is Carmen San Diego?	PBS			
Why Why Family	WB			
Wishbone	PBS	X	X	X

Notes: * APPC = Annenberg Public Policy Center, University of Pennsylvania
[1] Favorite children's programs according to parents in 1997 APPC Survey (Stranger, 1997)
[2] Favorite children's programs according to 10- 17-year-olds in 1997 APPC Survey
[3] Programs parents encourage children to watch as reported in 1997 APPC Survey
Source: Jordan, A., & Woodard, E. (1997). *The 1997 State of Children's Television Report: Programming for Children over Broadcast and Cable Television.* Report No. 14, The Annenberg Public Policy Center of the University of Pennsylvania.

TABLE 6.5. Top Ten Educational TV Programs from Scoring of Broadcaster Labeled Educational Program

1. *Bill Nye the Science Guy*
2. *The New Adventures of Captain Planet*
3. *Gladiators 2000*
4. *Nick News*
5. *PE TV*
6. *Madison's Adventures Growing Up Wild*
7. *Bananas in Pajamas*
8. *News for Kids*
9. *C-Bear and Jamal*
10. *Hang Time*

Source: Jordan, A., & Woodard, E. (1997). *The 1997 State of Children's Television Report: Programming for Children over Broadcast and Cable Television.* Report No. 14, The Annenberg Public Policy Center of the University of Pennsylvania.

C-Bear and Jamal, a story about an African-American boy and his hip teddy bear, was one of the top ten educational TV children's programs rated by the Annenberg Public Policy Center of the University of Pennsylvania.

12 minutes of commercials on weekday children's programs and more than 10.5 minutes on weekend children's programs (Hayes, 1994). From 1992–94, approximately 25 percent of the nation's 900 television stations violated advertising rules for children's television (Farhi, 1995a). Forty-four stations were fined an overall total of 1 million dollars, 98 stations were admonished, and 100 stations received written warnings for minor infractions (Farhi, 1995b).

PARENT ADVISORIES AND PROGRAM RATINGS

As we discussed in Chapter 2, the networks are also rating their programs for different kinds of content (Farhi, 1997a). Initially, these ratings were rather general: *TV-Y* (for all children), *TV-Y7* (for children at least age 7), *TV-G* (for general audiences), *TV-PG* (parental guidance suggested), *TV-14* (for adolescents at least 14 years old), and *TV-M* (for mature audiences). However, researchers such as Cantor (1997) found that parents wanted more specific information so that they could make informed decisions about their children's viewing.

In July 1997, all major networks except for NBC agreed to provide additional voluntary ratings about the content of their programs beginning October 1, 1997. These ratings are *V* for violence, *S* for sexual content, *L* for coarse language, *D* for suggestive dialogue, and *FV* for fantasy violence, which is found in some children's programs (Farhi, 1997a). NBC was concerned that the purpose of additional codes was ultimately to dictate television programming content (Farhi, 1997a). These codes are now available on most television programs and enable parents to monitor their children's television viewing.

ROADBLOCKS TO QUALITY TELEVISION PROGRAMS

Roadblocks to quality children's television programs include broadcaster beliefs, financial blockades, and distrust between broadcasters and social scientists. After interviewing broadcasters, Jordan and Sullivan (1997) identified several pervasive beliefs that impede the development of quality children's television programs. Specifically, broadcasters held five beliefs: (1) that children won't watch educational television programming after school or on the weekend because they just spent all day or all week in school—they want to be entertained, not educated, during their leisure time; (2) educational programs are too expensive to replace the toy-based programs given to them at very low costs; (3) educational programs do not reap commercial profits because the content must appeal to a smaller audience to transmit an educational message effectively, and smaller audiences mean smaller revenues; (4) educational television programs appeal to young children, but older children won't watch them; and (5) the public has little interest in educational television programs.

Educational programs may be more attractive to parents and to children than the broadcasters believe. In surveying parents' and children's attitudes about television, Stranger (1997) found that programs identified as educational would be more likely to attract than to drive away viewers between the ages of 2 and 17. About 70 percent of parents were aware of network program ratings of *TV-Y, TV-Y7, TV-G, TV-PG, TV-14, TV-M*, and about one-third of these parents used these ratings to encourage and/or discourage their children from viewing programs. However, only about 2 percent of parents and children knew that the E & I logo stands for educational and informational programming. Overall, parents were more concerned with what their children watched, not how much they watched. These findings suggest there is an audience for quality television programs for children.

Currently, we are creating an Internet site to evaluate what children 7 to 11 years old are learning from programs broadcasters identify as educational and informational. This age group is one that broadcasters believe have little interest in educational programs. The Internet site, called the *Georgetown Hoya TV Reporters*, elicits children's comments about their favorite educational programs each week in a game format. Specifically, children are asked to identify the programs that they view, to select their favorite program, and to write about what they learned from that favorite program. By gaining this information, we can assess what they understand and learn. Younger children are designated as *Junior Bulldogs* and older children as *Senior Bulldogs*. Points are awarded each time a child sends us a report. We also produce a weekly newspaper with reports from our *Top Dogs*, the best reporters of the week. Over time, we will develop a database about the kinds of educational programs that are most effective from the children's perspective.

CREATING A MARKET FOR QUALITY TELEVISION PROGRAMS

Since commercial television programs only exist to deliver an audience to an advertiser, most advertisers really don't care much about the kind of content shown in the program. Advertisers simply want viewers to buy products.

Parents can potentially use this information to get better programming for their children. For example, parents could write advertisers and tell them that they will purchase the advertised products if the advertiser sponsors quality educational television programs for their children. Parents could then buy the products advertised by sponsors who are responsive to their request, as well as watch the programs with their children to ensure maximum effectiveness.

This strategy builds on the current network practice of selling blocks of advertising rather than selling time in specific programs. Since several networks are presenting their educational and informational programming in a block on Saturday morning, for example, advertisers could buy into that block of educational television programming. This strategy also allays network fears about losing a commercial audience when they broadcast quality programs for

The *Georgetown Hoya TV Reporters* is an Internet site where researchers collect information from children about their favorite educational television programs.

children. Even if the audience is smaller, the viewers become more responsive to purchasing the advertiser's products and show more loyalty to that advertiser.

Commercials are not the only way to make profits from children's television programs. Good television programs inevitably lead to spin-off products that can provide educational benefits for children and profits for advertisers. For example, parents will purchase videocassettes and numerous other products from programs without ever seeing advertisements for these products; *Sesame Street* and *Barney* products are an example. If parents identify, look for, and buy these kinds of products, they can also subsidize or encourage businesses to support quality programs.

Quality television programs require financial support from viewers. Public television is financed by the government, by viewers, and by commercial businesses. However, businesses **underwrite** rather than advertise on public television. In this arrangement, a company provides a grant to a program and is acknowledged for their support at the beginning of the program. Libby's Juicy Juice, for instance, contributes to the PBS program *Arthur.* Many corporations are involved in underwriting children's programs and have been for many years. Parents can write to these companies, praise them for their efforts, and purchase their products. Parents can also buy products associated with certain PBS programs, such as *Sesame Street;* revenue from these products is then funneled back into the creation of educational programs for children. In these ways, consumers can directly support their children's favorite PBS educational programs. Parents can also make financial contributions to public television and support governmental budget decisions that fund public television.

A remaining problem is the false dichotomy that classifies television programs as either educational or entertaining. Programs can be both. A promising trend is occurring as industry leaders and social scientists collaborate on how to create television programs that will both entertain and educate children.

Nickelodeon, a cable station, created three programs, *Allegra's Window, Gullah Gullah Island,* and *Blue's Clues* with Dr. Daniel Anderson, a social scientist, acting as consultant. Dr. Jennings Bryant is the evaluator of the programs. Cable stations like Nickelodeon have no legal obligation to broadcast educational programming for children. As a business decision, they targeted the child audience, creating a mixture of entertaining and educational programs. Their strategy was successful, for Nickelodeon's children's programs are very competitive (Friend, 1997). That means there is an audience for quality children's programs. In fact, ABC's ratings have improved since they introduced their new Saturday morning programs, which are predominantly educational (Jordan, 1997b).

In response to the passage of the Children's Television Act and the implementation of the three-hour rule, some networks have set up advisory boards which include social scientists. These boards provide advice to the networks about how to implement the Children's Television Act and about their overall children's schedule. Other social scientists serve as consultants for some of

Blue's Clues, an educational television program developed by Nickelodeon, represents a successful collaborative effort between academics and business to create an educational and entertaining program for young children.

these programs. ABC, for example, worked with Harvard Project Zero to create several new children's programs. These collaborative efforts could lead to better programs for children.

Identifying quality programs is important in creating a market for quality television programs. Stations are required by law to disseminate information to the public about which programs are educational and informational. Although educational and informational logos do identify programs, they appear quickly and are not always accurate (Jordan & Woodard, 1997). *TV Guide* has published educational and informational identifiers, but newspapers rarely publish them (Aday, 1997). Newspapers are reluctant to provide identifiers in part because they are concerned that the television industry will mislabel some programs as educational (Aday, 1997). Newspapers are also reluctant to review children's television programs, for they are not the most "important" aspect of programming to newspaper readers. Parent groups could request reviews of children's programs from newspapers.

Independent academic and consumer groups, such as the **Annenberg Public Policy Center (APPC)** and the **Center for Media Education (CME),** are taking steps to ensure the successful implementation of the Children's Television Act. Researchers from the Annenberg Public Policy Center rate television programs (Jordan & Woodard, 1997), examine industry beliefs that impede progress (Jordan & Sullivan, 1997), interview parents and children about television viewing behaviors (Stranger, 1997), examine newspaper and *TV Guide* coverage of children's programs (Aday, 1997), provide financial support to producers of children's programs (Jamieson, 1997), and organize conferences and press releases to bring interested parties together to improve children's television programming (Jamieson, 1997). This type of comprehensive effort increases public awareness of successes and failures in children's television.

After the passage of The Children's Television Act of 1990, Action for Children's Television (ACT) formally disbanded. The Center for Media Education has followed in ACT's footsteps as an advocate for children's television.

The Center for Media Education has an Internet site where people can access information about children's television. This site provides a place for a dialogue among those who are interested in quality children's television programs. Researchers and parents, for example, can tap into this cite and learn about the programs available to children. The site also contains information about other children's media issues, such as deceptive advertising directed at children over the Internet.

The strategies outlined here fit within the existing commercial and public funding system. Some researchers, however, advocate more radical change. For example, Huston et al. (1992) recommend the removal of economic pressures for programs to pay for themselves through advertising. One way to do so is to increase public and government funding of public television. Another way is to eliminate commercials in children's programs, a solution that seems unlikely to happen.

Ultimately, though, the litmus test of educational television will be whether children watch it in large numbers. Parents have a responsibility to make sure their children choose to view quality programming.

IMPLICATIONS FOR THE INTERACTIVE TECHNOLOGIES

It will be difficult to enforce regulation of content in the interactive technologies. It will also be difficult to get legislation to protect children from controversial material. Issues have already arisen about children's access to hardcore pornographic content. Although the Telecommunications Act of 1996 made it a federal crime to expose minors to indecent material on the Internet (Sussman, 1996), judges from New York and Pennsylvania ruled that the Communications Decency Act, one part of this law, was too broad (Schwartz, 1996). Specifically, Internet users could be prosecuted for disseminating materials that are generally protected under the First Amendment (Schwartz, 1996), such as print materials like the *Canterbury Tales* (Sussman, 1996). On June 26, 1997, the Supreme Court overturned the Communications Decency Act (Chandrasekaran, 1997).

Issues about pornography on the Internet and in computer software are also occurring in other cultures. According to Frean (1994), three of ten boys' secondary schools in England have pornographic computer games that depict violent sexual acts such as rape and torture. Sexually explicit material is purchased on bootlegged compact discs or pirated computer game software. Pornographic software can also be transmitted directly to children via computer terminals. The cost of an international phone call gives children access to pornographic material. Britain is attempting to regulate this material under the Obscene Publications Act, but the police are ill-equipped to enforce it, for few know enough about computers to investigate the problem adequately. Hence, the computer games industry is itself attempting to slow down the spread of hard-core pornography in homes and at schools.

Software that blocks children's access to certain sites is one solution to the free access issue. Using blocking software such as *The Nanny*, parents can prevent their children from entering sites with adult content, while adults continue to have access to these sites. Rating systems can also be utilized; video game manufacturers took this step to advise parents about violent content.

SUMMARY

Although broadcasters have a responsibility to serve the good of the people and to provide programming for their entire audience, including the youngest members, broadcast television is designed to sell products. As such, it creates programs that can deliver specific audiences to advertisers. The benchmark for a successful television program is the number of viewers it has, not how much children learn from it. Serving the people and running a business are not always compatible.

Government agencies such as the Federal Communications Commission and the Federal Trade Commission have regulated broadcasters since the 1930s. Governmental legislation, such as the Children's Television Act of 1990, has mandated that broadcasters provide educational and informational programs and limit advertisements to child audiences as a condition for license renewal. Voluntary rating systems and screening devices for television and computer content also identify sexual and violent content.

Ultimately, the journeys children will take down the information highway depend strongly on political and economic forces that have limited interest in children's development. If parents do not support quality educational programs for their children in the television, computer, video game, and virtual reality technologies, few such programs will be developed. Parent groups and other political organizations can alter media practices over time, as the mandate for educational and informational television programming demonstrates.

The Form of the Information Highway

When we were children, my younger brother and I used to watch scary programs together. Just when the scary scenes climaxed, I hid my eyes behind a pillow so that I wouldn't see them. (I'm not sure what he did because I couldn't see him.) How did I know when to hide my eyes?

W hen you watch a television program, you are not seeing the world exactly as you would in real life. Instead, quick changes in visual perspectives take place, along with major shifts in time and place, and more often than not, music plays in the background. You understand this representation of reality because you understand the "grammar" of the medium, which we call *formal features*. Even young children know some of the basic production conventions of television and film, such as how to avoid looking at the scariest parts of a program. For example, I knew that the music builds tension and then crescendos at the point when the actions become most frightening. I used that formal feature to guide my visual attention, just as other viewers do now.

Formal features are audiovisual production features that structure, mark, and represent content (Huston & Wright, 1983). As adults, we take this symbol system for granted. When we see a dreamy dissolve, we know that a dream sequence is going to occur, just as we know that the letters on this page represent words and thoughts. Children, however, must master this media code to understand televised messages, just as they must master reading to understand the messages in books. Some of these codes are easier to understand than others, just as some words are easier to understand than others.

The representational codes of film, television, and now computer, video game, and virtual reality interfaces also include formal features such as language, action, sound effects, and music. Consequently, children's journeys through the information age depend on their ability to understand these media codes. In this chapter, we will begin by examining exactly what these features are. Then we will examine the cognitive skills that children of different ages bring to the media. Finally, we will examine the specific role form plays in the way children process media messages.

Children can use the production techniques on a television sound track, such as a crescendo in the music, so that they don't see the really scary television content.

WHAT ARE FORMAL PRODUCTION FEATURES?

When television came of age, McLuhan (1964) argued that the power of the medium was in its form, not in its content. By that statement, he meant that *how* information is presented (for example, visually) is more important than *what* is presented (for example, the news). In the past two decades, researchers have begun to examine McLuhan's thesis by studying the impact form has on viewers, particularly children.

A research group headed by Huston and Wright defined various formal features and then began to study their use in television programs. A detailed list of the features and their definitions appears in Table 7.1. Formal features include *macro features* such as action and pace; *visual micro features* such as pans, zooms, and fades; and *auditory micro features* such as dialogue, sound effects, and music.

Macro Formal Features

Action refers to how much physical movement is present on the screen, ranging from no motion at all to very rapid motion. Some (for example, Calvert, in press) believe moderate action, which involves movements at about the speed of a walk, carries the most comprehensible visual messages to children.

Pace refers to the rate of scene and character changes. One can think of pace as the setting on a stage, with a new scene occurring every time the stage setting is changed (Wright & Huston, 1983). Characters in television and in film portrayals can go to a novel new scene; or they can return to a familiar scene they have been to before. For example, Fred Rogers (of *Mister Rogers' Neighborhood*) comes home and enters his living room; the living room is scored as a new scene. He goes to his kitchen to feed his fish, another new

TABLE 7.1 Formal Features of Children's Television Programs

Category	Definition
Macro Level	
Action	Gross motor movement through space, including locomotion activities such as walking, running, or riding in vehicles
Pace	Change of scenes, sets, or characters (unfamiliar or previously shown)
Micro Level—Visual	
Cuts	Instantaneous shifts between cameras
Pans and trucks	Vertical or horizontal camera movements
Zooms	Camera moves continuously in (toward) or out (away from) a scene or object in the scene
Fades	Picture/scene to black, followed by a different picture/scene
Dissolves	One picture superimposed on top of another as the visual image changes
Visual special effects	Visual camera techniques such as freeze frames, special lenses, distorting prisms, slow motion, fast motion, superimposition, trick photography, instant appearances or disappearances
Micro Level—Audio	
Dialogue	Adult, child, or nonhuman (for example, animals or robots) speaking to one another
Narration	Explanatory speech from a person off screen
Vocalizations	Noises that are not speech
Music	Prominent foreground music vs. background music overlaid with speech
Laugh track	Sound of laughter from unseen audience
Singing	Music and language in combination
Sound effects	Prominent noises

Source: Calvert, S. L. (in press). The form of thought. In I. Sigel (Ed.). *Theoretical perspectives in the concept of representation.* Hillsdale, N.J.: Erlbaum. Adapted with permission from Lawrence Erlbaum Associates, Inc.

scene. Then he returns to his living room, which is now scored as a familiar scene, because he has already been there. Characters typically move into and out of a combination of new and familiar scenes. Pace also involves the changes in the actual characters moving in and out of the set. For instance, a character change occurs when the mailman enters Fred Rogers's living room, and again when the mailman leaves.

As the pace increases, so do the processing demands placed on the viewer, who must integrate information across rapid changes in time and place (Anderson & Smith, 1984; Wright et al., 1984). This may challenge the cognitive skills of an older viewer and enhance his or her skills at putting information together over time. But a younger viewer may experience difficulty integrating this information because the pace makes it too difficult to understand.

Visual Micro Features

Visual features at the micro level include the various ways cameras are used. Camera techniques often parallel the ways we use our eyes to gather information. For instance, a camera can *pan* across a scene; you can create a pan motion by looking out the window and turning your head from left to right so that you can see the entire scene in your visual field. A camera can also *zoom* in to emphasize program details, or zoom out to provide a broader perspective of a scene. You can create a zoom motion by holding an object such as a ball in your hand; bring it close to your eyes (a zoom in), and then move it away from your eyes (a zoom out). Cameras can *dissolve* from one scene to the next so that one scene gradually disappears as the edges of the picture blur and another visual scene appears in its place; dissolves often represent major time shifts, such as flashbacks in time (Calvert, 1988). Cameras can *fade* to black to shift to a different scene; an analog would be looking out the window as you rode on a train, seeing a city passing by, closing your eyes and taking a nap (fade to black), and opening your eyes to see a new scene of countryside and farms passing outside the window. Cameras can also shift scenes with a *wipe* across a scene; the familiar scene exits (stage right) as the new scene pushes its way onto the screen (stage left). A camera can quickly *cut* from one visual perspective to another, as when one looks at an airplane flying through the air and then sees a new scene depicted as the camera cuts inside to the airplane cabin. Finally, cameras can show *visual special effects* by depicting impossible events on the screen. In *Terminator 2*, for instance, the newest "machine" could morph into any person it touched, including a police officer, a security guard, and even a young boy's mom.

As experienced viewers, we barely notice these media conventions. Indeed, in an effective production, form fades into the background with the viewer demonstrating little conscious awareness of its presence. But you can easily bring form into your consciousness: simply pay attention to all the changes taking place on the screen as you watch a television program or film. A young child must master the media conventions in order to understand the story being presented. Nevertheless, if segments are brief and simple, even young children can comprehend visual techniques like cuts, pans, and zooms (Smith, Anderson, & Fischer, 1985).

Auditory Micro Features

We think of television as a visual medium, but television would be far less interesting if no one spoke. Huston and Wright (1983) classified audio formal features at two levels. One level involved dialogue or narration, forms that carry meaning and advance a story line; the second level involved interesting sounds and music that can highlight certain program content, such as a crescendo in music when exciting or scary events occur.

Dialogue and *narration* involve verbal-linguistic forms of communication. These presentational forms carry much of the meaning of a story plot, and thus, are often the most informative aspects of a presentation. *Dialogue* can involve *child, adult,* or *nonhuman* speakers (for example, dogs can talk in television programs). *Narration* involves a person speaking about the program without interacting with other characters. Narrators talk directly to the audience.

Musical forms include loud *foreground music,* which often crescendos when important actions are taking place in the story. Music also sets the tone of a story. Scary music, for example, creates a particular mood for a story and can elicit fearful feelings from viewers. *Background music,* which plays behind dialogue, can also serve as a mood setter. Melancholy background music, for example, conveys the sad mood of a character whose best friend is moving away. *Singing* combines music and language in children's television programs. Fred Rogers, for instance, has been singing about how special each and every child is for the past 25 years.

Sound effects are unusual noises that occur in a story. Zips, bangs, and train whistles are sound effects found commonly in children's television programs. *Character vocalizations,* such as Fat Albert's "Hey, Hey, Hey" or Scooby Doo's "Scooby Dooby Doo!" are also nonverbal audio features often used in children's productions.

Form exists in every media activity, for all media must convey information by some type of representation. Action, sound effects, and rapid pace are found in video games, in CD-ROM educational software, and in virtual reality games. The conceptual framework surrounding formal features has been exported from the television area to these other technologies. We turn next to the ways children think and how this dovetails with the formal features of the media.

CHILDREN'S COGNITIVE SKILLS: THEORETICAL UNDERPINNINGS

To understand how form impacts children's memory of content, we must first consider the cognitive skills children have at various ages and how they use these skills. All modern theories of cognition view the child as active from the very beginnings of life: a child perceives, encodes, thinks about, remembers, and uses information to organize his or her actions.

Information processing models trace the flow of information through the child from input (through perception and attention) to output (a child's actions, be they motoric or linguistic). Children can also store information in memory without acting on the content at that time. Because information processing models were initially based on the way adults think, developmental differences in children's thinking were not initially considered. More specifically, we considered verbal ways of thinking (more of an adult's way of thinking) more than visual ways of thinking (more of a child's way of thinking). The first to consider developmental changes in how a child thinks (visually versus verbally) were **cognitive developmental** theorists such as Piaget and Bruner.

The approach we will take here will be an information processing theory sensitive to developmental changes in thought. As we trace the flow of information, we will consider the way children perceive incoming information, their attention to that content, how that information is represented in memory, their later memories of the content, and what actions, if any, they eventually take.

Perception: The Intake of Information

We live in a sea of stimulation. Every moment, we make decisions about what information in our perceptual field we will consider further, and what information we will ignore. These decisions comprise **selective attention,** which is influenced by the perceptual qualities inherent in information.

Perceptual Salience

Certain properties of information are likely to elicit selective attention and active processing because being responsive to these features has survival value for our species. For instance, movement signals a change in the environment; those who attend to, and respond to, movement are more likely to survive a potential predator's attack than those who do not. In 1960, Berlyne identified a set of these attention-getting stimuli, which involved characteristics such as movement, contrast, surprise, incongruity, and novelty. He called these attention-getters **perceptually salient** stimuli.

Extending Berlyne's theory of perceptual salience, Wright and Huston (1983) argued that certain television formal features were perceptually salient. For example, rapid action involves movement; new scenes involve novelty; sound effects, visual special effects, and character vocalizations involve incongruity and surprise (Huston & Wright, 1983). These features, they believed, were especially likely to elicit attention and interest from viewers, particularly the youngest ones. With age and experience, children were likely to attend more to informative features (for example, dialogue that advances a story plot), regardless of perceptual salience. In this model, young children were expected to be more interested in what people did, not what they said. As they got older, they were expected to be more interested in what people said.

As new technologies emerged, other researchers used the framework of perceptual salience to describe the forms of new technologies. For instance, Malone (1981) argued that the perceptually salient features in video games could create an intrinsically interesting learning environment for children. That is, environments that contain features like action and music were more interesting, and hence more engaging, to children. Because of this motivational appeal, children should spontaneously interact with that content, and consequently, would be more likely to learn it. Similarly, Silvern and Williamson (1987) described the action and sound effects that characterize the video games children play. They argued that these features impact children similarly, whether they are playing a video game or watching a television show. I examined action, sound effects, and language in the context of educational computer simulations in an attempt to identify interesting and informative features to maximize children's learning. Examining the form of the information highway became an important avenue for exploring how children understood its content.

In summary, perceptually salient formal features are techniques that "make it through" children's initial perceptual systems, thereby making it more likely that children will notice, and then process, the content. We turn next to how form influences children's attention.

Attention: Passing through the Gatekeeper

Once information enters our awareness via our perceptions (seeing, hearing, and smelling), we must then attend to the content further, or we will forget the information. Attention is often an auditory and visual experience for media users. Children listen to the sound track, and then they deploy their visual attention to content if it seems comprehensible and interesting (Lorch, Anderson, & Levin, 1979).

Through certain features, children learn that the content is for them and that the information is *comprehensible* (Anderson & Lorch, 1983). For instance, childlike language signals that the content is for children, not adults. *Sesame Street* has many child speakers in the vignettes so that youngsters will attend to the program. By contrast, adult dialogue signals content for adults, not for children. The evening news, for example, is targeted at adults. Children learn these *signals* early in life, and they direct their attention accordingly. From viewing different television programs, children construct schemas about what they should attend to and what they should ignore.

In every television program, there is a great deal of information for children to make sense of. Some of that information is important, and some is not. The important information, which advances the plot, is known as **central content** (Collins, 1983). The information that is irrelevant to plot comprehension is known as **incidental content** (Collins, 1983). Young children have difficulty discerning between central and incidental content, so features that are perceptually salient, such as sound effects, can help signal the important content (Calvert et al., 1982). Attending at just the right moment can improve children's understanding of that information. Because young children often attend selectively to important content when it is presented with perceptually salient forms, using these forms to highlight important media content can and does enhance their information processing activities.

Attending for long periods of time is a cognitive skill the older child develops. By about age 10, children are more likely to pay attention to important content, regardless of perceptual salience. This growing skill at sustaining attention and at choosing the right moments to attend makes older children less reliant on salience than younger children are.

But what about video games? Do children know when to attend to these games? Do they attend for sustained periods of time? Does perceptual salience play any role?

Think about what games often do in arcades—even when no one is play-ing them. They make interesting noises so that someone will come look at them and play them. Sound effects elicit attention to video games, just as they elicit attention to television programs.

Once a child begins to play a video game, however, attention becomes an essential skill for "survival." That's not true when a child watches a television program. With a television program, a child can wander away for long peri-ods of time and still pick up the program in progress. But if a child stops pay-ing attention to a video game, the game quickly ends. Indeed, the game can end quickly even when the child is paying attention! Many video games and computer games now have a pause button so that the player can stop, catch his or her breath, and resume play at his or her leisure. Even so, the interactive nature of the new technologies makes sustained attention necessary for success.

Representation and Memory of Information

Once a child attends to information, the information must be represented in some form or the child will forget it. Developmental theorists, including Pia-get (Flavell, 1963) and Bruner (for example, Bruner, Olver, & Greenfield, 1968) advanced seminal ideas about how thought changes as children age. Using Bruner's levels of representation, children move from *enactive to iconic to sym-bolic modes of representing information.*

Enactive modes involve representing information with the body. For ex-ample, when a baby moves her or his head from side to side to avoid eating the food on a spoon, that action comes to represent the concept of "no." In the new technologies, pulling a symbolic trigger in a virtual reality game can be-come encoded in one's muscles—conveying that this is what it feels like to shoot a gun, to pull a trigger (Calvert & Tan, 1996). Although young children rely more on enactive modes than older children do, even adults continue to use them at times, as when we point to give directions to another person. Sports is another area that makes use of enactive modes of representation—I know how it feels to hit a forehand down the line in tennis because it is en-coded and understood in my muscles.

Iconic modes involve representing information in a visual form (icons). Young children often rely on visual ways of thinking because pictures are con-crete and easily understood. A neglected area of visual representation involves moving, as opposed to static, visual images (Calvert, in press). Action can be a dynamic form of thought, yet it is an area that has received virtually no empir-ical attention. I once interviewed a 10-year-old boy who told me he could put the pictures from a television story in order by going back and rewatching the program in his head (Calvert, 1992). These representational capacities, which allow children to capture dynamic moving images, parallel the ways informa-tion technologies present content to users.

Echoic modes are similar to icons, but they involve the sounds objects make rather than visual images of the objects. *Onomatopoeia,* a poetic device that uses words that sound similar to their meanings, provides some examples of echoic imagery. For example, we all know that the "choo choo" sound means a train.

The developmental progression from concrete to abstract thought is characterized by the use of language as a way to represent information. The **symbolic mode** of words, comprised of arbitrary alphabetic symbols, can connote virtually any thought. Abstract concepts such as *fidelity* are much easier to express in language than in a picture.

By middle childhood, language has emerged as the preferred mode of thought. Words win in American culture. Literacy is a prized goal of Western culture, and children are encouraged to express their thoughts in language. Even so, children best understand abstract concepts when a picture accompanies the language (Bandura, 1986).

Abstract thought also involves the capacity to go beyond the information given and make inferences about content that was never explicitly presented. For instance, at about ages 9 and 10, children begin to understand the motivations and feelings of other people (Collins, 1983). Not surprisingly, this age is also the time when they begin to understand the motivations and feelings of characters in television stories (Collins, 1983). As children develop inferential cognitive skills, they apply them to both real-life and symbolic media experiences.

Action as Output

So what do children do with all this information that they have collected? In some instances, they simply store the information and it remains available if it's ever needed (Bandura, 1986). This, as you may remember, is the **acquisition** of information. In other instances, children use that information to organize linguistic and behavioral actions. When children demonstrate behaviors they have learned, it is called **performance.** Visual actions are particularly potent stimuli, for they serve as organizers for what one does, for one's movements.

While older technologies, such as television and radio, allow children to learn without necessarily acting, the new technologies require children to act. Video and virtual reality games, for example, require children to "shoot" their enemies, often by pulling a trigger of some kind. When this type of encoding occurs, the line between acquisition and performance disappears, making action a more important aspect of information processing. Enactive representations of pulling triggers are easily reenacted long after the game is over.

Summary of Cognitive Skills

In summary, children live in a stimulating world, and they must make constant decisions about what to attend to. Their perceptual sensory systems, which allow them to see, hear, and smell, are the initial entry point. Perceptually salient stimuli, which embody characteristics such as movement and surprise, are likely to elicit attention in the early phases of information processing. Once children selectively attend to certain information, they must represent it in some form, or they will never remember it again. Children's representations depend on their age and their cognitive skills.

When a technology matches its information delivery system with the ways children can think, then children's attention and learning are maximized. Children initially think in very concrete, often visual, ways. Later, they depend more on abstract thoughts, made possible by language development. Therefore, enactive, iconic, and echoic ways of thinking take center stage for young children, whereas abstract symbolic ways of thinking command center stage by middle childhood. The eventual output of this information-gathering activity is some kind of potential action, which can take place now, tomorrow, or never.

With television, there is always a lag between observing and acting. By contrast, the new technologies have no lag. We act immediately on information, giving it direct access into our behaviors. As we move into increasingly interactive technologies, enactive forms of representation (for example, pulling the trigger of a gun) will be readily available for real-life action.

EMPIRICAL INQUIRIES IN THE TELEVISION AND COMPUTER AREAS

To examine the impact of formal features on children's information processing activities, we will examine the empirical literature in the television and computer areas. We will begin with a discussion of how perceptually salient formal features impact children's visual attention in the television area. We then will examine the role formal features play in children's memory of content. Finally, we will examine the use of formal features in the new technologies in which motivation and learning issues have been explored.

Children's Attention to, and Memory of, Television Content

For formal features to impact children's memory of television content, children must first attend to that content over competing stimuli, a process called **selective attention.** Selective attention, as you may recall, is influenced by perceptually salient formal features such as sound effects and crescendos in music. There are two ways formal features can call attention to certain content. The first involves a very primitive orienting response to changes in the environment. The second way occurs when children learn that these features serve as markers, or signals, of important content. These are called the **salience** and the **marker** functions of features, respectively (Calvert et al., 1982).

Attention is necessary, but not sufficient, for children to comprehend and remember television content (Huston & Wright, 1983). Children's memory of televised content is an active process, guided by their attempts to understand the stories that so rapidly progress. Formal features, especially those that are perceptually salient, can help them to understand those stories in two important ways. The first way is through **contiguous presentation,** when important television content immediately follows salient auditory features like sound effects. If children look up when they hear these salient features, then they are likely to see and to process the content that occurs next. The second way, **modes to represent content,** involves the parallel between how content is presented and how a child thinks. For example, a visual depiction of the content may be represented in visual, iconic modes, whereas a verbal description may be represented in verbal, symbolic modes of thought (Calvert et al., 1982).

Attention to Television Forms

When children are viewing television, they do not sit and watch the set all the time. Instead, they play with toys, siblings, and friends, and they look at the television program when interesting events occur (Anderson & Lorch, 1983). Perceptually salient features can tell them when to look (Huston & Wright, 1983).

Children are often highly attentive to television content when a perceptually salient technique, such as a sound effect, signals that something interesting is about to happen.

By their very nature, visual events cannot get a child or adult who is not looking to attend to the television set. The one exception is when rapid visual change occurs on a television screen, as when the camera cuts rapidly across several successive pictures in many television advertisements. By contrast, perceptually salient audio events, such as sound effects and vocalizations, reliably get children to look at television content when they have become inattentive (Huston & Wright, 1983).

Children of different ages may attend to perceptually salient events for different reasons. Consider children who are playing with their toys in a room where a television program is on. In the program, a fire engine screeches down the highway, its siren blaring. A very young child will look at the screen because of the loud noise. Attention is involuntary, occurring because we are prewired to attend to sudden changes in our perceptual field. This demonstrates the salience function of features. The marker or signal function of features emerges when older children learn that something important is associated with a particular sound. When an older child hears that siren, she looks to see what is wrong because she has learned that sirens mean an emergency. This built-in human response to attend to an unusual loud sound, because it is salient or because it serves as a marker, can be used to call attention to program material that is necessary for understanding a story

Contiguous Presentation of Important Content

If you use a sound effect to elicit children's attention and then present important television content immediately after that sound, then children remember the contiguous content. In both correlational and experimental studies, perceptually salient features like sound effects and character vocalizations are associated with improved memory of the program material.

In an early correlational study (Calvert et al., 1982), kindergarten and third/fourth graders watched an episode of *Fat Albert and the Cosby Kids*. The researchers scored the formal features of the program, as well as each child's visual attention to the features in that program. After viewing, children's visual attention to those features was related to their memory of program content. Content was classified on two dimensions: (1) whether the content was *central* (necessary) or *incidental* (irrelevant) to the program plot; and (2) whether the content was presented with *perceptually salient* (primarily action in this case) or *nonsalient* (no action) features. The young children who attended to character vocalizations recalled the central content presented with perceptually salient features better than those who were less attentive to character vocalizations. In this story, Fat Albert uttered the vocalization, "Hey, Hey, Hey." Then he said, "I've got something to say." After that, he told children an important lesson of the story. The "Hey, Hey, Hey" vocalization served as a marker for the important dialogue that immediately followed, thereby increasing children's memory of the important, contiguous verbal content.

In an experimental follow-up of this study (Calvert & Gersh, 1987), three sound effects that made a slide whistle noise were inserted into an episode of *Spanky and Our Gang*. Kindergartners and third/fourth graders viewed the

TABLE 7.2 Developmental Differences in Mean Number of Inferential Items Correct as a Function of Sound Effect Treatment

Treatment	Kindergarten (N = 32)		Fifth Grade (N = 32)	
	Mean	Standard Deviation	Mean	Standard Deviation
No Sound Effect	2.00[c]	1.37	5.75[a]	1.06
Sound Effect	3.38[b]	1.45	5.69[a]	1.25

Note: Means with different letter superscripts are significantly different at p < .05 (that is, 5 chances in 100 that the differences occurred by chance).
Source: Calvert, S. L., & Gersh, T. L. (1987). The selective use of sound effects and visual inserts for children's television story comprehension. *Journal of Applied Developmental Psychology, 8,* 363–375. Copyright © 1987 by the Ablex Publishing Corporation. Reprinted with permission.

program, and their memory of the content was examined. Kindergartners who saw the version of the program with the sound effects selectively attended to the important story transitions. More importantly, as Table 7.2 shows, the kindergartners who heard sound effects understood the central, inferential story content better than their peers who saw the same program without sound effects. Older children, by contrast, did not need sound effects to remember the important story content. This finding suggests that with development, children can identify and remember important television content without the aid of attention-getting features. Young children, by contrast, are dependent on attention-getting features for accurate memories of televised stories.

In a second experimental study (Calvert & Scott, 1989), these same sound effects were inserted in two programs that varied in pace, the rate of scene and character change. After viewing, children were asked to put a series of pictures from the story in order—just as it happened in the story. As Table 7.3 indicates, sound effects increased children's attention to important story events, but only for those who viewed the rapidly-paced television programs. Children who attended to the marked story events also sequenced the program material better. The results suggest that slowly-paced programs are easy for children to understand; rapidly-paced programs, by contrast, may be passing by so quickly that the additional focus of a sound effect is needed to elicit selective attention.

Taken together, these studies suggest that producers of children's television programs can take a feature as simple as a sound effect, place it just before important story content, and improve story comprehension for their youngest viewers. This kind of technique is very inexpensive and could easily be added to existing children's television programs.

Modes to Represent Content: Visual Features Representing Time Shifts

Formal features also represent changes in time. A fade to black commonly represents a major shift in time and place (Huston-Stein et al., 1981). Dreamy dissolves represent even more distal events, as when flashbacks take one back to an earlier time and place (Calvert, 1988).

TABLE 7.3 Mean Selective Attention to Marked Story Events as a Function of Sound Effect Treatment and Program Pace

| | Sound Effect Treatment | | | |
| | Off | | On | |
Pace Level	Mean	Standard Deviation	Mean	Standard Deviation
Slow	3.31[b]	1.15	3.25[b]	1.30
Rapid	2.38[c]	1.50	4.08[a]	1.55

Note: Means with different letter superscripts are significantly different at $p < .05$ (that is, 5 chances in 100 that the differences occurred by chance). Each mean is based on 16 subjects.
Source: Calvert, S. L., & Scott, M. C. (1989). Sound effects for children's comprehension of fast-paced television content. *Journal of Broadcasting and Electronic Media, 33,* 233–246. Reprinted with permission from the publisher, the Broadcast Education Association.

Flashbacks are a particularly interesting time displacement in television portrayals because you can see visual events and scenes that others are remembering. This type of experience is not possible in real life, but it is in film and television.

Julia was a film that moved continuously between major shifts in time. Lilly was an elderly woman reflecting on her life, particularly her friendship with a woman named Julia whom the Nazis killed during World War II. As Lilly thought about her friend, she moved from the "present" to two time frames in the "past": her earlier childhood and her earlier adulthood. Transitions between time frames were represented by one of two camera techniques: either a *dreamy dissolve* or a *camera cut.* Mysterious music and sound effects, such as a train whistle waking her from a reverie, also marked time transitions. How would children understand these major shifts in time? Would they find it easier to understand dreamy dissolves than avant-garde techniques like camera cuts? Would they better comprehend flashbacks marked by sound effects than flashbacks with no attention-getting sounds?

Although *Julia* was too difficult for a young audience, some children's programs do use flashbacks. So to answer these questions, I edited two flashbacks in an animated children's television program named *Tarzan, Lord of the Jungle* so that the time shifts were marked with: (1) dreamy camera dissolves or camera cuts; and (2) sound effects or no sound effects (Calvert, 1988). Kindergarten and first- versus fourth- and fifth-grade children viewed the program in one of four treatment conditions: (1) cut and no sound effect; (2) cut and sound effect; (3) dissolve and no sound effect; or (4) dissolve and sound effect. The researchers then scored the children's selective attention to the content that was presented immediately after the beginning of each flashback.

After the viewing, the investigators examined the children's understanding of the flashbacks. To do so, they asked the children to tell about something that happened to them when they were little. After each child completed his or her story, the experimenter said, "That was something that happened in the past. Can you tell me anything that happened in the past in this television program?"

As expected, children who viewed the television program with dreamy camera dissolves understood that a change in time had taken place more often than children who viewed the television program with camera cuts. Not surprisingly, older children understood that a time shift had occurred more often than younger children did, particularly when the more difficult camera cut was used to mark the time shift. The sound effect had no impact on children's understanding of the flashback, perhaps because the mysterious background music ensured that all children were watching when the flashback occurred. The results of this study suggest that children come to understand the typical media conventions of time representation during the early grade school years, and that they are able to understand violations of those conventions by middle childhood (Calvert, 1988).

Slow motion is another representation of time that never occurs in real life. Yet slow motion videotapes have become a part of courtroom proceedings. For instance, several years ago, members of the Los Angeles Police Department were tried for beating a man named Rodney King. A person with a camcorder happened to be at the site and videotaped the arrest scene. The jury and American television viewers repeatedly viewed the beating, which was often shown in slow motion. King was on the ground, and some of the police continued to hit him. The defense attorney argued that King kept trying to get up, so the police officers had to hit him again. The prosecution argued that King was moving because he was being hit. The event was shown repeatedly in slow motion to determine whether King was trying to get up or to avoid the blows. Greenfield (1995), however, argued that this slow motion presentation was misleading to viewers and to the jury because no one could really evaluate King's behaviors in slow motion; only real-time portrayals could present what the police had experienced. The implication is that while slow motion can allow us to analyze the minute details of another's actions, our inferences about another's real-time perceptions of those events may well be inaccurate.

Action as a Mode to Represent Content

When children see information visually, such as the Road Runner racing down the road, they may well remember that information in a visual, iconic mode. That is, they may see the Road Runner racing in their "mind's eye" when they think about that content. On the other hand, when children listen to verbal story content, such as Arthur's sister talking about how afraid she is of the water, children may remember what she said in a verbal mode. That is, they may "hear" Arthur's sister talking in their mind. Children may also see and listen to content and remember it as both a visual and verbal image. For instance, children might view Winnie the Pooh and later "see" him eating his honey and "hear" his voice exclaiming that "I love my honey, Piglet!" The visual and auditory forms of television programs may thus serve as **modes to represent content,** thereby assisting children in understanding stories.

Many researchers, however, think that visual images distract children from listening to and remembering verbal story messages. This interference effect is called the **visual superiority hypothesis.**

Hayes and Birnbaum (1980), who advanced the visual superiority hypothesis, conducted three studies to examine children's memory of audio and visual information, particularly when the two types of information conflict. In the first study, preschoolers viewed the video portion from an episode of *Superfriends* but heard the audio portion of *Scooby Doo.* After viewing, children were asked if anything was wrong with the television program. Only one young girl found a problem with the program; she said that the color wasn't very good—she was right, for it was a black and white program. When children were tested for their comprehension of the program material, they recalled the visually presented material better than the verbally presented material.

In the second study, preschoolers were shown a 6-minute episode of *Scooby Doo.* Five questions assessed children's recognition of visually presented events; five questions assessed their recognition of aurally presented events; and five questions assessed their recognition of information presented in an integrated audiovisual format. The children remembered information presented visually or in an integrated audiovisual form better than they recalled information presented aurally.

The third study used 6-minute episodes of *Scooby Doo* and *Fangface.* Using the original intact *Fangface* program as a control, the researchers created composite experimental conditions by mixing a video *Fangface* with an audio *Scooby Doo* and a video *Scooby Doo* with an audio *Fangface.* As in the first study, children who viewed the programs with mixed audio and visual tracks remembered the visual content better than the audio content. Only one child identified a problem with the program, which she described as their "funny voices." This pattern of recall became known as the *visual superiority effect:* the children *processed visual material at the expense of the aural material.*

Later researchers questioned whether a reliance on visual modes of thought was truly a distractor from children's memory of aural material. Consider the first books children learn to read, which often match pictures of objects with the names of the objects. If a picture of a ball is mismatched with the word *cat,* can we infer that visual presentation interferes with verbal comprehension? We can, but only if we mismatch visual and auditory material. In real life, visual and auditory content rarely present conflicting messages.

Researchers in the television area increasingly studied children's memory of visual and audio material when the audio and visual tracks matched one another as well as when the tracks were mismatched. If the tracks are mismatched, the results inevitably support the visual superiority hypothesis: children remember the visually presented content better than the aurally presented content (Pezdek & Hartman, 1983). However, when children hear an audio track of a television program or see and hear the original program, no differences occur for their memory of the content presented from the audio track (Pezdek & Hartman, 1983; Pezdek & Stevens, 1984). If visuals were truly distracting children, then they should understand and remember the audio-only

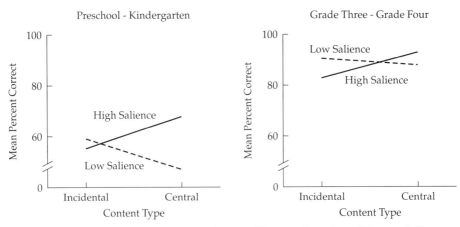

FIGURE 7.1 Mean Proportion on Comprehension Test as a Function of Feature Salience and Content Centrality

presentation better than the audiovisual presentation. Such findings cast doubt on the thesis that a visual presentation *interferes* with how children process auditory content. Instead, visual content appears to be more salient and memorable than audio content.

Indeed, when visual and auditory material present the same message, children's memory of content increases. We examined the thesis that action provides a visual mode that can help children process linguistic content using an episode of *Fat Albert and the Cosby Kids* (Calvert et al., 1982). In this program, we divided the content into *central* material essential for understanding the plot and *incidental* material that was irrelevant to the plot. We then looked at whether the central and incidental content was paired with formal features that were *perceptually salient,* such as action, or *nonsalient,* such as dialogue and narration. Because young children often think visually, we predicted that younger children (kindergartners) would rely more than older children (third and fourth graders) on perceptually salient features like visual actions to understand the central content. Older children, we thought, would be able to understand the verbal content without perceptually salient features like action. As Figure 7.1 shows, both age groups remembered the central content better when it was paired with actions than the central content without action (Calvert et al., 1982). These findings suggest that a visual mode such as action supports, rather than hinders, children's understanding of important verbal television content.

As research studies accumulated, researchers began to wonder if visual superiority should really be called *action superiority.* Visual presentation may not be the most salient aspect of a televised presentation; it may well be the *movement* of those visual images. For example, 4- and 7-year-olds reproduced more of the characters' actions than their speech, even when they had only heard a story (Gibbons et al., 1986). We will return to the question of action superiority later in this chapter, when we examine the computer technologies.

Children may also best remember information in the form in which it is initially presented. For example, children who saw *visual preplays* of a story that presented the upcoming plot were more attentive to these inserts and more successful at sequencing pictures from the story than those who only heard a narrator describe the story. However, children who heard the narrator use *inferential language,* summarizing the abstract verbal narration, understood the implicit verbal program content best (Calvert, Huston, & Wright, 1987). Similarly, children who saw an audiovisual story recalled more actions that occurred during story telling and were better able to sequence pictures from the story than those who heard the story as a radio presentation. However, those who heard the radio story remembered more verbal story material and drew more inferences about the hidden story content than those who saw the television version (Beagles-Roos & Gat, 1983). Comparable findings are reported when children hear a storybook compared to watching the story on television. Children who saw a televised version of a story remembered more visual material, whereas children who heard that story remembered more of the verbal story content (Meringoff, 1980).

Summary of the Empirical Evidence

Taken together, these studies suggest that visual presentation typically enhances children's memories of television presentations, particularly when children are asked to perform visual memory tasks, such as sequencing the pictures of a story. Visual superiority, as an interference effect, occurs primarily when audio and visual tracks are mismatched, and these effects are the most pronounced for very young children who probably rely more on visual ways of thinking. Visual superiority may actually be action superiority. Still visual frames do not capture the dynamic moving forms television, films, and the newer computer technologies make possible. Finally, children tend to remember information in the way they experienced it. That is, they often remember visually presented information in a pictorial form, whereas they often remember aurally presented information in a verbal form.

PRODUCTION FEATURES AND THE NEW TECHNOLOGIES

The computer area uses the same formal presentational features to present content as television does. Two lines of research have emerged that target information processing activities as a function of computer presentational features. The first line targets the motivational aspects of computer features (Malone, 1981). The second line examines action as a way to enhance children's memory of computer content (Calvert, 1991).

Motivational Aspects of Features

Malone (1981) examined the impact of a dart game on children's motivation and interest in educational video games. In doing so, he found gender differences in the forms that most interested children. Boys liked the action-oriented fantasy of popping balloons with darts, while girls preferred the musical reward that played after they won the game. After children played a game called *Breakout,* Malone (1981) found that the driving force of player interest was the visual goal of knocking out bricks.

Based on these findings, Malone (1981) began to construct a theory of intrinsic motivation. In the construction of **intrinsically interesting learning environments,** Malone (1981) targeted three domains: **challenge, fantasy,** and **curiosity.** Challenge involves goals, uncertain outcomes, hidden information, and randomness. Fantasy involves both cognitive and emotional aspects of imaginary experiences.

Of particular interest in the discussion of formal features is the dimension of curiosity. Curiosity involves an optimal level of information complexity, creating an environment that is novel and surprising, but not incomprehensible. Sensory curiosity can be generated through the use of audio and visual special effects. Cognitive curiosity can be generated by using knowledge structures that are complete, consistent, and parsimonious; cognitive curiosity is also increased through informative feedback that is both surprising and constructive. These elements bear close resemblance to Berlyne's (1960) theory of perceptual salience in that novelty, surprise, incongruity, and complexity are the foundations of attention and interest.

When Malone (1981) argued that the stimulus property of curiosity could be found in computer games via audio and visual special effects, he was specifying the same features identified as perceptually salient in the television area (Huston & Wright, 1983). Audio and visual special effects can serve as a decoration, as a way to enhance fantasy, and as a representational device (Malone, 1981). As representational devices, audio tones can tell a player if a response is right or wrong; visual features can represent an in-basket and an out-basket. The Macintosh and Windows icon of a trash can is a visual feature that depicts an action on information. One puts a discarded file into the trash can, which then grows fatter; the trash can be recovered from the can until it is emptied; and the trash can then returns to its normal size, signifying that the "trash" is gone.

Motivation and Learning

One reason motivation is important in the video game area is because we expect it to increase children's learning. If children are interested, do they learn more?

Lepper and Malone (1987) found that children chose to play the dart video game about fractions (which contained the features of action and music) about 50 percent more of the time than a simple drill-and-practice version of the same material. In this instance, playing the game resulted in more learning.

However, if children interacted with both versions for a similar amount of time, no difference in learning occurred. Thus, motivation increased learning only when children had the freedom to choose their activities. Nevertheless, children may be more likely to play a game than to drill at fractions during their free time. If children are more interested and motivated when they interact with video games that have interesting features, then those features could be used to make learning a more enjoyable experience for them. Why not make learning fun?

Computer games also increase motivation and learning more than traditional lecture formats. Calvert and Littman (1996) either exposed children to: (1) a computer game about the brain; (2) a lecture about the brain; or (3) math problems. Playing the audiovisual computer game increased children's motivation more than the other conditions. Moreover, the increased motivation translated into increased learning about the brain. The implication is that the new technologies can present content with audiovisual features that spark both interest and learning.

Action Superiority in Computer Interactions

Another way to examine the interface of children and computers is to compare the skills children bring to the computer in relation to the processing requirements the software makes. In this instance, we are looking at the match between a child's cognitive skills and the representational codes the computer software requires.

This approach extends the television research about perceptual salience, particularly in the form of action, to the computer area. Specifically, it examines the thesis that *action can provide a developmentally appropriate code that children can use to represent visually presented content.* Because children increasingly use language to represent content as they grow older, action should be especially memorable to young children and to those who are developmentally behind their peers.

Computer Microworlds

A computer **microworld** is a representation of a real-life scene, such as a beach or a park, depicted on the computer screen. The program is often written in a language called Sprite LOGO.

Lawler (1982) recognized the importance of computer interactions for children's literacy when he created a microworld called *Beach World* to teach his 2-year-old daughter, Peggy, to read. Peggy's beach world depicted a beach and ocean scene as the background. Objects such as a pony and the sun would appear on her beach when she keyed in the name of the object. She could animate these objects and set them in motion by keying in other commands like *up* and *run.* For instance, Peggy could make the sun move through the sky by keying in the command *sun up.* New objects and actions could easily be added by having her father modify the program. Thus, Peggy had a computer world personalized to her particular interests. It was *her* beach world.

Peggy did, in fact, increase her written vocabulary and learn to read by interacting with *Beach World*. However, Lawler never examined the specific properties of *Beach World* that made the environment so effective for learning.

Action-Oriented Microworlds

To answer this question, my colleagues and I decided to examine the facets of microworlds that enhance children's learning. In particular, we hypothesized that the *actions* of objects were particularly relevant to young children's learning. In a series of studies, we examined the impact of such computer presentational features as action, verbal labels, and sound effects on children's information processing activities.

We created a computer microworld with a background scene of a park, comprised of a green grassy area, a lake, a road, a blue sky, and a train track. Objects would appear in *Park World* when the user keyed in the name of the object. However, instead of having the child set the objects in motion, as Lawler had done, we designed the program to make some objects move (action) while others remained stationary (no action). In this way, we could examine the impact of formal features on children's information processing activities.

In the first study (Calvert et al., 1989), preschoolers were exposed to *Park World* for a four-day period. Each day, an experimenter read a story and keyed in the targeted words to make objects appear in *Park World*. The objects belonged to one of six categories: (1) *vehicles* (car, truck, train, plane); (2) *land animals* (dog, cat, horse, bird); (3) *water animals* (duck, frog, turtle, fish); (4) *nature* (sun, flower, cloud, tree); (5) *people* (mom, dad, boy, girl); and (6) *toys* (ball, wagon, boat, kite).

Four versions of *Park World* were created. Across versions, objects from each category assumed all combinations of action and sound effects. For example, the train simply appeared on the train track in one version (no action and no sound); it moved along the train track without noise in another (action and no sound); it stayed still but made a choo-choo noise in a third version (no action and sound); and it moved along the train track and made a choo-choo noise in the fourth version (action and sound). By making objects appear in different ways, we could tell if the features were interesting and memorable to children rather than just being a particularly attractive object.

After her daily reading of the story, the experimenter hid the objects, leaving only the computer background of the park. Children then selected one object that they wanted in their world from each set of the 6 categories. Preschoolers *preferentially selected* objects that *moved* over stationary objects. On the fifth day, the experimenter asked the preschoolers to recall all the objects they could from *Park World*. They also *recalled* objects that *moved* better than stationary objects. *Action, then, emerged as an important computer feature that facilitates preschoolers' preferential selection and verbal recall of information.*

In the second *Park World* study (Calvert et al., 1990), we replaced the sound effects with actual verbal labels of the information. A computer voice synthesizer was programmed to say the words the user keyed into the computer. Because the program could now vocalize, we called this program *Talk World*. The background scene was still the same park, and the same objects appeared when keyed into the computer. This time we asked kindergartners and second graders to participate. Some of these children were good readers, and some were poor readers. We thought that action might help the poor readers to remember the objects since their language skills were relatively undeveloped, particularly for somewhat older children. Kindergartners are just learning to read, so reading level should have less impact on their memory.

Once again, the teacher read the story, and the objects appeared in *Talk World*. This time, however, children came only one time. After the story was read, the teacher hid the objects and asked the children to remember all the objects they could. Second graders who were poor readers *recalled* as many objects as the good readers did, but only when objects appeared with action. Kindergartners were not affected.

In the next *Talk World* study (Calvert, 1991), I decided to see if the computer itself was necessary for features to affect learning. A felt board version of *Talk World* was constructed that was exactly the same size as the computer version. The background depicted the same park scene, and the objects looked just like the objects on the computer. The objects were so little we had to move them with tweezers. This time, we used only one version of *Talk World* since it had become clear that the presentational features, not the individual objects, affected recall.

Preschoolers and kindergartners participated in this study. Once again, an experimenter read a story and objects appeared in *Talk World* immediately after each target word was read. In the computer version, the program made the objects move or stay still and the voice synthesizer either said the object name or remained silent. In the felt board version, the experimenter provided the same movements and verbal labels. As the experimenter read the story, she kept track of whether the child *produced* (that is, spontaneously said) the object names or not. Naming objects is an early strategy children use to remember information. After the story, the experimenter hid the objects and asked the child to *recall* all the objects he or she could.

As the story progressed, kindergartners were more likely to produce the names of objects; by contrast, preschoolers did not. This suggests that kindergartners are just beginning to master simple rehearsal activities like naming objects. As Table 7.4 reveals, preschoolers had difficulty recalling any objects without the aid of action or verbal labels.

Kindergartners recalled the most objects when both action and verbal labels were used to present the content. These findings suggest that age changes occur in how children use features to remember information. Specifically, while the youngest children are dependent on some assistance from either action or language to remember the names of objects, slightly older children successfully remember object names when both action and labels are used simultaneously. The findings suggest that children integrate visual and verbal information in memory by age 5, and they use these dual codes to remember content.

Interestingly, no differences occurred for recall of information presented on a felt board versus a computer. On the one hand, this finding is a bit disheartening since we spent more than $2,000 to develop the computer version of *Talk World* and only $6.86 to create the felt board version. On the

TABLE 7.4 Mean Number of Words Recalled as a Function of Grade, Verbal Labels, and Action

		Preschoolers *Verbal Labels*		Kindergartners *Verbal Labels*	
		Absent	Present	Absent	Present
Action	Absent	1.20[d]	2.30[bc]	2.10[bc]	2.60[b]
	Present	1.80[c]	2.30[bc]	2.00[bc]	3.35[a]

Note: Means with different letter superscripts are significantly different at $p < .05$ (that is, 5 chances in 100 that the differences occurred by chance). Each mean is based on 20 subjects.
Source: Calvert, S. L. (1991). Presentational features for children's production and recall of information. *Journal of Applied Developmental Psychology, 12,* 367–378. Copyright © 1991 by the Ablex Publishing Corporation. Reprinted with permission.

other hand, it is encouraging to note that feature effects generalize beyond a specific technology. That means that action may be useful in a variety of contexts, including television and felt board stories. One kindergartner repeatedly told me how much fun the felt board version of *Talk World* was, and I think the movement of the objects was the key reason this felt board story was unique and interesting to her. Historically, teachers have not animated their felt board stories with actions, and this procedure has obvious value as a memory aid for children. One school in which I conducted this study now animates their felt board stories, a practice that could be helpful in other schools as well.

In the last *Talk World* study (Calvert, 1994b), we compared kindergartners' and second graders' recall of objects for a story versus a list format. One computerized version of *Talk World* was used. This time the experimenter read the story as before, or she simply keyed in the names of each object in that same order. Again, she recorded children's *production* of the names of objects during the session and tested their *recall* after completion of the story. The main finding this time was that kindergartners' production and recall benefitted from action and verbal labels, but second graders did not need these features to produce or recall information. Once again, then, the kindergartners benefited the most from these features, but this time more so than a slightly older, rather than slightly younger, age group. The list or story presentation had little impact on either production or recall of objects.

Taken together, this series of computer studies supports the thesis that *action facilitates children's processing of verbal information.* Action never interfered with children's memory of verbal information. Instead, action benefitted the youngest children and even older children who read poorly. Specifically, children are likely to *select, name,* and *remember* objects that move.

Computer presentational features like action and labels should be used judiciously in developing computer software for children. By interfacing the cognitive skills of young learners (in this instance, a preference for visual, iconic modes of representation), with similar modes of information delivery (in this case, computerized action to supplement verbal labels), software designers can maximize children's learning from new technologies. The implication is that we should use visual menus and visual software, such as those developed for the Macintosh or Windows menus, to transmit information to young computer users.

Visually based systems such as Windows have replaced verbally based operating systems such as DOS. Visual ways of interacting with information technologies, including the content on the World Wide Web, will become more prevalent in the future. Those who use these new visual technologies may increasingly use visual, iconic ways to think about that content.

INTERACTIVE EXPERIENCES: WILL THE MEDIUM BECOME THE MESSAGE?

A question that has interested researchers since the early 1960s (McLuhan, 1964) is *how* media exposure influences children's thinking. Although television does not seem to have strong effects on whether children think in visual or verbal forms (Huston et al., 1992), the interactive technologies seem to have more influence. Video game research provides the strongest evidence that media can cultivate visual modes of thought (Greenfield, 1996).

Several years ago, Greenfield (1993) was playing a video game called *Castle Wolfenstein* with her son. She was doing terribly, and he was doing quite well. When they discussed their performances, he told her the mazes of the castle were connected. She had not recognized these spatial relationships, while her son took them to be essential for winning the game—he had constructed a map of the game in his head. When Greenfield asked a friend of her son to draw the maze for her, he provided a quite accurate drawing of the castle mazes, which he revised slightly after playing the game. In *Castle Wolfenstein,* the player moves through several rooms and has to exit through particular doors from each room to reach the ultimate destination: freedom! Clearly, spatial integration skills were required for successful performance at this game. By repeatedly playing the game, these boys had constructed an internalized map to guide their performance, which was an iconic visual representation of that space. Greenfield then decided to study spatial skills in relation to video game play.

Video Games and the Cultivation of Visual Spatial Skills

Visual spatial skills involve the ability to construct and manipulate pictorial images of objects and places in one's mind. For example, having a map in your head as you drive makes use of visual spatial skills. You use this information to move through space. Adolescents and adults who have good visual spatial skills may perform well when driving to new places, in part, because they represent information in visual rather than verbal modes. That is, they think about where they are going in a visual spatial image, such as a "map in their head."

Video games frequently call upon the user to construct visual representations of space in order to win the game. Does video game play therefore cultivate visual spatial skills? Or do children with good visual spatial skills tend to play video games because they already have the prerequisite skills to do well?

To answer these questions, Greenfield, Brannon, and Lohr (1996) began with a naturalistic study in which they went to a video parlor and waited for players to complete a game called *The Empire Strikes Back*. This game requires the player to navigate through three-dimensional space from a two-dimensional video game depiction. The player is a pilot who flies a starship through enemy territory. Points are accumulated by shooting opponents and avoiding asteroids or other fatal obstacles. After students had finished their games, the experimenters asked them to perform a mental paper-folding task, a test of visual spatial skills. Students who were extremely proficient on the computer game were also more proficient on the mental paper-folding task. The results suggest that the visual spatial skills required in video games are linked to more general visual spatial skills like paper folding.

While it was becoming clear that expert players of video games are more proficient at using visual spatial skills, it was unclear whether they were initially more proficient at creating mental maps or if they developed (cultivated) the skill by playing the game. In an experimental follow-up of this study, the authors pretested students to see how proficient they initially were at using visual spatial skills. They then gave an experimental group $10 in quarters and told them to play *The Empire Strikes Back* until they were proficient at the game. They could get more quarters if they needed them. Students had a ten-week academic quarter to complete the study. When subjects became proficient at the game (or the term ended, whichever came first), they took a posttest assessing visual spatial skills. Although students who were initially good at the paper-folding task were also good at the video game, short-term exposure to the game did not improve students' posttest performance on the paper-folding task. The results suggest that visual spatial skills are certainly not developed overnight. It takes practice to build these skills, as it does with every other cognitive skill. Interestingly, men reached criterion levels of expertise in playing the game much more often than women did. This led Greenfield to study gender differences in video game play and in visual spatial skills.

Ongoing debates have occurred about why males often perform better on visual spatial tasks than females do. Is it a genetic difference between the sexes, or a matter of environmental differences in experience? If it is a matter of experience, then playing video games might improve girls' skills at visual spatial tasks.

Subrahmanyam and Greenfield (1996) attempted to reduce gender differences in visual spatial skills by exposing 10- and 11-year-old children to a maze-based video game called *Marble Madness*. *Marble Madness* requires children to move a marble along a path on a three-dimensional grid. Obstacles include falling off the grid, attack by a black ball that pushes the player off the grid, and worm creatures that make the marble disappear upon contact. The spatial skills this game requires include moving objects, figuring out the speed and distance of moving objects, and intercepting objects.

Children were initially pretested on three spatial skill tasks to control for prior levels of expertise. At the beginning of the study, boys were better at visual spatial tasks and had played more video games. However, boys and girls played *Marble Madness* at about the same level of expertise.

Children in the experimental group then played *Marble Madness* for three 45-minute sessions, resulting in a total of 2 hours and 15 minutes of game play. A control group played a word game called *Conjecture* on the computer. After they finished their three game sessions, children were posttested on two of the three pretests on spatial skills. All children who played the video game became more proficient at visual spatial tasks. By contrast, those who played the word game did not improve. Moreover, the children who were initially lowest in visual spatial scores (mostly girls) had the most improved visual spatial skills. Nevertheless, the children who were strong in visual spatial skills to begin with continued to have stronger visual spatial skills after training. This pattern would certainly be expected given the short exposure time to the video game. With repeated exposure to the game, boys became the better players of the video game, even though both genders were equally proficient when the study began. In short, although girls' performance increased in the more general spatial task tested after video game exposure, boys outperformed girls at the actual computer game.

In summary, although it does appear that those who initially have strong visual spatial skills choose to play video games, video game play also enhances these skills. This pattern suggests a bidirectional relation. For example, a child who has good visual spatial skills will enjoy playing video games because he or she has the prerequisite skills for doing well. As play time accumulates, the child's visual spatial skills also improve. This creates a successful pattern of skill enhancement. On the other hand, some children may like to play video games more than others do—perhaps because of the content. By playing more, their visual spatial skills improve, and they get better at the game. Both patterns lead to better visual spatial skills.

But an opposing pattern can also occur. Here, for example, a child who has poor visual spatial skills does not do well at video games, and therefore, will not play the games. If the games are uninteresting to him or her, then there is no enticement to continue to play. If the child does not play the games, his or her visual spatial skills do not improve. The good news is that children, including those who are not particularly good at using visual spatial skills, can be taught to think in visual spatial ways by playing video games. The implication is that we need to make games that appeal to *all* children.

Video game play can also impact the way participants reconstruct their memories of tasks (Greenfield et al., 1996). Subjects in this study, who were from the United States and Italy, took a pretest, either played an action-oriented video game or were involved in a control condition, and then took a posttest. The tests involved viewing a moving representation of computer circuitry and then answering questions about the display. Subjects could answer questions in words, drawings, or both.

All subjects exposed to the video game improved at these tasks. By contrast, the subjects exposed to the control conditions improved the least. For our purposes, the most important findings involved how subjects presented their responses. Specifically, those who played the computer game tended to present their responses in visual, iconic displays. Americans, who had more exposure to video games than their Italian counterparts, also used iconic representations more often than the Italians did. The authors concluded that skills at decoding and encoding the iconic codes of video games transfer to other scientific tasks, and that these iconic skills are becoming increasingly important to our future.

Creating Video and Computer Programs: Windows to the Mind

Perhaps the most direct way computers can impact children's cognitive skills is when children become creators, rather than simply users, of a technology. Programming a computer requires children to use logical skills, procedural thinking, and hierarchical structure. Therefore, when children program computers, that experience may impact the way they structure and represent thought.

Video Game Programs

Kafai (1996) had boys and girls create programs in which they had to perform educational activities, in this case solving fraction problems. She tracked the progress children made on their video games over the course of several months.

In Figure 7.2, you can observe the structure of a child's thoughts. The figure depicts a schematic diagram of his game. Logic and planning are necessary skills to create a flowchart like his. Branching techniques are displayed as he depicts how one will move from one screen to the next. Children who master the logical skills required to make video games could become more logical thinkers themselves.

LOGO programs

Empirical research has also been conducted on the cognitive skills of children who use **LOGO,** a computer programming language developed at the Massachusetts Institute of Technology. To use LOGO, children type in commands at a keyboard to move a screen cursor called a turtle. There is also an optional robot turtle that can make movements, which are driven by LOGO commands, on paper placed on the floor. The turtle, or cursor, moves when children give commands such as Forward (FD), Right Turn (RT), or Left Turn (LT). These commands combine with distance and angles to move the turtle Forward 50 spaces, make a Right Turn of 90 degrees, and so on. If a child duplicates this

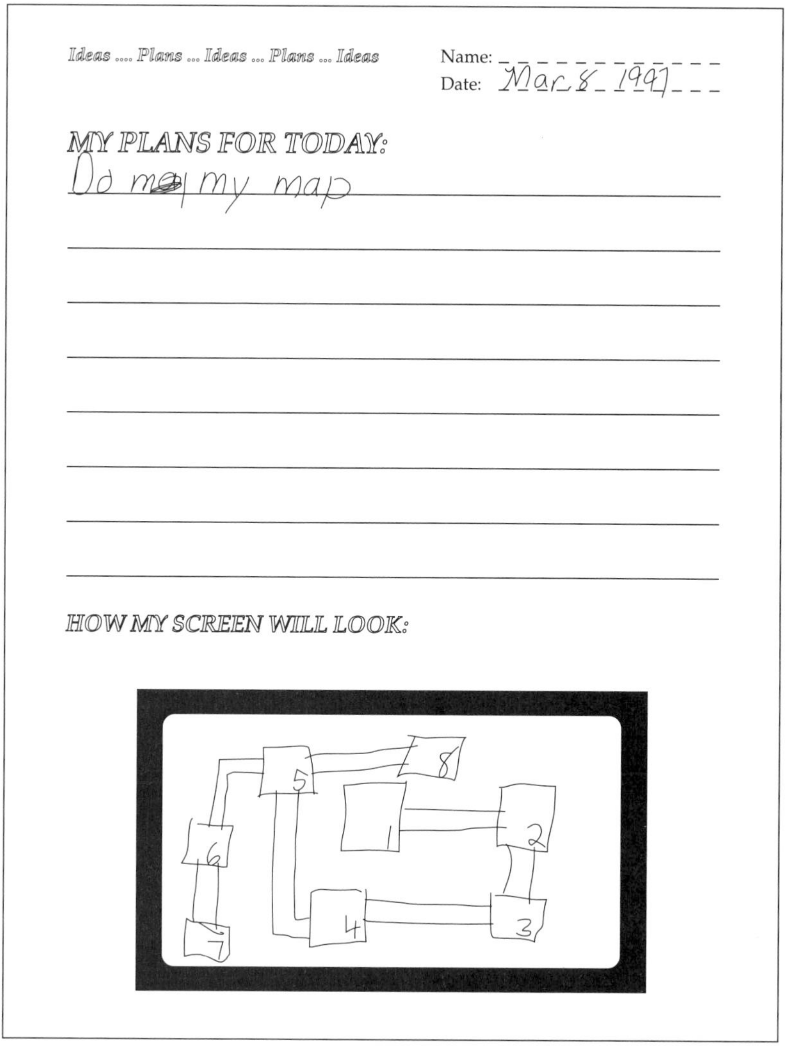

Ideas .... Plans ... Ideas ... Plans ... Ideas   Name: _ _ _ _ _ _ _ _ _ _ _ _
Date: Mar 8 1991 _ _

MY PLANS FOR TODAY:

Do me my map

HOW MY SCREEN WILL LOOK:

FIGURE 7.2 Maze Depicting the Structure of a Video Game Design by a 10-Year-Old Boy

command four times, the turtle creates a square. Using LOGO, children can program geometric patterns such as squares, rectangles, and stars. These kinds of programming experiences are thought to cultivate children's problem-solving skills (Papert, 1980).

Although many researchers expected children to benefit cognitively from using LOGO, findings have been mixed (Poulin-Dubois, McGilly, & Shultz, 1989). Some studies demonstrate clear effects (Gorman & Bourne, 1983), others demonstrate partial effects (Poulin-Dubois et al., 1989), and still others demonstrate no effects (Pea, 1983).

Poulin-Dubois and her colleagues (1989) concluded that studies reporting the clearest positive effects examined concepts similar to those that children learned in LOGO. For example, these researchers found that children learned to use procedures and debugging skills, which require children to analyze, to learn from, and to correct mistakes, though they did not transfer those skills beyond the LOGO context. By contrast, studies that found mixed or no effects often examined concepts that were more distant from LOGO. These findings suggest that LOGO training results in the acquisition of specific skills that do not readily generalize to other areas.

Virtual Reality Experiences: Enactive Representations of the Future

The newest frontier of information technologies, virtual reality, may influence how children and adults think by moving the player through a symbolic reality (Calvert, in press). In contrast to past television, computer, or video game experiences, the player is embodied. You look out of the character's eyes and move from inside the character.

In one study of virtual reality (Calvert & Tan, 1996) described earlier, we examined the impact of this kind of experience on the arousal and aggressive thoughts of college-aged students after playing an aggressive game. Game players were more aroused and had more aggressive thoughts than those who observed others' play or who simulated game movements. We did not study player actions, but it may well be that playing the game made "pulling the trigger" an enactive representation, readily available for future actions.

Medical applications are becoming prevalent in virtual reality programs. Programs, for example, allow doctors to practice procedures, such as a heart catherization, to gain the "feel" of the technique before they actually perform it on patients. This experience creates an enactive representation of a surgical technique which doctors can then apply to real-life procedures.

These enactive representations, encoded into the muscles, foreshadow a new age in representational media. The link between acquiring a response and performing a response may virtually disappear in the future, making action an integral outcome of symbolic experiences.

In summary, the bold thesis that the medium is the message received only weak support in the age of television. By requiring children to participate, computers may well produce stronger support. Already we see that children who play video games develop better visual spatial skills than those who play less often—although research on children who play LOGO suggests that cognitive effects are specific, rather than general. As children become able to choose media interactions consistent with their own developing cognitive skills and interests, cultivation effects may become more pronounced. Such effects are already noticeable as boys select video games and computer programming activities that require and cultivate visual spatial thinking.

SUMMARY

Form is the gateway to content in the information age. Perceptually salient forms alert our sensory systems to information that is potentially important; they elicit attention to that content; and they provide ways for children to encode, think about, and remember that content. Children and adults can also participate in action scenarios, and in the future, their real-life actions may be increasingly influenced by these symbolic interactions. These effects cross television, radio, computer, and even storybook presentations on felt boards. Interactive media can also influence the way children think about information. The implication is that *how* we present content in the information age may be every bit as important as *what* we present.

Children are far more sensitive to form than adults are because they are just developing the representational capacities to comprehend media codes and signals. Successful journeys in the information age will require us to be sensitive to how we present information, for information technologies will increasingly present and rely on multiple forms of delivery, thereby cultivating the use of multiple modes of thought and action. Television and computer software programs that appeal to a diverse group of children increase the opportunities for multiple modes of thought to develop for all users.

Educational Media

When my 4-year-old niece and 8-year-old nephew visited me, they discovered that I had two videotapes from *Blue's Clues*, an educational television series. Blue, a dog, helps Steve solve mysteries. Steve pauses after the clue of a paw print appears so that viewers have the opportunity to guess the right answer. My niece and nephew wanted to view these two episodes repeatedly. As they did, they quickly began to answer the clues aloud and solve the problems. This type of educational activity was fostered by a videocassette recorder, which allowed them to repeatedly view the vignettes, and by an innovative program format that encourages children to interact with the content.

Since its inception, educators have attempted to harness the power of television to educate a mass audience. Instantaneously, millions of viewers can view material that will benefit their cognitive development. Not surprisingly, these efforts occurred for educational radio in an earlier era, and are being put into educational computer interfaces today. The promise of educational media is coming closer to fulfillment, particularly with the rehearsal and interactive options newer technologies make possible.

In this chapter, we will explore children's educational television and computer programs. First, we will define what an educational television and computer program is. Then we will turn to the history of educational television, complete with its potentials and its limitations. We will examine the kinds of characteristics that make an educational television or computer program effective. Finally, we will explore the impact of educational television and computer programs on children's learning, and a theoretical model that has emerged in this area. The major thesis is that we can educate and entertain our children at the same time, and that learning can be fun.

WHAT IS AN EDUCATIONAL TELEVISION OR COMPUTER PROGRAM?

It would seem that the definition of an educational television program would be rather straightforward. An educational program should transmit the type of academic content children are taught at school. However, the decision about what is educational became a thorny issue when the Children's Television Act was being enforced (Huston & Wright, in press). School readiness can include a broad range of skills, including: (1) physical well-being and motor skills; (2) social and emotional development; (3) approaches to learning; (4) language skills; (5) cognitive skills; and (6) natural and social science knowledge (Neopolitan & Huston, 1994b).

The Children's Television Act of 1990 broadly defined educational and informational programming as "any television programming that furthers the educational and informational needs of children 16 years of age and under in any respect, including the child's intellectual/cognitive or social/emotional needs" (FCC, 1996, p. 1160). Historically, those of us who study television would call this definition *a combination of educational and prosocial programming,* rather than educational and informational programming. Educational and informational programming focuses on the cognitive development of the child, whereas prosocial programming focuses on the social and emotional needs of the child.

Certainly programs can be both educational and prosocial, as *Barney* is. However, many television programs do not teach any academic content and still include prosocial messages. Thus, the two concepts are not identical, and they do not always overlap. While both educational and prosocial programming are valuable in a child's development, we will define and examine educational programming in a narrow sense in this chapter and then focus on prosocial programming in the next.

For our purposes, an **educational television** or **computer program** is one designed to teach children academic concepts, such as reading, math, science, history, or geography, that can also be a part of school experiences (Calvert, Gallagher, & McGuckin, 1997). These programs are based on **curriculum goals,** which organize age-appropriate concepts to build on each other. For instance, number identification must precede solving addition problems. Not surprisingly, when a mass audience views a television program such as *Sesame Street,* it's difficult to match cognitive demands with the skills of individual viewers. This is a past limitation of educational television that videocassette recorders have remedied somewhat. With a videocassette recorder, children can watch and rewatch the parts of a program that are comprehensible and interesting and skip over the parts that are too difficult, too easy, or just downright boring to them.

Educational television programs can be independent of school classes, or they can be integrated into school classes. In fact, programs for older children often work best when integrated within the school curriculum. For example, *The Electric Company,* a television program designed to teach reading skills (Lesser, 1976), was viewed by children in their homes, but it was also used with curriculum materials in school classrooms. The experiences at school maximized children's learning. To accomplish learning goals, then, children should view these programs both at school and at home so that information is repeated sufficiently for children to master it.

Videocassette recorders allow teachers to tape and show educational programs at their discretion so that they can integrate the programs into classroom curriculum goals. In addition, videocassette recorders allow repetition of important messages to foster children's comprehension of the material, as I described in my opening scenario.

HISTORY OF EDUCATIONAL TELEVISION PROGRAMS

Over the years, many educational programs have been created for adult and child audiences. Early efforts often targeted adults in college courses (Watkins, Huston-Stein, & Wright, 1981). While effective, the presentations were often slow-paced programs with little supportive action to enhance the message.

"Talking heads" were the norm, and boredom was often the outcome. When summarizing the literature on these early programs, Schramm (1962) pointed out that educational programs were most effective when they taught subjects such as math and science in concrete ways. For example, students should see pictures of how an airplane flies, with graphic depictions of the laws of aero-dynamics, to maximize their learning.

Educators did make some attempts to create educational programs for children in the early days of television. *Captain Kangaroo,* an early television program that was recently reintroduced with a new cast, featured an adult television star who introduced and reinforced some academic lessons to preschool-aged children. Similarly, *Romper Room* was a television series about a preschool classroom, complete with a teacher who taught children academic lessons.

But there were inherent problems in using television as an educator that limited its influence on children's cognitive development. First, it was difficult to teach many children of different ages the kinds of information that a partic-ular child was ready to learn. Second, it was difficult to build on past lessons, because there was no way to tell who had seen which programs. Third, the format was often live, precluding the animated imaginary elements prevalent in children's cartoons, a major source of entertainment for young viewers. (I remember, for example, being especially interested in the "Tom Terrific" car-toon that appeared in the *Captain Kangaroo* program. Live programs were in-teresting, but animated programs often capture the imaginations of children.) Last, but not least, was the difficulty experienced when educators tried to cre-ate educational programs on their own. The productions were often too aca-demic, without sufficient entertainment value to appeal to a broad audience (Watkins et al., 1981).

While these obstacles have not disappeared, a major breakthrough in edu-cational television occurred in the late 1960s and early 1970s. The program was called *Sesame Street*. While you who grew up watching this program take *Sesame Street* as an everyday experience, the thought and effort required to cre-ate this program was truly amazing.

Sesame Street began when a group of researchers, television producers, and broadcasters joined together in the late 1960s to create a program that could entertain as well as educate very young children (Lesser, 1974). Almost no one thought they could do it. More that twenty-five years later, the program con-tinues to attract young viewers, as well as their parents, many of whom viewed the program themselves as children (Mielke, 1989). This pattern of intergenerational transmission, in which one generation passes on a family and cultural heritage of viewing *Sesame Street,* is one that benefits children.

Sesame Street received criticism as well as praise. Critics argued that the program is fast-paced, offering little opportunity for children to reflect and re-hearse its lessons (Singer & Singer, 1983). Others argued that it promotes su-perficial, rote learning (Cook et al., 1975).

In spite of these criticisms, *Sesame Street* became a prototype for future ed-ucational programs. The revenues *Sesame Street* generated, in part from selling products and toys associated with the program, funded new educational series. These series targeted an older audience, and none has ever had the longevity or popularity of *Sesame Street*. These included *The Electric Company*, designed to teach reading skills to children as they begin primary school; *3–2–1 Contact*, designed to teach science to middle elementary-school children; and *Square One*, designed to teach math skills to middle elementary-school children. Existing programs, such as *Mister Rogers' Neighborhood* and *Captain Kangaroo*, also incorporated more educational content into their scripts (Watkins et al., 1981).

During the 1970s, broadcasters also created some programs that were educational or prosocial because of pressure generated from the Surgeon General's Report on the impact of television violence on children (Murray, 1997). As we saw in Chapter 6, that pressure came to a halt when President Reagan selected Mark Fowler as the chair for the Federal Communications Commission. In the early 1980s, the children's television market was expected to regulate itself (Fowler & Brenner, 1982). Protections for the child audience disappeared, and television programs increasingly reflected the goals of commercial broadcasters: to sell products to a mass audience (Kunkel & Canepa, 1994). Programs to sell products, called product-based programming, proliferated in this deregulated atmosphere. In the 1980s, children's educational television disappeared from broadcast television.

With political and philosophical changes in Congress and the presidency, children's television again became a focal point of legislative action. The Children's Television Act of 1990 legislated that broadcasters must provide educational and informational programming for children.

After the passage of the Children's Television Act of 1990, many scholars and educators expected more educational television programs to appear on network television. But change is often slow, mired in politics. Some broadcasters attempted to do the least amount of new educational programming legally required. As late as 1996, the networks had developed few new programs to educate children. Calvert, Gallagher, and McGuckin (1997), for example, examined a 1995-96 sample of Saturday morning television programs. They found only about 30 minutes of educational programming per network, even when using a definition that included both educational and prosocial programs. Two networks in the Washington metropolitan area had abandoned children's television almost entirely, replacing the traditional children's line-up with adult news programming rather than educational children's programs.

Changes in programming did come in September 1997, when broadcasters were required to show a minimum of three hours of educational and informational television programming each week. If you want to know what kinds of educational television programs are currently available for children, I recommend you watch Saturday morning television and also examine what's on the air before and after children are in school. The educational and informational offerings the major networks were broadcasting in the fall of 1997 appear in Table 6.3 of Chapter 6.

PBS has continued to be a major developer of children's educational television programs. A major initiative by PBS began in the late 1980s when Congress told them to begin a new enterprise known as Ready to Learn (Huston & Wright, in press).

Ready to Learn (Corporation for Public Broadcasting, 1993) targets the preschool audience and prepares them for school entry by exposing them to educational television programs throughout the day. Programs such as *Sesame Street, Mister Rogers' Neighborhood, Lamb Chops Play-Along* with Shari Lewis and her puppets, *Barney,* and *Shining Times Station* target children who are not yet in school. These kinds of programs are thought to prepare children for school by teaching them the skills they need to succeed. These programs are broadcast during the mornings and afternoons each weekday on PBS stations, and they represent an effort to educate our preschoolers for the demands of school. Children who watch these programs are expected to be better prepared for school entry, and they are expected to succeed in school more than children who do not watch these programs or who watch these programs very little (Corporation for Public Broadcasting, 1993).

Middle childhood is an age few educational programs target, but there are a few important exceptions. PBS programs for children in elementary school include *Arthur, Wishbone, The Magic School Bus,* and more established programs such as *Reading Rainbow,* with a host who introduces children to classic children's stories to inspire them to read books, and *Bill Nye, the Science Guy. Arthur* is an animated story involving prosocial and educational themes. In *The Magic School Bus,* Ms. Frizzle and her class learn science by exploring amazing places, ranging from the planets to the inside of the human body, traveling on an animated school bus. *The Magic School Bus* will be broadcast by FOX, beginning Fall, 1998. *Wishbone* introduces children to great literature, such as *Romeo and Juliet,* via a story about a dog who travels in time to portray classic literary tales.

Nickelodeon, a cable station, has also taken a leadership role in developing children's educational and prosocial programs. The *Blue's Clues* series that we described earlier introduces young children to academic concepts and encourages them to participate with the characters in educational activities. *Blue's Clues* is a mystery series that invites children to figure out problems. As you can see in the picture, Steve, the main character, sits in his thinking chair as he and Blue solve the mystery of the week. Steve elicits active participation from viewers by asking them questions. Many children, including my niece and nephew, respond to these queries. *Gullah Gullah Island* and *Allegra's Windows* are other programs Nickelodeon has developed for children.

Given the popularity of many of these programs, one might ask why the networks have not adapted these formulas for their programs. The answer lies in profits and profit margins. The networks perceive the production of children's television programs as a major financial liability, resulting in a market disincentive to create or broadcast educational programs (Jordan, 1997a). By necessity, educational television programming must target a narrow age range to be effective, and a smaller audience means smaller profits. Educational programming also costs more to create. For example, each hour of children's

Steve, of *Blue's Clues,* solving the mystery of the day.

programming on PBS costs between $152,000 and $811,000, averaging $380,000 (Corporation for Public Broadcasting, 1993). By contrast, advertisers virtually give programs to networks when the characters represent a commercial product.

CHARACTERISTICS OF EFFECTIVE EDUCATIONAL TELEVISION AND COMPUTER PROGRAMS

With the advent of personal computers, many educators believed we gained a renewed opportunity to use technologies in constructive ways. Computers, unlike television, are interactive, can respond to personal learning styles, can repeat lessons as often as necessary, and can tutor each child. A new era in educational media is upon us. What makes an educational television or computer program effective? Table 8.1 summarizes the kinds of characteristics that make a program educational as well as entertaining.

Age-Appropriate Content

The first characteristic of an effective program is **age-appropriate content.** Does the content target an age group who should be on the verge of mastering this type of information? To determine the answer, we can call upon the idea of a sensitive period. **Sensitive periods** are windows of time in which children should be ready to learn certain concepts. Television programs have focused on age-appropriate content, but computer programs have been even more diligent in doing so.

Many educators and psychologists have targeted early childhood as a sensitive period for acquiring the skills they will need for successful performance

TABLE 8.1 Characteristics of Effective Educational Television and Computer Programs

Characteristic	Description
Age-appropriate content	Children should be able to understand the information
Gender- and ethnic-appropriate content	Children should be able to relate to the characters
Perceptually salient production techniques	Program should include action, sound effects, and visual special effects
Comprehensible language	Language should be easy for children to understand
Repetition	Program should frequently repeat main themes and messages
Interactivity	Children should participate in the educational activity
Familiar host and cast	All episodes should feature one or more characters children like
Familiar setting	Some of the action should take place in the same setting across episodes
Theme	Each show should emphasize a specific lesson
Learning is fun!	Program should portray learning as interesting and enjoyable, not dry and boring
Multimedia materials	Complimentary materials such as books, videotapes, and CD-ROM programs should support the educational messages

in school. For example, learning vocabulary explodes from ages 2 to 5. Mastery occurs because of a sensitive period in the acquisition of language. Therefore, vocabulary acquisition should be a focus of educational content during this age period. *Sesame Street* focuses on language and vocabulary during this time frame. Not surprisingly, *Sesame Street* offers a medley of parallel educational computer programs, including *Elmo's Preschool,* a program which teaches basic numbers and letter skills; *Art Workshop,* which teaches creativity; *Let's Make a Word,* a spelling game; and *Get Set to Learn,* a program focusing on patterns, shapes, and sizes.

Because early childhood is an important time for developing scholastic skills, CD-ROM programs often focus on 3- to 6-year-olds. Educational games for young children focus on the same kinds of basic cognitive skills that educational television programs emphasize (for example, letter recognition, reading, number recognition). *Reader Rabbit's Interactive Reading Journey,* for example, teaches children to read by exposing them to 40 storybooks that target different age groups. As a child masters easy reading lessons, he or she progresses to the next level of difficulty automatically. *Let's Start Learning,* from the makers of the Reader Rabbit series, teaches preschoolers the skills they need to begin kindergarten. For instance, they learn to identify numbers, patterns, shapes, and colors via attention-getting and fun computer activities. Basic math skills, such as addition, subtraction, and counting, are taught by a program called *James Discovers Math* (Oldenburg, 1995).

A series of storybooks by Broderbund focuses on early reading skills with a picture book accompanying each CD-ROM. In this series, Arthur, based on the book series and the PBS television series, celebrates his birthday; Ruff, a playful dog, goes in search of his bone; and Grandma takes her granddaughter to the beach. The user can play these programs in English or in Spanish; Grandma can also be played in Japanese. By switching from one audio track to another, children can learn foreign languages. All of these programs cultivate, emphasize, and expand the educational lessons available in other forms of media, and they are an important resource for parents who are preparing their children for school entry.

Educational television programs are not numerous for elementary school children, yet children continue to achieve important developmental accomplishments during this time frame. At around age 6, Condry (1989) argues that a sensitive period occurs in the development of reading skills. Television and computer programs could promote reading skills, such as blending sounds to create words, in programs for children this age. For instance, *The Electric Company*, a program designed to teach reading skills, taught word blending in the following way. Two silhouettes appeared, facing each other, from a side view. One said "Kuh" and the letter *C* floated across the left side of the screen; the other character said "Ow" and an the letters *ow* floated from the right side of the screen. They ended by saying "Cow" together, with the word appearing directly over their heads. In another vignette, Letterman, an animated character, foils a villain by changing the letters in a story. For instance, a damsel imprisoned in a tower is rescued when Letterman changes the *t* to an *fl*, thereby changing the tower to a flower. The visual images change as the letters are altered.

Television and computer programs can also foster reading skills by presenting books that children can then check out and read from the library. Most of us have seen a good movie and then gone to the bookstore or to the library to get the book to read. In *Reading Rainbow,* children are explicitly told that the book that they just heard, and more like them, are available in the library. Now children can also be motivated to read a good book by experiencing it first as a CD-Rom story, such as *Arthur's Birthday.*

Although educational television programs for grade schoolers have not been prevalent, software packages for this age group are. *JumpStart First Grade* teaches 5- to 7-year old children early school subjects such as music, art, math, and reading via activities. *The Magic School Bus* presents science concepts to grade schoolers, based in part on the lessons taught in the educational television series. Children who are in second through fifth grade can learn English, math, and science with *Adi's Comprehensive Learning Systems* (Oldenburg, 1995). Sim Series software, such as *Sim Town* and *Sim City*, teaches children about pollution, city planning, and the creation of healthy environments in an interactive format. Interest is fostered when children encounter "eco-villains" who lurk in wooded backgrounds where they cut down trees. The child can transform polluted cities into healthy landscapes by planting trees and creating bike trails. These games encourage problem-solving skills and creativity.

During middle childhood, from ages 8 to 10, children begin to understand hidden information in television presentations and in other areas of life. During this time frame, children can be taught to search for hidden meanings in stories. Series designed to activate children's problem-solving skills are rare, but they have been created in the past. For example, the animated story version of *Where in the World Is Carmen San Diego?* challenged children to figure out where the thief Carmen was, based on geography cues, as they chased her across the United States and around the world.

For this age group, science and math areas should be taught with concrete lessons with visual emphasis. For example, *Bill Nye, The Science Guy* teaches middle elementary-school children science concepts. The series develops one theme per episode, such as information about the moon, and it richly sprinkles humor throughout the fast-paced format. A central host links the program together as he discusses one concept. Visual depictions of science concepts, long known to be an effective facet of educational television (Schramm, 1962), are featured throughout each episode. For example, Bill Nye uses a baseball field to illustrate how the moon travels around the earth. The earth is the pitcher, and the sun is behind home plate. The moon dashes with Bill in fast motion as he runs to first base (half moon), second base (full moon), third base (half moon), and home (new moon). The episode repeatedly emphasizes the concepts of the moon, earth, and sun's rotations in different vignettes to ensure that children will get the concept.

Adventure games are popular for grade school children. Planning skills, which are cultivated by these programs, are part of the metacognitive skills children acquire and use in the later grade school years to organize successful performance in scholastic settings. For example, in a program called *Oregon Trail I*, children travel West by wagon, as the pioneers did more than 100 years ago. Along the way, they have to solve math and logic problems as the pioneers encounter obstacles such as navigating rivers and purchasing adequate provisions for the journey. The computer tells children how far they have traveled and whether they need food, water, or supplies. An old woman gives advice to children if they click on her image. *Oregon Trail II* extends these concepts and increases the level of difficulty for a successful journey, focusing on a man who is planning a move West with his family during the 1800s.

Adolescents become capable of using formal operational thought to master abstract concepts. The kinds of academic skills that adolescent programs should focus on include abstract reasoning about verbal, mathematical, and scientific concepts. The few academic educational television programs for adolescents are basically quiz shows that test what adolescents know in competitive contests. This approach focuses on what children have learned. No programs, however, aired on PBS or network television provide a model of how children should be thinking. A program that puts an adolescent in a problem-solving situation, that challenges the audience to figure out the answer, could be useful. For example, a mystery problem-solving story, with an amateur sleuth, could promote problem-solving skills.

In summary, throughout development, there are particular times when children should be exposed to particular kinds of content. I have provided a few illustrations to consider when developing age-appropriate material. Teachers have spent many years creating age-appropriate curricula in the classroom. Those who create educational television and computer programs for children can learn a few lessons from them.

Gender- and Ethnic-Appropriate Content

Not only should educational content be age-appropriate, it should also be gender-appropriate and appropriate for children of varying ethnic backgrounds. Children, like adults, often look to those who seem similar to themselves. If we want girls to excel in math and science, they must see female characters who participate in these activities.

Similarly, children from ethnic minorities need to see African Americans, Hispanics, Native Americans, or Asian Americans involved in educational lessons. Put another way, children are looking for someone they can identify with and use as a model for behavior. As Chapter 4 discussed, African-American children are especially interested in programs with African-American television characters. That's one reason that *Sesame Street* has been so effective. People from many cultures live and interact with each other in *Sesame Street*. Similarly, *Barney, Wishbone,* and *The Magic School Bus* create television, and in some instances computer programs, that have boy and girl characters from diverse ethnic backgrounds. Programs that present a diverse cast can appeal to many children in the viewing audience.

Perceptually Salient Production Techniques

Many of the early problems with educational television related to how the content was presented. When people stand still and talk about abstract events, children are rarely interested. Yet this style was common in educational television productions (Watkins et al., 1981).

With the advent of *Sesame Street*, the television industry began to use much more interesting production techniques in the creation of educational programs (Lesser, 1974). More specifically, moderate levels of action, singing, and catchy visual and auditory special effects were used to present the important content. The producers deliberately used electronic embellishments to emphasize the important program content (Bryant, Zillmann, & Brown, 1983).

Comprehensible Language

Effective educational programs use comprehensible language: that is, language children can understand (Anderson & Lorch, 1983). Language that is concrete and that has visual referents to accompany the verbal message are within a child's range of comprehension. By contrast, language that is abstract and that has no interesting visual referent accompanying the content is incomprehensible to children. For example, a character talking on the telephone about the aardvark he saw at the zoo is incomprehensible to young viewers.

Steve interacts with his audience.

All you can see on the television screen is a person talking. This kind of language is very difficult for young children to understand. However, if you place the speaker's thoughts in a cartoon bubble over his head so that children could see the aardvark, young children would understand the words more easily.

Interactivity

One criticism leveled at educational television has been the passive learning mode the medium fosters. However, new computer technologies require students to act on content. In addition, children's television programs are now eliciting interaction from the audience in more deliberate ways. As we saw earlier, *Blue's Clues* effectively gets children to interact with Steve as they solve the weekly puzzle. As you can see in the picture, Steve looks directly at the audience to get them to interact with him and solve problems. These types of interactions help children remember educational lessons.

Repetition

Television is a medium that presents content quickly. It provides little opportunity for review or rehearsal of the important content. When a program repeats content, children have an additional opportunity to go over it. One way to do this is by developing the same theme in many different ways. For instance, *Bill Nye, the Science Guy* might spend an entire program on the weather. Parts of the presentation will come back to a topic like "the wind" in many different vignettes so that children come to understand that concept. Programs for very young children, such as *Teletubbies* and *Blue's Clues*, even repeat some of the content within an episode, or show the same exact program for an entire week.

Videocassette recorders allow children to view programs as many times as they like. This allows them to master content, particularly content of interest to them, for that is the information they will be most likely to review. Similarly, CD-ROM games allow children to interact with, and to rehearse, content as much as they desire.

Familiar Host and Cast

Successful children's television programs have a host or cast that children recognize. Mister Rogers, Shari Lewis in *Lamb Chops,* Bill Nye, the Science Guy, Captain Kangaroo, and Steve from *Blue's Clues* are all recognizable hosts. Other programs use nonhuman or multiple hosts—for example, *Wishbone* presents a dog, three adolescents, and one boy's mothers as key characters.

When children see the same host and cast over time, they may become more interested in the program. It's familiar to them. They come to know the characters. In some instances, they may come to like and to identify with some of these characters, and thus, become more likely to watch the program regularly and learn from it.

Familiar Setting

Just as familiar characters are important in educational television, so too is a familiar place. *Sesame Street* is a place, a setting in which the action occurs. From that street, children can venture off with characters to novel places and new settings. Similarly, the dog Wishbone lives in the present time with Joe and his mother in their house in their neighborhood; however, he travels in time to other places and acts out classic novels, such as *Huckleberry Finn,* with different characters. Only Wishbone and the theme of the program are constant across the two settings and the two plots.

Themes

Themes provide continuity and make the program "hang together" for children. Television and computer programs are presented in two basic formats: **story** or **magazine format.** In stories, the theme involves a plot organized around many hidden causal elements, such as motives and feelings, that propel the characters into action. Stories involve drama, and children enjoy listening to stories from the preschool years onward. *Science Court* innovatively teaches grade school children science lessons about subjects such as condensation and air pressure by bringing a case to court. In these cases, the defendant always goes free because an expert witness teaches them a science lesson which explains the purported crime. These explanations are presented both visually and verbally. Similarly, the Broderbund CD-ROM series presents a story to enhance children's reading skills. Embedding academic content in story themes is an underused mode of delivering educational messages; it might well be expanded in future productions.

Television has historically presented educational material in a magazine format, merging independent vignettes together to create a program. Each vignette, called a "bit," stands independently. Programs like *Sesame Street, The Electric Company, 3–2–1 Contact,* and *Square One* all used a magazine format to present educational lessons.

When *Sesame Street* is presented by the letters "A" and "D" and by the number "3," this means these concepts will be featured over and over in that episode. Similarly, *Bill Nye, the Science Guy* develops a theme about the weather or the moon in numerous vignettes. When one bit is not attention-getting, producers can easily replace it with one that is. Bits present information concretely to maximize children's comprehension of the educational material.

Learning Is Fun!

One of the most important lessons an educational television program can convey to children is how much fun it is to learn. Learning should be presented as an exciting and interesting enterprise, not a dry and tedious ordeal to be endured.

To make learning fun, characters should be excited, involved, and interested in what they are doing. Attractive production techniques also make learning fun. Some believe we should "hide" the educational message so that children do not understand we are educating them. "Stealth education" may maximize children's interest in activities that traditionally take place during leisure time.

Multimedia Learning Environments

Multimedia environments—in which print, televised, and interactive software support an educational message—can flourish around a successful television program. Take, for example, the PBS program *The Magic School Bus.* Children take imaginary journeys to learn science lessons, such as how the digestive system works. CD-ROM programs and storybooks support educational television lessons by allowing children to rehearse and to interact with the same material.

Educational computer programs can build upon the interest generated when children view parallel television programs. Take a trip to WETA Learning Smith, an outgrowth of PBS initiatives. Here you will find computer programs such as *Where in the World Is Carmen San Diego?, Arthur,* and *The Magic School Bus.* Children can rehearse and master the kinds of lessons they viewed. Playing these games should not only promote learning, it should foster more interest in the educational television program. In this way, a multimedia educational curriculum can build on the program's strengths to engage and excite children and stimulate them to learn educational material.

Many educational television programs also refer children to the library for books, to videotapes they can view to emphasize and repeat messages, or to

CD-ROM computer games that allow children to interact with educational messages. These additional resources reinforce and enhance the educational lesson.

The same qualities that create effective television programs also apply to educational computer programs. For example, age-appropriateness is important throughout these software applications. Adventure, interesting graphics, and entertainment are also key ingredients in making the educational material interesting for children, thereby increasing the chances that they will use it, particularly during their free time.

EFFECTIVENESS OF EDUCATIONAL TELEVISION PROGRAMS

Educational television programs should be broadcast if these programs foster children's cognitive development. Children who are regular viewers of these types of programs are expected to do better in school. Do they?

Research on educational television programming can be divided into two broad categories: formative or summative. **Formative research** aids initial production decisions, providing quick feedback to producers to improve the production. For example, I once collected data on *Sesame Street* to examine the appeal of new bits. A group of researchers went to a child care center, and a group of 3-, 4-, and 5-year-olds viewed the program from several rows of chairs. Every 30 seconds, when I heard a beep in my ear from a tape recorder, I recorded whether each individual in my small group of children was looking or not looking at the television screen. Other researchers did the same thing with different groups of children. After collecting and analyzing this data, the researchers could tell the producers which bits were appealing, capable of attracting and holding children's attention, and which bits were not appealing. Focus groups of older children provide verbal feedback to producers about the program's appeal. This type of formative research is provided quickly so that producers can make changes in the program before costly production decisions continue unchecked.

Summative research examines the final product. The goal is to discover whether the program is accomplishing its educational mission. Studies can be undertaken in children's homes or in schools, depending on the setting in which the children are supposed to view the program. In addition, laboratory studies can be conducted to test specific predictions about how the program should work. For instance, Anderson and Levin (1976) conducted a laboratory study of *Sesame Street* to examine the specific production features that attract children's visual attention. They found that certain features, such as child voices and women on the screen, increased children's attention, whereas men's voices decreased their attention. Because *Sesame Street* is one of the most researched programs ever made, I will highlight some of the more important studies only, focusing on research that examined the impact of the series on the child audience.

Evaluations of Sesame Street

From the beginning, evaluators examined the impact of *Sesame Street* on young viewers' learning. Two initial summative field evaluations (Ball & Bogatz, 1970, 1972; Bogatz & Ball, 1971) started during the first six months *Sesame Street* was broadcast. In the first study (Ball & Bogatz, 1970), 3- to 5-year old children viewed *Sesame Street* in their homes either with or without encouragement. The researchers contacted the parents of the encouraged group, told them about the program, and gave them toys from the program to facilitate their children's interest. The parents of the children who were not encouraged, that is, the control group, did not receive any information or toys. This strategy was expected to create differences in the amount of exposure children had to *Sesame Street*.

However, the researchers did not anticipate that *Sesame Street* would be a big hit. The result was that all children viewed the program, not just the encouraged group.

The researchers had to take another tack to understand how *Sesame Street* impacted children's learning. They decided to divide children into four groups, based on frequency of viewing. High viewers of *Sesame Street* learned more in the curriculum areas of letters, numbers, geometric forms, sorting, and classification than the low viewers did. Disadvantaged children learned just as much as advantaged children, and boys and girls learned equally well from the program.

In the second season of *Sesame Street,* the researchers went to areas where children did not have access to UHF stations without a special cable. At this time, *Sesame Street* was broadcast in these viewing areas on a UHF station. In this study, the encouraged group got the cable, while the control group did not. This manipulation was effective in creating different amounts of exposure to *Sesame Street*. The researchers examined twenty-nine goal areas from the curriculum. Viewing *Sesame Street* had a clear impact on 13 of these areas, a questionable effect on 10 areas, and no impact on 6 areas. The 13 areas that improved after children viewed *Sesame Street* were naming parts of the body, identifying numbers, knowing initial sounds, decoding, knowing left from right, counting strategies, knowing the correspondence between a number and a numeral, addition and subtraction, classifying by two dimensions simultaneously, and identifying emotions (Bogatz & Ball, 1971). Viewers of *Sesame Street* also improved in their Peabody Picture Vocabulary Test scores, a measure of language skills, more than nonviewers did.

In the second-year evaluation, the researchers studied the children who participated in the first-year evaluation again. Some of these children were entering school. Teachers, who did not know how much individual children had viewed *Sesame Street*, rated each child on school readiness. Frequent viewers of *Sesame Street* had better attitudes towards school and their peers than less frequent viewers did. Critics argued and continue to argue that children who view *Sesame Street* will be less prepared for school because school is less exciting than watching television programs. The data did not support this concern.

Instead, *Sesame Street* viewers were better prepared for school than nonviewers or low viewers of the program.

Success often breeds criticism (Watkins et al., 1981). Cook and his colleagues (1975) argued that it was not *Sesame Street* that improved children's learning. Instead, it was getting the mothers of these children involved in their learning through the encouragement condition. These researchers argued that the encouraged group should not be studied at all. They reanalyzed the data, using only the data from the control conditions. These children varied in how much they watched the program but did not receive any encouragement. While *Sesame Street* was still effective in teaching children, the impact of the program was more limited when researchers examined only the control groups. These children improved in number and letter recognition, but not in the more difficult conceptual tasks. The authors argued that without maternal intervention, performance improved primarily in rote learning tasks.

These authors also criticized *Sesame Street* for increasing, rather than decreasing, the achievement gap between advantaged and disadvantaged children. Although disadvantaged children who viewed the program gained just as much as advantaged viewers, middle-class children were more likely to view the program than poor children were when the program was initially broadcast. However, gap filling was never one of *Sesame Street*'s goals, and it would be difficult to create a program designed to assist only certain child viewers (Watkins et al., 1981).

Wright and Huston (1995) later addressed the role that encouragement versus no encouragement played in these evaluations in a longitudinal study. The study followed two groups of children from working class or disadvantaged homes for three years. One group was 2 years old when the study began; the other group was 4 years old. Forty percent of the sample was European American, 40 percent was African American, and 20 percent was Hispanic. None of the children were encouraged to view, thereby eliminating the problem inherent in the early evaluation studies. Instead, the researchers examined naturalistic viewing patterns in children's homes. Between ages 2 and 4, children viewed about two hours of educational television per week, and 80 percent of that viewing was *Sesame Street*. As Figure 8.1 shows, 2-year-olds who viewed more *Sesame Street* or the more general category of Child Informative Programming performed better in math, Peabody Picture Vocabulary Tests, and overall school readiness at age 5. Until age 5, there was a strong link between viewing educational television programs, particularly *Sesame Street*, and exposure to reading and other educational activities. At ages 6 and 7, children who were heavier viewers of educational programs, particularly *Sesame Street*, were better readers, as assessed by paragraph comprehension. Viewing educational television, particularly *Sesame Street*, was also associated with better teacher ratings for children's school adjustment in the first and second grades. These findings suggest that children should view educational television programs to prepare for school.

One reason *Sesame Street* viewers are better prepared for school is because they develop better vocabularies. Rice and colleagues (1990) tracked 3- and

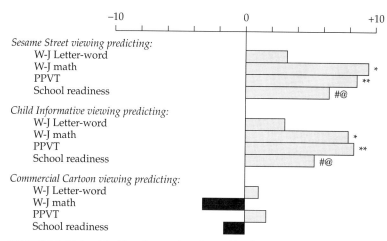

FIGURE 8.1 Cohort 1: Viewing at Age 2 as a Predictor of Test Scores at Age 5 (+ = advantage, – = disadvantage)
# p < .10; * p < .05; ** p < .01; @ p < .05 in step down regression.

5-year-olds' viewing patterns for two years. Prior to the beginning of the study, children took the Peabody Picture Vocabulary Test, a measure of vocabulary skills. As Table 8.2 indicates, children who began the study at age 3 and who were frequent viewers of *Sesame Street* knew more words two years later, again measured by the Peabody Picture Vocabulary Test, than those who were infrequent viewers. Viewing the program had less effect on the vocabulary of the 5-year-olds. These viewing effects remained after removing the effects of

TABLE 8.2 Cross-Time Regressions Predicting Final PPVT Scores from Early Viewing of *Sesame Street* (Waves 1 + 2)

Predictor	Cohort 1 (age 3)		Cohort 2 (age 5)	
	B	t	B	t
Initial PPVT-R	.387	4.81***	5.14	6.79***
Parent education	.142	1.80	.189	2.57***
Older siblings	−.076	−0.96	−.106	−1.45
Gender of child	−.205	−2.69**	−.170	−2.43*
Encourage *Sesame Street*	−.086	−1.09	.088	1.26
Parent positive attitudes to TV	−.133	−1.68	−.047	−0.67
Early viewing of *Sesame Street* (Waves 1 + 2)	.233	2.93***	.018	0.26

Note: PPVT-R = Peabody Picture Vocabulary Test-Revised. *Wave* means the time at which data are collected. *Waves 1 + 2* are the first two time frames when data were collected. *Cohort* means age group.
* p < .05 ** p < .01 *** p < .001
Source: Rice, M. L., Huston, A. C., Truglio, R., & Wright, J. C. (1990). Words from *Sesame Street:* Learning vocabulary while viewing. *Developmental Psychology, 26,* 421–428. Copyright © 1990 by the American Psychological Association. Adapted with permission.

Sesame Street's The Count.

Enduring Effects of Educational Television on Academic Success

One of the most important questions to ask about educational television involves its potential long-term effects on children's academic success. In the early 1980s, the research teams headed by Anderson and by Huston and Wright collected information about young children's television viewing habits. From that data, the researchers gained a wealth of information about the kinds of television programs children viewed when they were 5 years old. This data provided them with an opportunity to later explore how well these children were doing in school, based on their early television viewing habits.

In 1994, these researchers recontacted the original participants in their

initial Peabody Picture Vocabulary scores, parent education, gender, and other potential mediators of educational television effects. Not surprisingly, initial vocabulary scores were positively related to later vocabulary scores. Parent education also had a positive impact on 5-year-olds' subsequent vocabulary scores. For both age groups, boys performed better than girls.

Cook and his colleagues' (1975) criticisms were unsupported in this more recent evaluation, for *Sesame Street* was viewed just as much by poor as by middle-class or wealthy children, and maternal coviewing of the program was rare. Seventy-four percent of the younger age groups' and 82 percent of the older age groups' viewing took place when parents were not in the same room with their children. These findings suggest that viewing a program that focuses attention on age-appropriate vocabulary, in this case for 3- to 5-year-olds, has an educational impact on their mastery of language, even without parental assistance. It also suggests that *Sesame Street* is not widening the achievement gap between the socioeconomic classes (Rice et al., 1990).

Maternal encouragement is now taking a different form since children who viewed *Sesame Street* have grown up. Poor mothers from Caucasian, African-American, and Latino backgrounds are raising preschoolers who are home viewing studies. Five hundred and seventy of the original participants, or 87 percent of the original sample, participated in a 40-minute telephone interview. The subjects were now either in high school, had graduated from high school, or had left school. They were asked about the courses they took in high school, their grades, their academic expectations, their media usage patterns, and their extracurricular activities. The researchers also obtained high school transcripts for many of the students, allowing the researchers to adjust for the slightly inflated grades the students reported.

The educational television programs available to children in the early 1980s consisted of *Sesame Street, Mister Rogers' Neighborhood, The Electric Company,* and *3–2–1 Contact.* These shows were examples of *child-informative programs. Sesame Street* claimed 52 percent of all child-informative viewing.

Many critics of *Sesame Street* argued that its rapid pacing and use of visual special effects would yield negative school outcomes. The researchers, however, hypothesized that *Sesame Street's* carefully developed preschool curriculum would yield positive academic outcomes. The researchers were right. Children's early viewing patterns predicted their subsequent academic achievement during adolescence. Specifically, children who were frequent viewers of informative programs, primarily *Sesame Street* and *Mister Rogers' Neighborhood,* had better grades, higher levels of achievement in high school, better academic self-concepts, and better values regarding academic success than the less frequent viewers did. Children who viewed an hour of *Sesame Street* each weekday exhibited an increase of about one-quarter of a grade point on their high school transcripts. These results suggest that early viewing of educational television programs has lasting beneficial effects on children's academic success (Collins et al., 1997).

second-generation viewers of *Sesame Street.* Specifically, 40 percent of the mothers studied viewed *Sesame Street* as children, and they were more likely to discuss the program with their children than their nonviewing peers. Viewing was steady over time, with 92 percent of all the children viewing *Sesame Street* the previous week and 89 percent viewing the program within the past two weeks (Mielke, 1989). These findings suggest there is intergenerational transmission of viewing patterns, creating a constructive learning environment for children over time.

Although mothers who stay at home to raise their young children often provide opportunities for their youngsters to view *Sesame Street,* children who attend preschool or day care centers view less television programming, including *Sesame Street* (Pinon, Huston, & Wright, 1989). In addition, children with older siblings watched less *Sesame Street* than children with younger siblings. Based on the earlier research findings about the positive relationship between viewing *Sesame Street* and school readiness, preschools and day care centers might consider adding educational television as one facet of their curriculum.

One of the most important questions about educational television programs, including *Sesame Street,* asks whether viewers gain any long-term benefits (Comstock, 1991). That question is addressed in the box found on pages 196–197.

The Comprehensibility Hypothesis

Research on educational television programs like *Sesame Street* led to theoretical advances in the study of children and television. Based on early studies of *Sesame Street*, Anderson and his colleagues developed the **comprehensibility hypothesis:** the idea that children attend to certain types of televised information because they expect to understand it.

When Anderson and his colleagues began to study *Sesame Street*, it was commonly assumed that increases in the overall level of visual attention to a television program would result in better understanding of the program material. Put simply, scholars believed that the more children look, the more they will understand. This assumption is not necessarily true.

Lorch, Anderson, and Levin (1979), for instance, experimentally manipulated the overall amount of visual attention preschoolers paid to an episode of *Sesame Street* by showing the program with or without toys in the viewing room. Not surprisingly, children who viewed without toys watched twice as much of the program as those who watched with toys (88 percent versus 44 percent, respectively). What was surprising was that there were no differences in children's recall of the important program material. That is, watching twice as much of the program did not result in better comprehension of the important program messages. However, visual attention at the specific times when the program was presenting important content was related to recall of that content; that is, selective attention at particular program points did predict comprehension. The authors concluded that children attended when they expected the content to be *comprehensible*, and they used formal features such as peculiar voices to guide their attentional decisions.

The comprehensibility hypothesis was then tested in two related studies. The first experiment (Anderson et al., 1981) related preschoolers' visual attention to an episode of *Sesame Street* to three conditions: immediate dialogue in which events were visually depicted in the television program; nonimmediate dialogue with no visual referents (such as people talking about an event on a phone); and the absence of any dialogue. As expected, children attended most during segments with immediate dialogue, then during segments with no dialogue, and finally during segments with nonimmediate dialogue. The comprehensibility of the dialogue had a clear impact on children's attention to the program.

In the second experiment (Anderson et al., 1981), the researchers measured 3- and 5-year-olds' visual attention to *Sesame Street* with various changes related to the comprehensibility of the content. Children in a control condition saw the original program, with the dialogue and scenes in order. In one experimental condition, children saw program scenes randomly rearranged so that the sequence of actions was logically inconsistent and difficult to understand. In the second experimental condition, the children saw the program with dialogue manipulated so that speech utterances were reversed, thereby creating an incomprehensible verbal track. In the third experimental condition, characters spoke a foreign language. Visual attention was highest to the original program, followed by the randomly rearranged scenes, foreign dialogue, and the backwards dialogue, respectively. The 5-year-olds looked less than 3-year-olds did when the segments were presented with backwards or foreign dialogue, as compared to the segments presented with normal dialogue. This study demonstrated that children's visual attention was related to the comprehensibility of the program material, particularly to the verbally presented material.

These studies support the thesis that even young children are active, strategic processors of television content (Anderson & Lorch, 1983). This position contrasts sharply with earlier models that presented children as passive recipients of media content. It also emphasizes content, not form, as the reason for children's attention to, and memory of, television content.

Evaluations of School House Rock

Several years ago, as I told my class about the benefits of *Sesame Street*, one student inquired: "What about *School House Rock?*" And I replied, "What about it?" Those two questions led me to explore the impact of this educational series on children's learning.

School House Rock was a 1970s musical animated series about academic content. History, math, English, and science lessons were presented in three-minute segments. These vignettes were much like the *Sesame Street* format, but they were not part of a longer program. Instead, these vignettes were inserted into spots where commercial breaks typically appear. Because children's television was deregulated in the early 1980s, these vignettes did not air on commercial television for about ten years. I began to study the impact of this series on the original viewers as well as study those who had never seen the show.

The first bit examined, called *The Preamble,* depicted the Preamble to the Constitution in a song. The words to *The Preamble* appear in Table 8.3. There were two parts to this study. In the first part, we initially asked the undergraduate students in my class to write the Preamble to the Constitution. Then they reported how much they had viewed *School House Rock* as children. Students who had frequently seen the series remembered more of the words than those who had seen the series infrequently. One infrequent viewer began with "Four score and seven years ago . . ."; another wrote that he would have remembered more of the words had he seen the series more often. These naturalistic data supported the potential educational television has for very long-term memory of academic content.

In the second part of the study, we controlled for the amount of exposure to the series by studying undergraduates who had never seen the original vignettes. We altered whether the sound track was sung or spoken. After several exposures, we found that the students remembered the musical presentation of the Preamble better than the spoken one. Four weeks later, students still remembered the musical presentation well, while their memory of the spoken

TABLE 8.3 The Preamble to the Constitution

We the people of the United States, in order to form a more perfect Union, establish justice, ensure domestic tranquility, provide for the common defense, promote the general welfare, and to ensure the blessings of liberty to ourselves and our posterity, do ordain and establish this Constitution, for the United States of America.

Note: I sang the *School House Rock* preamble song in my head to write the preceding text. I initially left out "of the United States" in the first line because the song does not include these words. I went back and added them when I proofread the text. This same error of omission was made by subjects in the Preamble study.

version was deteriorating more rapidly. The results indicated that singing improves word-for-word recall of important verbal texts over extended periods of time (Calvert & Tart, 1993).

Next we (Calvert, Rigaud, & Mazzulla, 1991) examined how well children understood the content presented in *The Shot Heard 'Round the World*. This vignette was about the first shots of the Revolutionary War, including the famous ride of Paul Revere. Students who were in either the second grade or in college watched or listened to the script in a sung or a spoken condition. This procedure created four conditions: (1) spoken only; (2) sung only; (3) spoken and viewed; and (4) sung and viewed. Subjects heard or saw the vignette only once.

After exposure, subjects put a set of pictures about the program in order and then answered multiple-choice questions about the important, central content of the vignette. An example of a multiple-choice question is, "What were Paul Revere's famous words?" (A) "Give me liberty or give me death"; (B) "The British are coming! The British are coming!"; or (C) "Four score and seven years ago." Not surprisingly, college students performed better on both tasks than second graders did. The televised presentation was also more effective than the spoken presentation for sequencing visual pictures. Contrary to prediction, however, children who heard the spoken presentation understood the central program material better than those who heard it sung. The results of this study suggest that the children processed sung presentations at a relatively superficial level, based on sound and rhyme, rather than at a deeper level, based on meaning (Craik & Lockhart, 1972). If this is indeed the case, then the common practice of singing in children's educational programs may be far less effective than it is thought to be.

We (Calvert & Pfordresher, 1994) then studied the impact of *I'm Just a Bill* on several kinds of memory measures. *I'm Just a Bill* is an animated *School House Rock* history vignette about how a bill, depicted as a "living" piece of paper, a character with writing on it, becomes a law. The vignette traces the process from the time an idea is conceived to passage in the House, the Senate, and the president for a signature (or veto). This vignette included both sung and spoken material to present the content. Third-grade children and college students were exposed to this vignette either once or repeatedly (four times).

Students in the repetition condition recalled the words verbatim and verbally sequenced events about how a bill becomes a law better than those who saw the vignette only once. No differences were found, however, for recognition of important story content or for sequencing of important visual events.

Taken together, this series of studies suggests that *School House Rock* was effective in getting certain kinds of messages to the audience. If the goal is to remember information verbatim, then the material should be sung. If the goal is to think about material at a deeper level, then at least some of the material should be spoken. Moreover, beneficial effects depend on repeated exposure to a specific vignette. Four exposures appear to be sufficient if spaced within a period of about two weeks, suggesting that targeted vignettes should be broadcast often when they are initially introduced. After acquisition, vignettes can be reshown at longer intervals of time to remind children of the lesson.

Because of the Children's Television Act of 1990, *School House Rock* is now back on the air for a new generation of children. But, as is true with any broadcast medium, children in the audience will continue to differ in exposure levels. Using commercially available videotapes of the series in the home can help children to memorize information more readily.

Evaluations of Other Educational Programs

In addition to *Sesame Street,* several other educational series created for PBS by the Children's Television Workshop were evaluated for effectiveness. These include *The Electric Company, 3–2–1 Contact,* and *Square One.* Nickelodeon later evaluated their children's programs as well.

In one evaluation, first- through fourth-grade children who viewed *The Electric Company* in their schools improved in the specific skills taught in the program. Viewing at home, however, had no effect on reading skills, nor did viewing at school impact performance on a standardized reading test. It appears that related curriculum materials and in this instance, rehearsal led by teachers, increased the effectiveness of the series, but in a limited way (Ball & Bogatz, 1973).

A formative evaluation of *3–2–1 Contact,* a science series, was conducted with over 4,000 children who were in elementary school. Ten- and 11-year-olds learned more from the series than 8- and 9-year-olds did. This age difference may reflect the increased powers of abstraction that characterize the thought processes of older children (Mielke, 1983). Even though the series effectively transmitted science concepts, it did not maintain an audience, and thus, it was eventually dropped from production.

Square One, aimed at 8- to 12-year olds, is a series that teaches math. In one study of the program, fifth-grade children were pretested on math skills. Then an experimental group viewed 30 half-hour episodes of *Square One* in their school classrooms. A control group viewed none of these episodes. Math classes were not altered in any other way. After viewing, the experimental group increased in mathematical problem-solving skills more than the control group did. Similar effects were found for boys and girls and for members of different ethnic minorities (Hall, Esty, & Fisch, 1990).

Following the examples of the Children's Television Workshop, Nickelodeon also conducted evaluations of some of their educational programs. The goals of *Allegra's Window* and of *Gullah Gullah Island* are to increase preschool children's flexible thinking, problem solving, and prosocial behavior. Two samples of preschool children were compared to their respective control groups: one of the experimental groups was encouraged to view, and the other group was simply given access to the programs. Periodically, caregivers assessed the children's skills. After the programs were available in the experimental groups' homes for six months, children who viewed these educational programs had increased in flexible thinking, problem solving, and prosocial behaviors more than those in the control group. Within the experimental groups, the impact was strongest for those encouraged to view (Bryant et al., 1995).

Evaluations of *Blue's Clues* are indicating this program has positive effects on children's learning as well. The producers adopted a format in which they broadcast the same program every day for five days a week. In an evaluation of the series, Anderson and his colleagues (1997) reported that 3-year-olds continue to be attentive throughout the week, that attention peaks and then drops for 4-year-olds, but not significantly so, and does drop over the course of the week for 5-year-olds. Children who are exposed to the same episode five times remember the information better than those who are exposed to the information just once or not at all. Longitudinal evaluations of children's learning over time are now in progress.

Summary of Educational Television Programs

Taken together, the research studies document that children who are frequent viewers of educational television programs, particularly *Sesame Street*, acquire academic concepts earlier, are better prepared for school, have a richer vocabulary, have better attitudes about learning, and perform better in school up through the adolescent years. Maternal encouragement augments this relationship, but beneficial effects occur even when children view without encouragement. Although causality is difficult to determine, since viewing is rarely manipulated, other relevant background variables such as parent education are typically controlled. The results indicate that educational television programs like *Sesame Street* benefit children from all ethnic backgrounds, from all economic backgrounds, and of both genders. Other educational television programs can provide academic benefits as well. Maximum effectiveness often occurs in school or when teachers or parents encourage children to view.

While educational television is not the answer to educating our children, it could be part of the formula for accomplishing that goal. Perhaps encouragement to view should be expanded, rather than constrained, as we attempt to maximize the impact of educational programming on young viewers' academic readiness and success.

EFFECTIVENESS OF EDUCATIONAL COMPUTER PROGRAMS

Although most educational video applications on the computer are now on CD-ROM systems, most of the research is on the earlier and more expensive videodisc technology. Both operate in similar ways, so the videodisc literature should generalize to the newer CD-ROM applications children now use.

One of the early designers of videodisc multimedia environments was Bank Street, who developed the *Voyage of the Mimi*. The *Voyage of the Mimi* was a television series with accompanying books, computer games, and videodiscs. In the first season, the characters lived and worked on a tuna trawler that took voyages to track the migration patterns of whales. CJ, a child character, his mother, and his grandfather, who is the ship's Captain, explore science concepts with a group of preadolescent and adolescent children. Computer software and videodisc applications parallel the story lines. For instance, children can play a computer game about survival on an island, paralleling the shipwreck the crew experienced in the television episode. Books also present the stories, paralleling the television programs.

Videodisc applications focused on two themes from the series: navigational skills and whale identification. Bank Street created an early iconic rather than text-based menu for children to explore the videodisc. Formative research revealed that the visual menu was both comprehensible and interesting to children (Wilson, 1987). These kinds of visual menus, as you well know, have become a standard for both child and adult computer interfaces today. The multimedia approach has also become one that many educational developers use.

Videodisc applications on computers have also focused on teaching language skills to children. Chomsky (1990), for instance, believes that children may be motivated to read books when they initially see them in the very enjoyable format of television. To test her thesis, she put a Beatrix Potter story, *Peter Rabbit,* on videodisc. The program was constructed so that it read aloud to children, and children could look up definitions of words unfamiliar to them. They could also slow down or speed up the rate at which the program read the words. Children were expected to learn the words of the story through repeated readings. In preliminary testings, Chomsky found that children liked to read alone and in pairs. When alone, they often liked to have the book beside them and read along on the real pages as the computer read aloud. Slow readers chose to have the program read the story slowly. When children were in pairs, they liked to play games such as inserting the words that belong in a particular sentence. Many times they enjoyed inserting the wrong word because they thought it was funny. Then they completed the task and checked their work with the computer. These findings suggest that computer videodiscs can foster children's reading skills in diverse ways. They also provide a way for busy parents to read to their children by computer. This approach may be especially welcome by parents who have children who want to hear the same book read over and over. Even so, the computer should supplement, not replace, the essential and personal activity that takes place when a parent reads to his or her child.

Teaching children about how to use knowledge, rather than teaching them knowledge per se, is another initiative videodiscs have taken. Through **anchored instruction,** videodisc presentations anchor important concepts to the contexts afforded by visually presented stories, thereby fostering active modes of learning. Bransford and his colleagues have examined videodisc anchors in relation to math and science concepts. In one study (Bransford et al., 1988), one group of fifth and sixth graders who were behind their peers in math viewed segments about Indiana Jones from *Raiders of the Lost Ark.* Another group learned from a traditional, though more individualized, teaching method. After viewing, the students tackled math problems based on the story. For example, students tried to figure out how far Indiana Jones would have to jump to get over a pit. They could solve the problem by using Indiana Jones's height and the length of his bull whip, applying this information to create proportions. Those who viewed the videodisc were more successful at solving the math problems than those taught in a traditional manner. These students also generalized these solutions to other situations. For instance, they estimated the height of trees, based on their height and the height of their friends.

In another set of studies (Sherwood et al., 1987a), college students learned a science lesson by viewing the Indiana Jones videodisc. One group read about standard science information with the goal of learning the content. A second group read the same information embedded in the Indiana Jones story. Students who learned the information in an anchored videodisc context remembered more of the topics they had encountered, and they were also better able to use the information spontaneously in a different context. Similarly, seventh and eighth graders also demonstrated better mastery of information learned from the video than of information learned in a standard reading group. College students also demonstrated superior inferencing skills when visual, contextual anchors were provided from an episode of *Swiss Family Robinson* (Sherwood et al., 1987b).

In developing a CD-ROM program about the brain, grade-school children's interest in, and learning about, the brain was compared in three conditions: through exposure to a computer game, a traditional lecture, or a control group. The computer program portrayed the brain with visual images, such as "Sara Bellum," and children explored the brain by playing games. Children who interacted with the computer game were more interested in the brain and learned more about the brain than children who heard the lecture or were in a control group (Calvert & Littman, 1996).

The results of these studies are encouraging. By using films or television series children find entertaining, CD-ROM designers can create programs that teach children to reason about math and science information. These programs can teach concepts more effectively than traditional pedagogical approaches, excelling in both motivational appeal and learning. The implication is that education can be entertaining and that entertainment can enhance children's mastery of basic educational material, ranging from mastery of vocabulary to mastery of math and science concepts.

EDUCATIONAL PATHWAYS ON THE INTERNET

Internet access has become a buzzword for academic success as we move into the twenty-first century. Schools currently linked to the Internet provide students with access to vast amounts of information. They can study the latest bills introduced in Congress or learn about foreign countries such as Argentina or Mongolia by exploring different web sites (Farhi, 1996c). Cable companies plan to connect elementary and secondary schools to the Internet using high-speed modems. Similarly, phone companies are paying for schools to connect their students to the Internet. In so doing, companies hope to entice teachers and students to use their companies for paid Internet services in their homes (Farhi, 1996c). Wiring the schools is the most expensive part of the venture, and competition for home business may fuel efforts to accomplish this task (Farhi, 1996c).

We know from early efforts that computer networking for educational purposes yields positive results. At the University of California San Diego, an Intercultural Learning Network was developed to link students, teachers, and researchers from several locations, including San Diego, Hawaii, Alaska, Tokyo, and Jerusalem. Students collaborated on research projects, such as learning about the weather or exploring family histories. On the weather project, the students exchanged data and analyzed it across different sites. Students at various sites also wrote a collaborative newspaper (Laboratory for Comparative Human Cognition, 1988).

Bank Street was also involved in early efforts to coordinate children's academic activities across long distances. An initial effort to establish pen pals between elementary-aged children in New York City and San Diego was largely unsuccessful, in part because of time lags between the two sites and in part because of the difficulty of coordinating the activities of two specific children. When one failed to respond, the activity broke down. An undergraduate student who took on this project shifted the emphasis from personal letters to news-oriented events. Children exchanged editorial opinions on current events, such as the bombing of Libya, and the project began to flourish. The new format also shifted from individual to collaborative exchanges, making the replies of individual children unnecessary (Newman, 1987).

In recent years, Internet access has spread from the classroom to the home, making the Internet available to parents and their children. Information about educational television programs is available on the Internet. For example, PBS has a web site where you can call up information about many of their educational television programs. Parents or children can obtain information about the series, including comments from those who host the show. A greeting from Shari Lewis, from *Lamb Chops Play-Along,* describes the educational philosophy

Many educational television programs, such as *Wishbone*, have parallel sites set up on the Internet to enhance children's learning of the program content.

of her series—to involve the child in active learning of the concepts she is teaching. The programs that you can obtain information about at this PBS site include *Bill Nye, the Science Guy, Mister Rogers' Neighborhood, Reading Rainbow, Shining Times Station, Storytime, Tots TV,* and *Wishbone* (see the photograph showing an overview page for the *Wishbone* site). In one story, Wishbone, a Jack Russell Terrier, and Rosie, a Beagle, are star-crossed lovers, paralleling the classic play, *Romeo and Juliet.* The Internet site describes activities in language arts, science, problem solving, and social studies. For example, a language arts activity asks children to reenact the balcony scene from the episode. Children are then asked to describe their own individual reactions to the scene in a diary.

There is an entire section in the main menu of America Online called *For Kids Only* where children can access web sites for Nickelodeon and other children's programs. Nickelodeon, for example, has a site based on *Blue's Clues,* their educational mystery series. Children can download Blue's picture and print it out. Children can also paint small and large elephants at this site. This area is directed at preschool-aged children, and it's a good way to get children started on the Internet. Currently, visual programs on the Internet are slower than televised images, but faster modems and connections in the future should remedy this problem.

Children can also access the Internet with Sega Saturn equipment linked to a television set and a computer modem. Because children often play video games when they first interact with computers, Sega believes their joystick will be easier to operate than the traditional computer keyboard. This type of interface is also less expensive than buying a computer. "To play is to learn" for Sega, and this type of interface to the Internet makes it possible for children to play and to learn about diverse, interesting activities.

SUMMARY

While the potential for using media to educate our children has existed for several decades, we now live in an opportune time when we can make that vision a reality. The Children's Television Act of 1990 set the stage for broadcasters to provide educational enrichment in an entertaining way. PBS pioneered innovations such as Ready to Learn with many well-made programs for young audiences. Specialized cable services, such as Nickelodeon, have invested in quality children's television programs as well. Educational television programs can attract a child audience. Even so, to effectively focus on cognitive lessons, the content must target a smaller viewing audience than a purely entertainment program or even a prosocial program, thereby yielding smaller profits for broadcasters.

Because television series often spawn additional multimedia materials, educational messages can be transmitted in optimal ways to teach children. CD-ROM programs and videotapes are part of these new frontiers, but educational television also steers children toward traditional modes of learning, notably books. Multimedia materials can much more easily target a narrow age range than broadcast television programs can. By the year 2000, most schools and many homes will also be linked to the Internet, opening up a new world of educational media for children, parents, and teachers.

With this window of opportunity upon us, the main question is whether we will use the media to educate our youth. Will parents encourage their children to use educational media? Will they purchase ancillary materials to make educational media work to capacity? Will children watch and interact with these programs, and will they learn from them? Will children and their parents use the Internet to enhance their children's educations, to expand their horizons? That choice, which people like you and I will make, will determine whether educational media ever fulfill their promise.

Prosocial and Imaginative Media

Remember the *Itchy and Scratchy Show?* After her daughter imitated the attack on her father with a mallet, Mrs. Simpson pressured the program to stop showing aggressive content. Later we see Itchy and Scratchy sitting on the porch rocking and pouring lemonade for one another. The Simpson baby then offers lemonade to her father. She can imitate sharing, just as she can imitate aggression.

This imaginary but realistic illustration teaches us that children can learn either aggressive or prosocial behavior from watching television. Does prosocial programming require us to give up drama, action, or other program qualities viewers find arousing and interesting? Are we reduced to watching boring characters who sip lemonade on the porch as they sit in their rocking chairs?

In this chapter, we will begin by defining what prosocial content is. We will then examine the prevalence of prosocial content in children's television programs. Because of the three-hour rule for children's television, which requires the local affiliates to provide at least three hours of educational and informational programming per week, prosocial programming is becoming more prevalent. Then we will explore the impact of prosocial content on children's actions, and we will examine ways to maximize children's learning and performance of prosocial behaviors. Finally, we will evaluate the new technologies as tools for increasing prosocial action, focusing on the collaborative and cooperative interactions that children engage in on the computer. The potential prosocial computer programs have to enhance children's social skills is clearly present, but few software developers have initiated efforts to make this idea a reality.

WHAT IS PROSOCIAL BEHAVIOR?

Prosocial behavior encompasses socially desirable activities that our society generally values. Prosocial actions include several classes of behavior, including: (1) *positive social interaction skills* such as cooperation, sharing, kindness, helping, showing affection, and verbalizing feelings; (2) *self-regulation and achievement behaviors* such as persistence, independence, responsibility, and a willingness to tolerate minor delays; and (3) *creative fantasy and imaginative play* (Friedrich-Cofer et al., 1979). These behaviors benefit society, sometimes at the expense of the individual. For example, when a child shares a toy with another child, he or she may be giving up personal enjoyment.

While most people value these kinds of prosocial activities, others may question their utility. Some, for example, prefer rugged individualism to cooperation, or they value the ability to seize the moment over the ability to resist temptation (Mares, 1996). Moreover, it may be maladaptive to be friendly and help a stranger in an inner-city neighborhood (Lovelace & Huston, 1982). There are also times when aggression may be socially appropriate, as when a mother uses force to protect her children. Thus, while society usually values prosocial behaviors, important exceptions and limits to this support do exist.

CONTENT ANALYSES OF TELEVISION PROGRAMS

If we want our children to learn and act in prosocial ways, then our society should convey this value by portraying television characters who carry out prosocial actions. **Prosocial television programs** are designed to promote positive social behaviors. Content analyses of television programs have not charted prosocial actions as systematically as they have violent content, but we do have some information about the prevalence of prosocial television over time.

In the early days of television, prosocial programs abounded. *Captain Kangaroo*, which was designed to enhance the early social development of children, *Lassie* and *Rin Tin Tin*, which were stories about boys and their heroic dogs, and action programs like *Sky King*, who was an airplane pilot in the West, were prevalent. These kinds of programs continued into the 1960s, and many are still broadcast to this day. Even so, I heard a mother interviewed on a talk radio show who had viewed an old episode of *Lassie* with her son. She lamented the loss of this type of quality program. She then pointed out that television once *helped* parents to socialize their children; now parents have to be increasingly vigilant to *protect* their children from television fare.

Her point is well taken, but the 1960s also had its share of violent television programs, as you may remember from Chapter 2. Prosocial television programs became more prevalent during the 1970s because of government hearings that increased the pressure on networks to reduce violent television content.

Several content analyses were conducted during this era. One study (Poulos, Harvey, & Liebert, 1976) compared prosocial activity on Saturday morning network television (ABC, CBS, & NBC) to programming on PBS. The study examined several prosocial categories: altruism (sharing, helping, cooperation); sympathy and explaining feelings; reparation for negative behavior; resistance to temptation; and control of aggressive impulses. Altruism was the most frequently portrayed prosocial behavior, occurring about 7 times each half-hour in network television and about 10 times per half-hour on PBS. Sympathy and explaining feelings occurred about 2 times per half-hour on the networks and once per half-hour on PBS. Reparation for negative behavior, resistance to temptation, and control of aggressive impulses rarely appeared. Twenty-five percent of the programs in this sample were low in violent content, which is important in creating effective prosocial programs.

In a later content analysis (Greenberg et al., 1980), the favorite programs of fourth, sixth, and eighth graders were examined. Although portrayals of altruism, empathy, and disclosures about feelings appeared in the majority of these programs, aggression did as well. Thus, many programs that children view contain a combination of antisocial and prosocial messages, which may send the wrong message to young children.

Coates and Pusser (1975) compared two PBS programs, *Mister Rogers' Neighborhood* and *Sesame Street*, for the frequency of positively reinforcing behaviors versus punishing behaviors. *Mister Rogers* presented 95 percent positive reinforcement, such as giving physical affection and praise, but only 5 percent punishment. *Sesame Street* presented 78 percent positive reinforcement and 22 percent punishment. While both programs on balance were prosocial, *Mister Rogers* was especially positive for children.

With the deregulation of children's television in the early 1980s, prosocial television programs declined. The Children's Television Act (1990) was supposed to alter this situation by requiring commercial broadcasters to transmit educational and informational programming, including prosocial programming, to children. However, few educational or prosocial programs were broadcast on Saturday morning, probably because the FCC required only 30 minutes of educational and informational programming per week for license renewals. In a 1995 content analysis of Saturday morning television programs broadcast by the four major network affiliates (ABC, CBS, NBC, and FOX), only two programs, *Fudge* and *Santa Bugito,* were rated as prosocial (Calvert, Gallagher, & McGuckin, 1997). To be rated as a prosocial program, the program had to present a nonviolent, moral message. Most of the children's programs had little prosocial or educational value, and in fact, many programs in the Washington, D.C. metropolitan area targeted adults in a time frame that once belonged to children.

Prosocial programs appeared with more frequency during the fall of 1997 when the Federal Communications Commission increased the requirement to 3 hours of educational and informational programming by each station per week. In fact, the trend now is to broadcast more prosocial than academic programs (Jordan, 1997b). Well-made older programs are reemerging, such as a new *Captain Kangaroo* that integrates educational and prosocial messages for a later generation of children.

The reappearance of prosocial programming in the context of the Children's Television Act, however, comes with some caveats. For one thing, it is easier to define an educational program that counts or identifies letters than to define appropriate moral messages. The greater ambiguity of a prosocial definition gives broadcasters more flexibility in designating programs "educational" and "informational." For example, some broadcasters mix violence with a little prosocial content in a program and argue that it teaches a moral lesson, such as "distinguishing the difference between right and wrong."

In summary, the early programs developed for children contained many prosocial themes and messages. In the 1970s, prosocial programs were prevalent on children's Saturday morning television, focusing primarily on altruistic behaviors such as helping, sharing, and cooperating, but these programs disappeared during the 1980s. By the 1990s, prosocial programs were rarely shown on Saturday mornings. This pattern may be due, in part, to market forces that encourage broadcasters to transmit profitable aggressive, action-packed programs to young viewers, or news programming to adult audiences. Programming patterns are again changing since the FCC new time requirements were implemented for children's television programming.

Allowing prosocial programs to meet the requirements of the Children's Television Act is based on the belief that prosocial television benefits children's

Captain Kangaroo, now played by a
new actor, continues the heritage of
presenting educational and prosocial
content for young children.

behavior. What prosocial effects, if any, occur, and how can we maximize the
beneficial effects?

CAN TELEVISION VIEWING INCREASE CHILDREN'S PROSOCIAL BEHAVIORS?

Social cognitive theory has been the most useful paradigm for studying the effects of prosocial television content on children's behavior (Bandura, 1986).
Through the process of modeling, children imitate the actions of those they
have observed. Specifically, children acquire and learn prosocial behaviors by
watching others do them. They translate this information into their own behavioral repertoires by performing the actions they have observed (Bandura,
1986).

The first study that examined the impact of prosocial television compared
Mister Rogers' Neighborhood to violent television programs (Stein & Friedrich,
1972). For a nine-week period, children in preschool classrooms watched either: (1) prosocial episodes from *Mister Rogers' Neighborhood;* (2) violent *Superman* and *Batman* cartoons; or (3) neutral nature films. The researchers observed
their behavior before the treatments began, and observers continued to rate
their behaviors throughout the course of the experiment. In comparison to the

other two groups, the preschoolers who watched *Mister Rogers* increased in task persistence, tolerating delays, and rule obedience, all facets of achievement behavior. The children from low socioeconomic backgrounds who viewed *Mister Rogers* also increased in prosocial interpersonal behaviors such as cooperation, nurturance, and verbalization of feelings more than their counterparts in the other groups. The beneficial effects for prosocial interpersonal behaviors were not present for children from higher socioeconomic backgrounds. This study was important because it demonstrated the potentially positive effects television can have on children's social behavior. In a later study, preschoolers from middle-income families who viewed either *Mister Rogers' Neighborhood* or a prosocial cartoon demonstrated more prosocial behavior in their play than those who watched neutral programming (Forge & Phemister, 1987). Thus, prosocial television has beneficial effects for many young children.

Children in grade school also benefit from well-made commercial programming. For example, first-grade children viewed either: (1) a prosocial episode of *Lassie* in which Jeff rescues a runt puppy from a mine shaft; (2) a neutral episode of *Lassie* in which Jeff tries to avoid taking violin lessons; or (3) a competitive episode of *The Brady Bunch* featuring a seesaw contest. After viewing the television program, children could win points and prizes by playing a game. During the game, they were told, they could stop to press a "help" button to call someone to assist barking dogs the children could "hear" in a kennel. Over time, the dogs barked with increased distress. As Table 9.1 shows, children who viewed the prosocial *Lassie* episode helped the dogs in the kennel more often than those who saw either the neutral Lassie or the *Brady Bunch* episodes. In a follow-up study of first graders, the researchers found that children attended to the prosocial *Lassie* more than to the neutral *Lassie* (Sprafkin, Liebert, & Poulos, 1975). Thus, prosocial programming is both interesting and memorable to children.

Children's viewing behaviors at home are also related to their prosocial behaviors at school. Sprafkin and Rubenstein (1979) examined the prosocial content in various television programs. Then they related the prosocial content to children's viewing behaviors, to peer ratings of children's prosocial behaviors at school, and to teacher ratings of the children's academic success. Children who watched less television were rated as more prosocial by their peers. More importantly, the more prosocial a child's favorite programs were, the more prosocial the child was at school. The children who were the most prosocial were also the best students, suggesting an important link between children's scholastic and social success.

Verbal Labeling and Role Playing as Aids for Prosocial Activity

Studies have shown that additional rehearsal activities help children to understand and to enact the prosocial behaviors they have viewed. These are **verbal labeling** and **role playing.** In verbal labeling, an adult rehearses the important

TABLE 9.1 Means (and SD) of Helping Scores in Seconds for All Groups

	Sex of subject		
	Female	Male	Combined
Prosocial *Lassie*	105.48	79.80	92.64
	(20.37)	(47.38)	(39.94)
Neutral *Lassie*	34.80	68.20	51.50
	(46.30)	(53.36)	(50.28)
Brady Bunch	8.50	66.50	37.50
	(14.18)	(45.55)	(44.13)

Source: Sprafkin, J. N., Liebert, R. M., & Poulos, R. W. (1975). Effects of a prosocial televised example on children's helping. *Journal of Experimental Child Psychology, 20,* 119–126. Copyright © 1975 by Academic Press, Inc. Reprinted with permission.

verbal content of a television program, sometimes by summarizing the key material and sometimes by reading a book to emphasize the important concepts. Verbal labeling is expected to increase children's learning or acquisition of prosocial messages by providing a verbal mode for children to represent content. In role playing, children enact the behaviors they have observed on television. Enactment can occur through the child's own behaviors, through using small toys to represent the story content, or through using puppets to reenact the central story themes. Role playing is expected to improve children's performance of prosocial behaviors because it provides a motoric way to represent content.

Friedrich and Stein (1975) compared the effectiveness of verbal labeling and role playing in helping children understand and enact the prosocial behaviors portrayed in *Mister Rogers' Neighborhood*. Kindergartners viewed either four episodes of *Mister Rogers' Neighborhood* or control films. After viewing, children who viewed *Mister Rogers* participated in four different rehearsal conditions: (1) verbal labeling only; (2) role playing only; (3) verbal labeling and role playing; or (4) irrelevant activities. In the verbal label condition, adults read stories that emphasized the prosocial messages to the children; in the role playing condition, children participated in puppet play to rehearse the prosocial actions.

Afterwards, the researchers assessed children's learning by testing their recognition of program content and their skill at generalizing the program themes to other situations. Friedrich and Stein assessed helping, the focus of the performance measure, by asking children to help during a puppet interview and to help a child who needed assistance in repairing a collage. All children who had viewed *Mister Rogers* performed better on both measures than children who had viewed the control films. Verbal labeling increased children's understanding of the prosocial messages, particularly among girls. As Table 9.2 reveals, prosocial television in combination with verbal labeling and role playing increased girls' helping behaviors, but boys helped the most

TABLE 9.2 Means Scores for Program-Related Helping

Sex	Role Playing Treatment	Verbal Labeling		Neutral Condition
		No VL	VL	
Male	No RP	11.50[a,b]	9.13[a,b]	
	RP	15.25[a]	9.86[a,b]	7.88[b]
Female	No RP	5.86	9.00	
	RP	6.00	13.00	10.29

Note.—Means that include the same superscript are not significantly different. RP = role playing; VL = verbal labeling.
Source: Friedrich, L. K. & Stein, A. H. (1975). Prosocial television and young children: The effects of verbal labeling and role playing on learning and behavior. *Child Development, 46,* 27–38. Copyright © 1975 by the Society for Research in Child Development, Inc. Reprinted with permission.

when they viewed the television program and engaged only in the role playing rehearsal activities. The authors suggested that the verbal labeling procedures, which required children to sit still and listen, probably favored girls over the more restless behaviors typical of young boys. For those same reasons, boys probably responded best to the role playing activities, which required them to enact behaviors in physical ways.

In another study, Friedrich-Cofer et al. (1979) examined the relative effectiveness of viewing *Mister Rogers,* engaging in teacher-led interaction about the program, and playing with toys related to the program in producing prosocial behavior in children. In the study, children who were enrolled in Head Start programs viewed *Mister Rogers* in one of four viewing conditions: (1) prosocial television with relevant teacher training and relevant play materials in the classroom; (2) prosocial television with relevant play materials in the classroom; (3) prosocial television with irrelevant materials in the classroom; and (4) neutral films with irrelevant play materials in the classroom. Each day for two months, children viewed a 30-minute television program. The researchers observed the children's natural social behaviors in the classroom before the treatments began and continued to observe them throughout the study. The teacher-training condition made use of songs and chants as well as verbal labeling books during circle time to assist the teacher in teaching the prosocial lessons to the children. In addition, the teacher used picture puppets to elicit story telling from the children. Positive social interactions with peers increased the most when children viewed prosocial television programs and the teachers and children participated together in rehearsing that material. Self-regulation skills were unaffected. Prosocial television alone led to few differences in children's behaviors. For low-income children, then, prosocial television is most effective when adults in the child's environment reinforce the messages.

Role playing has a positive impact on children's prosocial behavior, either with or without prosocial televised programs. Ahammer and Murray (1979) compared the effects of live and televised training programs on the development of altruism. Preschool children either: (1) enacted altruistic behavior with a live model in one of three role-playing conditions; (2) viewed episodes of commercial television programs such as *I Love Lucy*, *Lassie*, and *Gilligan's Island* that contained altruistic behavior; or (3) viewed neutral television programs. Although live models were more effective than televised models in promoting altruistic behaviors, prosocial television was superior to neutral television in promoting altruistic behaviors. Boys who viewed the prosocial television programs helped more than those who viewed the neutral programs, but girls showed no differences. This study suggests that role playing conveys important behavioral lessons, particularly to boys, by getting them to enact socially desirable behaviors.

Verbal labeling also increased children's understanding of the prosocial themes depicted in an episode of *Fat Albert and the Cosby Kids* (Watkins et al., 1980). Children watched this program, sometimes with three pauses inserted. In one condition, an adult verbally labeled the abstract material directly on the audio track of the tape during the pauses. In another condition, he personally viewed the program with the children and gave them the same information during the pauses. Children who heard these verbal labels with the adult present understood the important story content better than those who heard the content summarized on the audio track. These results suggest the importance of a live adult who views and summarizes important television content with children.

When summarizing content, however, adults must provide information children will not spontaneously produce themselves. For example, Collins, Sobol, and Westby (1979) provided children with either concrete or abstract program summaries as they viewed a television program. Only the summaries of the abstract program material improved comprehension.

In an effort to increase prosocial programming for the junior high school age group, Singer and Singer (1994) examined the influence of a television series called *Degrassi Junior High* on 11- to 15-year-olds' problem-solving skills and attitudes about drugs. The students viewed five episodes in classroom settings, either with or without teacher-led discussions. Although adolescents grasped the point of some episodes more readily than others, teacher assistance did not improve the students' comprehension of the main program points. The program did not affect the students' attitudes about drugs, either with or without teacher-led discussions. The authors argued that these adolescents were already against drugs before the study began. Moreover, it seems likely that adolescents are quite capable of understanding the program messages without teacher-led discussion.

In summary, both role playing and verbal labeling can improve young children's memory of television content. To be most effective, adults should participate with children directly, fostering active rehearsal and labeling. For older children, adults must label and explain information that is still too difficult for the children to understand, or the intervention will be relatively ineffective. Adolescents, by contrast, do not seem to derive measurable benefits from teacher-led discussions, probably because they are quite capable of understanding television content on their own.

Previewing and Reviewing Content to Aid Comprehension

Verbal labeling and role playing rely on adults who actively view television with children, but many children view without adults or with adults who do not necessarily explain the ongoing story content well. Because of the complexity of understanding a televised story, which unfolds quickly, another technique may be used to improve comprehension—**previewing** or **reviewing** the content for children. This type of intervention can be built right into the program. On the one hand, previews of content provide advance organizers of information that may help children to search for the most important program material. On the other hand, reviews of content provide summaries of the important points in the story the children have just seen. Both previews and reviews enhance children's learning of television content.

To examine previews of a televised story on children's comprehension, Neuman, Burden, and Holden (1990) provided a one-and-a-half minute **advance organizer,** or preview, of the plot for second graders. The preview included the following elements: (1) information to activate prior schemas and to generate interest in the program; (2) background information essential to understanding the story; (3) story information, including information about the plot; and (4) questions to prompt inferencing activities. Second graders were randomly assigned to a preview or a no preview condition. The reviewers assessed children's comprehension after the children viewed *Soup and Me,* a prosocial program from the ABC Afterschool Special series. Second graders who had viewed previews remembered more central, plot-relevant program material than those who had not viewed previews, but memory did not differ for the more complex inferential content and the irrelevant, incidental content. In a second study, first graders viewed an episode of *Soup and Me* in preview or no preview conditions. After viewing, children were asked to retell the story. First graders retold the central story events better when they had seen previews. The studies indicate that children's comprehension of central story content benefits when children see brief previews of the essential story events.

Advance organizers were also used to create **preplays,** audiovisual inserts that were used to preview the key concepts in a prosocial episode of *Fat Albert and the Cosby Kids* (Calvert et al., 1987). In these preplays, which varied in the use of visual and verbal features, a gypsy forecast coming story events by looking into her crystal ball. Visual preplays either involved actions from the cartoon or footage of the gypsy narrator. Verbal preplays involved her use of concrete versus inferential language to describe the upcoming story actions. First through fourth graders who viewed visual action preplays were better able to sequence the important visual events of the story. Children who heard the inferential narration also understood the implicit story content better than those who heard the concrete narration. Put another way, preplays improved children's comprehension the most when visual action sequences were combined with inferential narration that described the implicit program events.

Summaries of program content, in the form of **intraprogram synopses,** also improve children's comprehension of important story content. Synopses summarized important content after commercials interrupted the flow of the story. Young children who had the benefit of these synopses understood the central story content better than those who viewed the program without them (Kelly & Spear, 1991).

Taken together, these studies suggest that short summaries of important program content can improve children's comprehension in the early grade school years. These summaries can come prior to the presentation of story segments, as in previews or preplays, or between story segments, as in intraprogram synopses. These techniques provide an advance organizer for children to use, calling up prior schemas for processing incoming information. Review techniques provide a rehearsal mechanism to help children pull out and go over the essential content again.

Mixing the Message: Combining Prosocial and Aggressive Content

A common dramatic technique is to mix aggressive and prosocial content, particularly in children's Saturday morning television programs (Liss & Reinhardt, 1980). For instance, some programs embed prosocial behavior in aggression when the hero rescues the damsel in distress by fighting the villains. What message does the child take away when antisocial and prosocial messages are combined?

Collins and Getz (1976) edited an action-adventure television program so that the original aggressive outcome was compared to a prosocial, constructive response to the same threat. The story involved a police captain framed for bribery. In the aggression version, the police captain responded with force by refusing to cooperate with investigators and by confronting the gangster who framed him. Aggressive scenes involved fist fighting and gunfire. By contrast, the prosocial, constructive version deleted the aggression and replaced it with scenes in which the investigators collected evidence and cooperated with each other to resolve the case. There was also a control condition that presented a wildlife documentary.

Children in the fourth, seventh, and tenth grades viewed one of these three programs. Then they were measured on a "help/hurt" machine which tested their interpersonal behavioral tendencies. Children who viewed the constructive outcome chose more positive responses than children who saw the aggressive outcome or the control condition.

These children were older. What impact might we expect from a younger viewing audience? When superheroes demonstrate both prosocial and antisocial actions, young children take away mixed messages. For example, Liss, Reinhardt, and Fredriksen (1983) showed kindergartners an episode of *Superfriends* or of *Popeye*. In one cartoon, the Superfriends used both aggression and prosocial actions; in another cartoon, the Superfriends used only prosocial behavior; in the third cartoon, Popeye used only aggressive behavior. After viewing, children played the "help/hurt" game, which measured children's willingness to hurt others, and answered questions assessing their comprehension

TABLE 9.3 **Behavioral and Comprehension Scores, Cell Means, Experiment II**

Condition	Grade	Sex	Behavioral Measure		Comprehension Score
			Help	Hurt	
Purely Prosocial	K	male	5.833	4.085	10.3
		female	4.595	2.861	10.1
	2	male	5.758	2.428	11.9
		female	8.452	5.798	12.1
	4	male	6.312	2.608	12.2
		female	10.671	4.044	13.1
Prosocial/Aggressive	K	male	2.144	7.028	4.2
		female	3.550	5.721	4.6
	2	male	5.264	3.700	7.0
		female	3.558	4.115	4.9
	4	male	7.220	2.629	7.8
		female	4.458	4.235	6.7

Source: Liss, M. B., Reinhardt, L. C., & Fredriksen, S. (1983). TV heroes: The impact of rhetoric and deeds. *Journal of Applied Developmental Psychology, 4,* 175–187. Copyright © 1983 by Ablex Publishing Corporation. Reprinted with permission.

of the program content. Kindergartners who viewed the Superfriends performing only prosocial acts helped more than they hurt others, but kindergartners who viewed the Superfriends performing both prosocial and aggressive acts hurt others more than they helped them. However, kindergartners who viewed the purely aggressive program, who should have been the most aggressive and least helpful, did not differ in their willingness to help or hurt another.

To examine possible age effects on this relationship, the authors then had kindergartners, second graders, and fourth graders view the prosocial only or the mixed prosocial and aggressive cartoon. As Table 9.3 shows, children who viewed the prosocial only program were more helpful and less hurtful than children who viewed a mixed prosocial and aggressive message. They also understood the story message the best. Kindergartners who viewed the mixed prosocial and aggressive message were more hurtful than helpful; by contrast, the second and fourth grade boys were more helpful than hurtful. The more boys understood the story message, the more helpful they tended to be. These findings suggest that story comprehension is an important mediator of prosocial and aggressive behavior when there is a mixed message.

Further evidence to support the age-related problems young children experience with mixed messages comes from a study of *Sesame Street*. Preschoolers who viewed *Sesame Street* vignettes featuring only prosocial outcomes cooperated more when they played a game than a group of children who viewed vignettes in which the characters resolved conflicts (Silverman & Sprafkin, 1980). Taken together, these studies suggest that a mixed message is difficult for very young children to understand, often leading to aggression. However, age-related improvements in story comprehension which occur in grade school tend to reduce harmful outcomes and increase prosocial ones, particularly for boys.

One reason a mixed message may be difficult for children to interpret involves the salience of the message. More specifically, aggressive content often appears with loud music and other attention-getting techniques, whereas prosocial content, particularly the moral of a story, is far more subtle. Abelman (1987; 1991) addressed this problem by creating a school curriculum to teach children to identify prosocial behaviors in television programs. For three weeks, children viewed 8-minute excerpts of current television programs under the supervision of a teacher. Each segment targeted a specific concept, such as altruism, cooperation, reparation, sympathy, or sharing. Fourth-grade children who were guided by a teacher in labeling prosocial acts on television could later identify prosocial behaviors better than those who did not participate in the school-based intervention. Beneficial effects occurred for intellectually gifted, normal, and learning disabled children (Abelman, 1987; 1991). These kinds of intervention techniques could be extended to assist younger viewers.

Effective Formats for Presenting Prosocial Television Programs

Prosocial television programs can be presented in different ways. Lovelace and Huston (1982) describe these as: (1) a combination of antisocial and prosocial actions, the most common dramatic technique on television; (2) prosocial behavior only; and (3) programs with unresolved conflicts. From the studies just cited, we know that strictly prosocial content works much better than the combination of prosocial and antisocial content. However, producers are wary of using prosocial only content because they are concerned that children will be bored when no conflict occurs. Itchy and Scratchy sipping lemonade and rocking on the porch will not hold viewer interest. Yet we know that children enjoyed the prosocial *Lassie* episode. Thus, the prosocial only formula can be effective in sustaining interest from child viewers.

Programs with unresolved conflicts, which are broadcast infrequently, occur when a program poses a problem without presenting a solution (Lovelace & Huston, 1982). The viewer must then resolve the problem. This type of program has been used only in school settings with a teacher's guidance. Without adult input, children can easily select an antisocial outcome that defeats the purpose of the programming.

Other aspects of format also seem to make a difference in producing prosocial behaviors. Story formats involve emotions and plot lines that evolve over a period of time. Magazine formats, by contrast, use brief vignettes to present content to viewers. Magazine formats can teach children specific social skills, but the skills often do not generalize to children's play activities. For example, Paulson (1974) examined the second season of *Sesame Street*, in which prosocial models taught cooperation in a magazine format of brief vignettes.

In one vignette, two children figure out it's easier to button up a paint smock when you help each other. Later, children who viewed these vignettes were presented with similar dilemmas. Three- and 4-year-old children imitated specific cooperative acts they had observed, but did not carry cooperative behaviors over into their play. Similarly, preschoolers who viewed *Sesame Street* increased in positive social behaviors, but only if their initial skill mastery was low; by contrast, those who viewed *Mister Rogers' Neighborhood*, which embeds prosocial behavior in a story, all increased in positive social behaviors (Coates, Pusser, & Goodman, 1976). Children also learn the messages embedded in prosocial stories, particularly after ages 9 and 10. For example, a CBS evaluation of *Fat Albert and the Cosby Kids* found that 90 percent of the children they interviewed could identify at least one prosocial theme from the stories they had recently viewed at home (Columbia Broadcasting System, 1974). The implication of these studies is that magazine formats work well in teaching children educational material, but story formats seem better suited for teaching children prosocial lessons and behaviors.

Influences of Television Content on Children's Imagination

Imagination is another type of prosocial behavior. Valkenberg and van der Voort (1994) organized the literature in this area into three types of studies: (1) *imaginative play,* in which children transcend reality and pretend that objects mean something out of the ordinary; (2) *daydreaming,* in which children and adolescents focus their attention on internal rather than external stimuli, including internal musings and fantasies; and (3) *creative imagination,* in which children and adolescents create novel or unusual ideas. Studies in all three subcategories predict either *stimulation* (that is, enhancement effects) or *reduction* (disruptive effects) on imagination when children view television.

Imaginative Play

Through imaginative play, children create a shared reality and work together to sustain a dramatic episode. Children assume various pretend roles, such as the teacher or the family dog, thereby learning to see the world from the perspective of others. Such role-taking skills can promote empathy, kindness, and understanding.

As Table 9.4 indicates, various researchers have hypothesized that television viewing either stimulates or reduces children's imaginative play. According to the **stimulation hypothesis** (van der Voort & Valkenburg, 1994), television can provide the raw material to stimulate children's play. By exposing children to other children and places, for example, television programs can elicit play about this content, thereby helping children to encode and understand the material.

The **reduction hypothesis** suggests that television disrupts children's imaginative play. According to van der Voort & Valkenburg (1994), several explanations may account for this disruptive effect. One is that television

TABLE 9.4 Hypotheses on the Impact of Television Viewing on Children's Imaginative Play

Hypotheses	Predicted Effects
Stimulation Hypothesis	Children use televised material as a source of ideas to increase their level of imaginative play.
Reduction Hypotheses	
Displacement hypothesis	Children watch television instead of engaging in imaginative play.
Passivity hypothesis	Children become lazy processors when they view television, so they do not engage in effortful activities like imaginative play.
Rapid pacing hypothesis	The images of television pass by so quickly that children have little time to rehearse and to reflect, necessary ingredients for imaginative play.
Arousal hypothesis	Television viewing overstimulates children, leading to hyperactivity and impulsive behavior rather than to reflective imaginative play.
Anxiety hypothesis	Television viewing frightens children and makes them anxious, thereby interfering with imaginative play.

displaces imaginative play activities; children have less time to pretend when they are watching television, so the more they watch, the less they pretend. A second explanation is the *passivity* hypothesis; in this model, television is a lazy medium, eliciting minimal efforts to master effortful tasks such as imaginative play. The *rapid pacing* hypothesis is a third explanation for reduced imaginative play. In this model, the images of television speed by so quickly that children have little time to reflect on the content. Reflection is a necessary activity for imaginary play to occur. The *arousal* hypothesis links television viewing to impulsive and hyperactive behavior, in part because of the arousing aggressive content. Planning activities, a necessary aspect of imaginary play, are hindered in such situations. Finally, the *anxiety* hypothesis suggests that violent television programs reduce imaginative play because children are anxious after viewing aggressive television content.

After reviewing the literature in this area, van der Voort and Valkenburg (1994) conclude that there is little evidence that television viewing stimulates the imaginative play of young children. Children do incorporate television and other media-related material into their own play, particularly boys and older preschool children (James & McCain, 1982). The themes of children's play now involve more heroic adventures, and today's children have more fantasy heroes than children who grew up without television (French & Pena, 1991). But these studies tell us that television content has become incorporated into children's imaginary play, not that television viewing has stimulated or increased it.

The evidence supporting reduction effects is more prevalent than the evidence supporting stimulation effects (van der Voort & Valkenburg, 1994). In particular, some evidence suggests that television displaces children's play time, though imaginative play is not measured separately from overall play time each day. For example, children gave up about one-and-a-half hours of play time each day to view television after it was first introduced (Maccoby, 1951). Children who lived in towns in which television had been recently introduced also played less than children living in similar towns who still had only radios (Schramm, Lyle, & Parker, 1961). But not all researchers find these negative effects. Murray and Kippax (1978), for instance, reported an increase in play as television became more available in Australia.

Depriving children of television viewing is another way to examine its impact on play. Changes in leisure time activities do occur during the actual weeks of deprivation (van der Voort & Valkenburg, 1994), but one week later, no changes in imaginative play are present (Gadberry, 1980). Overall, then, television seems to displace the imaginative play activities of young children, but children do often play as they view television (Anderson & Collins, 1988). It is conceivable that children now combine television viewing and imaginative play activities, rather than giving up one for the other (van der Voort & Valkenburg, 1994).

Other reduction hypotheses have received little, if any, empirical support. For example, a study that showed two versions of *Sesame Street* to preschoolers examined the rapid pacing hypothesis. Children who viewed a rapidly paced version did not reduce imaginative play when compared to children who viewed a slowly paced version of the series or to children who viewed no *Sesame Street* at all (Anderson, Levin, & Lorch, 1977). Nor did children who viewed the slowly paced *Mister Rogers' Neighborhood* play less imaginatively than children who viewed the more rapidly paced *Sesame Street* program (Tower et al., 1979). Similarly, Greer et al. (1982) found that pacing had no effect on children's imaginative play.

Empirical research has also failed to support the arousal hypothesis. For instance, one study examined children's imaginative play before and after they viewed either a (1) high-action and high-violence program; (2) high-action and low-violence program; or (3) low-action and low-violence program. There was also a control group. According to the arousal hypothesis, imaginative play should decline after viewing any arousing content, including high-action and high-violence or high-action and low-violence programs. Instead, imaginative play declined only for the group who viewed the high-action and high-violence program (Huston-Stein et al., 1981). A later study found that action and violence had little impact on children's imaginative play (Potts, Huston, & Wright, 1986). These studies suggest that the arousal hypothesis does not explain why television viewing reduces children's imaginative play.

The passivity hypothesis predicts that children will be lazy processors after watching television programs (van der Voort & Valkenburg, 1994). Not only is the empirical base for this hypothesis absent, we know that children actively process the programs they view (Anderson & Lorch, 1983). Moreover, fifth graders used similar patterns of inferencing strategies when thinking about a written or a video presentation of a story (Neuman, 1992). Thus, there is no evidence that children are passively viewing television programs.

Finally, there is no empirical evidence supporting or contradicting the anxiety hypothesis, which predicts that television content frightens children, makes them anxious, and thereby interferes with their imaginative activity. Cantor (1991) finds that certain television themes frighten children, and anxiety does suppress play. However, no research directly tests the thesis that aggressive programs reduce imaginative activity because they cause children to feel anxious (van der Voort & Valkenburg, 1994).

It is important to draw a distinction between the overall amount of television a child views versus the kinds of television programs he or she watches. Some television programs are designed to stimulate imaginative play (van der Voort & Valkenburg, 1994). For example, *Mister Rogers' Neighborhood*, in which children learn imaginative skills by journeying to the Land of Make Believe, does stimulate imaginative play in some circumstances. Specifically, children who are initially less imaginative engage in more imaginative play after exposure to *Mister Rogers' Neighborhood* (Tower et al., 1979). Singer and Singer (1976) found increases in imaginative play for children who viewed *Mister Rogers' Neighborhood*, with or without adult intervention; but for some children, environmental aids such as play materials related to the program were necessary to promote imaginative play (Friedrich-Cofer et al., 1979). On the other hand, a heavy diet of aggressive television programs at home (Singer & Singer, 1981) or exposure to aggressive television programs or violent video games in laboratory studies (Huston-Stein et al., 1981a; Silvern & Williamson, 1987) is typically linked to declines in imaginative play. Therefore, it's not *how much* children view, but *what kinds of programs* children view, that is crucial in determining the impact television has on children's imaginative play.

In summary, the displacement hypothesis has received the most empirical support when explaining the association between reduced imaginative play and television viewing (van der Voort & Valkenburg, 1994). Little evidence supports the arousal, passivity, anxiety, rapid pacing, or stimulation hypotheses. The kind of programming also influences the way television impacts children's imaginative play (van der Voort & Valkenburg, 1994). Aggressive programming is often associated with reductions in imaginative play, but most benign programs have little impact. Programs that attempt to increase imaginative play, such as *Mister Rogers' Neighborhood*, often do.

Daydreaming

In another review of the literature, Valkenburg and van der Voort (1994) examine the impact of television viewing on daydreaming and creative imagination. The stimulation hypothesis predicts that children and adolescents will fantasize more after viewing television because the content provides the raw material to construct daydreams. Once again, the reduction hypothesis includes several competing hypotheses (the visualization hypothesis, the passivity hypothesis, and the rapid pacing hypothesis) that attempt to explain the interference effect of television viewing on daydreaming. However, since the authors conclude there is no evidence that television reduces daydreaming, we will focus on the stimulation hypothesis.

The available evidence suggests that television is more likely to stimulate than to disrupt daydreaming. For instance, children who are heavy television viewers report aggressive, heroic daydreams (Huesmann & Eron, 1986). This effect has also been linked to the specific programs that children view—that is, children who watch aggressive television programs report the most aggressive, heroic daydreams (Valkenberg et al., 1992). Moreover, watching nonviolent children's programs stimulates positive daydreams (Valkenberg et al., 1992). Therefore, it seems that the type of program viewed plays a central role in the kinds of fantasies children create. Prosocial programs may contribute to the construction of pleasant internal thoughts.

Creativity

When investigators turn to creative thought, they find the evidence points more toward a reduction effect, not a stimulation effect (Valkenberg & van der Voort, 1994). Evidence supports one of three possible reasons for this reduction: (1) the visualization hypothesis; (2) the arousal hypothesis; or (3) the displacement hypothesis (Valkenberg & van der Voort, 1994).

In the visualization hypothesis, the ready-made visual images television provides inhibit children's own tendencies to form visual images. Cross-media studies that compare children's creativity when they watch television versus read books or listen to the radio support the visualization hypothesis (Valkenberg & van der Voort, 1994). More specifically, children who watch television generally make fewer creative responses, as measured by novel responses for the end of a story, than children who read books or listen to radio stories (Greenfield & Beagles-Roos, 1988; Greenfield, Farrar, & Beagles-Roos, 1986).

According to the arousal hypothesis, viewing rapidly paced programs increases impulsiveness and restlessness. Moreover, the viewer has little time to reflect, a necessary ingredient for imaginative thought. Although no one has directly tested this hypothesis, evidence does support the underlying reasons for this position (Valkenberg & van der Voort, 1994). For instance, viewing violent television programs creates more arousal (Zillmann, 1991), restlessness (Singer, Singer, & Rapaczynski, 1984), and intolerance for delays (Friedrich & Stein, 1973).

The displacement hypothesis argues that television displaces other activities, including creative ones. The underlying rationale for this hypothesis has received some support, though the hypothesis itself has not been directly tested (Valkenberg & van der Voort, 1994). For instance, when television comes to a town, children decline in creative imagination scores as time passes, suggesting that time spent with television is time not spent in creative activities (Harrison & Williams, 1986). The collective evidence suggests that heavy television viewing interferes with creative thought (Valkenberg & van der Voort, 1994).

However, the kind of program viewed, which has rarely been studied, may again play a pivotal role in understanding how television influences creativity. For instance, a longitudinal follow-up of adolescents examined their early viewing behaviors as 5-year-olds in relation to their later creativity, measured by ideational fluency (that is, naming numerous uses of objects or interpretations of a pattern), participation in creative activities, enrollment in art classes, and grades in art (Schmitt et al., 1997). The authors found that the type of program children viewed was more important than how much they viewed. Specifically, frequent viewing of *Sesame Street* and *Mister Rogers' Neighborhood* was positively related to creativity in adolescence, but frequent viewing of commercial entertainment programming was negatively related to creativity.

Summary of Prosocial Effects

Overall, the literature suggests that television most often increases the kinds of prosocial behavior children have observed. Through modeling and imitation, children cooperate, share, delay gratification, and incorporate other forms of socially desirable behaviors into their own actions.

Two meta-analyses have statistically analyzed the impact of prosocial television programs on children's behavior (Hearold, 1986; Mares, 1996). In a meta-analysis, the researchers combine and analyze the data from numerous studies. In the first meta-analysis, Hearold (1986) reported stronger effects for prosocial than for antisocial programs. That is, the positive effects of prosocial viewing were stronger than the negative effects of viewing aggressive programs. Altruism, defined as helping and giving, showed the strongest effects. In a later meta-analysis of the positive effects of television on children's prosocial behaviors, Mares (1996) reported a small-to-medium effect for children who viewed prosocial television content versus those who did not, and a moderate improvement for those who viewed prosocial rather than antisocial content. Once again, the strongest effects of prosocial television were found for children's altruistic behaviors. Given these beneficial effects on children's social behaviors, Hearold (1986) recommended that we focus our attention on the creation of prosocial programs for young audiences.

The picture for imaginative play is less favorable than for the other prosocial behaviors. Imagination, in the form of imaginative play or creativity, declines when children become heavy television viewers, particularly if they view violent television programs. By contrast, daydreams appear to be stimulated by television viewing. It seems that the kind of content children view is more important than how much they view. For example, young children who watch imaginative programs like *Mister Rogers' Neighborhood* increase in imaginative play; later, as adolescents, they are also more creative.

Prosocial and imaginative effects are strongest for young children when environmental aids, such as related play materials and verbal labeling prompts, are included in the program, or when previews or reviews of essential material are integrated into the program. These results document the beneficial effects of television on children's positive social behaviors, effects that could be increased by newer interactive technologies that require children to act out and rehearse prosocial activities. We turn next to the unrealized potential of our new technologies for promoting children's prosocial behaviors.

THE NEW TECHNOLOGIES AND CHILDREN'S PROSOCIAL BEHAVIORS

Have you ever seen a prosocial video game? Does the thought bring a smile to your face? No one seems to consider the possibility of engaging children in prosocial activity in this area, yet interesting presentational forms combined with prosocial content could yield a viable video game. Even more surprising is the lack of attention to this area in the world of computer games.

Computer games, and computer interaction in general, have almost always been studied as a force that can decrease children's social interactions. The reduction hypothesis has drawn considerable attention, but little information supports the thesis that children live in an asocial world in the computer age (Hicks, 1989).

Instead, accumulating observational data suggest that children are interacting with each other on the information highway. Children communicate with other groups of children to share current events and to learn about each other (Laboratory for Comparative Human Cognition, 1988). Moreover, software packages such as *Where in the World Is Carmen San Diego?* are designed to foster thinking skills through group collaboration (Hicks, 1989). Computer programs can cultivate these kinds of prosocial behaviors in the information age.

Cooperative and Collaborative Computer Activities

Because computer interaction has shifted learning paradigms to group rather than individual work (Hooper et al., 1989), one area under study is cooperative and collaborative activities. **Collaborative work** requires children to cooperate as they solve computer problems.

Not surprisingly, researchers and curriculum designers have been concerned with creating a formal structure for using computers in the classroom. The National Curriculum Council of the United Kingdom asks teachers to be sure that children can work together collaboratively on computers (McMahon, 1990). Through collaborative computer work, the Department of Education and Science suggests, children will develop personal qualities such as social responsibility and the ability to work cooperatively with others (DES, 1987).

Obviously, certain kinds of computer activities are designed to promote collaboration, whereas other programs have no properties that make them intrinsically collaborative. We expect programs that elicit cooperation to have the greatest impact on children's prosocial skills. However, most computer studies simply describe children's and adolescents' prosocial activity during school-based computer activities. Control groups and quantitative assessments are rare. We will begin by describing the kinds of prosocial activity that take place when groups of children interact with computers. We will then examine the characteristics of groups that lead to optimal collaborative functioning and mastery of material. We will also consider how computers can improve a child's achievement-related behaviors.

Cooperation During Computer Activities

When groups of children interact with computers, they can engage in prosocial activities. For example, children who were usually quiet cooperated and participated in playing adventure games (DES, 1987). Similarly, 10-year-old British children were mutually supportive and cooperative in collaborative word-processing activities (Broderick & Trushell, 1985).

Eraut (1995) reported on 8- to 12-year-old children's collaborative computer activities based on case studies of sixteen classes in ten British primary schools. In these schools, computers were in short supply; hence, children had to share them in classroom activities. Eraut observed children as they worked in small groups of two to five students for several months in their classrooms. Children took turns as the keyboarder, a valued role, often sharing the role quite successfully. As an observer noted:

> The children shared the keyboard throughout—it happened so naturally that I wasn't aware they had decided on a rota system. It was over half way through the session before one of the children commented "It's your turn now, I think." It was only then I realized they were sharing the keyboard! It all seemed so easy and smoothly done—remarkable. (R3: 17) (p. 67).

Eraut (1995) used **group ownership,** in which all members work together and feel responsible for the project outcome, as one standard for evaluating positive collaborative interactions. Mutual help, in which children assisted each other in understanding the programming decisions, was another. Consider the following assistance one boy provided to a less able student:

> One boy was the enabler of the other two. He actually sat at an angle to the computer almost facing them. He insisted that they took turns in using the keyboard. He constantly enquired as to whether or not they understood what was happening. He took particular care over the least able member of the group. I recorded no less than six occasions (in seven questions) when he asked "Now, did you understand that, K . . . .? Can we go on now?" in some form or other. (R2: 29) (p. 65).

Ultimately, the most successful collaborative interactions involved synergy, in which members stimulated each other's thoughts, jointly worked on the problem at hand, and demonstrated mutual sensitivity to one another (Eraut, 1995). The implication of this research is that collaboration is a necessary social skill for successful computer interactions, particularly when the computer is a scarce resource in the classroom. Prosocial skills such as cooperation, being sensitive to the perspective of another, and helping are common experiences of children in these situations.

Optimal Group Characteristics

The construction of the group is one area that influences group success (Eraut, 1995). Issues of size, gender, dominance, ability, and teacher construction of groups all play roles in creating a successful group structure.

Problems can occur when social dominance patterns emerge between two children using the same computer (Hoyles, Healy, & Pozzi, 1994; McMahon, 1990). In these instances, children often talk very little to one another, focusing instead on their own specific roles (Anderson & O'Hagan, 1989). Dominance patterns are more difficult to contain in groups of two than in larger groups. When only two children are in a group, a child who takes control of the keyboard can easily dominate the other child (Eraut, 1995). Most children are brought into line by peers in larger groups, even if one person still plays a more dominant role (Eraut, 1995).

Gender issues can emerge in mixed-gender groups of three, with the two children of the same gender often leaving out the other child. Collaborative group functioning is often best when children are in groups of four or more, but optimal group size also depends on the complexity of the task. For example, when the task required children to practice keyboarding skills to become skilled in basic commands, small groups worked best. By contrast, reflective decisions that required children to generate ideas and perform more complex tasks favored larger groups (Eraut, 1995).

When two children share a computer, dominance patterns can emerge—one child may control the keyboard while the other child watches.

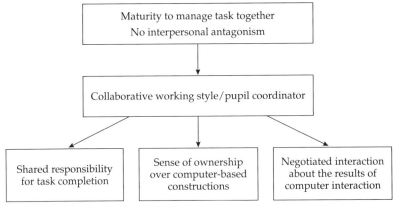

FIGURE 9.1 Successful Group Settings.

Teachers play an important role in group formation. If left to their own choices, children often create same-sex groups. Most low-ability children also end up in one group. Teachers use gender, friendship, ability, and personality factors to create groups. A particularly effective strategy is to create a group of seven or eight children, breaking the group down into smaller groups with different children performing different tasks. This group size minimized the problems of gender-segregated groups, particularly when the teacher empha- sized egalitarian opportunities. Moreover, at least one "computer expert" can be present in each larger group to coordinate programming activities (Eraut, 1995).

Knowing how to create effective groups is important in part because it promotes prosocial behavior and effective group functioning. Figure 9.1 depicts the group style that was most effective in collaborative computer interactions in Hoyles et al.'s (1994) research. Initially, children must be able to figure out the task and have no hostility within the group. Children do not have to be best friends, but they should not be enemies (Eraut, 1995). Older children are more successful at figuring out the task than younger children are. Understanding the task and having low levels of conflict within the group yields a collaborative working style in which one student emerges as the coor- dinator. The collaborative style then yields: (1) shared responsibility for com- pleting the task; (2) a sense of ownership over the product that the children created on the computer; and (3) negotiated interaction about their computer interactions (Hoyles et al., 1994). These outcomes are all facets of prosocial behavior.

Even when computer interactions emphasize collaborative work, individ- ual competence should also be assessed to see whether each child is mastering the lessons. When Hoyles et al. (1994) examined both group and individual outcomes in computer interactions, they found no relation between the two measures. In these situations, some individual children, particularly the less able ones, fail to master the targeted material (Hooper et al.,1989). This problem is especially likely to occur if the low-ability learners do not actively participate in the collaborative computer activities; the group can solve the problem, but not all members of the group can do so. Low-ability members sometimes coast, for only one person has to master the activity for successful group performance. Mastery for all group members increases when individual, as well as group, performance measures are administered. This can be accomplished by giving children individual quizzes as they complete successive phases of the group project (Hooper et al., 1989).

Achievement-Related Prosocial Behavior

Because computer interactions can sustain children's interest, computers may also cultivate task persistence, an achievement behavior. Although no one has examined task persistence per se, we do know that kindergarten and third-grade children demonstrate sustained attention to educational computer software even when a competing television program serves as a distractor (Calvert, 1994a). This area is one in which computers may well have an important prosocial impact, and we need to study it systematically.

Summary of the New Technologies

In summary, collaborative computer activities can promote prosocial behaviors such as cooperation, sharing, and sensitivity to others' perspectives. Group size should be a minimum of four, unless children of the same gender comprise smaller groups of two or three. Teachers can play a key role by creating flexible groups whose members tend to get along with one another. They can also create larger groups and break them down into smaller groups to accomplish particular tasks. Placing children of similar rather than mixed ability levels in groups yields mixed results. Some studies find that low-ability learners benefit from exposure to high-ability learners, but others do not. Clearly, individual as well as group performance measures must be taken to ensure that all students master the task. In addition, researchers need to make efforts to compare the prosocial behaviors of children interacting with computer games designed to facilitate prosocial activity to the behaviors of children interacting with neutral or even competitive programming.

Imaginative Activities on the Computer

McMahon (1990) suggests that we will not use computers as effectively as possible in group settings unless we begin to consider the perspectives of the children using them. He points out that children attribute lifelike qualities to computers and treat them as if they were alive. Piaget (1962) calls this tendency *animism.* Computers, after all, do interact with us. McMahon's point raises some of the potential ways children can use computers imaginatively. One way is by creating their own computer programs.

Children bring their own imaginative and creative skills to all situations they experience, and they display these skills in their programs. In addition, actively engaging in imaginative activities should further cultivate these skills. Consider the following imaginative content from an excerpt of a boy's computer game (Kafai, 1995):

> The rules are fairly simple. You are Jose, a third grade kid who gets lost and must find his way home. You will go on many different adventures. Along the way, people (or beasts, creatures, etc.) will ask you questions about fractions. (You will type A, B, or C, remember to press enter.) If you get the question right, you will go on safely, but beware! Danger lurks if you get the question wrong. Have fun if you dare! Type play and press enter.
>
> "Where am I?" "I have to get home."
>
> A mysterious man approaches you. "Hey, kid, I'm Marley the Magician and I'm going to make you disappear if you don't tell me how much of this square is colored!, says the man.
>
> YES! Go free says the man.
>
> A man comes out of a hot air balloon and approaches you. "I'm going to take you prisoner in my balloon if you don't tell me which one of these fractions is equal to two-thirds." says the man.
>
> Yes! See ya' (p. 64, © 1995 Erlbaum Associates, Inc.).

These kinds of programs demonstrate the imaginative thoughts integral to children's software creations.

Virtual reality games provide an amazing array of outlets for children's imaginative play. Children can literally become cartoon or other imaginary characters, enter imaginary worlds, and act in ways that are impossible in real life. For instance, children can take a trip to Mars or fly like a bird. Only our imaginations and, of course, our programming skills limit our virtual reality experiences. No one has yet examined the kinds of imaginary adventures children are experiencing in this new technology. Some of these games are played in groups. If we promote cooperative, helpful activities in virtual reality settings, then children should enact and master these prosocial skills.

Communicating on the Internet

Little has been done to promote prosocial activity through the Internet, but it is clearly a vehicle with great potential for older children and adolescents to learn about and to interact with others. Internet mail systems are a popular way for adults to communicate. Similarly, mail systems now allow adolescents from various parts of the country to communicate quickly and efficiently to others.

For those who have little social interaction or even those desiring to make new friends with similar interests, the Internet is a quick way to contact others online. A shared reality that fulfills individual needs can be constructed in cyberspace. The computer user can easily access chat groups organized around all kinds of topics, and adolescents are indeed accessing them, though no one has studied their communications. Children and adolescents can help others who are in need of advice. Children with special needs, for example, can reach out to others experiencing a similar problem, such as a physical handicap, thereby diminishing their sense of isolation.

We can also access additional information about prosocial television programs via the Internet. While some of this information is for adults, some is for children. For example, if you go to http://www.pbs.org, select the kids' option, and explore the prosocial television program *Arthur,* you can write stories to Arthur, learn how to understand stories better by asking certain questions, send pictures to Arthur, or download software so that you can color pictures of Arthur and his friends. A picture a child sent to Arthur's home page is on the cover of your book.

The interactivity the Internet affords dovetails nicely with the activities in the *Arthur* television program. Vignettes about real children appear between the two Arthur cartoons broadcast in each episode. In these live vignettes, children draw pictures, or they write and then read their own comments to Arthur and his friends. Sometimes they engage in problem solving and moral reasoning as they tell Arthur what he should have done. For instance, in one episode, Arthur accidentally portrays himself as a thief; children wrote and told him about why he should always tell the truth. These vignettes provide a model for how children should incorporate the prosocial lessons of Arthur. They also present models of other children commenting on Arthur's behaviors; viewers can then follow suit by writing to Arthur themselves.

SUMMARY

The information highway provides many opportunities for children to experience prosocial activities, particularly cooperation, sharing, and helpfulness. The literature in both the television and computer areas documents that children learn these skills after viewing or interacting with prosocial content. Effects are especially pronounced when adults or teachers assist young children in translating the prosocial messages into their own behaviors. Similarly, prosocial achievement-related behaviors, such as delaying gratification and persisting at tasks, increase after children view televised models they can imitate.

Imaginary content tells a more complex story. Television can promote imaginative play, but, not surprisingly, that only occurs when the content is designed to enhance imagination. The negative effects of television viewing on imagination are stronger. Children who view lots of television content often play less imaginatively and are less creative than their peers, but television content does stimulate daydreaming. The new technologies elicit imaginative activity as the child interacts with imaginary characters in faraway places. Although no one has examined imaginative play within this new interactive context, it seems likely that children will develop more imaginative skills from such experiences.

Prosocial and imaginative content both provide avenues for socially constructive emotional expression. Moreover, by learning and using prosocial behaviors, children learn alternative actions to violence. For example, it is here that children learn to put themselves in another child's shoes, thereby making it more likely they will understand one another rather than attack one another when a conflict occurs. As a society, our challenge is to provide interesting media experiences that will encourage children's constructive social responses as they travel through the information age.

The Convergence of Information Technologies

Alan Alda, an actor, visits the Media Lab at the Massachusetts Institute of Technology. In one project, researchers are studying how computers can tell what we are doing and intending.

Alda interacts with a virtual dog, Silas, who has needs built into his program. He gets thirsty and drinks. He wants to play ball, and Alda throws it for him. Silas even has complex emotions programmed into his behavior. For example, he acts jealous when the virtual hamster gets attention, and he acts sad when Alda sends him away to punish him for his behavior.

The information age involves a rapid explosion of hardware and software developments where nothing remains constant for long. Change is the only constant. Yet we can predict some of the coming changes in technology, in part because of new technological developments on the horizon, and in part based on themes that have recurred in other media throughout this century.

In this closing chapter, we will address two themes that we began with: (1) *the media are messengers;* and (2) *the medium is the message.* The types of content we have examined in this book have recurred across a variety of media, such as television, video games, and the Internet. We get much of our information from various media; media serve as messengers that quickly transmit information throughout the global community. What has changed and will continue to change are the media that deliver those messages, such as virtual reality simulations that create imaginary dogs who act in lifelike ways.

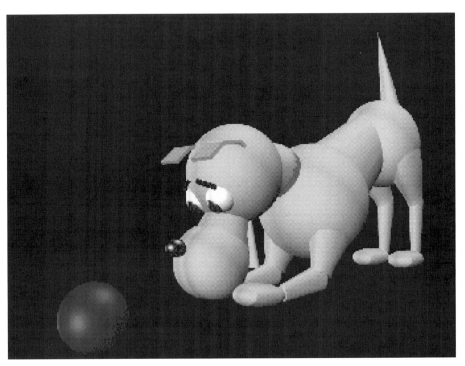

At the Massachusetts Institute of Technology, virtual dogs like Silas roam the Media Lab.

We begin this chapter by exploring the messages the media deliver to us. We end with a look at technological developments of the future, with a particular emphasis on how they will impact education. We will focus on two future trends: (1) video images will become increasingly prevalent and realistic; and (2) media will converge, making multimedia presentations the norm.

THE CONTENT

While no single theory explains all media effects, individual theories provide insight into how media exposure impacts children's learning and social behavior. For example, *cultivation theory* predicts that media depictions, be they violent, prosocial, stereotypical, or educational, provide information that shape our views of society and the roles we play in it (Gerbner, 1996; 1993). *Schema theory* suggests that these depictions are embedded within our culture and that television portrayals can amplify or reduce these cultural beliefs (Calvert & Huston, 1987). We will review content areas through the lenses of the theories that shed the best insight into how the media affect children.

Concerns about violent television content arose in the 1950s and have joined more recently with concerns about violent video games and virtual reality game content (Calvert & Tan, 1996; Huston & Wright, in press). In spite of these concerns, there has been no appreciable decline in the levels of aggressive media content over time (Murray, 1998).

Arousal theory, social cognitive theory, and *cultivation theory* provide the best fit with the data. According to arousal theory, children and adults habituate and become desensitized to violent content after viewing it over time. The data support this prediction (Murray, 1998). Moreover, with exposure, audiences seem to require increased levels of aggressive content to remain aroused and interested in violent programs. Social cognitive theory predicts that children who view aggressive content will acquire and perform the aggressive actions they have observed, primarily when motivational incentives are available for imitative performance (Bandura, 1986). Considerable data support this prediction as well (Friedrich-Cofer & Huston, 1986; Huston et al., 1992; Murray, 1998). Children also become more fearful after viewing violent television content (Murray, 1998), a finding that supports the cultivation hypothesis if viewers are identifying with the victim rather than the perpetrator of crimes. These theories will continue to guide future research in the effects of media aggression, but interactive technologies may require that some theories be modified. For example, virtual reality games require players to act on content, not just observe it, thereby placing aggressive behaviors at the players' disposal. Put another way, performance occurs as learning takes place, not afterwards, which requires modifications in social cognitive theory to explain interactive technological effects (Calvert & Tan, 1996).

Although sexual content and gender-stereotyped content were not originally issues in television, they have become so over the past 30 years. Until the 1970s, gender-stereotyped male and female roles were the norm in American culture, and sexual content was rarely shown (Calvert & Huston, 1987). But that has changed. Gender-stereotyped television content has been controversial since the Women's Movement began in the 1970s because stereotyped depictions were linked to gender discrimination (Huston, 1983). Even though the social roles of men and women are changing, stereotyped portrayals of women and men are still common on television and in video games (Calvert et al., 1997). Sexual content in television programs shifted from little more than innuendo in the 1950s to explicit sexual scenes in the 1990s. Computer content also portrays sexual interactions, particularly on the Internet.

Children who view and interact with gender-stereotyped content tend to construct traditional rather than nontraditional gender schemas of men and women (Calvert & Huston, 1987). Exposure to counterstereotypical television programs, however, can alter children's beliefs about men and women (Calvert & Huston, 1987). Children of either gender who have high levels of self-efficacy, a construct from social cognitive theory, are also more proficient computer users.

Media content also provides children with material they use to construct racial schemas. Racial portrayals have progressed from invisibility or stereotyped presentations to greater visibility and more diverse presentations for African-American males, but other minority groups remain relatively invisible (Calvert et al., 1997). On the Internet, specific sites are available for minority groups, but they are relatively rare. At present, African Americans and Americans of Spanish descent are less likely to purchase computers than Asian Americans and Caucasians (Marriott with Brant, 1995). As the Internet expands, sites pertaining to the interests of particular minority groups will become more common. Failure to provide such content, however, can increase the racial gap between those who are computer-literate and those who are not (Montgomery, 1995). There is some indication from the drench hypothesis that a few nonstereotyped and consistent television images about minority groups will have more impact on children than the more pervasive stereotyped images (Greenberg, 1988). If this is the case, then children may seek out programming and sites that improve their own sense of self-efficacy and self-worth.

What will our identities be like in this new symbolic reality? In everyday experience, we have certain personal characteristics that define who we are. But in cyberspace, those limits are not imposed (Donath, in press). You can change gender, age, or any other personal quality as you create your own character symbolically. Donath (in press) argues that people may deceive others about who they are in order to gain advantage over them.

The commercialization of television, and now the Internet, means that the programs that deliver a large audience to advertisers will drive the content we see. As predicted by *uses and gratification theory*, we often use our information technologies for *entertainment*, and that pattern is likely to continue. Consequently, violence, gender stereotypes, and racial stereotypes are likely to be present in future media presentations, and they will continue to be a focus of ongoing research inquiry and social advocacy. Even so, options for new stations will allow broadcasters to develop and distribute more nonstereotyped programs for viewers as well.

REGULATION AND DEREGULATION

With new issues emerging about the content and the underlying commercial base of the media, regulation and legal challenges to regulation will be an ongoing theme. Government agencies like the Federal Communications Commission (FCC), and to a lesser extent the Federal Trade Commission (FTC), will walk a fine line between regulating technologies and preserving the right to free speech on television and over the Internet (Huston et al., 1992; Williams et al., 1997).

Regulatory and deregulatory cycles will continue, depending on who is in power. When proregulatory groups control the White House, the House of Representatives, the Senate, and the FCC, they will make efforts to restrict violence, sexually explicit material, and advertising. By contrast, when marketplace groups control the Presidency, the House of Representatives, the Senate, and the FCC, fewer restrictions will occur. In deregulatory cycles, parents will have more responsibility for monitoring their children's media experiences. If parents don't have time to supervise children's media experiences, they will be able to purchase software that blocks their children's access to certain television programs and Internet sites (Williams et al., 1997). Even so, without the content ratings that software uses to screen out content, computer blocking programs cannot prevent children from accessing any content they choose to find (or accidentally find) as they are surfing the television or the Internet.

FCC rulings also impact who will deliver services and hence regulate the competitive aspects of information delivery. For example, a 1992 FCC ruling allowed telephone companies to compete with cable television systems to deliver television programming to homes, thereby opening up a range of options for integrating voice, data, and video signals (Murray, 1993). Similarly, the FCC ruling which required broadcasters to air three hours of educational and informational television programming per week to meet the guidelines of the Children's Television Act changed children's television programs, particularly on Saturday morning.

TECHNOLOGICAL CHANGES IN INFORMATION DELIVERY

Although the issues surrounding the regulation of media content will remain similar in the future, the way we transmit and experience those messages will change. The information superhighway consists of hardware, software, and interconnecting communications, such as phone lines (Meyers, 1996). Technological developments in these areas are driving changes throughout the television and computer industries. One such innovation has been the Internet, which has integrated telegraph, telephone, radio, and computer technologies (Leiner et al., 1997). The next innovation is digital television, which may eventually merge television and computer hardware (Farhi, 1997b).

Digital transmissions, the language of computers, will soon be available from American television stations (Farhi, 1997c). Digital transmissions allow high-quality pictures and auditory tracks by transmitting programs in the computer code of 0s and 1s. This transmission format allows flexibility for sending broadcasts in high-definition or standard format (Brinkley, 1996). In 1997, the FCC gave a second channel to television station owners to transmit digital television over the public airwaves (Farhi, 1997b; 1997c). Broadcasters will pursue one of two directions: they will each establish one new station broadcasting high-definition television, or they will divide the channel into four or five standard-definition stations with interactive capabilities (Farhi, 1997c).

High-Definition Television

If a station chooses to use its new channel for high-definition broadcasting, then the realism of portrayals will become more pronounced in the future. The clarity of digital high-definition television far surpasses that of current analog television. Digital images will be presented in rectangular configurations, as we now see when viewing films, rather than in the square configurations we see when viewing television programs. Some networks, notably CBS and NBC, who will begin to broadcast some programs in high-definition format in 1998, have already made this choice (Farhi, 1997c). The cost of converting industry equipment and television sets to high-definition format, however, makes this an expensive decision for broadcasters and consumers alike (Farhi, 1997c). However, the clarity of the images and the ease of use make high-definition television attractive to manufacturers (Brinkley, 1996).

Viewers of high-definition television may experience at least two effects. First, the clarity of the images may increase the overall amount of viewing as well as attention to the programming, thereby increasing the amount of time children spend with media each day. Secondly, the realism of the images may

LCD (liquid crystal display) technology advances will soon yield tiny, thin televisions with near-perfect pictures that can be hung on walls like paintings.

result in less distinction between reality and fantasy as well as increase the probability that children will copy the vivid acts they see. From earlier research, we know that television influences younger children more than older children (Huston & Wright, in press), and high-definition television may make these effects even more pronounced. The specific impact will depend on the kinds of content children view.

Interactive Television

If a television station decides to divide its new channel into four or five standard-definition television stations, media experiences in the near future will become interactive. Television programs will have interactive areas at the side of the screen where users can "click" to explore the content of the program, making television an increasingly active medium.

The interactive nature of television technology in the future will make mastery of the content on the screen far easier, with computer technology capable of tailoring feedback to individual users. As active processing increases, the choices children make may have more impact than those that happen simply because they are in a viewing audience.

The only shark that can swim in fresh water and salt water is the bull shark.

Show   The Lab

E-mail   Chat

A young great white shark eats mostly fish; while an older great white has a much bigger appetite... seals and sea lions.

Photo by Stephen Frink/Corbis

Photo by Stuart Westmoreland/Corbis

Interactive television programs will make it possible for children to actively control the content they experience in programs like *Sci Squad*.

If broadcasters choose this option, computer companies will build digital television receivers into personal computers, making computers and television sets virtually identical (Brinkley, 1996). Children will be able to explore the Internet from their television screens, or watch television programs or movies on their computer screens. Children will choose programs to view, games to play, and worlds to construct via their television sets or their computers. This technological direction will challenge many of the past criticisms of television as a medium that promotes passive, rather than active, involvement with content (Singer & Singer, 1983). Future media experiences will require children to make more active efforts to see and to interact with the content.

The major drawback of taking this direction is that insufficient advertising revenue is available for tripling or quadrupling the number of channels available to consumers (Farhi, 1997c). As the audience becomes smaller, the efficiency of delivering content to market commercial products decreases. This means that other sources of financing television programs, such as underwriting television programs, may become more prevalent.

Virtual Reality Interfaces

Virtual reality experiences will also be available over computers or television sets. Virtual reality creates a three-dimensional rather than the current two-dimensional media representation of reality. These representations will likely elicit stronger emotional reactions than the same images on current television sets (Calvert & Tan, 1996). In the future, you will be able to experience virtually any thought you can imagine. If you can program it, you can experience it in the future. Because the images and experiences will be increasingly vivid and realistic, the boundaries between reality and fantasy will become increasingly blurred (Calvert & Tan, 1996). Computer networks should allow three-dimensional virtual reality interactions within the next decade (Adam et al., 1997). Some already exist, such as the three-dimensional dog developed at MIT.

Summary on Changes in Delivery

Regardless of who wins the debate over the new digital channels, it is clear that television is going to change. Pictures will become more vivid, and options for interactivity will become increasingly available. It seems likely that different stations will select different options, making both interactive television and high-definition television a reality before the year 2000.

Seamless environments will develop as the moving audiovisual images of television merge with the interactive capabilities of computers in an increasingly realistic format. Children will be able to explore the Internet on their television sets, or watch movies, play video games, write papers, and perform innumerable other tasks on their computer screens. Real-time video clips will allow children to see cartoons, music videos, and film clips online. Eventually, children will be able to watch entire movies and television shows online. VRML (Virtual Reality Modeling Language) will be used to construct three-dimensional worlds in which children can interact in real-time with others (Montgomery & Pasnik, 1996).

UBIQUITOUS ACCESS

Television access is already ubiquitous in the United States (Huston & Wright, in press). Not only do 98 percent of Americans have television sets in their homes, they find them in schools, banks, hotels, dental offices, video arcades, and airports (Farhi, 1997d).

Computers must eventually provide the same kind of universal access and ease of use. One facet of the Telecommunications Act of 1996 will make computer access ubiquitous for all American citizens. "Universal Service" mandates that basic computer communication services be affordable for all, much as the telephone is (Weingarten, 1996). Schools, libraries, and public health providers are institutions this legislation targets (Weingarten, 1996).

The implication of this legislation is that computers will be integrated into every aspect of daily life. Computers will be in our homes, our schools, and our workplaces. Computers will be mobile, as current laptops are, so that we can take them everywhere we go. Computers will also become smaller and smarter so that we can carry a computer on a wristwatch, much as the character Dick Tracy once did.

Many children will have network computers so that they can plug into the Internet for all programs and services (Clark, 1997). Network computers provide few actual programs. Instead, users link to the network for all information. Such computers can currently be purchased for as little as $500.

Just having a computer, however, does not ensure ubiquitous access. Computer software often makes computing activities awkward and difficult. Thus, *ease of use* is a second prerequisite for computing to become ubiquitous. This means that the computer needs to be as easy to operate as a car, telephone, or television. The user does not have to understand how any of these technologies work to use them, and they should be able to use computers just as easily (Adam et al., 1997).

Raskin (1997) targets awkward computer interfaces as a key reason they are not easy to use. An **interface** is an arrangement of words, pictures, or sounds that allows users to interact with content. When using computers, children must shift back and forth between the content of their activities and the demands of the interface. For instance, a user must know how to save a file or use a spell checker to use a computer easily. Information processing theory gives us a clear framework for understanding the interference effects users encounter as they navigate between these competing cognitive activities. Specifically, when a user encounters a difficult command, thought has to shift from the content of the task to figuring out how to make the software do what the user desires. This shift can disrupt cognitive processing, making the user lose his or her train of thought. These complications often arise when the user encounters new hardware or software, making many users resist changes in technology that presumably should make tasks easier.

Raskin (1997) recommends that the user interface require only habitual operation, thereby making it an automatic task for the user. In information processing theory, automatic processing allows the human computer—that is, the brain—to perform more than one cognitive activity at a time. As the commands to interface the computer become automatic, the user can focus his or her attention and processing activities on the task. These points are especially important for young users, who need interfaces that allow quick access to tools that are easy to use. Only when computers become easy to use will they become an integral part of most children's lives. Moreover, the computer interface must fulfill certain needs children have, which may well be educational, as children often use computers to meet educational needs (Ancarrow, 1986).

EDUCATIONAL AND PROSOCIAL CONTENT

The educational media will continue to lag behind commercial areas of development, but their development is inevitable. Education as we know it will change dramatically in the twenty-first century.

As information technologies are integrated, children will experience a seamless environment with smooth transitions between different media. When an environment is seamless, it is easier to sustain attention across boundaries because no abrupt transitions interrupt media activities. This quality should result in more on-task behavior.

Computers will become the norm for educating children at school and at home. The World Wide Web, a network where people can interact and access text, visual images, animation, and sounds throughout the world (Berners-Lee, 1996), will become a learning environment. The interactive nature of learning in the future means major changes in the role the teacher will play. Instead of giving lectures, teachers will be guides to the vast amount of information available to children. Children will explore databases, not perform drill-and-practice exercises (Wulf, 1997).

Access to this information will begin early in development. As children grow up with computers in their homes, they will use computers much as you used television. Students will have their own computers throughout the school years and into college. The cost of computers will decrease, but the demand for updated hardware and software will create pressures to buy new computers on a regular basis. This will continue to divide the "haves" and the "have nots" in terms of access to information technologies.

By the year 2000, all schools and libraries should be wired to the Internet and have access to the World Wide Web. In places where wiring is difficult, wireless options will be utilized. In the past, children explored faraway places by reading books and by watching television programs and films. In the future, they will "visit" these places on the Internet. Student desks will provide electronic links for computers, which will link up to other computers (Sachem Web Slingers, 1997). With this development, the world will become a smaller and a more accessible place for children.

Children will have access to **digital libraries,** electronic libraries where they can experience multimedia presentations of topics they want to explore (Marchionini & Maurer, 1995). Vast amounts of information that have been traditionally unavailable to children and teachers will be at their fingertips. For instance, children will be able to take field trips vicariously or have famous virtual guests talk to them in their classrooms or in their homes (Marchionini & Maurer, 1995). This type of access to the same courses, the same teachers, and the same databases will give students who are attending different schools a level playing field for educational success (Sachem Web Slingers, 1997).

Although the Internet provides a vast library for instructional purposes, its organization is currently fragmented. Search engines are required for successful navigation to needed materials (Marchionini & Maurer, 1995). A **search engine** is computer software that quickly looks through large indexes to find the information a user seeks (Berners-Lee, 1996). To do so, the user designates key words, such as *technology and education.* Unfortunately, search engines do not "sort out the wheat from the chaff," leaving it to the user to sort through materials to find the most relevant documents (Berners-Lee, 1996).

Intranets will also become widely available in the future, including networks within school settings. An **intranet** is an in-house computer network where employees or students are all part of one system. An intranet will allow students and teachers to use one suite of software packages. Often the intranet provides access to the Internet as well. The advantage of this type of network is that students can all use the same software, making computing and collaborative activities easy for students (Berners-Lee, 1996). In the future, students will use intranets for a range of activities, including test taking, daily lessons, and logging on to gain access to class materials and assignments (Sachem Web Slingers, 1997).

Computers will make access to information easier for children by incorporating voice recognition, so that children will simply talk to interact with the computer. Three-dimensional speech and visual holographic displays will become typical output devices (Parrish, 1997). These alterations will make the Internet available to preschool-aged children who cannot yet read or write. Learning environments will tailor the pace and level of difficulty to match an individual learner's particular characteristics (Parrish, 1997).

E-mail will become a standard way of communicating with other people. The Web Slingers, a club based in New York, already has created an environment in which teachers, students, and administrators are connected by e-mail (Sachem Web Slingers, 1997). Increasingly, children will be electronically linked with those who provide their education.

Rapid technological change also means that students will periodically return to school to update their skills (Adam et al., 1997). This return need not be physical, but instead can be accomplished by distance learning, which links users by telecommunications technology over long distances (Adam et al., 1997). The World Wide Web allows these interfaces to cross international boundaries to facilitate universal student access to information.

Because most television stations have chosen to develop prosocial rather than academic content to meet the requirements of the Children's Television Act, prosocial children's programs will be widely available on network television through the end of this century. Interactive television and computer experiences will make prosocial content more available for the child to encode and learn. Just as violent virtual reality experiences encode directly into behavior (Calvert & Tan, 1996), so too can socially constructive behaviors such as helping, sharing, and cooperating.

Computers will also promote collaborative, prosocial activities more readily than they currently do. At present, most computer interfaces focus on user-software applications rather than user-user applications. In the future, user-user applications will become commonplace, and authors will be able to interact and work together on projects online. These types of developments will foster direct social interactions, allowing users to learn from each other online.

IMPLICATIONS FOR THE FORM OF THOUGHT

The information age may also influence the way children think. If one looks back through history, writing has long been understood as the representation of speech (Davis, 1997). However, writing is really comprised of two elements: **glottographic writing,** a communication system focusing on the notational system for recording and duplicating human speech; and **semasiographic writing,** a communication system focusing on the meanings of words, including visual images as well as speech (Davis, 1997). Historically, writers have focused on glottographic writing and ignored visual aspects of semasiographic writing. This neglect occurred in part because technological innovations such as the printing press made it possible to write with language systems, but moving visual symbol systems lagged behind in development until the twentieth century (Davis, 1997).

As motion pictures, camcorders, and computational technologies merge so that users can create moving visual depictions of their thoughts, a shift may take place in how we represent our thoughts to one another (Davis, 1997). Certainly, we have been able to view the representations of film makers and television producers in the twentieth century. What will change is that *computing will allow us to create and transmit our own moving representations of reality.* Because children tend to think in pictures (Bruner et al., 1968), cognitive advances may become apparent at younger ages because the form of children's thought will easily map onto the way the message is transmitted to others.

These representations will be constructed in "garages," much as the early Apple computers were (Davis, 1997). Users will download video images from the Internet, from television, and from their own camcorder videotapes. They will then merge these images into their own unique perceptions of reality. As computational video technology becomes a part of daily experience, semasiographic forms of thought, which have been dormant for ten thousand years, will begin to develop (Davis, 1997).

Early efforts to convey our thoughts are already present with camcorder depictions that are integrated into broadcast television programs, yet other distribution outlets are emerging. For example, integrated visual and auditory thoughts will have a ready-made publication and distribution facility on the **Internet II.** The Internet II, the next generation of the Internet, will allow faster transmission of visual images and will permit real-time images of events to be captured and transmitted. This will allow multimedia network technologies to play an increasingly important role in education (Adam et al., 1997). As three-dimensional virtual reality interfaces become commonplace, these experiences will increasingly be lifelike as well as visual and interactive.

In the past, we saw that observational experiences of television viewing had limited ability to alter the way children think (Huston et al., 1992), but that interactive experiences with computer games were having greater impact (Greenfield, 1996). The next generation of integrated "garage cinema" and computational interfaces may also impact the form of thought. Visual literacy, a long neglected form of experience that could not easily be captured or transmitted to others, may emerge in future technologies. Davis (1997) believes that the popularization and distribution of personalized motion pictures will impact culture with the same force as the printing press did centuries ago.

SUMMARY

In the future, the technology will be in the hands of the user. Technologies will be less tools of the masses, and far more individualized as computers respond to the individual needs of each child.

As with television, children will be able to travel around the world without leaving their homes. But in the future, the images will be interactive and personalized. The symbol systems will be visual, verbal, musical, and interactive. They will be three-dimensional, and children will be able to enter virtual realities they create. Mobile computers will allow children to take and to access information everywhere they go.

The images children will take with them and that they will access will depend on the decisions our culture, and increasingly the world culture, makes about how we will use information technologies. Will future information technologies be our entertainers, our educators, or both? What will they teach our children? What will the future hold?

My parents grew up listening to a radio. My generation grew up watching television. Your generation grew up watching television, but also began to spend increasing amounts of time interacting with computers. The convergence of information technologies, which will make multimedia options the norm, will provide the coming generations with far more possibilities than we can currently imagine.

Glossary

Achievement-related behaviors Prosocial behaviors, such as delaying gratification, task persistence, and impulse control, that are likely to facilitate academic success.

Action Physical movement.

Action-and-violence formula A television story formula which pairs character movement with aggressive content.

Action for Children's Television (ACT) A nonprofit organization that advocated for quality television programs for children.

Action superiority hypothesis The thesis that action facilitates, rather than interferes with, children's comprehension of verbally presented content.

Activation The process of pulling information into consciousness and thinking about it.

Active exposure Making an intentional, deliberate choice to experience an information technology.

Advance organizer A preview of coming events that guides children's processing activities.

Advertisements Commercial messages designed to get consumers to purchase specific products.

Age-appropriate content Content targeted at an age group that should be on the verge of mastering this type of information.

Anchored instruction Videodisc presentations that "anchor" important concepts to the contexts of visually presented stories, thereby linking abstract lessons with clear contextual referents.

Androgyny A blend of traditionally "masculine" and "feminine" personality characteristics, or an absence of gender-based judgments.

Annenberg Public Policy Center (APPC) A group of scholars who study public policy issues, such as the implementation of the Children's Television Act, within the Annenberg School for Communication at the University of Pennsylvania.

Arousal theory A theory that attributes reactions to various stimuli, including media experiences, to physiological changes in the body.

Assistive intent The concept that commercials intend to provide consumers with helpful information about products.

Attention Visual orientation to the television or computer screen.

Attentional inertia A phenomenon observed with visual orientation to television programs. Specifically, the longer a child looks, the more likely he or she is to keep looking. In addition, the longer a child does not look, the more likely he or she is to not look at the television.

Autonomic arousal Physiological responses—measured by heart rate, blood pressure, and skin conductance—related to affect and emotion.

Banners Material on the Internet, somewhat like billboards, that are used to advertise to consumers.

Behavior What children or adults do.

Behaviorism The study of how reinforcements and punishments mold behavior.

Bidirectional relation   A causal relationship between variables that goes in both directions.

Catharsis   A psychoanalytic process that harmlessly releases aggressive drives through symbolic acts of aggressive fantasy.

Celebrity endorsements   A commercial practice in which famous celebrities are paid to be spokespersons in the advertisements for particular products.

Center for Media Education (CME)   A media-related children's advocacy group.

Central content   Information essential for understanding a story plot.

Challenge   The domain of an intrinsically interesting learning environment that involves goals, uncertain outcomes, hidden information, and randomness.

Children's Television Act of 1990   A law which requires television stations to (1) broadcast educational and informational programming for young viewers; and (2) broadcast commercials no more than 10.5 minutes per hour on weekends and 12 minutes per hour on weekdays during children's programming as a condition for license renewal.

Cognitive developmental theory   Piaget's theory that identifies stages in the way children think.

Cognitive scripts   Expectations stored in memory as guides for future actions.

Cohorts   Groups that are similar in age.

Collaboration   Working together on a group project with a shared goal.

Commercial separators   Brief, often animated segments presented just after a program goes to commercials and just before the program returns.

Communications Decency Act   A law, overturned by the U.S. Supreme Court, that made it a crime to transmit indecent material to minors over the Internet.

Comprehensibility hypothesis   A theory, developed from television research, that predicts that children will attend to certain televised information because they expect to understand it.

Comprehension   Understanding material.

Concrete operational thought   The third stage in Piaget's cognitive developmental theory. At this stage (from about ages 7 to 12), children think logically, as adults do, but only in concrete terms; they are not yet capable of abstract thought.

Content analyses   Studies in which large numbers of television programs are periodically sampled and then analyzed for various kinds of content, such as aggression and stereotyped gender roles.

Content indifference   Watching television to pass the time rather than to select particular programs for viewing.

Contiguous presentation   Presenting important content immediately after a perceptually salient formal feature to maximize memory and comprehension of that material.

Core educational programming   A type of programming mandated by a provision of the recent guidelines of the Children's Television Act. Specifically, a program must have educational value for children age 16 or under as a significant purpose to qualify as core educational programming; also, the station must broadcast the program on a regular basis between 7:00 A.M. and 10:00 P.M., and the program must be at least thirty minutes long.

Correlational study   A type of experimental design in which the researchers manipulate nothing; they simply study variables as they exist in the natural environment.

Cortical arousal   Physiological responses related to attention, perception, alertness, and vigilance.

Counterstereotypical content   Nontraditional information about men and women.

Creativity   The expression of novel and interesting ideas (for example, artistic endeavors).

Cultivation effect A belief or attitude about the world that television viewing fosters.

Cultivation theory A theory of communication that holds that viewers exposed to television content cultivate a world view consistent with the dominant media images. *Resonance* and *mainstreaming* are the mechanisms by which this process takes place.

Curiosity The domain of an intrinsically interesting learning environment that involves an optimal level of information complexity in which information is novel and surprising, but not incomprehensible.

Curriculum goals Academic content goals that develop age-appropriate concepts to build on specific areas of expertise, such as math or English.

Daydreams Internal thoughts and fantasies.

Debugging skills The skills by which a person analyzes and corrects errors to make a computer program run.

Defensive safeguards The protective mechanisms children develop to prevent advertisers from manipulating them.

Deregulation The removal of rules and regulations. During the 1980s, the FCC rescinded most of the rules that govern television; according to the deregulatory philosophy, the competitive marketplace would regulate itself.

Desensitization An arousal process that causes children to become less responsive to intense stimuli due to overexposure and habituation.

Diary A measure of audience viewing behavior that allows people to log in their program selections as they watch.

Digital libraries An electronic library where children can experience multimedia presentations of topics they want to explore.

Disinhibition A social learning process that causes the internal controls that prevent children from acting aggressively to be overridden when children repeatedly see aggressive television

models who are either rewarded for their aggression or go unpunished.

Displacement The replacement of one activity by another, as when television viewing replaces going to the movies.

Drench hypothesis The hypothesis that a few salient media images can overshadow the more prevalent images in the media.

Drip hypothesis The belief that the media impact viewers most through a steady stream of consistent, prevalent images.

Echoic modes Forms of communication that represent an object by replicating the sounds it makes (for example, a "choo choo" sound for a train).

Educational and informational logos (E & I logos) Logos at the beginning of television programs that identify them as meeting the requirements of the Children's Television Act.

Educational programming According to the FCC (1991), content that serves to "further the positive development of the child in any respect, including the child's cognitive/intellectual or emotional/social needs."

Educational strength A measure of a program's lesson clarity, lesson salience, lesson involvement, and lesson applicability.

Educational television or computer program A program designed to teach children academic content and concepts, such as reading, math, science, history, geography (areas of content) or problem solving and planning (concepts).

E & I logos Educational and informational logos.

Enactive learning When a person's own behaviors and actions cause her to encode certain behaviors.

Enactive modes Forms of communication that rely on the body to represent information.

Fantasy The domain of an intrinsically interesting learning environment that entails both cognitive and emotional aspects of imaginary experiences.

Federal Communications Commission (FCC) The government agency charged with granting licenses and overseeing communications in the television and radio industries.

Federal Trade Commission (FTC) The government agency charged with enforcing rules of interstate commerce, including the fairness rules and the prevention of deceptive practices by television advertisers. The FTC's powers to rule on fairness issues in the children's television area were restricted in 1981.

Femininity Stereotypical female personality characteristics such as compassion, loyalty, and sensitivity.

Field experiment A type of experiment conducted in a child's natural environment.

First Amendment A legal right in the Bill of Rights that guarantees freedom of speech and of the press.

Formal features Visual and auditory production features that structure, mark, and represent content.

Formal operational thought The fourth and final stage of Piaget's theory of cognitive development. During this stage (from age 12 on), children can think abstractly and consider hypothetical situations, not just concrete ideas.

Formative research Research that aids the initial production decisions made during the development of an educational program.

Gender consistency The knowledge that physical transformations, such as changing the clothing one wears, will not alter one's gender.

Gender constancy Knowledge that your gender will never change, a concept gained at around age 7.

Gender identity Knowledge that you are a boy or girl, a concept gained by about age 2.

Gender roles The kinds of behaviors and occupations expected of males and females, based on gender.

Gender schemas Expectations and beliefs of people based on whether they are male or female.

Gender stability The knowledge that gender does not change over time (that is, boys do not grow up to be mothers).

Gender-stereotyped content Television or computer content that portrays traditional values about men and women.

Gender stereotypes A simple type of gender schema reflecting traditional beliefs about men and women.

Glottographic writing Writing which focuses on the notational system for recording and reproducing human speech.

Grazing Using a remote control to flip through channels; also called channel surfing.

Group ownership A process in which all members of a group work together to accomplish a goal and feel responsible for the project outcome.

Habituation An arousal process by which children who are overexposed to exciting stimuli cease to respond physiologically to it.

High-definition television (HDTV) Digital television transmissions, using the computer codes of 0 and 1, which allow high-quality pictures and auditory tracks to be broadcast to viewers.

Host selling A technique in which a program host sells products within or during blocks of time adjacent to the program. The separation principle prohibits this in children's programming.

Iconic modes Forms of communication that represent information in visual form.

Imagination The divergent, original aspects of cognitive functioning expressed in *daydreams, creative activities,* and *imaginative play.*

Imaginative play Individual or group play in which a child suspends reality and extends the immediate perceptual field through pretense and fantasy.

Implicit content Content that is hidden but is also essential for plot comprehension. Implicit content includes character motivations, feelings, and knowledge of how events link together across a story; this material is also called *inferential content.*

Incidental content Content irrelevant to understanding a story plot.

Information processing theory A theory about how children and adults understand information as a function of perception, attention, and memory processes.

Interface An arrangement of words, pictures, and sounds that allows a user to access information.

Internet Interconnected computers that provide access to data and programs from any connected site in the world.

Internet II The next generation of interconnected computers. Internet II will allow faster transmission of visual images, thereby permitting real-time, moving images of events to be transmitted and captured.

Intranet An in-house computer network where everyone is part of one closed system.

Intraprogram synopses Summaries of program content inserted after commercials to enhance children's learning of televised material.

Intrinsically interesting learning environments A theory based on the qualities of educational environments that generate spontaneous interest and discovery-based learning in children.

Learning Acquiring a response.

LOGO A computer programming language children can use to create geometric patterns and shapes.

Magazine format A format that merges independent vignettes together to create a program.

Mainstreaming The shared vision of the world created by heavy television viewing (a cultivation effect).

Majority group A group of people who are numerically more prevalent in a society than other groups.

Major role The role of a television character who speaks and is present on the screen during at least 20 percent of the program.

Markers Features used as highlighters of important television or computer material.

Masculinity Stereotypical male personality traits such as dominance, aggression, independence, and ambition.

Memory Constructions of information children and adults create after experiencing their environment.

Microworld A computer-based scenario in which children interact with educational content.

Minority group A group of people who are less numerous, and/or less powerful, than other groups.

Minor role A background television character.

Modality-specific processing Processing of content that parallels the way that content was initially experienced (visual input-visual output; verbal input-verbal output).

Modes to represent content The use of visual action and verbal language to represent content.

Motivation Interest in performing certain activities.

Motivational incentives The rewards or motivators used to arouse interest in performing an activity. A social learning theory subprocess.

Multimedia learning environments The combination of books, television, videotapes, CD-ROM software, videodiscs, and/or the Internet to teach an educational message in diverse yet complementary formats.

Observational learning When children learn behaviors by watching someone else do them.

Occupational role models Media characters that influence children's future occupational choices.

Pace, pacing The rate of scene and character changes in a television production.

Parental advisories and program ratings Verbal symbols placed at the beginning of a television program which inform viewers about the kind of content contained in the program.

Passive exposure Being present and experiencing a medium because another person selected it, not because you did.

People meter A Nielsen measure of audience viewing behaviors based on electronic tracking of people's viewing activities.

Perception The initial intake of information based on stimulus qualities associated with sensory systems, such as vision, hearing, and smell.

Perceptual salience The quality of having properties involving movement, contrast, incongruity, complexity, and surprise, all of which are likely to elicit visual attention and processing.

Performance Responding with action.

Persuasive intent The concept that commercials intend to sell products to consumers.

Positive interpersonal behaviors Prosocial behaviors, such as cooperation, sharing, kindness, empathy, sympathy, and helping, that benefit another individual.

Prejudice Negative attitudes about a group of people that stem from perceived differences, such as differences in ethnic or racial backgrounds.

Premiums Small toys included with a designated product to increase its appeal to young buyers.

Preoperational thought The second stage of development in Piaget's cognitive developmental theory. During this stage (from about ages 2 to 7), children are illogical, intuitive thinkers.

Preplays Advance organizers of television programs that are inserted prior to seeing the corresponding program material.

Preview A television technique that shows summaries of information before the actual program content.

Procedural skills The skills that allow a person to break a computer task into smaller subroutines in order to create a program.

Program-length commercials Longer commercials developed to look like programs but actually meant to sell particular commercial products. The FCC ruled against this practice in 1974 with the separation principle, but rescinded the restriction in the 1980s.

Program separators Segments, typically animated in children's programming, that separate the program from the commercial.

Prosocial behavior Socially desirable behaviors that include *positive interpersonal behaviors,* such as helping, sharing, and cooperating, that benefit other individuals; *achievement-related behaviors,* such as delaying gratification, task persistence, and controlling impulses, that increase the likelihood of academic success; and *imagination,* as expressed by imaginative play, creativity, and daydreaming.

Prosocial television Television programming designed to enhance children's positive interpersonal behaviors, achievement-related behaviors, and imagination.

Psychoanalytic theory The theory that predicts that children who view media aggression experience catharsis, draining away their aggressive impulses in harmless fantasy.

Qualitative research Research that describes relationships without statistically analyzing outcomes.

Quantitative research Research that describes and explains relationships by statistically analyzing outcomes.

Questionnaire A paper-and-pencil measure people fill out to provide information, for example, indicating their media usage patterns.

Racial stereotyping Depictions of people from different ethnic groups that rely on composite images, often negative in tone, to present images of an entire group of people.

Ratings A measure of the percentage of the total population watching a given television program.

Ready to Learn A PBS initiative which targets the preschool audience and prepares them for school entry by exposing them to educational television programs throughout the week.

Regulation Rules and guidelines by federal agencies, such as the FCC and the FTC, which prescribe acceptable and unacceptable ways to conduct business and use the public airwaves.

Relational marketing Commercial advertising practices on the Internet in which the advertiser attempts to create an interactive, personal relationship between the consumer and the advertiser.

Reliability The accuracy of a measure.

Resonance A type of cultivation effect in which media images reinforce viewers' real-life impressions.

Review A television technique that shows summaries of information after the actual program content.

Role models Persons, either live or symbolically presented on television, who serve as guides for children's behaviors.

Role playing A rehearsal activity in which children are taught to actively perform certain behaviors, such as those that they have observed on television.

Salience functions Aspects of formal features that activate primitive orienting responses to changes in the environment.

Schemas Cognitive beliefs that children construct based upon the events that happen to them.

Schema theory A cognitive information processing theory in which children use their prior conceptions, such as beliefs about others, to guide selective attention and memory of content. Children construct schemas about gender, race, and aggression as well as about other areas of experience.

School readiness A concept that examines whether children have mastered the kinds of skills they need to succeed in school, such as knowing their ABC's, counting, and classifying.

Script theory The theory that children create expectations and scripts about behavior, such as aggression, that come to guide their behavior over time.

Seamless programming A practice that provides no sharp defining line between parts of a program or between the program and the advertisements.

Search engine Computer software that quickly looks through large indexes to find information that a user requests.

Selective attention The selection of certain content for processing at the expense of other material.

Selective exposure hypothesis The prediction that individuals will choose to view programs in keeping with their own beliefs and values.

Selective perception hypothesis The prediction that viewers who are high or low in prejudice will perceive a program in different ways.

Self-concept Beliefs about the self that are predominantly descriptive, with little evaluation present.

Self-efficacy The belief that one can control the events in one's life.

Self-esteem Beliefs about the self that are predominantly evaluative.

Self-regulation A policy, favored by broadcasters, that lets industry set policies for itself.

Semasiographic writing "Writing" that focuses on meaning, be it written or visual in form.

Sensitive periods Windows of time in which children are ready to learn certain concepts.

Sensorimotor thought The first stage of Piaget's theory. In this stage (from about ages 0 to 2), children think about information through their bodies. For instance, turning the head back and forth represents the concept "no."

Separation devices Techniques that divide programs from commercials; a part of the separation principle requires broadcasters and advertisers to use consistent markers to divide the two.

Separation principle   FCC guidelines that require broadcasters and advertisers to use techniques that help children to divide programming from commercial content. These techniques involve rules about host selling, program-length commercials, and separation devices.

Sexual behavior   Intimate physical interactions.

Share   A measure of the available television audience at a given point in time.

Short-form programs   Television program formats less than 5 minutes in length.

Social cognitive theory   A social theory that explains children's actions in terms of their exposure to models who act as guides for their behavior.

Sound effects   Unusual noises added to a sound track for effect.

Spatial tasks   Activities that require visual processing skills, such as reading a map.

Story format   A format in which a coherent message or theme is presented around a narrative plot.

Summative research   Research that examines a finished educational television program or series to discover if the program is accomplishing its educational mission.

Symbolic modes   Forms of communication that represent information with language.

Telecommunications Act of 1996   A legislative act that regulates the communications technologies.

Three-hour rule   A 1996 FCC ruling which mandated that each television station broadcast a minimum of three hours of educational and informational programming each week beginning in the fall of 1997; this rule was part of the implementation procedures for the Children's Television Act of 1990.

Tombstone shot   A view of an unadorned product shown at the end of a commercial. Tombstone shots are required in advertisements surrounding children's programming.

Underwrite   A business arrangement; to provide a grant to a program in exchange for acknowledgment at the beginning or ending of the program.

Uses and gratification theory   A communications theory that predicts that children and adults select certain media experiences (the uses) to satisfy particular needs they have (the gratifications).

Validity   Whether a measure is really assessing what it claims to measure.

Verbal labeling   A rehearsal activity that teaches children the verbal messages of television programs as an adult discusses and places emphasis on key program content.

Videodisc   A technology in which audiovisual images are put on a disc, much like a record, and then accessed in any sequence desired.

Viewing   Being present when television programs are being broadcast, or more specifically, actually watching those programs.

Violence   Any overt act or threat to hurt or kill a person.

Violence Index   A measure of the frequency and rate of violent representations in network television drama.

Virtual reality   A three-dimensional computer simulation in which a player wears glasses and gloves that allow him or her to interact with computer-generated images.`

Visual sequencing   Placing visual events from a television program in order—from the first event viewed to the last.

Visual spatial skills   The ability to construct and manipulate pictorial images of objects and places in one's mind.

Visual special effects   Impossible visual events that appear to happen on television or in films.

Visual superiority hypothesis   The hypothesis that visual presentation interferes with children's comprehension of auditory, verbal content.

Working memory A type of memory that encompasses what one is conscious of at this moment.

World Wide Web Text, visual images, animation, and sounds that can be accessed through a global network of information connected by computers and phone lines.

References

ABC Nightline. (1995 October 3). ABC, Inc.

Abelman, R. (1987). TV literacy II—Amplifying the affective level effects of television's prosocial fare through curriculum intervention. *Journal of Research and Development in Education, 20,* 40–49.

Abelman, R. (1991). TV literacy III—Gifted and learning disabled children: Amplifying prosocial learning through curriculum intervention. *Journal of Research and Development in Education, 24,* 51–60.

Adam, N., Awerbuch, B., Slonim, J., Wegner, P., & Yesha, Y. (1997). Globalizing business, education, culture, through the Internet. *Communication of the ACM, 40,* 115–121.

Aday, S. (1997). *Newspaper coverage of children's television: A 1997 update.* Philadelphia, Penn.: The Annenberg Public Policy Center of the University of Pennsylvania.

Adler, R. P. (1980). Children's television advertising: History of the issue. In E. L. Palmer & A. Dorr (Eds.), *Children and the faces of television.* New York: Academic.

Ahammer, I. M., & Murray, J. P. (1979). Kindness in the kindergarten: The relative influence of role playing and prosocial television in facilitating altruism. *International Journal of Behavioral Development, 2,* 133–157.

Alvarez, M., Huston, A. C., Wright, J. C., & Kerkman, D. (1988). Gender differences in visual attention to television form and content. *Journal of Applied Developmental Psychology, 9,* 459–476.

Ancarrow, J. (1986). *Use of computers in home study* (US Department of Education Statistics). Washington, D.C.: U.S. Government Printing Office.

Anderson, A., & O'Hagan, F. J. (1989). Dyadic interaction at the microcomputer interface: A case of computer-assisted learning. *Journal of Computer Assisted Learning, 5,* 114–124.

Anderson, B., Mead, N., & Sullivan, S. (1986). *Television: What do national assessment results tell us?* Princeton, N.J.: Educational Testing Service.

Anderson, C. A., & Ford, C. M. (1986). Affect of the game player: short-term effects of highly and mildly aggressive video games. *Personality and Social Psychology Bulletin, 12,* 390–402.

Anderson, D. R., Bryant, J., Crawley, A., Santomero, A., Wilder, A., & Williams, M. E. (1997, May). Comprehensive research on Nick Jr.'s *Blue's Clues.* Symposium presented at the annual meeting of the International Communication Association, Montreal, Canada.

Anderson, D. R., & Collins, P. A. (1988). *The impact on children's education: Television's influence on cognitive development* (Working Paper No. 2). Washington, D.C.: Office of Educational Research and Improvement. (ERIC Document Reproduction Service No. ED 295 271).

Anderson, D. R., Field, D. E., Collins, P. A., Lorch, E. P., & Nathan, J. G. (1985). Estimates of children's time with television: A methodological comparison of parent reports with time-lapse video home observation. *Child Development, 56*, 1345–1357.

Anderson, D. R., & Levin, S. R. (1976). Young children's attention to *Sesame Street. Child Development, 47*, 806–811.

Anderson, D. R., Levin, S. R., & Lorch, E. P. (1977). The effects of TV program pacing on the behavior of preschool children. *AV Communication Review, 25*, 159–166.

Anderson, D. R., & Lorch, E. P. (1983). Looking at television: Action or reaction? In J. Bryant & D. R. Anderson (Eds.), *Children's understanding of television: Research on attention and comprehension.* New York: Academic Press.

Anderson, D. R., Lorch, E. P., Field, D. E., Collins, P. A., & Nathan, J. G. (1986). Television viewing at home: Age trends in visual attention and time with TV. *Child Development, 57*, 1024–1033.

Anderson, D. R., Lorch, E. P., Field, D., & Sanders, J. (1981). The effects of TV program comprehensibility on preschool children's visual attention to television. *Child Development, 52*, 151–157.

Anderson, D. R., & Smith, R. (1984). Young children's TV viewing: The problem of cognitive continuity. In F. J. Morrison, C. Lord, & D. F. Keating (Eds.), *Advances in applied psychology.* New York: Academic Press.

Arch, E. C., & Cummins, D. E. (1989). Structured and unstructured exposure to computers: Sex differences in attitude and use among college students. *Sex Roles, 20*, 245–254.

Atkin, C. (1980). Effects of television advertising on children. In E. L. Palmer & A. Dorr (Eds.), *Children and the faces of television: Teaching, violence, selling* (pp. 287–306). New York: Academic Press.

Atkin, C. (1982). Television advertising and socialization to consumer roles. In D. Pearl, L. Bouthilet, & J. Lazar (Eds.), *Television and behavior: Ten years of scientific progress and implications for the eighties. Vol. 2: Technical reviews* (pp. 191–200). Washington, D.C.: U.S. Government Printing Office.

Atkin, C. K., Greenberg, B. S., & McDermott, S. (1983). Television and race role socialization. *Journalism Quarterly, 23*, 407–414.

Ball, S., & Bogatz, G. A. (1970). *The first year of* Sesame Street: *An evaluation.* Princeton, N.J.: Educational Testing Service.

Ball, S., & Bogatz, G. (1972). Summative research on *Sesame Street:* Implications in the study of preschool children. In A. D. Pick (Ed.), *Minnesota symposia on child psychology* (Vol. 6). Minneapolis: University of Minnesota.

Ball, S., & Bogatz, G. (1973). Reading with television: An evaluation of *The Electric Company* (2 vols). Princeton, N.J.: Educational Testing Service.

Bandra, A. (1965). Influence of models' reinforcement contingencies on the acquisition and performance of imitative responses. *Journal of Personality and Social Psychology, 1*, 589–595.

Bandura, A. (1986). *Social foundations of thought and action.* Englewood Cliffs, N.J.: Prentice Hall.

Bandura, A. (1989). Regulation of cognitive processes through perceived self-efficacy. *Developmental Psychology, 5*, 729–735.

Bandura, A. (1997). *Self-efficacy: The exercise of control.* New York: W. H. Freeman & Co.

Baptista-Fernandez, P., & Greenberg, B. S. (1984). The context, characteristics, and communication behaviors of blacks on television. In B. S. Greenberg (Ed.), *Life on television: Content analyses of U.S. TV drama.* Norwood, N.J.: Ablex.

Barcus, F. E. (1980). The nature of television advertising to children. In E. Palmer & A. Dorr (Eds.), *Children and the faces of television: Teaching, violence, selling.* New York: Academic.

Beagles-Roos, J., & Gat, I. (1983). Specific impact of radio and television on children's story comprehension. *Journal of Educational Psychology, 75,* 128–137.

Beentjes, J. W., & Koolstra, C. M. (1995, May). Combining homework with television or sound media. Paper presented at the annual meeting of the International Communication Association, Albuquerque, New Mexico.

Bem, S. (1981). Gender schema theory: A cognitive account of sex typing. *Psychological Review, 88,* 352–364.

Berlyne, D. E. (1960). *Conflict, arousal, and curiosity.* New York: McGraw-Hill.

Berners-Lee, T. (1996). WWW: Past, present, and future. *IEEE,* 69–77.

Berry, G. L. (1980). Children, television, and social class roles: The medium as an unplanned curriculum. In E. L. Palmer & A. Dorr (Eds.), *Children and the faces of television.* New York: Academic Press.

Berry, G. L. (1988). Multicultural role portrayals on television as a social psychological issue. In S. Oskamp (Ed.), *Television as a social issue: Applied social psychology annual 8.* Newberry Park, CA: Sage.

Beuf, A. (1974). Doctor, lawyer, household drudge. *Journal of Communication, 24,* 142–145.

Blatt, J., Spencer, L., & Ward, S. (1972). A cognitive developmental study of children's reactions to television advertising. In E. Rubenstein, G. Comstock, & J. Murray (Eds.), *Television and social behavior* (Vol. 4). Washington, D.C.: U.S. Government Printing Office.

Bogatz, G. A., & Ball, S. (1971). *The second year of* Sesame Street: *A continuing evaluation.* Princeton, N.J.: Educational Testing Service.

Boush, D. M., Friestad, M., & Rose, G. M. (1994). Adolescent skepticism toward TV advertising and knowledge of advertiser tactics. *Journal of Consumer Research, 21,* 165–175.

Bransford, J. D., Hasselbring, T., Barron, B., Kulewicz, S., Littlefield, J., & Goin, L. (1988). The use of macro contexts to facilitate mathematical thinking. In R. Charles & E. Silver (Eds.), *The teaching and assessing of mathematical problem solving.* Hillsdale, N.J.: Erlbaum.

Brinkley, J. (1996, December 25). FCC approves standards for HDTV. *The New York Times.*

Broderick, C., & Trushell, J. (1985). Problems and processes—junior high school children using word processors to produce an information leaflet. *English in education, 9,* 29–35.

Brown, J. D., Childers, K. W., Bauman, K. E., & Koch, G. G. (1990). The influences of new media and family structure on young adolescents' television and radio use. *Communication Research, 17,* 65–82.

Bruner, J. S., Olver, R. R., & Greenfield, P. M. (1968). *Studies in cognitive growth.* New York: Wiley.

Bryant, J., McCollum, J., Maxwell, M., McGavin, L., Love, C., Raney, A., Mundorf, N., Mundorf, J., Wilson, B., & Smith, S. (1995, September). Effects of six–months viewing of *Allegra's Window* and *Gullah, Gullah Island.* Report submitted to Nick Jr., NY, NY.

Bryant, J., Zillmann, D., & Brown, D. (1983). Entertainment features in children's educational television: Effects on attention and information acquisition. In J. Bryant & D. R. Anderson (Eds.), *Children's understanding of television: Research on attention and comprehension.* New York: Academic Press.

Calvert, S. L. (1988). Television production feature effects on children's comprehension of time. *Journal of Applied Developmental Psychology, 9,* 263–273.

Calvert, S. L. (1991). Presentational features for young children's production and recall of information. *Journal of Applied Developmental Psychology, 12,* 367–378.

Calvert, S. L. (1992). Pictorial prompts for discursive analyses: Developmental considerations and methodological innovations. *American Behavioral Scientist, 36,* 39–51.

Calvert, S. L. (1994a). Children's attentional involvement and distractibility during educational computer interactions. *Journal of Educational Technology Systems, 22,* 251–258.

Calvert, S. L. (1994b). Developmental differences in children's production and recall of information as a function of computer presentational features. *Journal of Educational Computing Research, 10,* 131–143.

Calvert, S. L. (In press). The form of thought. In I. Sigel (Ed.), *Theoretical perspectives in the concept of representation.* Hillsdale, N.J.: Erlbaum.

Calvert, S. L., & Billingsley, R. L. (1998). Young children's recitation and comprehension of information presented by songs. *Journal of Applied Developmental Psychology, 19,* 97–108.

Calvert, S. L., Gallagher, K., & McGuckin, B. (1997, April). Educational and prosocial programming on Saturday morning television. Poster presented at the biennial meeting of the Society for Research in Child Development, Washington, D.C.

Calvert, S. L., & Gersh, T. L. (1987). The selective use of sound effects and visual inserts for children's television story comprehension. *Journal of Applied Developmental Psychology, 8,* 363–375.

Calvert, S. L., & Huston, A. C. (1987). Television and children's gender schemata. In L. Liben & M. Signorella (Eds.), *Children's Gender Schemata: Origins and Implications.* In the quarterly series, *New Directions in Child Development, 38.* San Francisco: Jossey-Bass.

Calvert, S. L., Huston, A. C., Watkins, B. A., & Wright, J. C. (1982). The relation between selective attention to television forms and children's comprehension of content. *Child Development, 53,* 601–610.

Calvert, S. L., Huston, A. C., & Wright, J. C. (1987). The effects of television preplay formats on children's attention and story comprehension. *Journal of Applied Developmental Psychology, 8,* 329–342.

Calvert, S. L., & Littman, K. G. (1996, May). Computer versus lecture presentations for children's comprehension of content. Paper presented at the annual meeting of the International Communication Association, Chicago, Illinois.

Calvert, S. L., & Pfordresher, P. Q. (1994, August). Impact of a televised song on students' memory. Poster presented at the annual meeting of the American Psychological Association, Los Angeles, California.

Calvert, S. L., Rigaud, E., & Mazzulla, J. (1991, April). Presentational features for students' recall of televised educational content. Poster presented at the biennial meeting of the Society for Research in Child Development, Seattle, Washington.

Calvert, S. L., & Scott, M. C. (1989). Sound effects for children's temporal integration of fast-paced television content. *Journal of Broadcasting and Electronic Media, 33,* 233–246.

Calvert, S. L., Stolkin, A., & Lee, J. (1997, April). Gender and ethnic portrayals in children's Saturday morning television programs. Poster presented at the biennial meeting of the Society for Research in Child Development, Washington, D.C.

Calvert, S. L., & Tan, S. L. (1996). Impact of virtual reality on young adults' physiological arousal and aggressive thoughts: Interaction versus observation. In P. M. Greenfield & R. R. Cocking (Eds.), *Interacting with video.* Norwood, N.J.: Ablex.

Calvert, S. L., & Tart, M. (1993). Song versus prose forms for students' very long-term, long-term, and short-term verbatim recall. *Journal of Applied Developmental Psychology, 14*, 245–260.

Calvert, S. L., Watson, J. A., Brinkley, V., & Bordeaux, B. (1989). Computer presentational features for young children's preferential selection and recall of information. *Journal of Educational Computing Research, 5*, 35–49.

Calvert, S. L., Watson, J. A., Brinkley, V., & Penny, J. (1990). Computer presentational features for poor readers' recall of information. *Journal of Educational Computing Research, 6*, 287–298.

Campbell, N. (1988). Correlates of computer anxiety of adolescent students. *Journal of Adolescent Research, 3*, 107–117.

Cannon, W. B. (1927). The James-Lange theory of emotions: A critical examination and an alternative theory. *American Journal of Psychology, 39*, 106–124.

Cantor, J. R. (1991). Fright responses to mass media productions. In J. Bryant & D. Zillmann (Eds.), *Responding to the screen: Reception and reaction processes*. Hillsdale, N.J.: Erlbaum.

Cantor, J. R. (1997, August). Impact of television ratings and advisories. Paper presented at the annual meeting of the American Psychological Association, Chicago, Illinois.

Cantor, M. G. (1977). Women and public broadcasting. *Journal of Communication, 25*, 107–131.

Caplan, J., & Watkins, B. A. (1981). The relationship between children's use of television and stereotypes about occupations and personality attributes. Paper presented to the Status of Women Committee, Association for Education in Journalism, East Lansing, Michigan.

Center for Media Education & Institute for Public Representation, Georgetown University. (1992, September 29). *A report on station compliance with the Children's Television Act*. Washington, D.C: Center for Media Education.

Chambers, J., & Ascione, F. (1987). The effects of prosocial and aggressive video games on children's donating and helping. *Journal of Genetic Psychology, 148*, 499–505.

Chandrasekaran, R. (1997, December 1). Online firms to offer own curbs on net. *The Washington Post, 1*, A17.

Char, C., Hawkins, J., Wootten, J., Sheingold, K., & Roberts, T. (1983). *"The voyage of the Mimi": Classroom case studies of software, video, and print materials*. (Report to the U.S. Department of Education). New York: Bank Street College of Education, Center for Children and Technology.

Charren, M. (1994, July). Testimony to the Federal Communications Commission at the En Banc Hearings on Children's Television, Washington, D.C.

Children's Television Act of 1990. (1990). Publ. L. No. 101–437, 104 Stat. 996–1000, codified at 47 USC Sections 303a, 303b, 394.

Children's Television Workshop. (1997, April). Teaching mutual respect in Israel and the Palestinian Territories. *Research Roundup*, Children's Television Workshop/ Research Department, *8*, 1–2.

Chomsky, C. (1990). Books on videodisc: Computers, video, and reading aloud. In D. Nix & R. Spiro (Eds.), *Cognition, education, and multimedia*. Hillsdale, N.J.: Erlbaum.

Christenson, P. G. (1982). Children's perceptions of TV commercials and products: The effects of PSA's. *Communication Research, 9*, 491–524.

Citron, C. C., Serbin, L. A., & Conner, J. M. (1979, March). Children's observational learning of same and opposite sex models' behaviors. Paper presented at the conference of the Association for Women in Psychology, Dallas, TX.

Clark, C. C. (1972). Race, identification, and television violence. In G. A. Comstock, E. A. Rubenstein, & J. P. Murray (Eds.), *Television and social behavior. Vol. V: Television's effects: Further exploration*. Washington, D.C.: U.S. Government Printing Office.

Clark, J. F. (1997). The next 50 years of computing: Will we recognize them? *Computer*, 18–19.

Cline, V., Croft, R., & Courrier, S. (1973). Desensitization of children to television violence. *Journal of Personality and Social Psychology, 7*, 360–365.

Coates, B., & Pusser, H. E. (1975). Positive reinforcement and punishment in *Sesame Street* and *Mister Rogers' Neighborhood*. *Journal of Broadcasting, 19*, 143–151.

Coates, B., Pusser, H. E., & Goodman, I. (1976). The influence of *Sesame Street* and *Mister Rogers' Neighborhood* on children's social behavior in the preschool. *Child Development, 47*, 138–144.

Cole, C. F. (1997, May). Formative research in Russia, Israel, and the Palestinian territories. Paper presented at the annual meeting of the International Communication Association, Montreal, Canada.

Colley, A. M., Gale, M. T., & Harris, T. A. (1994). Effects of gender role identity and experience on computer attitude components. *Journal of Educational Computing Research, 10*, 129–137.

Collins, P. A., Wright, J. C., Anderson, D. R., Huston, A. C., Schmitt, K. L., McElroy, E., & Linebarger, D. L. (1997, April). Effects of early childhood media use on academic achievement. Paper presented at the biennial meeting of the Society for Research in Child Development, Washington, D.C.

Collins, W. A. (1973). Effect of temporal separation between motivation, aggression, and consequences: A developmental study. *Developmental Psychology, 8*, 215–221.

Collins, W. A. (1983). Interpretation and inference in children's television viewing. In J. Bryant & D. R. Anderson (Eds.), *Children's understanding of television: Research on attention and comprehension*. New York: Academic Press.

Collins, W. A., & Getz, S. K. (1976). Children's social responses following modeled reactions to provocation: Prosocial effects of a television drama. *Journal of Personality, 44*, 488–500.

Collins, W. A., Sobol, S., & Westby, S. (1979). Effects of adult commentary on children's comprehension and inferences about a televised aggressive portrayal. *Child Development, 52*, 158–163.

Collins, W. A., Wellman, H., Keniston, A. H., & Westby, S. D. (1978). Age-related aspects of comprehension and inference from a televised dramatic narrative. *Child Development, 49*, 389–399.

Columbia Broadcasting System Group. (1974). *A study of messages received by children who viewed an episode of* Fat Albert and the Cosby Kids. New York: Office of Social Research, Department of Economics and Research, CBS Broadcast Group.

Communications Act of 1934. 47 U.S.C. 151–610 (1982).

Comstock, G. (1991). *Television and the American child*. San Diego: Academic.

Comstock, G., & Cobbey, R. (1979). Television and children of ethnic minorities. *Journal of Communication, 29*(1), 104–115.

Condry, J. (1989). *The psychology of television*. Hillsdale, N.J.: Erlbaum.

Condry, J., Bence, P., & Scheibe, C. (1988). Nonprogram content of children's television. *Journal of Broadcasting and Electronic Media, 32*, 255–270.

Cook, T. D., Appleton, H., Conner, R. F., Shaffer, A., Tamkin, G., & Weber, S. J. (1975). *Sesame Street revisited*. New York: Russell Sage.

Corcoran, E. (1996, June 30). On the Internet, a worldwide information explosion beyond words. *The Washington Post*, A1, A14–A15.

Cordua, G. D., McGraw, K. O., & Drabman, R. S. (1979). Doctor or nurse: Children's perceptions of sex-typed occupations. *Child Development, 50,* 590–593.

Corliss, R. (1993). Look! Up on the screen! It's a galaxy! It's a killer robot! It's . . . Virtual, man! *Time,* 80–83.

Corporation for Public Broadcasting. (1993). *Public broadcasting: Ready to teach: How public broadcasting can serve the ready-to-learn needs of America's children.* A report to the 103rd Congress and the American People. Washington, D.C.: Pursuant to P.L. 102–356.

Corteen, R. S., & Williams, T. M. (1986). Television and reading skills. In T. M. Williams (Ed.), *The impact of television: A natural experiment in three communities* (pp. 39–85). Orlando, FL: Academic Press.

Costley, C. L., & Brucks, M. (1986). Product knowlege as an explanation for age-related differences in children's cognitive responses to advertising. *Advances in Consumer Research, 14,* 288–292.

Courtney, A. E., & Whipple, T. W. (1974). Women in TV commercials. *Journal of Communication, 24,* 110–118.

Courtright, J. A., & Baran, S. J. (1980). The acquisition of sexual information by young people. *Journalism Quarterly, 57,* 107–114.

Craik, F., & Lockhart, R. (1972). Levels of processing: A framework for memory research. *Journal of Verbal Learning and Verbal Behavior, 11,* 521–533.

Crocker, F., Fiske, S. T., & Taylor, S. E. (1984). Schematic bases of belief change. In J. R. Eiser (Ed.), *Attitudinal judgment.* New York: Springer-Verlag.

Cross, W. E., Jr. (1991). *Shades of black.* Philadelphia: Temple University Press.

Davidson, E. S., Yasuna, A., & Tower, A. (1979). The effects of television cartoons on sex-role stereotyping in young girls. *Child Development, 50,* 597–600.

Davis, M. (1997). Garage cinema and the future of media technology. *Communication of the ACM, 40,* 43–48.

DeBell, C. (1993, August). Occupational gender-role stereotyping in television commercials: A nine-year longitudinal study. Paper presented at the annual meeting of the American Psychological Association, Toronto, Canada.

DES. (1987). *Aspects of work of the microelectronics education programme.* London: Department of Education and Science.

Dodge, K. A. (1985). A social information processing model of social competence in children. In M. Perlmutter (Ed.), *Minnesota symposia on child psychology.* Hillsdale, N.J.: Erlbaum.

Dominick, J. R., & Greenberg, B. S. (1970). Mass media functions among low-income adolescents. In B. S. Greenberg & B. Dervin (Eds.), *Use of the mass media by the urban poor.* New York: Praeger.

Donath, J. S. (In press). Identity and deception in the virtual community. In P. Kollock & M. Smith (Eds.), *Communities in cyberspace.* Berkley, CA: University of California Press.

Donnerstein, E., Kunkel, D., Linz, D., Potter, W. J., & Wilson, B. (1997, May). Violence in television programming overall. Paper presented at the annual meeting of the International Communication Association, Montreal, Canada.

Dorr, A. (1982). Television and the socialization of the minority child. In G. L. Berry & C. Mitchell-Kernan (Eds.), *Television and the socialization of the minority child.* New York: Academic.

Dorr, A. (1986). *Television and children: A special medium for a special audience.* Beverly Hills: Sage.

Dorr, A., & Kunkel, D. (1990). Children and the media environment. *Communication Research, 17*, 5–25.

Downs, A. C. (1981). Sex-role stereotyping on prime-time television. *The Journal of Genetic Psychology, 138*, 253–258.

Drabman, R. S., & Thomas, M. H. (1974). Does media violence increase children's tolerance of real-life aggression. *Developmental Psychology, 10*, 418–421.

Drabman, R. S., & Thomas, M. H. (1976). Does watching violence on television cause apathy? *Pediatrics, 57*, 329–331.

Durkin, K. (1985). Television and sex-role acquisition: 3: Counter-stereotyping. *British Journal of Social Psychology, 24*, 211–222.

Elmer-DeWitt, P. (1993, September). The amazing video game boom. *Time*, 67–72.

Eraut, M. (1995). Groupwork with computers in British primary schools. *Journal of Educational Computing Research, 13*, 61–87.

Eron, L. (1963). Relationship of TV viewing habits and aggressive behavior in children. *Journal of Abnormal and Social Psychology, 67*, 193–196.

Essa, E. (1987). The effects of a computer on preschool children's activities. *Early Childhood Research Quarterly, 2*, 377–382.

Farhi, P. (1995a, October 13). FCC's Hundt pushing for tougher TV station license renewal standards. *The Washington Post*, 1, A33.

Farhi, P. (1995b, October 13). Children's advertising: The rules not followed: FCC finds violations of commercial time limits are widespread. *The Washington Post*, A33.

Farhi, P. (1996a, February 2). BET, Microsoft plan interactive online venture. *The Washington Post*, F1.

Farhi, P. (1996b, July 30). Broadcasters pledge 3 hours of 'educational' TV a week. *The Washington Post*, A1, A7.

Farhi, P. (1996c, July 9). Cable TV firms to link schools to Internet. *Washington Post*, D1, D3.

Farhi, P. (1997a, July 10). TV ratings agreement reached: NBC refuses to join deal for stronger advisories. *The Washington Post*, 1, A16.

Farhi, P. (1997b, April 13). FCC to approve plan for digital television. *The Washington Post*, E1–E2.

Farhi, P. (1997c, April 28). TV's wave of the future takes on a digital look. *The Washington Post*, A1, A10.

Farhi, P. (1997d, May 5). TV channels its energy all over town. *The Washington Post*, A1, A12.

Federal Communications Commission. (1974). Children's television programs: Report and policy statement. *Federal Register, 39*, 39396–39409.

Federal Communications Commission. (1984). Revision of programming and commercialization policies, ascertainment requirements, and program log requirements for commercial television stations, 49 *Federal Register 33*, 588.

Federal Communications Commission. (1991). Report and order: In the matter of policies and rules concerning children's television programming. 6 *Federal Communications Commission Reports*, 2111.

Federal Communications Commission. (1996, August 8). *Action in docket case: FCC adopts new children's TV rules.* (MM Docket 93–48). Report No. DC 96–81.

Federal Communications Commission. (1996). *Policies and rules concerning children's television programming: Revision of programming policies for television broadcast stations.* MM Docket No. 93–48.

Federal Trade Commission. (1978). *FTC staff report on television advertising to children.* Washington, D.C.: U.S. Government Printing Office.

Federal Trade Commission. (1981). *FTC final staff report and recommendation.* Washington, D.C.: U.S. Government Printing Office.

Feshbach, S., & Singer, R. (1971). *Television and aggression.* San Francisco: Jossey Bass.

Fiske, S. T., & Taylor, S. E. (1984). *Social cognition.* Reading, Mass.: Addison-Wesley.

Flavell, J. H. (1963). *The developmental psychology of Jean Piaget.* Princeton, N.J: Van Nostrand.

Forge, L. S., & Phemister, S. (1987). The effect of prosocial cartoons on preschool children. *Child Study Journal, 17,* 83–87.

Fowler, M., & Brenner, D. (1982). A marketplace approach to broadcast regulation. *Texas Law Review, 60,* 207–257.

Frean, A. (1994, September 6). Computer games firms to fight porn in schools. *London Times.*

Freedman, J. L. (1984). Effects of television violence on aggression. *Psychological Bulletin, 96,* 227–246.

Freeman, J., & Huston, A. C. (1995, April). The effects of positive portrayals of black television characters on black children's racial attitudes, self-perception, and racial identification. Paper presented at the biennial meeting of the Society for Research in Child Development, Indianapolis, Indiana.

French, J., & Pena, S. (1991). Children's hero play of the 20th century: Changes resulting from television's influence. *Child Study Journal, 21,* 79–94.

Frey, K. S., & Ruble, D. N. (1992). Gender constancy and the "cost" of sex-typed behavior: A test of the conflict hypothesis. *Developmental Psychology, 28,* 714–721.

Friedrich, L. K., & Stein, A. H. (1973). Aggressive and prosocial television programs and the natural behavior of preschool children. *Monographs of the Society for Research in Child Development, 38,* 1–110.

Friedrich, L. K., & Stein, A. H. (1975). Prosocial television and young children: The effects of verbal labeling and role playing on learning and behavior. *Child Development, 46,* 27–38.

Friedrich-Cofer, L., & Huston, A. C. (1986). Television violence and aggression: The debate continues. *Psychological Bulletin, 100,* 364–371.

Friedrich-Cofer, L. K., Huston-Stein, A., Kipnis, D. M., Susman, E. J., & Clewett, A. S. (1979). Environmental enhancement of prosocial television content: Effect on interpersonal behavior, imaginative play, and self-regulation in a natural setting. *Developmental Psychology, 15,* 637–646.

Friend, B. (1997, September). Roundtable discussion about the measurement of children's television viewing. New York: Annenberg Public Policy Center.

Frueh, T., & McGhee, P. E. (1975). Traditional sex-role development and amount of time spent watching television. *Child Development, 11,* 109.

Gadberry, S. (1980). Effects of restricting first graders' TV viewing on leisure time use, IQ change, and cognitive style. *Journal of Applied Developmental Psychology, 1,* 45–57.

Gailey, C. W. (1996). Mediated messages: Gender, class, and cosmos in home video games. In P. M. Greenfield & R. R. Cocking (Eds.), *Interacting with video.* Norwood, N.J.: Ablex.

Galst, J. P., & White, M. A. (1976). The unhealthy persuader: The reinforcing value of television and children's purchase attempts at the supermarket. *Child Development, 47,* 1089–1096.

Geiogamah (Kiowa), H., & Pavel (Skokomish), D. M. (1993). Developing television for American Indian and Alaska Native children in the late 20th century. In G. L. Berry & J. K. Asamen (Eds.), *Children and television: Images in a changing sociocultural world.* Newberry Park, CA: Sage.

Gerbner, G. (1972). Violence in television drama: Trends and symbolic functions. In G. A. Comstock & E. A. Rubenstein (Eds.), *Television and social behavior. Vol 1.: Media content and control.* Washington, D.C.: U.S. Government Printing Office.

Gerbner, G. (1993, June). *Women and minorities on television* (a report to the Screen Actors Guild and the American Federation of Radio and Television Artists). Philadelphia: University of Pennsylvania, Annenberg School of Communications.

Gerbner, G. (1996). TV violence and what to do about it. *Nieman Reports,* Fall, 10–12.

Gerbner, G. (1997, March 2). Personal communication. Unpublished table and graph. Philadelphia: The Cultural Environment Movement.

Gerbner, G., Gross, L., Jackson-Beeck, M., Jeffries-Fox, S., & Signorielli, N. (1978). Cultural indicators: Violence profile No. 9. *Journal of Communication, 28,* 176–207.

Gerbner, G., Gross, L., Morgan, M., & Signorielli, N. (1980). The mainstreaming of America: Violence profile no. 11. *Journal of Communication, 32,* 100–127.

Gerbner, G., Gross, L., Morgan, M., & Signorielli, N. (1994). Growing up with television: The cultivation perspective. In J. Bryant & D. Zillmann (Eds.), *Media effects: Advances in theory and research.* Hillsdale, N.J.: Erlbaum.

Gerbner, G., Gross, L., Signorielli, N., & Morgan, M. (1986). *Television's mean world: Violence profile no. 14–15.* Philadelphia: University of Pennsylvania, Annenberg School of Communications.

Gerbner, G., Gross, L., Signorielli, N., Morgan, M., & Jackson-Beeck, M. (1979). The demonstration of power: Violence profile no. 10. *Journal of Communication, 29,* 177–196.

Gerbner, G., Morgan, M., & Signorielli, N. (1994, January). *Television violence profile No. 16: The turning point from research to action.* Philadelphia: The Cultural Environment Movement.

Gerbner, G., & Signorielli, N. (1990). Violence profile, 1967 through 1988–89: Enduring patterns. Unpublished manuscript, University of Pennsylvania, Annenberg School of Communication.

Gibbons, J., Anderson, D. R., Smith, R., Field, D. E., & Fischer, C. (1986). Young children's recall and reconstruction of audio and audiovisual material. *Child Development, 57,* 1014–1023.

Goldberg, M. E., Gorn, G. J., & Gibson, W. (1978). TV messages for snack and breakfast foods: Do they influence children's preferences? *Journal of Consumer Research, 5,* 73–81.

Gorman, H., & Bourne, L. E. (1983). Learning to think by learning LOGO: Rule learning in third-grade computer programmers. *Bulletin of the Psychonomic Society, 21,* 165–167.

Gorn, G. J., & Goldberg, M. E. (1980). Children's responses to repetitive television commercials. *Journal of Consumer Research, 6,* 421–424.

Gorn, G. J., Goldberg, M. E., & Kanugo, R. N. (1976). The role of educational television in changing the intergroup attitudes of children. *Child Development, 47,* 277–280.

Graves, S. B. (1980). Psychological effects of black portrayals on television. In S. B. Withey & R. B. Ables (Eds.), *Television and social behavior: Beyond violence and children.* Hillsdale, N.J.: Erlbaum.

Graves, S. B. (1993). Television, the portrayal of African Americans, and the development of children's attitudes. In G. L. Berry & J. K. Asamen (Eds.), *Children and television: Images in a changing sociocultural world.* Newberry Park, CA: Sage.

Graves, S. B. (1996). Diversity on television. In T. M. MacBeth (Ed.), *Tuning in to young viewers: Social science perspectives on television.* Newberry Park, CA: Sage.

Graybill, D., Kirsch, J., & Esselman, E. (1985). Effects of playing violent versus nonviolent videogames on the aggressive ideation of aggressive and nonaggressive children. *Child Study Journal, 15,* 199–205.

Graybill, D., Strawniak, M., Hunter, T., & O'Leary, M. (1987). Effects of playing versus observing violent versus nonviolent video games on children's aggression. *Psychology: A Quarterly Journal of Human Behavior, 24,* 1–8.

Greenberg, B. S. (1972). Children's reactions to TV blacks. *Journalism Quarterly, 47,* 277–280.

Greenberg, B. S. (1988). Some uncommon television images and the drench hypothesis. In S. Oskamp (Ed.), *Television as a social issue: Applied social psychology annual 8.* Newberry Park, CA: Sage.

Greenberg, B. S., & Atkin, C. K. (1982). Learning about minorities from television. In G. L. Berry & C. Mitchell-Kernan (Eds.), *Television and the socialization of the minority child.* New York: Academic.

Greenberg, B. S., Atkin, C. K., Edison, N. G., & Korzeny, F. (1980). Antisocial and prosocial behaviors on television. In B. S. Greenberg (Ed.), *Life on television: Content analysis of U.S. TV drama.* Norwood, N.J.: Ablex.

Greenberg, B. S., & Baptista-Fernandez, P. (1984). Hispanic-Americans—The new minority on television. In B. S. Greenberg (Ed.), *Life on television: Content analyses of U.S. TV drama.* Norwood, N.J.: Ablex.

Greenberg, B. S., & Brand, J. E. (1993). Cultural diversity on Saturday morning television. In G. L. Berry & J. K. Asamen (Eds.), *Children and television: Images in a changing sociocultural world.* Newberry Park, CA: Sage.

Greenberg, B. S., & Brand, J. E. (1994). Minorities and the mass media: 1970s to 1990s. In J. Bryant & D. Zillmann (Eds.), *Media effects: Advances in theory and research.* Hillsdale, N.J.: Erlbaum.

Greenberg, B. S., & Dominick, J. R. (1970). Television behavior among disadvantaged children. In B. S. Greenberg & B. Dervin (Eds.), *Use of the mass media by the urban poor.* New York: Praeger.

Greenberg, B. S., & Neuendorf, K. (1980). Black family interactions on television. In B. S. Greenberg (Ed.), *Life on television.* Norwood, N.J.: Ablex.

Greenfield, P. M. (1993). Representational competence in shared symbol systems: Electronic media from radio to video games. In R. R. Cocking & K. A. Renninger (Eds.), *The development and meaning of psychological distance.* Hillsdale, N.J.: Erlbaum.

Greenfield, P. M. (1995, July). *Media, children, and society.* Capitol Hill Science and Public Policy Seminar Series, Washington, D.C.

Greenfield, P. M. (1996). Video games as cultural artifacts. In P. M. Greenfield & R. R. Cocking (Eds.), *Interacting with video.* Norwood, N.J.: Ablex.

Greenfield, P. M., & Beagles-Roos, J. (1988). Radio vs. television: Their cognitive impact on children of different socioeconomic and ethnic groups. *Journal of Communication, 38,* 71–92.

Greenfield, P. M., Brannon, C., & Lohr, D. (1996). Two-dimensional representational movement through three-dimensional space: The role of video game expertise. In P. M. Greenfield & R. R. Cocking (Eds.), *Interacting with video.* Norwood, N.J.: Ablex.

Greenfield, P. M., Camaioni, L., Ercolani, P., Weiss, L., Lauber, B. A., & Perucchini, P. (1996). Cognitive socialization by computer games in two cultures: Inductive discovery versus mastery of an iconic code? In P. M. Greenfield & R. R. Cocking (Eds.), *Interacting with video.* Norwood, N.J.: Ablex.

Greenfield, P. M., Farrar, D., & Beagles-Roos, J. (1986). Is the medium the message? An experimental comparison of the effects of radio and television on imagination. *Journal of Applied Developmental Psychology, 7,* 201–218.

Greer, D., Potts, R., Wright, J. C., & Huston, A. C. (1982). The effects of television commercial form and commercial placement on children's social behavior and attention. *Child Development, 53,* 611–619.

Griffiths, M., & Alfrey, M. (1989). A stereotype in the making: Girls and computers in primary schools. *Educational Review, 41,* 73–79.

Gross, L., & Jeffries-Fox, S. (1978). What do you want to be when you grow up, little girl? In G. Tuchman, A. K. Daniels, & J. Benet (Eds.), *Hearth and home: Images of women in mass media.* New York: Oxford University Press.

Gross, L., & Morgan, M. (1980, March). Television and enculturation. Paper presented at the meeting of the National Workshop on Television and Youth. Washington, D.C.

Hall, C. (1954). *A primer of Freudian psychology.* New York: World.

Hall, E. R., Esty, E. T., & Fisch, S. M. (1990). Television and children's problem-solving behavior: A synopsis of an evaluation of the effects of *Square One TV. Journal of Mathematical Behavior, 9,* 161–174.

Hamamoto, D. Y. (1993). They're so cute when they're young: The Asian-American child on television. In G. L. Berry & J. K. Asamen (Eds.), *Children and television: Images in a changing sociocultural world.* Newberry Park, CA: Sage.

Harrison, L. F., & Williams, T. M. (1986). Television and cognitive development. In T. M. Williams (Ed.), *The impact of television: A natural experiment in three communities.* San Diego, CA: Academic Press.

Hawkins, J. (1985). Computers and girls. *Sex Roles, 13,* 165–180.

Hawkins, J., Sheingold, K., Gearhart, M., & Berger, J. (1982). Microcomputers in schools: Impact on the social life of elementary classrooms. *Journal of Applied Developmental Psychology, 3,* 361–373.

Hay, D., & Lockwood, R. (1989). Girls' and boys' success and strategies on a computer-generated hunting task. *British Journal of Developmental Psychology, 7,* 17–27.

Hayes, D. A. (1994). The children's hour revisited: The Children's Television Act of 1990. *Federal Communications Law Journal, 46,* 293–326.

Hayes, D. S., & Birnbaum, D. (1980). Preschoolers' retention of televised events: Is a picture worth a thousand words? *Developmental Psychology, 17,* 230–232.

Hearold, S. (1986). A synthesis of 1043 effects of television on social behavior. In G. Comstock (Ed.), *Public communication and behavior: Vol. 1.* New York: Academic Press.

Hess, R., & Miura, I. (1985). Gender differences in enrollment in computer camps and classes. *Sex Roles, 13,* 193–203.

Hicks, J. S. (1989). What's new in software? The social nature of computers in the classroom. *Reading, Writing, and Learning Disabilities, 5,* 133–137.

Hooper, S., Ward, T. J., Hannafin, M. J., & Clark, H. T. (1989). The effects of aptitude composition in achievement during small group learning. *Journal of Computer Based Learning, 16,* 102–109.

Hoyles, C., Healy, L., & Pozzi, S. (1994). Groupwork with computers: An overview of findings. *Journal of Computer Assisted Learning, 10,* 202–215.

Huesmann, L. R., & Eron, L. D. (Eds.). (1986). *Television and the aggressive child: A cross-national comparison.* Hillsdale, N.J.: Erlbaum.

Huesmann, L. R., Eron, L. D., Lefkowitz, M. M., & Walder, L. O. (1984). Stability of aggression over time and generations. *Developmental Psychology, 20,* 1120–1134.

Huesmann, L. R., Lagerspetz, K., & Eron, L. (1984). Intervening variables in the TV-violence-aggression relation: Evidence from two countries. *Developmental Psychology, 20,* 746–775.

Huesmann, L. R., & Miller, L. S. (1994). Long-term effects of repeated exposure to media violence in childhood. In L. R. Huesmann (Ed.), *Aggressive behavior: Current perspectives*. New York: Plenum Press.

Hundt, R. (1995, December). Reading the First Amendment in favor of children. Speech presented at the Brooklyn Law School, Brooklyn, NY.

Hur, K. K., & Robinson, J. P. (1978). The social impact of *Roots*. *Journalism Quarterly, 55*, 19–23.

Huston, A. C. (1983). Sex typing. In E. M Hetherington (Ed.), P. H. Mussen (Series Ed.). *Handbook of child psychology, Vol. 4: Socialization, personality, and social development*. New York: Wiley.

Huston, A. C., Donnerstein, E., Fairchild, H., Feshbach, N. D., Katz, P. A., Murray, J. P., Rubenstein, E. A., Wilcox, B. L., & Zuckerman, D. (1992). *Big world, small screen*. Lincoln and London: University of Nebraska Press.

Huston, A. C., Greer, D., Wright, J. C., Welch, R., & Ross, R. (1984). Children's comprehension of televised content with masculine and feminine connotations. *Developmental Psychology, 20,* 707–716.

Huston, A. C., Watkins, B. A., & Kunkel, D. (1989). Public policy and children's television. *American Psychologist, 44,* 424–433.

Huston, A. C., & Wright, J. C. (1983). Children's processing of television: The informative functions of formal features. In J. Bryant & D. R. Anderson (Eds.), *Children's understanding of television: Research on attention and comprehension*. New York: Academic Press.

Huston, A. C., & Wright, J. C. (in press). Mass media and children's development. In W. Damon, I. Sigel, & K. A. Renninger (Eds.), *Handbook of child psychology, Vol. 4: Child psychology in practice* (5th ed.). New York: Wiley.

Huston, A. C., Wright, J. C., Rice, M. L., Kerkman, D., & St. Peters, M. (1990). The development of television viewing patterns in early childhood: A longitudinal investigation. *Developmental Psychology, 26,* 409–420.

Huston, A. C., Wright, J. C., Wartella, E., Rice, M., Watkins, B. A., Campbell, T., & Potts, R. (1981b). Communicating more than content: Formal features of children's television programs. *Journal of Communication, 31,* 32–48.

Huston-Stein, A., Fox, S., Greer, D., Watkins, B. A., & Whitaker, J. (1981a). The effects of TV action and violence on children's social behavior. *The Journal of Genetic Psychology, 138,* 183–191.

Huston-Stein, A. C., Wright, J. C., Wartella, E., Rice, M. L., Watkins, B. A., Campbell, T., & Potts, R. (1981b). Communicating more than content: Formal features of children's television programs. *Journal of Communication, 31,* 32–48.

James, N. C., & McCain, T. A. (1982). Television games preschool children play: Patterns, themes, and uses. *Journal of Broadcasting, 26,* 783–800.

Jamieson, K. H. (1997, June). Closing comments at the second annual Annenberg Public Policy Center's Conference on Children and Television, Washington, D.C.

Johnston, J., & Ettema, J. S. (1982). *Positive images: Breaking stereotypes with children's television*. Beverly Hills, CA: Sage.

Jordan, A. B. (1996). *The state of children's television: An examination of quantity, quality, and industry beliefs*. Annenberg Public Policy Center Report No. 2, University of Pennsylvania.

Jordan, A. (1997a, May). Industry perspectives on the challenges of children's educational television. Paper presented at the annual meeting of the International Communication Association, Montreal, Canada.

Jordan, A. (1997b, November 21). Personal communication.

Jordan, A. B., & Sullivan, J. L. (1997). *Children's educational television regulations and the local broadcaster: Impact and implementation.* Philadelphia: University of Pennsylvania, The Annenberg Public Policy Center.

Jordan, A. B., & Woodard, E. (1997). The 1997 state of children's television report: Programming for children over broadcast and cable television. Philadelphia: University of Pennsylvania, The Annenberg Public Policy Center.

Kafai, Y. B. (1995). *Minds in play.* Hillsdale, N.J.: Lawrence Erlbaum.

Kafai, Y. B. (1996). Gender differences in children's constructions of video games. In P. M. Greenfield & R. R. Cocking (Eds.), *Interacting with video.* Norwood, N.J.: Ablex.

Kaplan, P. (1997, June 21). Networks angry at Gore, but ratings talks aren't kaput. *The Washington Times,* C4.

Kelly, A. E., & Spear, P. S. (1991). Intraprogram synopses for children's comprehension of television content. *Journal of Experimental Child Psychology, 52,* 87–98.

Kerkman, D., Kunkel, D., Huston, A. C., Wright, J. C., & Pinon, M. F. (1990). Children's television programming and the "Free market solution." *Journalism Quarterly, 67,* 147–156.

Kimball, M. (1986). Television and sex-role attitudes. In T. M. Williams (Ed.), *The impact of television: A natural experiment in three communities.* Orlando, FL: Academic Press.

Kinder, M. (1996). Contextualizing video game violence: From *Teenage Mutant Ninja Turtles 1* to *Mortal Kombat 2.* In P. M. Greenfield & R. R. Cocking (Eds.), *Interacting with video.* Norwood, N.J.: Ablex.

Kippax, S., & Murray, J. P. (1977). Using television: Programme content and need gratification. *Politics, 12,* 56–69.

Kohlberg, L. (1966). A cognitive-developmental analysis of children's sex-role concepts and attitudes. In E. E. Maccoby (Ed.), *The development of sex differences* (pp. 82–172). Stanford, CA: Stanford University Press.

Kohlberg, L. (1984). *The psychology of moral development.* San Francisco: Harper & Row.

Koolstra, C. M., & van der Voort, T. H. A. (1996). Longitudinal effects of television on children's leisure-time reading. *Human Communication Research, 23,* 3–35.

Kramer, P. E. (1987). *Final report to the National Science Foundation, Grant no. SER-8160408.* Washington, D.C.: National Science Foundation.

Kramer, P. E., & Lehman, S. (1990). Mismeasuring women: A critique of research on computer ability and avoidance. *Signs, 16,* 158–172.

Krendl, K. A., Broihier, M. C., & Fleetwood, C. (1989). Children and computers: Do sex-related differences persist? *Journal of Communication, 39,* 85–93.

Kubey, R., & Larson, R. (1990). The use and experience of the new video media among children and adolescents. *Communication Research, 17,* 107–130.

Kunkel, D. (1988). From a raised eyebrow to a turned back: Regulatory factors influencing the growth of children's product-related programming. *Journal of Communication, 38,* 90–108.

Kunkel, D. (1994, June 28). Testimony to the Federal Communications Commission at the En Banc Hearings on Children's Television. (MM docket No. 93–48). Washington, D.C.

Kunkel, D., & Canepa, J. (1994). Broadcasters' license renewal claims regarding children's educational programming. *Journal of Broadcasting and Electronic Media, 38,* 397–416.

Kunkel, D., & Gantz, W. (1992). Children's television advertising in the multichannel environment. *Journal of Communication, 42,* 134–152.

Kunkel, D., & Roberts, D. (1991). Young minds and marketplace values: Issues in children's television advertising. *Journal of Social Issues, 47,* 57–72.

Kunkel, D., Wilson, B., Donnerstein, E., Linz, D., Smith, S., Gray, T., Blumenthal, E., & Potter, W. J. (1995a). Measuring television violence: The importance of context. *Journal of Broadcasting and Electronic Media, 39*, 284–291.

Kunkel, D., Wilson, B., Linz, D., Potter, W. J., Donnerstein, E., Smith, S., Blumenthal, E., & Gray, T. (1995b). The effects of exposure to media violence. In *National Television Violence Study.* Los Angeles: Mediascope, Inc.

Kurland, D. M., & Pea, R. D. (1984). On the cognitive effects of learning computer programming. *New Ideas in Psychology, 2,*137–168.

Laboratory for Comparative Human Cognition. (1988, Winter). Computer networking for child development. *SRCD Newsletter*, 1–3.

Lawler, R. W. (1982). Designing computer-based microworlds. *Byte*, 138–160.

Leary, A., Huston, A. C., & Wright, J. C. (1983, April). The influence of television production features with masculine and feminine connotations on children's comprehension and play behavior. Paper presented at the biennial meeting of the Society for Research in Child Development, Detroit, Michigan.

Lefkowitz, M. M., Eron, L. D., Walder, L. O., & Huesmann, L. R. (1972). Television violence and child aggression: A follow-up study. In G. A. Comstock & E. A. Rubenstein (Eds.), *Television and social behavior.* Vol. III: Washington, D.C.: U.S. Government Printing Office.

Leiner, B., Cerf, V., Clark, D., Kahn, R., Kleinrock, L., Lynch, D., Postel, J., Roberts, L., & Wolff, S. (1997). The past and future history of the Internet. *Communication of the ACM, 38*, 102–108.

Lemish, D., & Rice, M. L. (1986). Television as a talking picture book: A prop for language acquisition. *Journal of Child Language, 13*, 251–274.

Lemon, J. (1977). Women and blacks on prime-time television. *Journal of Communication, 27*, 70–79.

Lepper, M. (1985). Microcomputers in education: Motivational and social issues. *American Psychologist, 40*, 1–18.

Lepper, M., & Malone, T. (1987). Intrinsic motivation and instructional effectiveness in computer-based education. In R. Snow & M. Farr (Eds.), *Aptitude, learning, and instruction: III. Conative and affective process analysis.* Hillsdale, N.J.: Erlbaum.

Lesser, G. S. (1974). *Children and television: Lessons from* Sesame Street. New York: Random House.

Lesser, G. S. (1976). Applications of psychology to television programming: Formulation of program objectives. *American Psychologist, 31*, 135–136.

Liebert, R. M., & Sprafkin, J. (1988). *The early window: Effects of television on children and youth* (3rd ed.). New York: Pergamon.

Liebert, D. E., Sprafkin, J. N., Liebert, R. M., & Rubenstein, E. A. (1977). Effects of television disclaimers on the product expectations of children. *Journal of Communication, 27*, 118–124.

Linn, M. C. (1985). Fostering equitable consequences from computer learning environments. *Sex Roles, 13*, 229–240.

Lipinski, J., Nida, R., Shade, D., & Watson, J. A. (1986). The effects of microcomputers on young children: An examination of free-play choices, sex differences, and social interactions. *Journal of Educational Computing Research, 2*, 147–168.

Liss, M. B., & Calvert, S. L. (1994). The development of gender identity: Making sense of the world. *Social Development, 3*, 82–87.

Liss, M. B., & Reinhardt, L. C. (1980). Aggression on prosocial television programs. *Psychological Reports, 46*, 1065–1066.

Liss, M. B., Reinhardt, L. C., & Fredriksen, S. (1983). TV heroes: The impact of rhetoric and deeds. *Journal of Applied Developmental Psychology, 4*, 175–187.

List, J. A., Collins, W. A., & Westby, S. (1983). Comprehension and inferences from traditional and nontraditional sex-role portrayals on television. *Child Development, 54*, 1579–1587.

Lorch, E. P., Anderson, D. R., & Levin, S. R. (1979). The relationship of visual attention to children's comprehension of television. *Child Development, 50*, 722–727.

Lovelace, V., Freund, S., & Graves, S. B. (In press). Race relations in *Sesame Street:* Racial knowledge, attitudes, and understanding in preschool children. In M. B. Spencer & G. K. Brookins (Eds.), *Research in minority child development.* Hillsdale, N.J.: Lawrence Erlbaum.

Lovelace, V. O., & Huston, A. C. (1982). How can television teach prosocial behavior? *Prevention in Human Services* by the Haworth Press, Inc.

Lovelace, V., Scheiner, S., Dollberg, S., Segui, I., & Black, T. (1994). Making a neighbourhood the *Sesame Street* way: Developing a methodology to evaluate children's understanding of race. *Journal of Educational Television, 20*, 69–78.

Loyd, B., Loyd, D., & Gressard, C. (1987). Gender and computer experience as factors in the computer attitudes of middle school students. *Journal of Early Adolescence, 7*, 13–19.

Luecke-Aleksa, D., Anderson, D. R., Collins, P. A., & Schmitt, K. L. (1995). Gender constancy and television viewing. *Developmental Psychology, 31*, 773–780.

Lyle, J., & Hoffman, H. R. (1972). Children's use of television and other media. In E. A. Rubenstein, G. A. Comstock, & J. P. Murray (Eds.), *Television and social behavior: Vol. 4: Television in day-to-day life: Patterns of use.* Washington, D.C.: Government Printing Office.

Maccoby, E. E. (1951). Television: Its impact on school children. *Public Opinion Quarterly, 15*, 421–444.

Maccoby, E. E. (1980). *Social development.* New York: Harcourt, Brace & Jovanovich.

Maccoby, E. E. (1988). Gender as a social category. *Developmental Psychology, 24*, 755–765.

Mackey, W. D., & Hess, D. J. (1982). Attention structure and stereotypy of gender on television: An empirical analysis. *Genetic Psychology Monographs, 106*, 199–215.

Macklin, N. C. (1987). Preschoolers' understanding of the informational function of television advertising. *Journal of Consumer Research, 14*, 229–239.

Malone, T. (1981). Toward a theory of intrinsically motivating instruction. *Cognitive Science, 4*, 333–369.

Marchionini, G., & Maurer, H. (1995). The roles of digital libraries in teaching and learning. *Communication of the ACM, 38*, 67–75.

Mares, M. L. (1996). Positive effects of television on social behavior: A meta-analysis. *Publications in the Annenberg Public Policy Center's Report Series, 3*, 1–26.

Marriott, M., with Brant, M. (1995, July 31). Cybersoul not found. *Newsweek*, 62–64.

Martin, C. L., & Halverson, C. F., Jr. (1981). A schematic processing model of sextyping and stereotyping in children. *Child Development, 52*, 1119–1134.

Martin, C. L., Wood, C. H., & Little, J. K. (1990). The development of gender stereotype components. *Child Development, 61*, 1891–1904.

Mays, L., Henderson, E. H., Seidman, S. K., & Steiner, V. S. (1975). An evaluation report on *Vegetable Soup:* The effects of a multiethnic children's series on intergroup attitudes of children. Unpublished manuscript, New York State Department of Education.

McArthur, L. Z., & Eisen, S. V. (1976). Television and sex-role stereotyping. *Journal of Applied Social Psychology, 6*, 329–351.

McDermott, S., & Greenberg, B. S. (1984). Black children's esteem: Parents, peers, and television. In R. Bostrom (Ed.), *Communication yearbook* (Vol. 8). Newbury Park, CA: Sage.

McGhee, P. E., & Frueh, T. (1980). Television viewing and the learning of sex-role stereotypes. *Sex Roles, 6,* 179–188.

McLuhan, H. M. (1964). *Understanding media: The extensions of man.* New York: McGraw-Hill.

McMahon, H. (1990). Collaborating with computers. *Journal of Computer Assisted Learning, 6,* 149–167.

Melody, W. (1973). *Children's television: The economics of exploitation.* New Haven, CT: Yale University Press.

Meringoff, L. K. (1980). A story: Influence of the medium on children's story apprehension. *Journal of Educational Psychology, 72,* 240–249.

Meringoff, L. K. (1983). How is children's learning from television distinctive? Exploiting the medium methodologically. In J. Bryant & D. R. Anderson (Eds.), *Children's understanding of television: Research on attention and comprehension.* New York: Academic.

Meringoff, L., & Lesser, G. (1980). Children's ability to distinguish television commercials from program material. In R. P. Adler, G. S. Lesser, L. K. Meringoff, T. S. Robertson, J. R. Rossiter, & S. Ward (Eds.), *The effects of television advertising on children* (pp. 29–42). Lexington, Mass: Lexington Books.

Meyers, W. (1996). On the road to the information superhighway. *IEEE,* 71–73.

Mielke, K. (1983). Formative research on appeal and comprehension in *3–2–1 Contact.* In J. Bryant & D. R. Anderson (Eds.), *Children's understanding of television: Research on attention and comprehension.* New York: Academic.

Mielke, K. (1989, November). Other current studies. Paper presented at *Sesame Street Research: A 20th Year Symposium.* Presented by the Children's Television Workshop at the Henry Chauncey Conference Center, Educational Testing Service, Princeton, N.J.

Miller, M. M., & Reeves, B. B. (1976). Children's occupational sex-role stereotypes: The linkage between television content and perception. *Journal of Broadcasting, 20,* 35–50.

Mintz, J., & Torry, S. (1998, January 15). Internal R. J. Reynolds documents detail cigarette marketing aimed at children. *The Washington Post,* A01.

Mischel, W. (1966). A social-learning view of sex differences in behavior. In E. E. Maccoby (Ed.), *The development of sex differences* (pp. 56–81). Stanford, CA: Stanford University Press.

Miura, I. (1984). Processes contributing to individual differences in computer literacy. Unpublished doctoral dissertation, Stanford University, 1984.

Miura, I. (1987). Gender and SES status differences in middle-school computer interest and use. *Journal of Early Adolescence, 7,* 243–254.

Miura, I., & Hess, R. (1984). Sex differences in computer access, interest, and usage: A summary of three studies. *Forum for Academic Computing and Teaching Systems, 2,* 3–4.

Miura, I., & Miura, J. (1984, August). Computer self-efficacy: A contributing factor to gender differences in the election of computer science courses. Paper presented at the Fifth International Congress of Mathematical Education, Adelaide, Australia.

Montgomery, K. C. (1995). *Children in the digital age.* Washington, D.C.: Center for Media Education.

Montgomery, K. C., & Pasnik, S. (1996). *Web of deception: Threats to children from online marketing.* Washington, D.C.: Center for Media Education.

Moore-Hart, M. A. (1995). The effects of multicultural links on reading and writing performance and cultural awareness of fourth and fifth graders. *Computers in Human Behavior, 11,* 391–410.

Mundy-Castle, A. C., Wilson, D. J., Sibanda, P. S., & Sibanda, J. S. (1989). Cognitive effects of LOGO among black and white Zimbabwean girls and boys. *International Journal of Psychology, 24,* 539–546.

Murray, J. P. (1993). The developing child in a multimedia society. In G. L. Berry & J. K. Asamen (Eds.), *Children and television: Images in a changing sociocultural world.* Newberry Park, CA: Sage.

Murray, J. P. (1997, January 28). Personal communication.

Murray, J. P. (1998). Studying television violence: A research agenda for the 21st century. In J. K. Asamen & G. L. Berry (Eds.), *Research paradigms, television, and social behavior.* Thousand Oaks, CA: Sage.

Murray, J. P., & Kippax, S. (1978). Children's social behavior in three towns with differing television experience. *Journal of Communication, 28,* 19–29.

National Commission on Working Women. (1986). *Women in focus: An analysis of TV's female characters and their jobs.* Washington, D.C.: Steenland.

Neopolitan, D. M., & Huston, A. C. (1994a). *Female and minority characters on educational and informative television programs for children: Report to the Public Broadcasting Service.* Lawrence, KS: Center for Research on the Influences of Television on Children, University of Kansas.

Neopolitan, D. M., & Huston, A. C. (1994b). *Educational content of children's programs on public and commercial television.* Lawrence, KS: Center for Research on the Influences of Television on Children, University of Kansas.

Neuman, S. B. (1988). The displacement effect: Assessing the relation between television viewing and reading performance. *Reading Research Quarterly, 23,* 414–440.

Neuman, S. B. (1991). *Literacy in the television age.* Norwood, NJ: Ablex.

Neuman, S. B. (1992). Is learning from media distinctive? Examining children's inferencing strategies. *American Educational Research Journal, 29,* 119–140.

Neuman, S. B., Burden, D., & Holden, E. (1990). Enhancing children's comprehension of a televised story through previewing. *Journal of Educational Research, 83,* 258–265.

Newcomb, A. F., & Collins, W. A. (1979). Children's comprehension of family role portrayals in televised dramas: Effects of socioeconomic status, ethnicity, and age. *Developmental Psychology, 15,* 417–423.

Newman, D. (1987). *Local and long-distance computer networking for science classrooms.* New York: Center for Children and Technology, Bank Street College of Education.

Nielsen Television Index. (1981). *Child and teenage television viewing* (Special Release). New York: NTI.

O'Bryant, S., & Corder-Bolz, C. (1978). The effects of television on children's stereotyping of women's work roles. *Journal of Vocational Behavior, 12,* 233–244.

Oldenburg, D. (1994, November 24). The electronic gender gap. *The Washington Post,* D5.

Oldenburg, D. (1995, October 17). Learning's the thing: New directions for kids' software. *The Washington Post,* C5.

Palmer, E., & McDowell, C. (1979). Program/commercial separators in children's television programming. *Journal of Communication, 29,* 197–201.

Palmer, E., & McDowell, C. (1981). Children's understanding of nutritional information presented in breakfast cereal commercials. *Journal of Broadcasting, 25,* 295–301.

Palmer, E. L., Smith, K. T., & Strawser, K. S. (1993). Rubik's Tube: Developing a child's television worldview. In G. L. Berry & J. K. Asamen (Eds.), *Children & television: Images in a changing sociocultural world.* Newberry Park, CA: Sage.

Papert, S. (1980). *Mindstorms: children, computers, and powerful ideas.* New York: Basic Books.

Parrish, E. A. (1997). The next 50 years of computing: Changes on campus. *Computer, 16.*

Paulson, F. L. (1974). Teaching cooperation on television: An evaluation of *Sesame Street* social goals programs. *AV Communication Review, 22,* 229–246.

Pea, R. D. (1983). LOGO programming and problem solving. Paper presented at the Annual Meeting of the American Educational Research Association, Montreal, Canada.

Pecora, N. (1995). Children and television advertising from a social science perspective. *Critical Studies in Mass Communication, 12,* 354–364.

Perse, E. M. (1990). Audience selectivity and involvement in the newer media environment. *Communication Research, 17,* 675–697.

Pezdek, K., & Hartman, E. F. (1983). Children's television viewing: Attention and comprehension of auditory and visual information. *Child Development, 54,* 1015–1023.

Pezdek, K., & Stevens, E. (1984). Children's memory for auditory and visual information on television. *Developmental Psychology, 20,* 212–218.

Piaget, J. (1962). *Play, dreams, and imitation in childhood.* London: Routledge & Kegan Paul.

Pingree, S. (1978). The effects of nonsexist commercials and perceptions of reality on children's attitudes about women. *Psychology of Women Quarterly, 2,* 262–277.

Pinon, M. F., Huston, A. C., & Wright, J. C. (1989). Family ecology and child characteristics that predict young children's educational television viewing. *Child Development, 60,* 846–856.

Potts, R., Huston, A. C., & Wright, J. C. (1986). The effects of television form and violent content on boys' attention and social behavior. *Journal of Experimental Child Psychology, 41,* 1–17.

Poulin-Dubois, D., McGilly, C., & Shultz, T. (1989). Psychology of computer use: Effect of learning LOGO on children's problem-solving skills. *Psychological Reports, 64,* 1327–1337.

Poulos, R. W., Harvey, S. E., & Liebert, R. M. (1976). Saturday morning television: A profile of the 1974–75 children's season. *Psychological Reports, 39,* 1047–1057.

Prime Time Live. (1991, September 19). American Broadcasting Corporation.

Raskin, J. (1997). Looking for a humane interface: Will computers ever become easy to use? *Communications of the ACM, 40,* 98–101.

Raymondo, J. C. (1997, March). Confessions of a Nielsen household. *American Demographics,* 24–31.

Renn, J. A., & Calvert, S. L. (1993). The relation between gender schemas and adults' recall of stereotyped and counterstereotyped television content. *Sex Roles, 28,* 449–459.

Rice, M. L., Huston, A. C., Truglio, R., & Wright, J. C. (1990). Words from *Sesame Street:* Learning vocabulary while viewing. *Developmental Psychology, 26,* 421–428.

Rice, M. L., & Sell, M. (1990). Exploration of the uses and effectiveness of *Sesame Street* home videotapes. Unpublished manuscript, University of Kansas, Lawrence, Kansas.

Rice, M. L., & Woodsmall, L. (1988). Lessons from television: Children's word learning when viewing. *Child Development, 59,* 420–429.

Roberts, D. F., Christenson, P. C., Gibson, W. A., Mooser, L., & Goldberg, M. E. (1980). Developing discriminating consumers. *Journal of Communication, 30,* 229–231.

Robertson, T. S., & Rossiter, J. R. (1974). Children and commercial persuasion: An attribution theory analysis. *Journal of Consumer Research, 1,* 13–20.

Robertson, T. S., & Rossiter, J. R. (1977). Children's responsiveness to commercials. *Journal of Communication, 27*, 101–106.

Ross, R. P., Campbell, T., Huston-Stein, A., & Wright, J. C. (1981). Nutritional misinformation of children: A developmental and experimental analysis of the effects of televised food commercials. *Journal of Applied Developmental Psychology, 1*, 329–347.

Ross, R. P., Campbell, T., Wright, J. C., Huston, A. C., Rice, M. L., & Turk, P. (1984). When celebrities talk, children listen: An experimental analysis of children's responses to TV ads with celebrity endorsement. *Journal of Applied Developmental Psychology, 5*, 185–202.

Rossiter, J. R. (1980a). Children and television advertising: Policy issues, perspectives, and the status of research. In E. L. Palmer & A. Dorr (Eds.), *Children and the faces of television: Teaching, violence, selling.* New York: Academic Press.

Rossiter, J. R. (1980b). The effects of volume and repetition of television commercials. In R. P. Adler, G. S. Lesser, L. K. Meringoff, T. S. Robertson, J. R. Rossiter, & S. Ward (Eds.), *The effects of television advertising on children: Review and recommendations* (pp. 153–184). Lexington, Mass.: Lexington Books.

Rossiter, J. R., & Robertson, T. (1974). Children's television commercials: Testing the defenses. *Journal of Broadcasting, 23*, 33–40.

Rubin, A. M. (1994). Media uses and effects: A uses-and-gratifications perspective. In J. Bryant & D. Zillmann (Eds.), *Media effects: Advances in theory and research.* Hillsdale, N.J.: Erlbaum.

Ruble, D. N., Balaban, T., & Cooper, J. (1981). Gender constancy and the effects of sex-typed televised toy commercials. *Child Development, 52*, 667–673.

Sachem Web Slingers (1997). Spinning webs into the 21st century. *Communication of the ACM, 40*, 125–128.

Schmitt, K. L., Linebarger, D. L., Collins, P. A., Wright, J. C., Anderson, D. R., Huston, A. C., & McElroy, E. (1997, April). Effects of preschool television viewing on adolescent creative thinking and behavior. Poster session presented at the biennial meeting of the Society for Research in Child Development, Washington, D.C.

Schramm, W. (1962). What we know about learning from instructional television. In L. Asheim (Ed.), *Educational television: The next ten years.* Stanford, Calif.: Institute for Communication Research.

Schramm, W., Lyle, J., & Parker, E. (1961). *Television in the lives of our children.* Stanford, Calif.: Stanford University Press.

Schutte, N., Malouff, J., Post-Garden, J., & Rodasta, A. (1988). Effects of playing video games on children's aggressive and other behaviors. *Journal of Applied Social Psychology, 18*, 454–460.

Schwartz, J. (1996, July 30). Internet law ruled invalid by U.S. judges. *The Washington Post*, C3.

Seggar, J. F., & Wheeler, P. (1973). World of work on TV: Ethnic and sex representation in TV drama. *Journal of Broadcasting, 17*, 201–214.

Sherwood, R. D., Kinzer, C. K., Bransford, J. D., & Franks, J. J. (1987a). Some benefits of creating macro-contexts for science instruction: Initial findings. *Journal of Research in Science Teaching, 24*, 417–435.

Sherwood, R. D., Kinzer, C., Hasselbring, T., & Bransford, J. (1987b). Macro-contexts for learning: Initial findings and issues. *Journal of Applied Cognitive Psychology, 1*, 93–108.

Siegel, A. E. (1956). Film-mediated fantasy aggression and strength of aggressive drive. *Child Development, 27*, 365–378.

Signorelli, N., Gross, L., & Morgan, M. (1982). Violence in television programs: Ten years later. In D. Pearl, L. Bouthilet, & J. Lazar (Eds.), *Television and behavior. Vol. 2: Technical Reports: Ten years of scientific progress and implications for the 80s.* Washington, D.C.: U.S. Government Printing Office.

Silverman, L. T., & Sprafkin, J. N. (1980). The effects of *Sesame Street's* prosocial spots on cooperative play between young children. *Journal of Broadcasting, 24,* 135–147.

Silvern, S. B., & Williamson, P. A. (1987). The effects of video game play on young children's aggression, fantasy, and prosocial behavior. *Journal of Applied Developmental Psychology, 8,* 453–462.

Simon, P. (1993, August). Invited address presented at the Television and Family Violence Conference, Los Angeles, CA.

Simon, P. (1995, July 12). Television interview on the MacNeil/Lehrer News Hour.

Singer, D. G., & Singer, J. L. (1976). Can television stimulate children's imaginative play? *Journal of Communication, 26,* 74–80.

Singer, D. G., & Singer, J. L. (1994). Evaluating the classroom viewing of a television series: *Degrassi Junior High.* In D. Zillmann, J. Bryant, & A. C. Huston (Eds.), *Media, children, and the family.* Hillsdale, N.J.: Lawrence Erlbaum.

Singer, J. L., & Singer, D. G. (1981). *Television, imagination, and aggression: A study of preschoolers.* Hillsdale, N.J.: Lawrence Erlbaum.

Singer, J. L., & Singer, D. G. (1983). Implications of childhood television viewing for cognition, imagination, and emotion. In J. Bryant & D. R. Anderson (Eds.), *Children's understanding of television: Research on attention and comprehension.* New York: Academic Press.

Singer, J. L., Singer, D. G., & Rapaczynski, W. S. (1984). Family patterns and television viewing as predictors of children's beliefs and aggression. *Journal of Communication, 34,* 73–89.

Sklorz-Weiner, M. (1989). Boys and girls and computers: Behavior and attitudes towards the new technologies. *Zeitschrift fur Padagogische Psychologie, 3,* 129–137.

Slaby, R. G., & Frey, K. (1975). Development of gender constancy and selective attention to same-sex models. *Child Development, 46,* 849–856.

Smith, R., Anderson, D. R., & Fischer, C. (1985). Young children's comprehension of montage. *Child Development, 56,* 962–971.

Smythe, D. (1954). Reality as presented on television. *Public Opinion Quarterly, 18,* 143–156.

Spence, J., & Helmrich, R. (1978). *Masculinity and femininity: Their psychological dimensions, correlates, and antecedents.* Austin, Texas: University of Texas Press.

Spencer, M. B., & Markstrom-Adams, C. (1990). Identity processes among racial and ethnic minority children in America. *Child Development, 61,* 290–310.

Sprafkin, J. N., & Liebert, R. M. (1978). Sex-typing and children's television preferences. In G. Tuchman, A. K. Daniels, & J. Benet (Eds.), *Hearth and home: Images of women in the mass media.* New York: Oxford University Press.

Sprafkin, J. N., Liebert, R. M., & Poulos, R. W. (1975). Effects of a prosocial televised example on children's helping. *Journal of Experimental Child Psychology, 20,* 119–126.

Sprafkin, J. N., & Rubenstein, A. (1979). A field correlational study of children's television viewing habits and prosocial behavior. *Journal of Broadcasting, 23,* 265–276.

Stein, A. H., & Friedrich, L. K. (1972). Television content and young children's behavior. In J. P. Murray, E. A. Rubenstein, & G. A. Comstock (Eds.), *Television and social behavior. Vol. II: Television and social learning* (pp. 202–317). Washington, D.C.: U.S. Government Printing Office.

Sternglanz, S. H., & Serbin, L. A. (1974). Sex-role stereotyping in children's television programs. *Developmental Psychology*, 1974, *10*, 710–715.

Stewart, D. W., & Ward, S. (1994). Media effects on advertising. In J. Bryant & D. Zillmann (Eds.), *Media effects: Advances in theory and research*. Hillsdale, N.J.: Erlbaum.

Stoneman, Z., & Brody, G. H. (1982). The indirect impact of child-oriented advertisements on mother-child interactions. *Journal of Applied Developmental Psychology, 17*, 853–858.

Stoneman, Z., & Brody, G. H. (1983). Immediate and long-term recognition and generalization of advertised products as a function of age and presentation mode. *Developmental Psychology, 19*, 56–61.

Stranger, J. D. (1997). *Television in the home. The 1997 survey of parents and children*. Philadelphia: University of Pennsylvania, The Annenberg Public Policy Center.

Streicher, H. W. (1974). The girls in the cartoons. *Journal of Communication*, 1974, *24*, 125–129.

Stroman, C. A. (1986). Television viewing and self-concept among black children. *Journal of Broadcasting and Electronic Media, 30*, 87–93.

Stutts, M., & Hunnicutt, G. (1987). Can young children understand disclaimers in television commercials? *Journal of Advertising, 16*, 41–46.

Subervi-Velez, F. A., & Colsant, S. (1993). The television worlds of Latino children. In G. L. Berry & J. K. Asamen (Eds.), *Children and television: Images in a changing sociocultural world*. Newberry Park, CA: Sage.

Subrahmanyam, K., & Greenfield, P. M. (1996). Effect of video game practice on spatial skills in boys and girls. In P. M. Greenfield & R. R. Cocking (Eds.), *Interacting with video*. Norwood, N.J.: Ablex.

Sussman, V. (1996, February). Unleashing the language police in cyberspace. *U.S. News and World Report*.

Swerdlow, J. L. (1995). Information revolution. *National Geographic, 188*, 5–36.

Telecommunications Act of 1996, Publ. No. 104-104, 110, STAT. 56, 1996.

Thomas, M. H., & Drabman, R. S. (1977, August). Effects of television violence on expectations of others' aggression. Paper presented at the annual meeting of the American Psychological Association, San Francisco, CA.

Thomas, M. H., Horton, R. W., Lippincott, E. C., & Drabman, R. S. (1977). Desensitization to portrayals of real-life aggression as a function of exposure to televised violence. *Journal of Personality and Social Psychology, 35*, 450–458.

Thomas, R. M. (1996). *Comparing theories of child development* (4th ed.). Pacific Grove, Calif.: Brooks Cole.

Tower, R. B., Singer, D. G., Singer, J. L., & Biggs, A. (1979). Differential effects of television programming on preschoolers' cognition, imagination, and social play. *Journal of Orthopsychiatry, 49*, 265–281.

Trias, J. (1994, June 28). Testimony to the Federal Communications Commission at the En Banc Hearings on Children's Television. (MM docket No. 93–48). Washington, D.C.

Turow, J. (1974). Advising and ordering: Day time, prime time. *Journal of Communication, 24*, 138–141.

United States Bureau of the Census (December, 1983). *1980 Census of Population. Characteristics of the Population: Part 1: United States General Social and Economic Characteristics. U.S. Summary*. Washington, D.C.: U.S. Government Printing Office.

United States Bureau of the Census (November, 1992). *1990 Census of Population. General Population Characteristics*. Washington, D.C.: U.S. Government Printing Office.

United States Bureau of the Census. (1986). *Statistical abstracts of the United States*. Washington, D.C.: U.S. Government Printing Office.

United States Bureau of the Census. (1994). *Statistical abstracts of the United States*. Washington, D.C.: U.S. Government Printing Office.

United States Bureau of the Census. (1996). *Statistical abstracts of the United States*. Washington, D.C.: U.S. Government Printing Office.

United States Commission on Civil Rights. (1977). *Window dressing on the set: Women and minorities on television*. Washington, D.C.: U.S. Government Printing Office.

United States Department of Commerce. Bureau of the Census. (1989). *Statistical abstract of the United States* (109th ed.). Washington, D.C.: U.S. Government Printing Office.

Valkenburg, P. M., & van der Voort, T. H. (1994). Influence of TV on daydreaming and creative imagination: A review of research. *Psychological Bulletin, 116*, 316–339.

Valkenburg, P. M., Vooijs, M. W., van der Voort, T. H., & Wiegman, O. (1992). Television's influence on children's fantasy styles: A secondary analysis. *Imagination, cognition, and personality, 12*, 55–67.

van der Voort, T. H., & Valkenburg, P. M. (1994). Television's impact on fantasy play: A review of research. *Developmental Review, 14*, 27–51.

Van Evra, J. (1990). *Television and child development*. Hillsdale, N.J.: Erlbaum.

Van Evra, J. (1995). Advertising's impact on children as a function of viewing purpose. *Psychology and Marketing, 12*, 423–432.

Vidmar, N., & Rokeach, M. (1974). Archie Bunker's bigotry: A study in selective perception and exposure. *Journal of Communication, 24*, 36–47.

Ward, S. (1972). Effects of television advertising on children and adolescents. In E. A. Rubenstein, G. A. Comstock, & J. P. Murray (Eds.), *Television and social behavior. Vol. 4: Television in day-to-day life: Patterns of use* (pp. 432–451). Washington, D.C.: U.S. Government Printing Office.

Ward, S. (1980). The effects of television advertising on consumer socialization. In R. P. Adler, G. S. Lesser, L. K. Meringoff, T. S. Robertson, J. R. Rossiter, & S. Ward (Eds.), *The effects of television advertising on children: Review and recommendations* (pp. 185–194). Lexington, Mass.: Lexington Books.

Ward, S., Levinson, D., & Wackman, D. (1972). Children's attention to television advertising. In E. A. Rubenstein, G. A. Comstock, & J. P. Murray (Eds.), *Television and social behavior: Vol. 4: Television in day-to-day life: Patterns of use*. Washington, D.C.: U.S. Government Printing Office.

Wartella, E. (1980). Individual differences in children's responses to television advertising. In E. L. Palmer & A. Dorr (Eds.), *Children and the faces of television: Teaching, violence, selling*. New York: Academic Press.

Wartella, E., & Ettema, J. (1974). A cognitive developmental study of children's attention to television commercials. *Communication Research, 1*, 46–69.

Wartella, E., Heintz, K., Aidman, A., & Mazzarella, S. (1990). Television and beyond: Children's video media in one community. *Communication Research, 17*, 45–64.

Watkins, B. A., Calvert, S. L., Huston-Stein, A., & Wright, J. C. (1980). Children's recall of television material: Effects of presentation mode and adult labeling. *Developmental Psychology, 16*, 672–674.

Watkins, B. A., Huston-Stein, A., & Wright, J. C. (1981). Effects of planned television programming. In E. L. Palmer & A. Dorr (Eds.), *Children and the faces of television*. New York: Academic.

Weingarten, F. W. (1996). Universal service: Fair access in the information age. *Computer*, 74–75.

Welch, A. (1995, May). The role of books, television, computers, and video games in children's day-to-day lives. Paper presented at the annual meeting of the International Communication Association, Albuquerque, New Mexico.

Welch, R., Huston-Stein, A., Wright, J. C., & Plehal, R. (1979). Subtle sex-role cues in children's commercials. *Journal of Communication, 29,* 202–209.

Wilkes, R. E., & Valencia, H. (1989). Hispanics and Blacks in television commercials. *Journal of Advertising, 18,* 19–25.

Williams, F., LaRose, R., & Frost, F. (1981). *Children, television, and sex-role stereotyping.* New York: Prager.

Williams, M., & Condry, J. (1989). Living color: Minority portrayals and cross-racial interaction on television. Unpublished manuscript, Cornell University, Ithaca, N.Y.

Williams, S., & Ogletree, S. (1992). Preschool children's computer interest and competence: Effects of sex and gender role. *Early Childhood Research Quarterly, 7,* 135–143.

Williams, T. M. (Ed.). (1986). *The impact of television: A natural experiment in three communities.* New York: Academic Press.

Williams, T. M., Baron, D., Phillips, S., Travis, L., & Jackson, D. (1986, August). The portrayal of sex roles on Canadian and U.S. television. Paper presented to the International Association for Mass Communication Research, New Delhi, India.

Williams, T. M., & Cox, R. (1995). Informative versus other children's TV programs: Portrayals of ethnic diversity, gender, and aggression. Paper presented at the biennial meeting of the Society for Research in Child Development, Indianapolis, IN.

Williams, W., Montgomery, K., & Pasnik, S. (1997). Alcohol and tobacco on the web: New threats to youth. Washington, D.C.: The Center for Media Education.

Wills, G. (1995, July). Discussion on *Meet the Press.*

Wilson, B. J., & Weiss, A. J. (1992). Developmental differences in children's reactions to a toy advertisement linked to a toy-based commercial. *Journal of Broadcasting and Electronic Media, 36,* 371–394.

Wilson, K. (1987). The Voyage of the Mimi *interactive video prototype: Development of an exploratory learning environment for children.* New York: Center for Children and Technology, Bank Street College of Education.

Winkel, M., Novak, D., & Hopson, H. (1987). Personality factors, subject gender, and the effects of aggressive games on aggression in adolescents. *Journal of Research in Personality, 21,* 211–223.

Wright, J. C., & Huston, A. C. (1983). A matter of form: Potential of television for young viewers. *American Psychologist, 38,* 835–843.

Wright, J. C., & Huston, A. C. (1995). *Effects of educational TV viewing of lower-income preschoolers on academic skills, school readiness, and school adjustment one to three years later: A report to Children's Television Workshop.* Lawrence: Center for Research on the Influences of Television on Children, The University of Kansas.

Wright, J. C., Huston, C., Ross, R. P., Calvert, S. L., Rolandelli, D., Weeks, L. A., Raessi, P., & Potts, R. (1984). Pace and continuity of television programs: Effects on children's attention and comprehension. *Developmental Psychology, 20,* 653–666.

Wroblewski, R., & Huston, A. C. (1987). Televised occupational stereotypes and their effects on early adolescents: Are they changing? *Journal of Early Adolescence, 7,* 283–297.

Wulf, W. (1997). Look in the spaces for tommorow's innovations. *Communication of the ACM, 40,* 109–111.

Yelland, N. (1995). Young children's attitudes to computers and computing. *British Journal of Educational Technology, 26,* 149–151.

Young, B. M. (1990). *Television advertising and children.* Oxford: Clarendon Press.

Zillmann, D. (1971). Excitation transfer in communication-mediated aggressive behavior. *Journal of Experimental Social Psychology, 7*, 153–159.

Zillmann, D. (1982). Television viewing and arousal. In D. Pearl, L. Bouthilet, & J. Lazar (Eds.), *Television and behavior. Vol. 2: Technical Reports: Ten years of scientific progress and implications for the 80s.* Washington, D.C.: U.S. Government Printing Office.

Zillmann, D. (1991). Television viewing and physiological arousal. In J. Bryant & D. Zillmann (Eds.), *Responding to the screen: Reception and reaction processes.* Hillsdale, N.J.: Erlbaum.

Zillmann, D., & Bryant, J. (1994). Entertainment as media effect. In J. Bryant & D. Zillmann (Eds.), *Media effects: Advances in theory and research.* Hillsdale, N.J.: Erlbaum.

Credits

Chapter 1

Figure 1.1, page 12: Reprinted by permission of Nielson Media Research

Figure 1.2, page 13: Reprinted with permission by Daniel R. Anderson, Department of Psychology, University of Massachusetts.

Chapter 2

Figure 2.1, page 30: Reprinted with permission from Cultural Indicators Project, George Gerbner, Director

Page 32: Reprinted with permission from The Broadcast Education Association, Publisher.

Chapter 7

Figure 7.1, page 164: From Calvert, S., Huston, A., Watkins, B., & Wright, J. (1982). The relation between selective attention to television forms and children's comprehension of content. *Child Development, 53,* 601–610. Copyright © 1982 Society for Research in Child Development. Reprinted by permission.

Figure 7.2, page 175: Reprinted by permission. Ablex Publishing Corporation.

Chapter 8

Figure 8.1, page 195: Reprinted by permission. John C. Wright and Aletha C. Huston. Center for Research on the Influences of Television on Children, Department of Human Development, The University of Kansas, Lawrence, KS 66045

Chapter 9

Figure 9.1, page 230: Reprinted by permission. Blackwell Science Limited.

Excerpt, page 228: From M. Eraut, "Groupwork with Computers in British Primary Schools," in *Journal of Educational Computing Research,* 13, 61–87, 1995. Copyright © 1995. Reprinted by permission.

Excerpt, page 232: From Y. B. Kafai, *Minds in Play.* Copyright © Lawrence Erlbaum & Associates, Hillsdale, NJ. Reprinted by permission.

Photo Research by Shirley Lanners

Chapter 1

Page 5: © 1996 *The Washington Post.* Reprinted with permission; **p. 6:** © Russell D. Curtis/Photo Researchers, Inc.; **p. 11:** © Alan Abramowitz/Tony Stone Images; **p. 19:** Courtesy of Zenith Electronics Corporation.

Chapter 2

Page 34: © Geoff Tompkinson/SPL/Photo Researchers, Inc.

Chapter 3

Page 62 (left): Carmen Sandiego TM & © 1998 Brøderbund Software, Inc. All Rights Reserved. Used with permission; **p. 62 (right):** Orly's Draw-a-Story TM & © Brøderbund Software, Inc. All Rights Reserved. Used with permission.

Chapter 4

Page 96: © Chip Henderson/Tony Stone Images.

Chapter 5

Page 116: © Tony Freeman/PhotoEdit.

Chapter 6

Page 139: © 1993 Film Roman, Inc. All rights reserved/courtesy Saban Entertainment; **p. 142:** Printed with permission of Sandra L. Calvert, Georgetown University; site programmer, William Murray. **p. 143:** Photographs from *Blues Clues* courtesy of Nickelodeon, a division of Viacom International, Inc. © 1999 Viacom International, Inc., All Rights Reserved.

Chapter 7

Page 149: © Bob Daemmrich/The Image Works; **p. 158:** © Ulrike Welsh/Photo Researchers, Inc.

Chapter 8

Page 184, 189: Photographs from *Blue's Clues* courtesy of Nickelodeon, a division of Viacom International, Inc. © 1999 Viacom International, Inc., All Rights Reserved; **p. 196:** © 1998 Children's Television Workshop Sesame Street Muppets and © 1998 Jim Henson Productions (Richard Termine, photographer); **p. 206:** courtesy Lyrick Studios, © 1997 Big Feats Entertainment, L.P. All rights reserved, Used with permission.

Chapter 9

Page 212: © 1998 Fox Kids Worldwide/courtesy Saban Entertainment; **p. 229:** © David Oliver/Tony Stone Images.

Chapter 10

Page 236: Courtesy of Bruce Blumberg, Massachusetts Institute of Technology Media Lab; **p. 240:** © Fujifotos/The Image Works; **p. 241:** © KCTS, Seattle, and Quest Productions/ courtesy Microsoft Digital Television (shark photos: left © Stephen Frink/Corbis; upper right © KCTS & Quest Productions; lower right © Stuart Westmoreland/ Corbis).

Author Index

Subject Index